Issues in Criminal Justice

A Reader for Critical Thought

FIRST EDITION

Issues in Criminal Justice

A Reader for Critical Thought

M.L. Dantzker and Rosalva Resendiz

University of Texas—Rio Grande Valley

cognella®

SAN DIEGO

Bassim Hamadeh, CEO and Publisher
John Remington, Executive Editor
Gem Rabanera, Senior Project Editor
Casey Hands, Production Editor
Jess Estrella, Senior Graphic Designer
Trey Soto, Licensing Coordinator
Natalie Piccotti, Director of Marketing
Kassie Graves, Vice President of Editorial
Jamie Giganti, Director of Academic Publishing

Printed in the United States of America.

cognella® | ACADEMIC PUBLISHING
3970 Sorrento Valley Blvd., Ste. 500, San Diego, CA 92121

CONTENTS

INTRODUCTION

Students who study Criminal Justice, whether in high school or college, generally start with an "Introduction to Criminal Justice" course. This course begins by indicating that the study of criminal justice primarily revolves around understanding the criminal justice system (CJS).

This system is comprised of three subsystems: police, courts, and corrections. As studies progress, students are often required to take at least one course on each of the three main elements. These courses are then enhanced and broadened through various other elements associated with the CJS. The completion of study generally includes a course that brings everything together, a capstone course. Unfortunately, this type of course may be no more than a review of what students were expected to learn throughout their studies. Thus, the type of book often used is the same "Introduction" text required in the first course. This book opposes that approach by offering a variety of issues within the requisite elements. The purpose of this book is to challenge students in a capstone course to think critically about aspects, concepts, perspectives, etc., related to criminal justice, instead of just memorizing facts.

This text's content and format, while designed specifically for a senior-level capstone or seminar, will also be useful for students in upper division and graduate classes, where the focus is critical thinking about contemporary issues, considering historical and institutional factors. The text is not intended to provide new knowledge as much as it is to provide the ideas and positions of others. Readers should approach this material with the mindset that the information offered is not necessarily wrong or right but open to debate and critically thought out discussion. The textbook includes scholarly articles from an academic perspective and a practitioner's point of view, therefore highlighting the multiple problems facing the CJS.

Understanding the Organization of Content

The organization of this text is based upon the order often discussed in an introductory criminal justice class. It includes six units. Each unit addresses a major element associated with the CJS. Each section begins with an introduction, followed by a set of readings, and ending with questions to assist in critical thinking.

Individuals reading this text should recognize that the first thing learned when studying criminal justice is the structure of the CJS. Generally, discussion includes its elements, process and procedures, actors, and other related aspects. Our unit on the CJS differs in that it offers perspectives and views about various issues within the CJS, which often may go unnoticed or receive little attention but are more important than given at face value. Topics include management, finance, economics, demographic factors, and the most recent need for attention, border issues.

With respect to policing or law enforcement, whole courses are offered just focusing on issues, and then one course is not enough considering that policing/law enforcement includes a vast network of federal, state, and local agencies, as well as corporate entities. The police are the gatekeepers of our society, who function as first responders, agents of social control, peace, and order. Since the police are required to take action against those who are believed to have violated a law, their actions are often more scrutinized than any other segment of the CJS. Of concern is how police may use force and against whom it is used. Unit Two looks at attitudes toward police, the use of excessive force, gender-related issues, and the organizational culture.

The second component of the CJS involves prosecution, trial, and sentencing, often recognized as the judicial system. Despite the expanse of this system across 50 states and a federal system, comprised of hundreds of courts, trial and appellate, most often recognized is the U.S. Supreme Court. However, while its role has strong constitutional ties, all the other courts devote more time to issues within the CJS. Many issues arise that are not always part of public knowledge yet are extremely relevant to the function and purpose of the courts. Unit Three looks at topics that often escape public scrutiny yet deserve attention, include funding, management, specialty courts, and the political environment which may or may not affect their decisions.

Component three of the CJS consists of punishment and corrections. Like the judiciary, this segment does not get the same attention as the police. Of interest is the composition of those who appear to be more often punished or ill-treated. Unit Four focuses primarily on demographic issues such as gender and race, as well as corruption and laws to address violent acts that occur within the correctional setting.

Until 1899, juveniles who violated the law were often punished and housed among adults. The formation of the Illinois Juvenile Court initiated the juvenile justice system. Some may suggest that it should be discussed as its own system; however, because there is crossover between the adult and juvenile components, juvenile justice is discussed as part of the CJS. Unit Five takes the approach that juvenile justice is its own entity, addressing topics specific to those individuals who experience the process and function of the juvenile system.

Finally, while the study of the CJS in the form of a criminal justice degree continues to be popular, another form of study requires recognition. Born out of sociology, criminology is the theoretical study of aspects of the CJS. The human component is the mainstay of criminology which includes sociology of law, penology, and victimology. Although the most recent aspect of criminology, victimology has been a fast-growing field of study in the CJS, practical and theoretical. Unit Six completes the text with the examination of just how victimology is linked to the CJS.

Overall, this text provides views and positions on issues related to some aspect of the criminal justice system. However, rather than just taking the information at face value, students are encouraged to take a critical thinking approach. The fact is that while issues will continue to exist, the specifics within change. This text offers one place to look at just some of the current specifics and is meant to spark inquiry into structural factors and policies that maintain and affect the system.

—M.L. Dantzker, Ph.D. and Rosalva Resendiz, Ph.D.
Co-editors

UNIT I

The Criminal Justice System

Unit Introduction

In the United States, the criminal justice system (CJS) is established by the three branches of government: executive, legislative, and judicial. As constitutional law has evolved, so has the role of the CJS, along with the challenges of an ever-changing democratic society. The text begins by highlighting some of the most recent issues facing the nation: mass incarceration, troubling police/citizen interactions (e.g., Ferguson, MO), and racial injustice. In addressing these issues, many efforts have been made by the CJS to provide resources for researchers and practitioners. One of the most recent efforts is the Marshall Project, named after Supreme Court judge and civil rights activist, Thurgood Marshall (Reading 1.1).

The CJS is guided by the legal system, but the Supreme Court has been criticized for not appropriately defining criminal law and its relation to constitutional law. Several authors note the need to examine the moral norms, legitimacy of law, the rule of law and human rights law in substantive criminal law in the modern state (Readings 1.2 and 1.3).

Another effort in advancing the reform of the CJS is the development of the Justice Index by the organization Measures for Justice, along with the Bureau of Justice. Some of the issues evaluated include the lack of comparative measures across counties, as well as the delivery of basic services (Reading 1.4).

In the last three readings, the authors examine the economic factors which impact the CJS, from the prison industrial complex to immigration and border security. The CJS is faced with multiple push-pull factors, which are framed by U.S. demands and policy. For example, the prison industrial complex is driven and sustained through racial profiling and police policies (Reading 1.5). The demand for drugs in the U.S. maintains profitability for Mexican organized crime, further increasing the violence among cartels as they compete for markets, resulting in the increase of illegal immigration and refugees (Reading 1.6). Although illegal immigration is partly driven by cartel violence, it is also a result of America's demand for cheap labor. Finally, in its efforts to curtail migration and drug trade, the CJS has responded with border security initiatives which have failed to provide safety and have produced some negative outcomes (Reading 1.7).

READING 1.1

Criminal Justice Sites Reflect Intense National Concerns

By Mick O'Leary

This review is being written 1 year after Ferguson. It's telling that I don't need to use more than that single word for you to know what I mean. "Ferguson" has entered the national vocabulary, similar to "Katrina" and "Newtown." It ignited an intense firestorm of attention to and criticism of the nation's criminal justice system, particularly over mass incarceration, troubling police/citizen interactions, and racial injustice.

Ferguson—both the incident and its larger significance—has been thoroughly covered by news and opinion media of all sorts: print, broadcast, cable, and the web (as well as others that may have escaped my notice). These recent discussions, however, are just the latest additions to a large and highly informative "content collection" that's been building for many years.

There are hundreds (if not thousands) of websites devoted to the panoply of criminal justice issues in the U.S. The large majority of these are concerned with a locality, a specific aspect of the larger issue, or advocacy rather than content aggregation. This leaves a much smaller number of websites that cover U.S. criminal justice from a national perspective; deal with the topic broadly; and have substantial, research-worthy content collections. These include a recent entrant, The Marshall Project, as well as older resources such as the Vera Institute of Justice, The Sentencing Project, the Justice Policy Institute, and the Prison Policy Initiative.

The Marshall Project

The Marshall Project (themarshallproject.org) launched in fall 2014 to considerable attention, due in part to its prominent editor-in-chief, Bill Keller, who was executive editor of *The New York Times* from 2003 to 2011. It is named after legendary civil rights attorney and Supreme Court justice Thurgood Marshall. The project's mission is "to raise public awareness around criminal justice issues and the possibility for reform." It is donor-supported.

Mick O'Leary, "Criminal Justice Sites Reflect Intense National Concerns," *Information Today*, vol. 32, no. 9, pp. 16-17.

Criminal Justice Sites

SYNOPSIS

The Marshall Project is a new, journalistically oriented website that covers pressing national issues in criminal justice, including incarceration, the courts, police/citizen interactions, and racial disparities, etc. Other sites—the Vera Institute of Justice, The Sentencing Project, the Justice Policy Institute, and the Prison Policy Initiative—cover the same topics but are based on the think tank model and have extensive research and commentary resources.

The Marshall Project follows the model of a newspaper; its three sections are Feature, News, and Commentary. It has more than 3 dozen feature articles (now known as "long-form" journalism), covering all aspects of the criminal justice system, with a slight emphasis on incarceration topics. They are probing, insightful, and compelling, in the best traditions of newspaper investigative journalism.

The News section contains short analyses of recent events and trends across the spectrum of criminal justice topics. The Commentary section, analogous to a newspaper op-ed section, has editorials from The Marshall Project's writers and external commentators.

The site itself suffers from what I've repeatedly decried as "Facebookization"—endless pages of posts, with poor browse and search functions. It has browsing by document type, but not by topic or date. The basic search function has no limiting, filtering, or sorting. While perhaps sufficient for posts from family and friends, this limited access structure weakens The Marshall Project's value as a serious information resource.

The Marshall Project's Predecessors

Unlike the newspaper model of The Marshall Project, four noteworthy predecessors—the Vera Institute of Justice, The Sentencing Project, the Justice Policy Institute, and the Prison Policy Initiative—follow the model of a think tank or nongovernmental organization by offering formal research and analysis, advocacy, and commentary. Each of these organizations has varying combinations of these three elements. Each, as mentioned previously, addresses the broad subject of criminal justice comprehensively, with attention to its varied aspects, and geographically, with projects at national and local levels. Each depends on a mixture of organizational and individual financial support.

(Author's note: This article does not cover important criminal justice resources that I have reviewed earlier. The National Registry of Exonerations and the Innocence Project, both of which deal with wrongly convicted people and those who have been exonerated, were covered in the September 2012

Database Review. Several officer-involved shooting databases, which catalog incidents of citizen deaths occurring during interactions with the police, were covered in the March 2015 Database Review.)

Vera Institute of Justice

The Vera Institute of Justice (vera.org), established in 1961, is a large organization with a long history of research and advocacy across a very broad range of criminal justice issues. Its database contains nearly 1,000 items, including many hundreds of research reports and smaller collections of other documents and videos. The database can be browsed by topic and source type and searched by title keyword and author. Since 2009, it has featured a blog that provides commentary from Vera analysts.

The Sentencing Project

The name of The Sentencing Project (sentencingproject.org) is slightly misleading. Founded in 1986, it does concentrate on sentencing issues, including unjust racial disparities and the need for sentencing alternatives, but it also covers other criminal justice issues. Its Publications database contains several dozen documents, including research reports, issue briefs, and position statements. Its News database provides links to relevant items from a variety of news and commentary sites. These two collections can be browsed by broad topic and resource type and searched by topic, resource type, and keyword. Its Racial Disparity section features the Race and Justice Clearinghouse, a large, separate database that contains more than 500 reports and studies on the intersection of race and the criminal justice system. These resources are from numerous research and policy organizations. Documents in the Clearinghouse can be searched by title, abstract, author, subject, and date.

Justice Policy Institute

The Justice Policy Institute (justicepolicy.org) was founded in 1997 and has a wide range of research and advocacy projects. Its Research database has almost 140 items, including reports, fact sheets, and briefings. Its Newsroom has links to hundreds of external sources. These sections can be searched by topic with a rudimentary search function. The institute's blog has commentary and news dating to 2011.

Prison Policy Initiative

The Prison Policy Initiative (prisonpolicy.org), founded in 2001, explores issues related to mass incarceration. It covers this topic widely, but gives particular attention to prison conditions and injustices. Its content includes dozens of research studies; videos, maps, and other graphics; and a blog. These sections have limited browse and search functionality. The initiative also produces two separate databases of criminal justice information: Research Clearinghouse and Legal Resources for the Incarcerated. The Clearinghouse contains links to hundreds of sources, representing, according to the institute, "virtually all the empirical criminal justice research available online." This may be a slight exaggeration, but the collection does cite a wide range of criminal justice research. Legal Resources for the Incarcerated is a directory of U.S. "law firms and organizations that provide free legal assistance to incarcerated people on civil (noncriminal) matters."

READING 1.2

On Management in Criminal Justice

By Ion Ristea

Introduction

The purpose of this paper is to gain a deeper understanding of the nexus between constitutional law and substantive criminal law, the possible interactions between constitutional law and criminal law, and the fundamental principles of substantive criminal law.

The Fairness and Rationality of Substantive Criminal Law Rules

Wattad discusses the constitutional grounds of substantive criminal law in American law. Addressing touchstone cases of the U.S. Supreme Court on substantive criminal law, Wattad proposes that the Court has consistently failed to provide a theory of substantive criminal law, and criticizes the Court's superficial understanding of fundamental principles of criminal theory, namely those that deal with the meaning of crime, guilt, punishment, *mens rea*, wrongdoing, attribution and others. In highlighting the inherent nexus between constitutional law and substantive criminal law, Wattad examines the American Supreme Court's reluctance to entangle with the constitutional aspects of substantive criminal law. Focusing on the meaning of "criminal prosecution" and "crime" of the Sixth Amendment, the Due Process Clause, and the Equal Protection Clause, Wattad suggests that the Constitution provides an obvious language of substantive criminal law. Inquiring into the possible interactions between constitutional law and criminal law, Wattad offers a complete theory of the fundamental principles of substantive criminal law, suggesting three basic tenets on which criminal law theory stands: guilt, crime, and wrongdoing. Understanding the meaning of these three pillars provides a wider and deeper panorama of the whole theory of criminal law, thus providing the vital legal tools for addressing many other criminal law questions in future.[1]

Ion Ristea, "On Management in Criminal Justice," *Economics, Management and Financial Markets*, vol. 6, no. 3, pp. 166-171.

Stein and Bierschbach challenge the conventional divide between substantive criminal law theory and evidence law, by exposing *an important and unrecognized function of evidence rules in criminal law*: throughout the criminal law, special rules of evidence work to mediate conflicts between criminal law's deterrence and retributivist goals, *by skewing errors in the actual application of the substantive criminal law to favor whichever theory has been disfavored by the substantive rule itself.* Stein and Bierschbach note that the mediating potential of evidentiary rules is particularly strong in criminal law: the substantive law's dominant animating theories—deterrence and retributivism—respond asymmetrically to the workings of those rules. Stein and Bierschbach analyze the features of "mediating rules," explore their effects across a range of substantive areas, and offer a tentative normative assessment of their role in a pluralistic criminal law system.[2] Frase holds that the Warren Court was much less active and progressive in its treatment of substantive criminal law and sentencing issues than it was in the area of criminal procedure. Frase examines the relatively small number of important Warren Court decisions relating to substantive criminal law and sentencing, and compares major decisions in these areas from earlier and later periods in order to identify specific topics that the Warren Court might have been expected to address: the requirement of proof beyond a reasonable doubt can be viewed as a substantive right closely related to core criminal law issues, the federal law of crimes was in terrible shape at the end of the Warren Court era, the indeterminate sentencing model reduced practical concerns about the fairness and rationality of substantive criminal law rules, and the Warren Court would not have been likely to slow or reverse the steady expansion of federal criminal jurisdiction and federal criminal laws.[3]

The Basic Moral Norms Embodied in the Criminal Law

Gans maintains that the Commonwealth may or may not be about to tread the oft-trodden path leading to a non-entrenched statute setting out and (to an extent) promoting human rights: criminal law is unlikely to feature in the debate on the adoption of a charter, which will instead focus on the theories of governance. Gans makes some observations about the effect of a Charter-like statute on criminal law, focussing on substantive criminal law rather than the probably vaster topic of criminal process. The interpretation of physical elements of crimes is a matter of ordinary statutory interpretation. Gans reasons that some of the public law doctrines developed overseas are geared towards a court nullifying a statutory provision. Human rights documents are known both for their vast scope and their almost-as-vast caveats.

> Human rights statutes actually have much more to offer substantive criminal law than some more robust readings of the words actually used in statutes. They can also offer robust set of principles designed to distinguish between good and bad forms of criminalisation and criminal responsibility, and a set of readymade doctrines that may convince courts or criminal justice decision-makers to bridge the gap between them.[4]

Bibas points out that criminal procedure is preoccupied with procedural values such as efficiency, accuracy, informed choice, and procedural fairness, using the terms substance and substantive criminal law to distinguish the body of law that defines crimes from the procedures used to enforce them: the criminal law's norms include honesty and responsibility for one's actions, many guilty-plea confessions are insincere or induced by extrinsic inducements or pressures, such as plea bargains, whereas if innocent defendants were fully informed, could accurately determine the likelihood of conviction and punishment at trial. Bibas holds that innocent defendants owe moral duties to themselves not to treat themselves unjustly, and the state should not facilitate such injustice. Society must not consciously promote guilty and nolo contendere pleas by innocent defendants. The justice system should forestall public cynicism by forbidding practices that openly promote injustice or even doubts about guilt. The system must be accurate to protect innocent defendants from injustice and to secure the community's confidence. Criminal procedure is detached from the moral moorings of the substantive criminal law. Bibas reviews the basic moral norms embodied in the criminal law, such as honesty and responsibility for one's actions, explores the psychological denial mechanisms of offenders (especially sex offenders) who refuse to admit guilt, discusses the therapeutic value of inducing confessions by encouraging and confronting defendants who refuse to admit guilt, contends that guilty pleas should be reserved for defendants who confess, because by confessing they take the first steps toward repentance and reform, and explains why defendants who refuse to admit guilt should have to undergo trials. The criminal law insists on moral culpability, in the form of mens rea and voluntariness, and excuses defendants who acted under duress, insanity, infancy, or other incapacity. Bibas puts it that criminal punishment seeks to educate the offender, induce repentance and reconciliation, vindicate the victim, achieve catharsis, and reinforce moral norms to society at large. Vindication of victims and moral norms are analytically tied to the message punishment sends. The criminal law seeks to a) lead offenders to repent by humbling them, b) exact moral sanctions, and then c) return them to the community as equals. The law's labels and ascriptions of blame influence rehabilitation and reform. Offenders who publicly accept responsibility for their crimes, even if they do so insincerely, are more likely to internalize that responsibility than those who persist in denying guilt. Bibas emphasizes that the hard work of admitting guilt and repenting may impress upon the defendant the wrongfulness and gravity of the crime: the value of confronting guilt and apologizing is a central insight of the restorative-justice movement, for those offenders who refuse to confess or repent, trials still bring catharsis and closure to victims and the community, and trials express respect for the law, communicate values, and justify punishment. Bibas reasons that the victim-vindication and expressive functions of the criminal law are not contingent on psychological probabilities. Trial verdicts send messages about the substantive moral norms underlying the criminal law. Judges at plea hearings could insist on more detailed allocutions and use more overtly moralistic language, driving home the wrongfulness of the crime.[5]

The Legitimacy of the Law

Bradley maintains that the pleading defendant sets himself on the path to moral reform. "By accepting responsibility for his actions, he cements his status as one who recognizes the basic ends of the law of crime and punishment."[6] Thurman claims that trials are like the miracle or morality plays of ancient times. "They dramatically present the conflicting moral values of a community in a way that could not be done by logical formalization."[7] The theory of criminal law has intimate normative connections with the theory of the criminal trial and theories of state punishment.[8] Barrozo claims that one of the effects of the focus on deviation is the overlegitimation of the norm, of the mainstream of our punitive practices: the distinction between norm and deviation fails to adequately capture the ideological and functional integration and complementarity of criminal law in modern societies.

> In the contexts of national and international criminal law and culpability, the concept of cruelty is sometimes used to identify and evaluate a particular state of mind of agents of criminal behavior in terms of delight or other form of hedonistic gratification in causing suffering. In the context of the prohibition of torture and other cruel punishment—or, less commonly, in the discrete area of executive decisions on whether to grant mercy—the idea of cruelty seeks to mark and check the behavior of the agents of punishment in cases in which it was unreasonably instituted, disproportionately applied, or excessively enforced.[9]

On Dyzenhaus's reading, legality makes government under the rule of law something worth having. *Judges should defer to public officials' interpretations of the law, as well as to legislative and administrative choice when it comes to institutional design, including the design of fair procedure.* Institutional arrangements are instrumental or functional to a larger purpose—the realization of principles.[10]

As Duff puts it, punishment tries to bring the criminal to understand the nature and implications of her crime, "to repent that crime and *thus*, by willing her own punishment as a penance which can expiate her crime, to reconcile herself with the Right and with her community."[11] Olusanya claims that after a long period of relative stagnation, substantive international criminal law has been invigorated primarily by the activities of the International Criminal Tribunals for the former Yugoslavia and Rwanda.

> Both ad hoc tribunals have made immense advancements to this area of international criminal law, by for instance laying down detailed rules on what constitutes culpable conduct and on when responsibility should be attributed for the conduct of others. These important advances notwithstanding, much remains in flux –the

elements of the core international crimes are still subject to controversy, theories of individual criminal responsibility such as command responsibility and joint criminal enterprise are highly controversial and there is as yet no knowledge of how international offences should be graded according to different levels and degrees of culpability and harm, etc.[12]

Raz writes that the claims that law makes for itself are evident from the language it adopts and from the opinions expressed by its spokesmen. "The law's claim to authority is manifested by the fact that legal institutions are officially designated as 'authorities', by the fact that they regard themselves as having the right to impose obligations on their subjects, by their claims that their subjects owe them allegiance, and that their subjects ought to obey the law as it requires to be obeyed."[13]

Conclusions

We seek to contribute to a wider understanding of contextual and cultural influences on the constitutional grounds of substantive criminal law, the constitutional aspects of substantive criminal law, and the meaning of criminal law.[14]

References

1. Wattad, M. (2007), "The Meaning of Criminal Law: Three Tenets on American and Comparative Constitutional Aspects of Substantive Criminal Law," DAI, 68-06 A, Columbia University, 2631.
2. Stein, A., & Bierschbach, R. A. (2007), "Mediating Rules in Criminal Law," *Virginia Law Review* 93(5): 1197–1258.
3. Frase, R. S. (2005), "The Warren Court's Missed Opportunities in Substantive Criminal Law," *Ohio State Journal of Criminal Law* 3: 75–103.
4. Gans, J. (2008), "Federal Criminal Law under a Rights Charter," speech presented at the *Federal Criminal Law*, conference run by the NSW Bar Association and the Law Counsel of Australia, Sydney, September 5: 8.
5. Bibas, S. (2003), "Harmonizing Substantive Criminal Law Values and Criminal Procedure: The Case of *Alford* and Nolo Contendere Pleas," *Cornell Law Review* 88: 1361–1407.
6. Bradley, G. V. (1999), "Plea Bargaining and the Criminal Defendant's Obligation to Plead Guilty," *South Texas Law Review* 40: 65.
7. Thurman, A. (1965), "The Criminal Trial as a Symbol of Public Morality," in Kamisar, Y. and Howard, A.E. (eds.), *Criminal Justice in Our Time.* Charlottesville, VA: University Press of Virginia, 141–144.
8. Duff, A. et al. (2004), "Introduction: Towards a Normative Theory of the Criminal Trial," in Duff, A. et al. (eds.), *The Trial on Trial*, Vol. 1. Oxford: Hart Publishing, Oxford, 11–17.

9. Barrozo, P. D. (2008), "Punishing Cruelly: Punishment, Cruelty, and Mercy," *Criminal Law and Philosophy* 2: 69.
10. Dyzenhaus, D. (2006), *The Constitution of Law: Legality in a Time of Emergency.* Cambridge: Cambridge University Press.
11. Duff, R. A. (1986), *Trials and Punishments.* Cambridge: Cambridge University Press, 259.
12. Olusanya, O. (ed.) (2007), *Rethinking International Criminal Law. The Substantive Part.* Groningen: Europa Law Publishing.
13. Raz, J. (1985), "Authority, Law, and Morality," *The Monist* 68: 295.
14. Ionescu, L. (2011), "The Economics of Anti-Corruption," *Contemporary Readings in Law and Social Justice* 3(1): 116–121.

READING 1.3

Criminal Justice and Economics of Crime

By Ion Ristea

Introduction

The main focus of this paper is the study of the moral foundations of the criminal law, the general ground for criminal liability, the principles underlying the substantive criminal law, and the appropriate role of the criminal law. In addition, this paper provides implications for practice and research to further explore the paradigm of the criminal law and the criminal trial, the shape of the procedural requirements of human rights law, the tasks of criminal law theory, the moral principles of obligation and duty, and the remedies of the civil law.

The Changing Role of the Criminal Law in the Modern State

Hampton holds that the *retributive* motive for inflicting suffering "is to annul or counter the appearance of the wrongdoer's superiority and thus affirm the victim's real value."[1] Stephen puts it that the sentence of the law is to the moral sentiment of the public in relation to any offence what a seal is to hot wax. "It converts into a permanent final judgment what might otherwise be a transient sentiment."[2] The criminal law represents an objective ethics which must sometimes oppose individual convictions of right.[3] Blackwell and Cunningham write that pretrial incarceration is the most punitive form of procedural punishment imposed by the lower courts: lower numbers of releases correlate with higher costs to taxpayers that result from full to overflowing jails, restorative justice has become a global movement, with applications in highly varied settings, whereas most defendants need restoration to a different or larger community than one defined as those harmed by the crime. Blackwell and Cunningham contend that the defense lawyer is likely the only person the defendant can speak to freely without risking criminal liability. Public discourse about whether

Ion Ristea, "Criminal Justice and Economics of Crime," *Economics, Management and Financial Markets*, vol. 6, no. 3, pp. 215-220.

to spend more resources on the lower criminal courts, particularly on indigent defense, tends to get stuck on "left v. right" distinctions. If the punishment is taken out of the process, and the processes of criminal justice become effective at restoration that would be a result both the "left" and the "right" (and everyone in between) would embrace.[4]

Ashworth and Zedner remark that some longstanding assumptions about the role and the place of the criminal trial and, it follows, the criminal law are under challenge, the shifting nature of the criminal law is bound up with certain changes in the nature and use of criminal trials, and the purpose of criminal law is to provide for the censure and sentencing of those who commit wrongs that have been (justifiably) criminalized. Ashworth and Zedner reflect on the changing role of the criminal law in the modern state: *this is partly bound up with growing skepticism about the fitness of the criminal trial to fulfill its purposes.* Ashworth and Zedner assess whether there is increased resort to the particular strategy, what its implications are for the role of the criminal law and the purpose of the criminal trial, and what reasons lie behind its greater use; and whether the development is to be applauded or not. *Whereas the system of reprimands and warnings for youths replaces police cautions, the conditional caution for adults has not replaced police cautions.*

> The practice of diversion compromises the right of defendants to be presumed innocent, relieves the prosecution of the burden of proving guilt, and may bring intolerable pressure to bear upon those eager to escape the police station or fearful of the prospect of prosecution to admit an offence they may not have committed. Where this admission is followed by further burdensome consequences, be it participation in rehabilitation programs or restorative justice conferences, the costs of diversion are even greater.[5]

Ashworth and Zedner affirm that the difference between fixed penalties and diversion itself is that the former may have penal consequences. *A new arrival in English law is what may be termed the hybrid civil–criminal process.* Hybrid orders like the ASBO are intended to lead to the decline of the criminal trial, by taking some cases away from that procedure and placing them in this hybrid category, strict criminal liability should be regarded as exceptional and in need of strong justification, particularly where the offence is serious, and in relation to sex offences there is little evidence of the efficacy of preventive orders. *What might be termed a full-dress criminal trial is increasingly regarded as an expensive luxury.*

> Economic analysis affects thinking about crime itself, regarding it less as a moral wrong than as a calculable cost to be averted, whose losses can be recovered through restitutionary payments or otherwise amortized. Thus where diversion has a greater likelihood of enabling offenders to make good the losses they have

> inflicted, and where this can be done more cheaply and without a higher reconviction rate, it is to be preferred over conventional punishment. This managerialist tendency is particularly dominant at the lower end of the tariff where the claim to normality is most plausible. Here, censure and hard treatment become less appropriate than the manipulation of costs or disincentives (hence penalty notices for disorder).[6]

Ashworth and Zedner argue that penalty notices for disorder and the greater use of strict liability are prime examples of the privileging of pace over process. The coercive provisions of an ASBO may be imposed without convicting the person of an offence. The paradigm of the criminal law and the criminal trial is being eroded by the state. Minor wrongdoing and other anti-social conduct should be dealt with outside the criminal law, there is public disquiet about the economic benefits to the criminal justice system being traded off too cheaply, whereas the pressure that the system creates on innocent defendants or those with an arguable case is too great. Ashworth and Zedner reason that at the level of justification, there is a necessary link between the censure of conviction, liability to punishment, and the need to respect the dignity of the individual defendant through the upholding of rights.

> Conviction of an individual for an offence is the strongest form of condemnation of conduct that the state can muster. Conviction for an offence also opens the possibility of a coercive sentence, ordered by a court within the limits of what legislation permits. To justify the creation of a certain crime is therefore to justify the imposition of the censure of conviction and the imposition of a punishment. It is the special significance and gravity of these consequences, with all their legal and social implications, that supports the argument for safeguards in the shape of the procedural requirements of human rights law—the presumption of innocence, the need for proper notice of the charge, adequate time and facilities for preparing a defense, state-funded legal assistance, the right to confront witnesses, the free assistance of an interpreter, the privilege against self-incrimination and various other rights."[7]

The Role of the Criminal Law

Green points out that it seems surprising that procedural protections are not allocated proportionally, so that, the more serious the offense charged, the more extensive the process due. The interest that citizens have in avoiding state incarceration is so great that certain basic procedural protections seem an imperative. Defendants charged with capital offenses are entitled to additional protections not generally available to defendants in non-capital cases. Procedural rights are allocated proportionally, varying according to the seriousness of the charge brought. Green maintains that offenders are diverted from the criminal justice system proper into rehabilitative or restorative programs of various sorts. By adhering to a one-size-fits-all approach to criminal procedure, and by insisting that defendants receive the full panoply of expensive procedural rights even in cases in which they face relatively minor penalties, we run the risk that these rights might be lost.[8] Grabosky and Sutton point out that regulation is essentially a charade, with businesses allowed to do largely as they please.

> Case after case suggests that regulatory authorities have failed in their role of protecting the public. [...] In some, the law is unable to address harmful corporate conduct. In others, the penalties available at law may have been inadequate. In others still, the legal apparatus may be sufficient but the enforcement agency may be co-opted by the industry which it oversees. Alternatively, the agency may be crippled by inadequate resources, by administrative incompetence, or by political forces.[9]

The Moral Foundations of the Criminal Law

Richards holds that the tasks of criminal law theory appear to be both explanatory and normative, concerned with both understanding and recommendations for change. The jurisprudence of rights directly challenges the existing state of constitutional theory and practice in the United States, taking seriously fundamental normative concepts of human rights. Certain human rights are convergently enforced by several legal institutions. The criminal law must be compatible with and express respect for basic human rights. The idea of human rights takes a normative attitude expressing respect for the capacity of persons, *as such*, for rational autonomy. Richards maintains that the idea of human rights expresses a normative point of view that puts an equal weight on each person's capacity for autonomy. The basic principles of political right must treat all persons as equals. To express equal respect for personal autonomy is to guarantee the minimum conditions requisite for autonomy. The criminal law rests on the enforcement of public morality. Both the criminal and civil law rest on the moral foundations of the moral principles of obligation and duty. Criminal sanctions must satisfy the underlying purpose of affording an effective symbolic statement of minimal moral standards of decency. The great virtue of a just legal system is that the distortions of judgment and execution, found with an individual in the state of nature, are significantly reduced. Richards views both the criminal law and the remedies of the civil law as means of enforcement (certain moral rights relating to keeping informal promises and the like may not be appropriately enforced either by the criminal or civil law). Richards examines how the proposed account of the moral foundations of the criminal law may be deployed in clarifying the substantive criminal law and cognate constitutional law doctrines, discussing *seriatim* the contribution this theory can make to understanding (a) decriminalization and the limits of the criminal sanction, (b) *actus reus* and the distinction between actions and omissions, (c) *mens rea* and excuses, including the novel idea of an excuse of socioeconomic deprivation, (d) legality, (e) the nature and place of justification, notably self-defense and necessity, (f) vexed issues relating to inchoate crimes, in particular, attempts, and (g) proportionality and the death penalty. The idea of human rights secures the minimum conditions which enable persons, with the dignity of freedom and rationality, to design their lives. Rights are defined independently of the good, and define the boundary constraints within which people on fair terms are free to define their own good. An autonomy-based ethics takes the normative attitude that the capacity is not only to be encouraged. Richards contends that the principles of justice play a role in clarifying the place of the *actus reus* requirement as a predicate of criminal liability. The criminal law is the way in which basic rights of moral decency, defined by ethical principles of obligation and duty, are enforced. The derivation of the moral principles of obligation and duty clarifies the proper interpretation of the action-omission distinction in the interpretation of *actus reus.* To limit the range of our moral duties to actions is a failure of moral reasoning and imagination. Defenses of justification are those which show that certain conduct, that is, *prima facie*, criminally wrong, is, in fact, justified (for example, on the ground of reasonable self-defense). Defenses of excuse are based not on the claim that the conduct is justified, but on the claim that the conduct, albeit unjustified, is not blameworthy or culpable. Forms of mental state would be required as necessary moral conditions of just punishment. The principle of legality does not go the whole way of supplying advance warning.

> From the point of view of an original position which expresses the idea of treating persons as equals, rational people would agree to or universalize certain coercively enforceable standards of conduct which, at little comparable cost to the agent, secure substantial interests of others, for example, a principle of nonmaleficence (not killing, harming, or inflicting gratuitous cruelty). For reasons of justice, once a centralized legal system exists, the use of coercion to enforce these principles would be monopolized by the state. A principle of justified self-defense would be agreed to or universalized, however, as an exception to non-maleficence and the prohibition of private coercion, in circumstances where such coercive force is necessary to preserve the substantial interests of an agent from an attack which he has not occasioned and where the use of force is both necessary and proportional to the harm inflicted; the duty of retreat might, within limits, be an application of necessity and proportionality.[10]

Conclusions

The theory that we shall seek to elaborate here puts considerable emphasis on the changing character of the criminal law, the moral foundations of the substantive criminal law, the role and the place of the criminal trial, and the purpose of the criminal trial.

References

1. Hampton, J. (1988), "Punishment as Defeat", in Murphy, J.G. and Hampton, J., (eds.), *Forgiveness and Mercy.* Cambridge: Cambridge University Press, 124–132.
2. Stephen, J. F. (1883), *A History of the Criminal Law of England.* London: MacMillan, 80.
3. Hall, J. (1960), *General Principles of Criminal Law*, 2nd edn. Indianapolis: Bobbs-Merill, 385.
4. Blackwell, B. S., & Cunningham, C. D. (2004), "Taking the Punishment out of the Process: From Substantive Criminal Justice through Procedural Justice to Restorative Justice," *Law and Contemporary Problems* 67: 59–86.
5. Ashworth, A., & Zedner, L. (2008), "Defending the Criminal Law: Reflections on the Changing Character of Crime, Procedure, and Sanctions," *Criminal Law and Philosophy* 2: 25.
6. Ibid., 39.
7. Ibid., 48.
8. Green, S. P. (2008), "Rationing Criminal Procedure: A Comment on Ashworth and Zedner," *Criminal Law and Philosophy* 2: 53–58.
9. Grabosky, P., & Sutton, A. (1990), *Stains on a White Collar.* Sydney: Federation Press, 240–247.
10. Richards, D. A. J. (1979), "Human Rights and the Moral Foundations of the Substantive Criminal Law," *Georgia Law Review* 13: 1446.

READING 1.4

Accounting for Justice

The US Criminal Justice System will Benefit from a New Tool that Collects and Compares Data on a County-By-County Basis

By Amy Bach

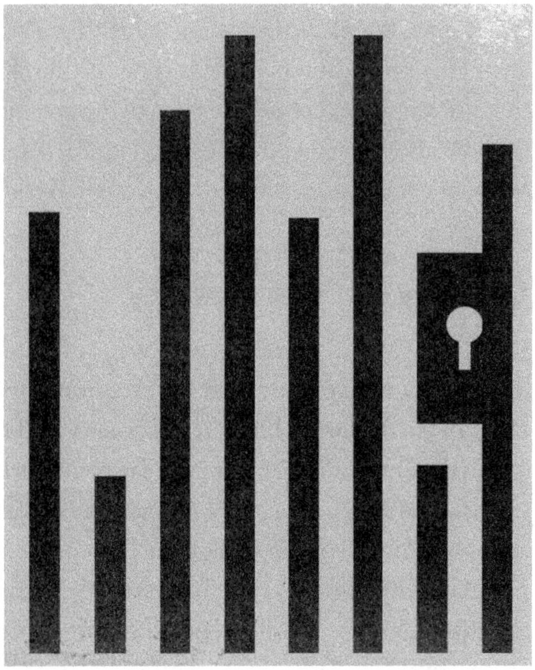

While doing research for a book, I met a woman in Mississippi who had been beaten by her boyfriend. She was in the hospital for days. But her case was never prosecuted. After some digging, I discovered that the local prosecutor hadn't prosecuted a single domestic violence case in 21 years.

"Has it been that long?" the prosecutor asked after I told him what I had found. Yes. That long. Resources were scarce, he explained, so he focused on prosecuting cases that he thought he could win. But in the process, he had let an entire category of cases fall by the wayside.

That prosecutor is far from alone. I spent eight years sitting in courts throughout the United States, and I saw how easy it is for well-meaning people to turn a blind eye to systemic problems. The US criminal justice system includes 3,143 counties, each with at least one state criminal trial court. Today, there is no accurate way to compare county-level performance to determine which courts need attention, or to evaluate which court practices work and which don't.

In April 2011, I founded Measures for Justice (MFJ), an organization that aims to create a Justice Index that will measure how criminal justice systems across the country are delivering basic services. For example, we created a measure to show prosecution rates of domestic violence arrests—in

Amy Bach, "Accounting for Justice," *Stanford Social Innovation Review*, vol. 11, no. 4, pp. 15-16.

Mississippi and elsewhere. Court insiders, criminal justice activists, journalists, and community members will be able to use data from the Justice Index to shed light on a given county's performance.

Nearly every public institution or resource in the United States—our schools, our hospitals, our water supply—is accountable to a watchdog system that provides comparative performance data. In education, measures such as student-teacher ratios and college admission rates have become standard tools for assessing the levels of opportunity that are available to students in different communities. In medicine, the Dartmouth Atlas of Health Care brings to light variations in resource allocation and in professional decision making, and it has become a common source of data for policy makers.

Criminal justice lags behind these realms, largely because there are no common measures that would allow one jurisdiction to compare its performance with that of other jurisdictions at each stage of the criminal justice process—from arrest to post-conviction. Federal, state, and local governments actually collect plenty of data. But there is no uniformity in the kinds of data that they collect or the way that they report that information. A county, for example, will typically count the number of people who enter its system. But its officials generally have no idea where the county ranks in terms of practices that prevent innocent people from being convicted, or practices that help to decrease recidivism. Nor do officials know how their county compares with others in money spent on holding people in jail. Without comparative data, we lack a crucial lever that would help us improve our system of due process.

County versus County

Our goal at MFJ is to create a wide array of measures that gauge performance in the areas that victims, defendants, legal professionals, and community members care most about. We are focusing on three areas in particular: public safety, equality and fairness, and efficient use of resources.

To develop indicators for each area, we worked with a multidisciplinary group of researchers and practitioners to draft a set of 50 measures. We then began to experiment with those measures in a series of pilots. In our first pilot, the Illustrative Measures Study, we selected 12 measures that we could populate with publicly available data. (We drew the data from the US Bureau of Justice Statistics and the FBI's Uniform Crime Reporting program, among other sources.) For many measures, we were able to find data for about half of the 100 largest US counties.

We found enormous differences between counties. Consider the example of average bail amounts. In 2004, Los Angeles County had an average bail of $169,047, whereas Broward County, Fla. (home to Ft. Lauderdale), had an average bail of $4,749. The purpose of bail is to ensure that a defendant will reappear in court. Even taking into account possible differences in patterns of criminal behavior, an average bail that's 35 times as high as that of another major metropolitan area counts as a big red flag.

Eventually, the Justice Index will become a system that's able to gather data from most, if not all, counties. It will create a picture that no single data point can provide.

Advocacy groups in California have long identified use of bail as a pressing issue. In the Illustrative Measures Study, five California counties were among those with the highest proportion of felony defendants who could not make bail or who were not assigned bail. Many counties in the state still rely on "bail schedules" to help judges process defendants quickly. San Bernardino County (whose average bail is $80,958) has a schedule that calls for assigning a bail of $25,000 to a defendant charged with delivering a check with insufficient funds. So a person who writes a bad check and who can't afford to pay that high bail amount might sit in jail for days or weeks or months. For years, legal experts have said that one-size-fits-all bail schedules are ill advised: They undermine judicial discretion and promote unnecessary detention. What's more, keeping people in overcrowded jails is costly—both for defendants, who lose valuable work time (and sometimes even lose their jobs), and for taxpayers.

Wouldn't it be beneficial to people in California to learn how other large US counties have tackled the challenge of setting bail? It's too soon to say exactly which counties have better practices than others. But of the counties in our study, Fairfax County, Va., stood out by having the lowest proportion of felony defendants in custody who were unable to make bail or who were not assigned bail. Here's one possible explanation for that result: Virginia has poured resources into a risk assessment tool that determines pre-trial release on the basis of a background investigation that screens for risk of flight and the risk of rearrest.

We shared the results of our Illustrative Measures Study with officials from counties that ranked either high or low on certain measures. Many officials, we discovered, are hungry for this information. Court administrators in St. Louis County, Mo., for example, asked to share our preliminary and incomplete data with their county's governing board. To them, these data were part of a success story: Among counties included in the study, St. Louis had the lowest percentage of defendants (4 percent in 2006) who were rearrested while awaiting trial—a sign that it had identified people with a high risk of reoffending and had taken necessary steps to reduce that risk.

King County, Wash., fell on the opposite end of the spectrum. It had the second-highest percentage of felony defendants (34 percent) who were rearrested while awaiting trial. But Dan Satterberg, the King County prosecutor, asked us for permission to share data from our study as well. "This could shame us into action," he said. Satterberg also highlighted the need for data that would allow counties to learn from one another about the design of effective re-entry programs, among other issues.

Better Data, Better Results

With the completion of the Illustrative Measures Study, our organization has moved beyond the proof-of-concept phase. We are now testing the measures to ensure that they are meaningful, accurate, and replicable. With support from the US Bureau of Justice Assistance, we have begun our first local pilot in Milwaukee County, Wis., where we will study the data that state and local officials collect and work to refine the measures. Then we will test those measures in other counties nationwide.

Eventually, we hope, the Justice Index will become a universal system that's able to gather data from most, if not all, counties. It will offer a bundle of measures that, taken together, will create a picture of the US justice system that no single data point can provide. We will use these data to identify best practices and to enable county officials to learn from each other. In short, better data will create better systems, which in turn will create better results.

We can't predict exactly how this initiative will play out. Take the example of the gross domestic product (GDP). An economist first unveiled the GDP model in 1937, and only after more than two decades of controversy did it become an established official metric. No one foresaw that it would become an established measure of national wealth. Our index will take time to develop, too. But its impact is potentially enormous. An estimated 65.7 million Americans—20 percent of the population—have a criminal record. And the number of Americans who are victims of crime is at least as high.

Bill Gates recently called for the adoption of a new, outcome-based model of philanthropy—one that is based on "setting clear goals, choosing an approach, measuring results, and then using those measurements to continually refine our approach." That model, he argued, will "[help] us to deliver tools and services to everybody who will benefit, be they students in the US or mothers in Africa."

Why not apply that model to the US criminal justice system? At MFJ, we are developing the tools to do so.

READING 1.5

Elaborating the Prison Industrial Complex

Race, Class, Gender and Social Control

By Kevin Wehr and Elyshia Aseltine

The American criminal justice system is often described as fulfilling one or more main goals of retribution, deterrence, incapacitation, and/or rehabilitation. The standard sanctions used to achieve these goals are intermediate sanctions (fines, community-based corrections, probation, parole), incarceration, and capital punishment. Since 1980, probation and incarceration have become the sanctions of choice in the United States—the United States now incarcerates 2.26 million people, or 732 out of every 100,000 people, and more than seven million people in the United States are under state supervision (Glaze 2011). Below we consider in more depth the various social groups that have borne the highest costs of our appetite for incarceration.

Race

The comedian Richard Pryor, in one of his stand-up comedy routines, jokes that he has finally figured out why they call it the "justice" system: Once you get inside you find out that it is "just us" (meaning African Americans). As Pryor's observation suggests, race is a deeply important social characteristic and in the criminal justice system. Racism has been a social fact in American society since its beginning. Our legacy of discrimination by **race** and **ethnicity** has profound effects on the criminal justice system, including policing and incarceration. The effect of race on the contemporary criminal justice system has led some to call it the "the new Jim Crow" (Alexander 2010).

Perhaps the best-known form of racial discrimination in the criminal justice system is racial profiling by police. In one scene of the film *Men in Black II*, Will Smith's character jokes that he used to have a black robotic driver, but switched to a white one because he kept getting pulled over. This scene suggests that racial profiling, or being targeted simply for "driving while black (or brown)," has become a common practice by law enforcement. Why is racial profiling and police policy significant for the Prison Industrial Complex? It is important because it is a clear demonstration of how we mobilize our resources based on ill-informed policy and ignorant cultural stereotypes—these processes are the very same processes that perpetuate racially disparate (or "just us") prisons.

What is the empirical reality for those guilty of "driving while black"? Statistical evidence indicates that black and Hispanic motorists are more likely to be pulled over, more likely to be asked to exit their vehicles, more likely to be searched, and more likely to receive harsh treatment from the police. In New Jersey, 35 percent of all drivers pulled over by state police were black, although they comprise only 13.5 percent of all drivers and 15 percent of driving law violators. In Maryland, only 17.5 percent of traffic violators were black, although black drivers accounted for 28.8 percent of those stopped and 71.3 percent of those arrested (Lamberth 2010). According to national data, young, Hispanic male drivers are 3.6 times more likely than white drivers to be searched, 2.3 times more likely to be arrested, and 3.4 times more likely to have force used against them during a traffic stop (Engel and Calnon 2004). Similar patterns were found for motorists in other states such as Ohio, Florida, Massachusetts, Rhode Island, North Carolina, and California. Racial profiling also appears to occur in pedestrian stops, with young black and Hispanic males more likely to be stopped and frisked on the streets (New York Attorney General's Office 1999). In summary, significant empirical evidence suggests that black and Hispanic people across the nation are subject to biased policing (Smith and Alpert 2007).

While some argue that police officers are "just doing their job," critics cry foul. Often traffic stops are initiated for non-hazardous reasons, such as a cracked tail light. Such minor problems are used as a pretext to find a reason to search the vehicle or its driver. There is an assumption that making vehicle stop decisions based on race or ethnicity is good policy because non-whites are more likely to participate in criminal activity, but this is erroneous—upon search, white and non-white motorists are equally likely to be found guilty of illegal possession of guns or drugs (Barnes and Kingsnorth 1996; Lamberth 2010). Think of police resources like a flashlight in a dark room. If you turn on the light and point it in any particular direction, you will see crime there. If you point it in another direction, crime is there, too. As a nation, we point our collective police resources toward poor communities of color and we find crime. This doesn't mean that there isn't crime elsewhere—we know there is—it just means we decided to shine the light in that direction.

If African Americans and Hispanics are subject to more **pretextual stops**, and are more likely to be searched during those stops, but are equally likely as whites to have committed a crime, why do police engage in this behavior? To address this question, we return to Patricia Hill Collins to consider her discussion of "**controlling images.**" Controlling images are stereotypical and degrading images that emphasize defective characteristics of a particular group to explain and justify cultural inferiority (Collins 1999). Much has been written about the controlling images of black men: common stereotypes cast them as aggressive, hypersexual, and criminal (Russell-Brown 1998). Similarly, controlling images of Hispanic men perpetuate stereotypes of dangerousness and illegality—largely by focusing on questionable citizenship and participation in gangs (Chavez 2008). Increasingly, young women of color are also being cast as dangerous and "unladylike" (Chesney-Lind and Jones 2010). Racial profiling cannot be understood without taking into account the existence of these culturally pervasive stereotypes of black and Hispanic dangerousness and criminality. The disproportionate number of people of color involved with the criminal justice system is then used to further justify increased surveillance and profiling. The result is a circular and cumulative cycle.

Although there certainly is a cultural bias that blacks are more likely to have guns or drugs and that there is more crime in the black community, does this bear out in the data? There is some amount of empirical research on this topic, but clear details are difficult to find on all types of crime. We know that 911 calls happen in inner-city and neighborhoods of color more than in the white suburbs, but this is likely an artifact of social conditions, such as density, heterogeneity, and mistrust, rather than black criminality. What also must be considered is the visibility of criminal activity and how increased visibility lends itself to increased chances of detection by the police (Goode 2002). For example, there is a great deal of interpersonal and intimate violence that goes on behind closed doors in the suburbs, while in the city center where pervasive segregation has relegated many of the nation's people of color, domestic violence is more likely to happen publicly, thus making it more visable to police and neighbors who might call 911.

The existence of, and reasons for, racial differences in criminal activity is hotly debated with the exception of one particular type of behavior: drug use. As it turns out, Americans use a lot of drugs. Some 20 million adults are current or recent users of illicit drugs, approximately 8 percent of the general population. When broken down by race, we see that 8.2 percent of whites report illegal drug use, Hispanics 6.6 percent, Blacks 9.5 percent, Asians 4.2 percent, American Indian/Alaska Natives 12.6 percent, and people of multiple races report a usage rate of 11.8 percent (Substance Abuse and Mental Health Services Administration 2008). What is remarkable about these numbers is the relatively tight range; Asians are low, American Indians are high, but most other races show little difference in drug usage.

What types of drugs are Americans using? There is some evidence that different groups prefer different types of drugs. In a study from the early nineties, the National Household Survey on Drug Abuse found that whites prefered Marlboro cigarettes by a huge margin, while blacks chose Newports (Office of National Household Survey on Drug Abuse 1991–1993). This might not be surprising given targeted advertising, but does it extend to illegal drugs? Since the eighties, there has been an assumption that crack cocaine is a black drug, while powder cocaine is a white drug. Sadly, most agencies that collect data on such topics do not differentiate between the two substances because chemically they are almost identical.

The law did differentiate, though. For most of the eighties and nineties, crack was punished more harshly than powder cocaine (the mandatory minimum punishment for possession of five grams of crack cocaine was five years in prison, while it required 500 grams of powder cocaine to get the same sentence). One study conducted during the early days of heavy anti-crack enforcement differentiates

Table 1.5.1 Drug Arrests by Race, Sacramento, 1987

	Drug involved by race of offender (in percent)			
Drug involved	**Caucasian**	**African American**	**Latino**	**Total cases**
Crack cocaine	2.9	78.3	7.5	
Powder cocaine	6.0	4.3	11.3	
Heroin	3.7	2.2	34.9	
Marijuana	13.3	9.2	11.3	
Methamphetamine	74.1	6.0	34.9	
Total	100.0	100.0	100.0	
Number of cases	517	414	106	1,037

Source: Barnes and Kingsnorth 1996; used with permission from Elsevier Science Ltd 1996 ©

arrests by race and type of drug. The results of the study, conducted in Sacramento County, are reproduced in Table 1.5.1. As the table reflects, black drug arrestees were much more likely to be arrested for crack offenses. Assuming that arrest rates mirror use patterns, there appears to be some truth to the idea that, at least for those arrested in Sacramento in the eighties, blacks used crack more than whites (Barnes and Kingsnorth 1996).

What is particularly interesting about this data is that the rates of methamphetamine use nearly reversed the trend in crack cocaine use—whites were much more likely to be arrested for meth. Remarkably, if you got arrested for either form of cocaine, you went to prison—a mandatory minimum sentence of 18 months for a first time possession offense. But if you were caught with methamphetamine the minimum sentence was just 12 months, meaning that you would go to county jail, not state prison, and were eligible for diversion, treatment, and other alternative programs. Thus, it is not patterns of drug use that cause differential rates of imprisonment by race, but rather, differential criminal justice responses to behaviors that vary by race (Beckett, et al. 2005). Although it may seem a subtle distinction, it is an important one.

The result of differential policing and unequal punishments is that 60 percent of inmates in American jails and prisons are people of color, and one out of every three black men will go to prison or jail sometime in their lives. In some places the percentage is even higher; for example, in California, 72 percent of prisoners are people of color (Petersilia 2008: 243). The national incarceration rate is 732 inmates per 100,000 people, but of course these are mostly men, and mostly black men—the incarceration rate for men is 1,352 per 100,000, whereas for black men it is a shocking 4,347 per 100,000 (Glaze 2011). Even more dramatic are the different likelihoods of going to prison at some point during one's lifetime. African-American men are eight times more likely to experience incarceration than white men (see Figure 1.5.2). Couple race with poor education, and incarceration is even more likely. By the end of the nineties, 21 percent of the nation's young black men without a high school degree were in a state or federal prison. This figure is astonishing, especially when compared to an imprisonment rate of less than 3 percent for white, poorly educated men. Incarceration has become such a frequent occurrence for young black men that some researchers describe it as "a normal stopping point on the route to midlife" (Pettit and Western 2004: 164).

Wrongful Convictions and Race: How Innocents Go to Jail

Ronald Huff (2002) interviewed judges, prosecutors, and law enforcement officials about error rates in the U.S. criminal justice system, and settled on the median response that mistakes are made about 0.5 percent of the time. Using this intentionally conservative estimate, this means that in any given year at least 7,500 people are wrongfully convicted of serious violent crimes. How does this happen?

The general public widely believes that eyewitness testimony is the gold standard of proof, yet witness error is the most frequent type of mistake that leads to wrongful conviction. Huff also identifies "overzealous law enforcement officers and prosecutors; ... false and coerced confessions; perjury; misleading lineups; inappropriate use of informants, or 'snitches;' ineffective assistance of counsellors" as well as outright incompetence and forensic errors (2002: 2). Deoxyribonucleic acid (DNA) evidence is commonly thought to solve such problems, but such evidence can be mishandled, and in most cases it simply doesn't exist. The Innocence Project and similar groups have used DNA to exonerate almost 300 wrongfully convicted innocent inmates, some of whom were on death row. They estimate that 84 percent were originally convicted from (clearly unreliable) eyewitness testimony (Scheck, Neufeld, and Dwyer 2000).

Since 1989, there have been 2,000 documented exonerations, half of which were African Americans. Most exonerations were for rape or murder cases (83 percent), which constitute only 2 percent of felonies but are more likely to include DNA evidence. Robbery and other crimes, where potentially exculpatory DNA evidence is comparatively rare, are under-represented in exoneration cases, yet logically they are equally likely to suffer from the error-causing factors described above (Gross and Shaffer 2012).

What can be done? Sadly, many of the factors that lead to the conviction of innocents will be difficult to undo. Of all exonerations, 27 percent stemmed from deliberate misidentification by eyewitnesses. People lie, and it will be hard to fix that. Official misconduct, inadequate defense counsel, and inappropriate use of informants might all be addressed through reforms to the way law enforcement and the judiciary do business—although this will take money and time. One disturbing problem is that of the sexual assault exonerations, 80 percent involved mistaken eyewitnesses and two-thirds of these had black defendants, while 72 percent had white victims. As Gross and Shaffer conclude:

> Most women who are raped are victimized by men of their own race. Interracial rape is uncommon and rapes of white women by black men are a small minority

> of all rapes, about 5%. But sexual assaults by black defendants on white victims were 53% of *all* exonerations in sexual assault cases with erroneous eyewitness identifications.
>
> Gross and Shaffer (2012: 49; italics in the original)

To say that solving the problem of cross-racial misidentification is difficult is an enormous understatement. Such issues of racial misperception are deeply entrenched.

Class

Today, as has been the case for the entire history of prisons, most inmates come from the ranks of the lower classes. When we examine the rates of those who are likely to experience incarceration, we see profound fractures not just by race but also by educational attainment—educational attainment is often used as a proxy, or substitute measurement, for class. In state institutions, 70 percent of inmates do not have a high school diploma; the average educational attainment is tenth grade (Western and Pettit 2010). Incarceration rates by level of education vary tremendously both within and between races. In 2008, 35 percent of black male high-school drop outs were in jail or prison, compared to 7 percent and 14 percent of Latino and white male high school drop-outs, respectively. Every group's incarceration rate has increased since the eighties (incarceration rates for each group in 1980: black, 10 percent; Latino, 4 percent; whites, 3 percent), suggesting that the patterns of incarceration for under-educated individuals are getting worse over time (Pettit, Sykes, and Western 2009).

In the preceding chapter we discussed the rise of the "tough on crime" movement. We return to this theme here, with the assistance of conflict theory, to elaborate on how class shapes criminal justice practices on a broader level. The famous slogan "Tough on crime" would be more accurate if a caveat was added: "Tough on some crime," or "Tough on crimes of the poor." Conflict theorists suggest that we have waged a war on crime *in the streets* for the last 50 years, while ignoring far more detrimental and extensive crime *in the suites.* Street crime consists of interpersonal crime such as murder, robbery, rape, and assault, while **suite crimes** are crimes "committed by a person of respectability and high social status in the course of his occupation" (Sutherland 1940: 9). Perhaps the boldest of **white-collar** criminals are corporations.

By almost any metric, corporate white-collar crime is far more costly and injurious than all street crime put together. It is difficult to estimate the costs of crime, but street crime costs society roughly $20 billion per year, and about 15,000 lives lost. Corporate crime costs society hundreds of billions of dollars, and kills perhaps 200,000 people per year (Coleman 2001). Although our murder rates are high compared to the rest of the developed world, these numbers pale in comparison to personal injury and death caused by corporations. Imagine if we could tally the number of workers injured or killed due to unsafe working conditions, such as the mine tragedy in Pennsylvania in 2009. What cost can be put on the explosion of the Deepwater Horizon oil rig in the Gulf of Mexico in 2008? Tobacco corporations have denied their products' harm for decades and used their economic and political influence to dismiss or water down regulations that could have saved the lives of millions.

Ironically, the light penalties for corporate crime may make corporate crime economically rational in many cases. Because fines are relatively low compared to the financial benefits gained by the corporation, there is a perverse incentive to break the law. Differential punishment between crimes on the street and crimes in the suites is a fundamental problem of the Prison Industrial Complex.

Gender

Women are both victims (often) and perpetrators (more rarely) of crime. Increasingly, women are prisoners. There were 205,165 women in prison or jail in the United States: in 2010, about 9 percent of the total prison population (Glaze 2011). This represents 126 women per 100,000 of the total female population, 10 times less then the incarceration rate for men. Yet this is 17 times the number of women who were incarcerated in 1980, when there were just 12,331 women incarcerated, or 11 per 100,000 of the total female population of the United States (BJS 2003). Minority women are being disproportionately imprisoned, and usually for non-violent property and drug conspiracy crimes. As illustrated in Figure 1.5.2, incarceration patterns within races demonstrate a dramatic mirroring between male and female incarceration.

There are several explanations for increased women's incarceration. Underlying many of these explanations is an implicit critique of the feminist movement of the seventies. The fundamental explanation is that there is a dark side to women's entry into the workforce and exit from the home. For example, the "**masculinity thesis**" posits that women today are behaving like men, that is, engaging

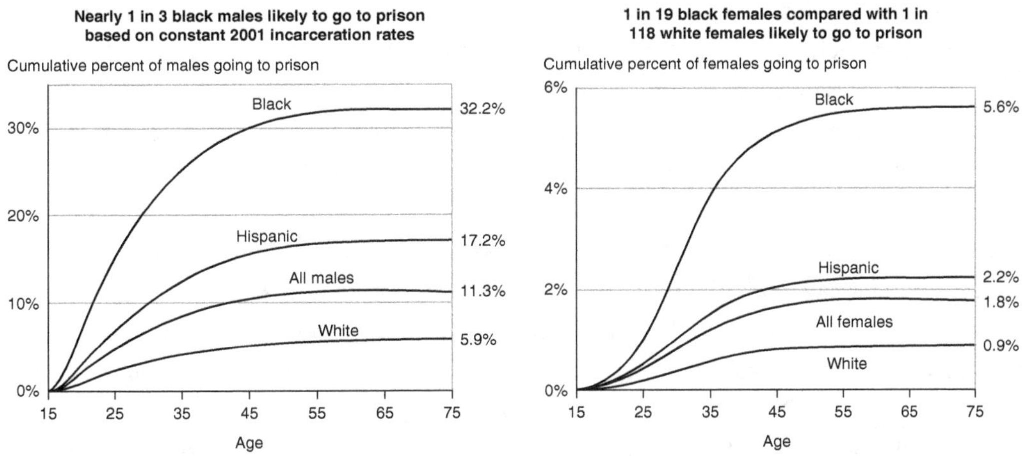

Figure 1.5.2 Lifetime likelihood of going to prison, by race and sex.

Source: Adapted from "**Prevalence of Imprisonment in the U.S. Population, 1974–2001**," Thomas P. Bonczar, BJS, Statistician, Bureau of Labor Statistics.

in crime. **Opportunity theorists** argue a similar vein, that as women enter the workforce in more diverse ways, they have more chances to commit crime. Lastly, the "equality thesis" indicates that there has been a shift in judicial and law enforcement attitudes to be tougher on female criminals—to treat them equally to men. The most persuasive approach to understanding the interaction of women and crime is the "**marginalization thesis**," which suggests that women suffer a continued lack of equal employment and equal pay, driving them toward crime and conspiratorial association with criminals (Akers 2004).

The feminist marginalization thesis identifies **patriarchy** as the most important form of inequality that shapes the everyday lives of women. Patriarchy is a system of oppression based on sex and gender: men have a disproportionate amount of social and economic power in most modern societies. Based on this understanding, a feminist analysis of crime focuses on the ways in which women's continued economic marginalization influences their participation in crime. It also points out the minimization or disregard for forms of victimization most commonly experienced by women, and the ways in which laws and their enforcement support and reproduce gender inequality. In short, criminal justice practices reinforce male dominance, as well as traditional sex roles, behaviors, and values. Rather than reflect advances in women's liberation, women's participation in crime is more heavily influenced by women's own histories of victimization and experiences of economic marginality (Steffensmeier 1996); for example, the sex trade, where enforcement against sex workers (overwhelmingly women) is more common than against their clients or "Johns" (mostly men). Such enforcement patterns resonate with larger social norms about how women and men are expected to behave (i.e., women are to be chaste while men may engage in frequent sexual activity with numerous partners).

A growing body of research about women's treatment by police and judges illustrates the complexity of interactions of race, class, and gender. Although some women may experience "softer" penalties for engaging in criminal activity, this experience is not universal. As shown in Figure 1.5.2, African-American women are more likely to be arrested and to experience harsh punishments, such as detention, than their white counterparts (MacDonald and Chesney-Lind 2001).

Women prisoners experience unique problems while in prison. Access to health care (as well as social, educational, and vocational services) remains more limited as compared to male prison populations. Furthermore, women are subjected to a great deal of discrimination and sexual abuse in detention facilities. There have been documented cases of improper viewing of women in cells by male guards and wardens, inappropriate or unnecessary full body searches, including searches of the breast and genital area, and, sadly, outright rape (Amnesty International 1999). One prison warden in California, when asked by a "Nightline" reporter about charges of frequent and unnecessary gynecological exams of female prisoners, replied that women liked the exams because "it's the only male contact they get" (Delsohn 1999: A4).

Patricia Hill Collins, with her notion of the matrix of domination, reminds us that three major lines of fracture within American society are so deeply interrelated as to defy any simple separate analysis. Race, class, and gender represent an interconnected matrix of domination where, in Collins' words, "each system needs the others in order to function" (Collins 1990: 222). Despite this insight, the reality is that experiences of women in general, and women of color in the criminal justice system specifically, are understudied. We know much less about crime and criminal justice patterns for women than we do for men.

Political Orientation

The criminal justice system has been used to suppress radical viewpoints and unaccepted religions, and to control subversive minorities. This has been done covertly and overtly, with the most famous example being the Federal Bureau of Investigation's (FBI's) counterintelligence program in the fifties and sixties. "**COINTELPRO**" engaged in illegal and unethical practices targeting activists such as Martin Luther King, Jr. and others associated with the civil rights and black nationalist movements, as well as the American Indian Movement, Students for a Democratic Society, the Communist Party of the USA, and the Puerto Rican Independencias (Churchill and Vander Wall 1990).

Many political activists have been jailed for their political views. There are names we recognize from the media: Mumia Abu-Jamal, Leonard Peltier, Assata Shakur, Angela Davis. Often the charges against political prisoners are "trumped up." Angela Davis was famously set free after facing the death penalty for three crimes she did not commit. Leonard Peltier and Mumia Abu-Jamal both have steadfastly maintained their innocence after being convicted in trials that were biased and unjust (Abu-Jamal 1996; Peltier 2000).

In some cases, the penalty far outweighs any harm done. Even in the absence of an actual crime, like the sensational murders that led to the arrests of Peltier, Davis, and Abu-Jamal, a person's political beliefs can become the focus of a prosecution and lead to a lengthy prison sentence. The case of Eric McDavid in Sacramento, California is such an example. In 2008, McDavid was found guilty of conspiring to commit arson. An FBI informant had befriended McDavid and two other young environmentalists, and over the course of 18 months pushed them to join a plot to bomb a dam on the American River near Sacramento. The two others agreed to plead guilty and testify against McDavid. Although action was never taken to implement the bombing plot, he was found guilty of conspiracy and sentenced to 20 years in prison. Critics argued that McDavid was entrapped—there would be no conspiracy if the FBI informant had not pressured the three for over a year. The first sentence of the criminal complaint against McDavid states: "Eric McDavid, 28, is an anarchist," suggesting that what was really on trial was Eric's political perspective.

What makes McDavid's case even more interesting is the comparison to an arson case involving the *same prosecutor* but another defendant. In 2010, Alexander Piggee started a fire in a Sacramento suburban shopping mall, causing $55 million in damages. In McDavid's case, the federal prosecutor Steven Lapham sought the maximum sentence for Eric, but let his two conspirators off with no jail time. In the Piggee case, Lapham argued for leniency: "Typically, in these cases there is a malevolent motive. None was apparent here." Lapham went on to say that this was a case of a "kid who did a stupid act" (Walsh and Stanton 2011).

Comparing the two cases brings out the manner in which political orientation can influence outcomes in the criminal justice system. When compared to the treatment of an actual arsonist by the same prosecutor, the political nature of the McDavid prosecution becomes apparent. Critics point out that in McDavid's case there was no action, no damage, no lives put in jeopardy. There was only a "conspiracy," driven by an FBI informant. In Piggee's case there were two fires that destroyed property and put lives in danger. For McDavid it was not just the possibility of an action (which never happened, and probably never would have), but instead his political motivations that brought about his harsh sentence.[1] Individual examples can be misleading as anecdotes, but good statistics are nearly impossible to find. Some critics estimate that there are 100 to 150 political prisoners in the United States today, but according to the government there are no political prisoners in America (James 2003; Kohn 1994). Critics of the American criminal justice system point out that certain forms of speech and action are harshly punished while others are not. With recent upsurges in protests like the "Occupy" and anti-globalization movements, there will be continued political repression.

Outside of the extreme cases of political prisoners, political control of prisoners happens every day through felon **disenfranchisement** (the denial of the right to vote). Incarcerated felons cannot vote in all states but Maine and Vermont; felons are barred from voting forever in nine states; and four more states bar certain felons forever (mostly those convicted of drug offenses). Almost all incarcerated people cannot vote due to a lack of access—prisons generally don't set up polling places in their exercise yards. Since prisons are overwhelmingly filled with people of color, some have argued that this is an effective way to keep black and Hispanic communities from participating in the political process. In fact, the passage of felon disenfranchisement laws is intimately linked to race—shortly after the Civil War these laws were introduced to prevent emancipated slaves from exercising their new political rights. Contemporary revivals of felon disenfranchisement laws are more common in places with higher proportions of non-whites. The effect of these laws is astounding. In the 2004 presidential election, approximately 5.3 million people were barred from casting their vote, including 13 percent of the nation's African-American males (Uggen and Manza 2006).

Conclusion

The number of people held in jails and prisons or under state supervision throughout the country has increased dramatically, with the long arm of the correctional system directly affecting 2.4 percent of Americans. Some groups are disproportionately exposed to this system. People of color, the poor, and those with unpopular political views are more likely to be targets of social control. Women, although incarcerated at lower rates than men, are increasingly being subjected to incarceration—the increase of women inmates is most devastating in communities of color. In the next section we consider the Prison Industrial Complex from another angle: the consequences of the incarceration boom for all those who fall prey to its grasp. We focus on both direct (inmates themselves) and indirect victims (families and communities of the incarcerated, and American democracy).

Note

1. The authors are indebted to Evan Tucker for his analysis of Eric McDavid's case.

Discussion Questions

1. Describe how mass incarceration has affected communities of color. How has it affected women and those with unpopular political views?
2. What is "patriarchy"? How does it affect women's incarceration?
3. What do you think are the common causes of criminal misidentification? What protections may be implemented in order to reduce the likelihood of misidentification?
4. How has the war on drugs affected incarceration in the United States? Do you think that a "war" on drugs is beneficial? Why or why not? What other ways might we address drug use in the United States?
5. What policies might governments and law enforcement administrators adopt in order to prevent racial profiling?
6. Why do law enforcement and the media seem to focus so little on corporate crime?
7. Do you agree or disagree with the differences in punishments of McDavid and Piggee (the two arson-related cases)? Explain.

References

Abu-Jamal, M. 1996. *Live from Death Row.* New York: Harper Perennial.

Akers, R. 2004. *Criminological Theories.* Los Angeles: Roxbury Publishing.

Alexander, M. 2010. *The New Jim Crow.* New York: The New Press.

Amnesty International. 1999. *USA: "Not Part of My Sentence:" Violations of the Human Rights of Women in Custody.* New York: Amnesty International USA.

Barnes, C. W., & R. Kingsnorth. 1996. "Race, Drug, and Criminal Sentencing: Hidden Effects of the Criminal Law." *Journal of Criminal Justice 24(1)*: 39–55.

Beckett, K., Nyrop, K., Pfingst, L., & Bowen. M. 2005. "Drug Use, Drug Possession Arrests, and the Question of Race: Lessons from Seattle." *Social Problems 52(3)*: 419–41.

Bonczar, T. P. 1997. "Prevalence of Imprisonment in the U.S. Population, 1974–2001." Bureau of Labor Statistics.

Bureau of Justice Statistics (BJS). 2003. *Sourcebook of Criminal Justice Statistics.*

Chavez, L. R. 2008. *The Latino Threat.* Stanford: Stanford University Press.

Chesney-Lind, M., & Jones, N. eds. 2010. *Fighting for Girls.* Albany: SUNY Press.

Churchill, W., & Vander Wall. 1990. *The COINTELPRO Papers.* Boston: South End Press.

Coleman, J. W. 2001. *The Criminal Elite.* New York: Worth.

Collins, P. H. 1990. *Black Feminist Thought.* Boston: Unwin Hyman.

———. 1999. "Mammies, Matriarchs, and Other Controlling Images." Pp. 142–52 in *Feminist Philosophies, 2nd ed.*, eds. J. Kournay, J. Sterba, and R. Tong. Upper Saddle River: Prentice Hall.

Delsohn, G. 1999. "Prison Doctor Loses Post over TV Comment—He Told Newsman Women Inmates Like Pelvic Exams." *Sacramento Bee* (October 15): A4.

Engel, R., & Calnon, J. 2004. "Examining the Influence of Drivers' Characteristics during Traffic Stops with Police: Results from a National Survey." *Justice Quarterly 21(1)*: 49–89.

Glaze, L. E. 2011. *Correctional Population in the United States, 2010.* Washington, D.C.: U.S. Bureau of Justice Statistics.

Goode, E. 2002. "Drug Arrests at the Millennium." *Society 39(5)*: 41–45.

Gross, S. R., & Shaffer, M. 2012. *Exonerations in the United States, 1989–2012.* Report by the National Registry of Exonerations, a joint project of the University of Michigan Law School and the Center on Wrongful Convictions at Northwestern University School of Law.

Huff, C. Ronald. 2002. "Wrongful Conviction and Public Policy: The American Society of Criminology 2001 Presidential Address." *Criminology 40(1)*: 1–19.

James, J., ed. 2003. *Imprisoned Intellectuals.* New York: Rowman and Littlefield.

Kohn, S. 1994. *American Political Prisoners.* Santa Barbara: Praeger.

Lamberth, J. 2010. "Driving While Black: A Statistician Proves That Prejudice Still Rules the Road." Pp. 32–35 in *Race, Ethnicity, and Policing: New and Essential Readings*, eds. S. Rice and M. White. New York: New York University Press.

MacDonald, J., & M. Chesney-Lind. 2001. "Gender Bias and Juvenile Justice Revisited." *Crime & Delinquency 47(2)*: 173–95.

New York Attorney General's Office. 1999. *The New York City Police Department's "Stop & Frisk" Practices.* New York: New York Attorney General's Office.

Office of National Household Survey on Drug Abuse. 1991–1993. Substance Abuse and Mental Health Services Administration, Office of Applied Studies (1996). *Substance Abuse in States and Metropolitan Areas: Model Based Estimates from the 1991–1993 National Household Surveys on Drug Abuse.* OAS Analytic Paper, DHHS Publication No. (SMA) 96-3095, Rockville, MD, September 1996.

Peltier, L. 2000. *Prison Writings.* New York: St. Martin's Press.

Petersilia, J. 2008. "California's Correctional Paradox of Excess and Deprivation." Pp. 207–78 in *Crime and Justice, Volume 37*, ed. Michael Tonry. Chicago: The University of Chicago Press.

Pettit, Becky, Sykes, B., & Western, B. 2009. *Technical Report on Revised Population Estimates and NLSY79 Tables for the Pew Public Safety and Mobility Project.* Boston: Harvard University.

Pettit, Becky, & Western, B. 2004. "Mass Imprisonment and the Life Course: Race and Class Inequality in U.S." *American Sociological Review 69(2)*: 151–69.

Russell-Brown, K. 1998. *The Color of Crime.* New York: New York University Press.

Scheck, Barry, Neufeld, P. & Dwyer, J. 2000. *Actual Innocence.* New York: Doubleday.

Smith, Michael, & Alpert, G. 2007. "Explaining Police Bias: A Theory of Social Conditioning and Illusory Correlation." *Criminal Justice and Behavior 34(1):* 262–83.

Steffensmeier, D. 1 996. "Gender and Crime: Toward a Gendered Theory of Female Offending." *Annual Review of Sociology 22*: 459–87.

Substance Abuse and Mental Health Services Administration. 2008. *Results from the 2007 National Survey on Drug Use and Health* (DHHS Publication No. SMA 08-4343). Rockville: Office of Applied Studies.

Sutherland, E. 1940. "White-collar Criminality." *American Sociological Review 5(1)*: 1–12.

Uggen, C., & Manza, J. 2006. "Democratic Contraction? Political Consequences of Felon Disenfranchisement in the United." *American Sociological Review 67(6)*: 777–803.

Walsh, D., & Stanton, S. 2011. "Galleria Arsonist Likely to Face 10 Years in Prison." Sacramento Bee. Retrieved March 8, 2011 (http://blogs.sacbee.com/crime/archives/2011/03/suspect-in-gall.html).

Wehr, K., et al. 2009. "Where Our Money Goes." *Sacramento News and Review* (June 25).

Western, B., & Pettit, B. 2010. "Incarceration & Social Inequality." *Daedalus 139*: 3, 8–19.

READING 1.6

How Mexican Cartels Are Changing the Face of Immigration

By Sylvia Longmire

One could argue that Ecuadorian immigrant Luis Fredy Lala Pomavilla is lucky to be alive. In August 2010, Luis and seventy-two other migrants from Central and South America were traveling north through Mexico in the back of two freight trucks. Some had paid up to USD 10,000 for safe passage to Texas through eastern Mexico, believing their *coyotes*, or paid human smugglers, knew this to be the safest route. Unfortunately, this route would take them through Tamaulipas state, the bloody battlefield of the rival Gulf and Los Zetas drug cartels.

At some point in the afternoon, the trucks were about nine miles north of the town of San Fernando—roughly ninety miles from the border with Texas—on Highway 101 when they came across a roadblock. Armed men wearing facemasks emerged from three vehicles parked across the road and identified themselves as members of Los Zetas. The men ordered all the migrants out of the freight trucks, put them into several pickup trucks, and took them to a warehouse on an abandoned ranch nearby. In all, fifty-eight men and fourteen women were lined up against a wall in the warehouse and interrogated about where they came from, where they were going, what they did for a living, and if they worked for the Gulf Cartel. All of them denied having any links to trafficking organizations.[1]

Not completely satisfied with their answers, the leader of the group, nicknamed "El Kilo," offered the migrants one last chance: they could work for Los Zetas as forced labor. All of them refused. In response to their refusal, the captors ordered the migrants to lie face down on the ground, then executed them with several rounds from assault rifles. To ensure everyone was dead, the men delivered a final shot into the head of every migrant. However, one of those *coup de grâce* shots went astray and caught Luis in the neck instead of in the head. Despite being in a massive amount of pain from the bullet that exited through his jaw, he played dead until his captors left the ranch.[2]

Sylvia Longmire, "How Mexican Cartels Are Changing the Face of Immigration," *The Fletcher Forum of World Affairs*, vol. 38, no. 2, pp. 109-114.

Luis managed to travel several miles to a Mexican Marine checkpoint, where he told the soldiers what happened. Once the Marines made it to the site of the massacre, they discovered the seventy-two bodies exactly as Luis had described. They also seized twenty-one firearms and detained a minor, most likely associated with the cartel.[3] El Kilo and his people avoided the Marine raid, and hid out in nearby Ciudad Victoria for several months. However, he and eleven of his accomplices were arrested in April 2011, although his boss, Salvador "La Ardilla" Martinez, remained at large.[4]

Los Zetas, in particular, are increasingly preying on vulnerable immigrants, viewing them as a potential source of ransom money or forced labor.

This massacre is just one example in which Mexican cartels are changing the nature of northbound human migration in Latin America. Los Zetas, in particular, are increasingly preying on vulnerable immigrants, viewing them as a potential source of ransom money or forced labor. But Los Zetas are certainly not the only drug trafficking group involved in reaping the profits of the human smuggling business. A report by the Woodrow Wilson International Center for Scholars stated, "Factions of many [organized crime groups] engage in similar activities, either directly or indirectly. The Gulf Cartel appears to be the most active, and works with both the Mexican police and Mexican migration officials in order to capture its victims." It also said, "Factions of the Juárez and Tijuana cartels also collect *piso* [a tax, or toll] from local smugglers and may, in the case of Juárez, be directly involved in trafficking. Portions of the old La Familia Michoacana, now called the Caballeros Templarios (the Knights Templar), and the Sinaloa Cartel have also reportedly displaced coyotes operating in their territories and have attempted to take over this business."[5]

Acclaimed journalist and producer for Al Jazeera America, Christof Putzel discovered this first-hand while filming a documentary for the now-defunct Current TV's *Vanguard* series. In November 2010, Putzel and Mexican-American filmmaker Juan Carlos Frey recorded their attempt to smuggle themselves across the southwest border in a manner as close as possible to that of hundreds of thousands of migrants every year. "What was nuts is that, when we initially planned to shoot this, we thought we would just get some 'mom and pop' *coyote* operation, and those things don't exist anymore. The cartels run the show," Putzel said about his experience. "So we needed to get permission from the cartels to do this [episode]. Part of the deal was, they would be okay with us doing it as long as we only talked about migrants and didn't mention anything about drug trafficking. They really didn't want us reporting on that at all."[6]

Immigration attorneys on the U.S. side of the border are seeing more and more cases of immigrants being coerced at gunpoint to work as drug mules. The cartels threaten them and their family members, giving them strict orders on where to haul drug loads as heavy as sixty pounds over unforgiving terrain and under penalty of death. Elizabeth Rogers, a federal public defender in West Texas, has said most of her recent backpacker cases claim coercion. "About a year and a half ago, ourselves as well as our investigators started seeing these clients that would say, *I don't care how long I'm going to get [in jail time], I can't go home—they'll kill me*," she told National Public Radio in 2011. "[We] have grown men, rawboned cowboy guys from Chihuahua, begging for protection from deportation."[7]

As a result of the increasing violence in Mexico and the targeting of innocent immigrants by drug cartels, the number of applications for asylum by Mexican nationals passing through U.S. immigration courts is skyrocketing.

Raul Miranda, a criminal defense attorney in Tucson, Arizona, has said about one-third of his clients have claimed they were unwilling drug mules. "They're told by the people—who obviously work for the cartels—that they have to carry the bundle, or they'll reduce the fee that they're going to have to pay, or they'll forgive the fee. But the people who are telling them this are armed, and the people feel threatened if they say no."[8]

As a result of the increasing violence in Mexico and the targeting of innocent immigrants by drug cartels, the number of applications for asylum by Mexican nationals passing through U.S. immigration courts is skyrocketing. In 2005, there were 2,670 applications filed, and that number rose to 2,818 in 2006. By 2010, applications had increased to 3,231, and nearly doubled to 6,133 in fiscal year 2012. However, between 2007 and 2011, only 2 percent of requests from Mexico were granted, compared to 38 percent of requests from Chinese nationals and 89 percent of Armenian applicants.[9]

Unfortunately, while the nature of cross-border migration has changed significantly in the last decade, immigration laws and the guidelines for granting asylum have not. Asylum has historically been associated with the Cold War and communism, and refugees fleeing the political and social oppression imposed on them by tyrants. In decades past, we would hear about "defectors" from places like the Soviet Union, Cuba, and North Korea. Today, China and Cuba are still popular countries for citizens with asylum requests, but U.S. courts are host to more and more applicants from countries like Afghanistan, Iraq, Iran, Somalia, and Pakistan—nations categorized as failed or failing states with governments that cannot protect their citizens, and in some cases, are actively oppressing their freedoms and rights.

Requesting asylum has not really been a popular or necessary option for Mexican immigrants until drug-related violence started spreading in earnest and the ties between government officials, law enforcement officers, and the cartels became stronger and more blatant. In some cases, it is very clear that the Mexican government is unable to provide adequate protection to an asylum applicant, the police are directly involved in the harm being caused, and the local government is obviously looking the other way while it happens. But in other cases, requesting asylum becomes a last-ditch effort by illegal immigrants to avoid deportation when they never would have considered applying if they hadn't gotten caught. This only delays the inevitable and

As the drug war continues in Mexico, fear may become the primary motivating factor for migrants heading north, rather than the lure of better economic opportunities.

clogs up the already backed-up immigration court system. As comprehensive immigration reform plans progress through U.S. political channels, it is important to keep an eye on asylum provisions and how they might change; it could have a huge impact on how these cases are processed in the future.

As the drug war continues in Mexico, fear may become the primary motivating factor for migrants heading north, rather than the lure of better economic opportunities. As one asylum applicant stated after her application was denied, "I will not hesitate to stay here illegally. I would rather do that than ever go to Mexico again, even if it means illegal re-entry. It's not that I want to live in the U.S. I never did. But I cannot go back. I do not want to die."[10]

Whether it is Mexicans, Cubans, Chinese, or Iraqis, foreigners will always want to come to the United States. Most of them will not be able to enter or stay here legally. Because the security situation in Mexico and Central America has deteriorated so badly over the last decade, citizens of those countries are more motivated than ever to run the risks of the northbound journey. And it does not matter to them how many border patrol agents get assigned to the border, or how many miles of fence the government builds. Maybe twenty years ago it was easier to detect undocumented immigrants along our borders, process them, and send them back to their home countries. But now our cross-border traffic has become a blur—a gray area where drug traffickers and migrants blend together and have become more difficult to separate.

It is clear that as long as the United States is safer than Mexico—which will be the case for the foreseeable future—Mexican and Central American citizens will go to great lengths to come here and avoid being returned home, no matter what border enforcement actions we take or laws we pass. It's also guaranteed that as long as the American demand for illegal drugs continues, Mexican cartels will exploit every aspect of cross-border migration for their own profit-seeking purposes.

Notes

1. "Their Dreams Ended in The San Fernando Massacre," August 24, 2012, <http://www.borderlandbeat.com/2012/08/their-dreams-ended-in-san-fernando.html> (accessed February 25, 2014).
2. Ibid.
3. "Survivor Details Massacre of 72 Migrants by Drug Cartel in Mexico," August 25, 2010, <http://www.foxnews.com/world/2010/08/25/mexican-government-migrants-dead-ranch-killed-zetas-drug-gang/> (accessed February 25, 2014).
4. "Their Dreams Ended in The San Fernando Massacre."
5. Steven Dudley, "Transnational Crime in Mexico and Central America: Its Evolution and Role in International Migration," Migration Policy Institute, Woodrow Wilson International Center for Scholars, November 2012.

6. Christof Putzel, Interview by Sylvia Longmire. Telephone interview. July 27, 2013.
7. John Burnett, "Migrants Say They're Unwilling Mules For Cartels," December 4, 2011, <http://m.npr.org/news/front/143025654> (accessed February 26, 2014).
8. Ibid.
9. Ioan Grillo, "Mexico's drug-war refugees seek asylum," September 15, 2011, <http://www.tucsonsentinel.com/nationworld/report/091511_mexico_asylum/mexicos-drug-war-refugees-seek-asylum/> (accessed February 26, 2014).
10. Chris Vogel and Patrick Michels, "Asylum Denied: Unlike Refugees from Other Troubled Countries, Only a Fraction of Mexicans Seeking U.S. Asylum Are Accepted—No Matter Their Wounds or Stories," August 26, 2010, <http://www.phoenixnewtimes.com/2010-08-26/news/asylum-unlike-refugees-from-other-troubled-countries-only-a-fraction-of-mexicans-seeking-u-s-asylum-are-accepted-no-matter-their-wounds-or-stories/4/> (accessed February 27).

READING 1.7

The Border Industry

By Ruben Andersson

Driving towards Mexico through Arizona, watchtowers rise out of the dry soil like tall cacti. The highway is adorned with clutches of cameras and blocked by a vast Border Patrol checkpoint. Down at the border itself, a tall fence of rust-brown steel drives a wedge between *ambos Nogales*—'both Nogales', as the interlinked US and Mexican towns are known. In the hinterland, drones buzz over the rattlesnake-infested ground, which is dotted by sensors whose antennae sprout like desert weed.

'You have to watch where you step,' says one middle-aged Central American man at a shelter in Nogales, Mexico, as he mimics a mine-clearing movement. The other migrants around us murmur and nod. Some of them are new to the route, some veterans, others deportees bent on returning home to the US. All are caught up in the 'cat-and-mouse game' of the border, where they are chased like prey while also playing another, complementary role: as guinea pigs in a state-of-the-art border control laboratory.

Across the industrialized world, public debate on migration is focused on numbers and the drama of recurrent border 'crises': massed arrivals and crowded camps; the saved, the drowned, the deported. How many people can we accept? How can we make them stay away? Republican presidential candidates such as Donald Trump assure voters the solution is to 'secure the border'. In Australia and Israel, militarized borders have also proved to be a vote-winner and a growth sector. The same goes for Europe, where bickering politicians only seem able to agree on one thing—beefed-up borders. As the European Council president, Donald Tusk, said last November, the means of saving the Schengen system of passport-less travel within the European Union (EU) was to 'first and foremost, restore external border control'.

However, what politicians like Trump and Tusk fail to mention is that border security has been booming for many years already, generating a large public-private industry. The US spends some $12 billion a year on customs and border protection, including massive increases in Border Patrol

Bordernomics

Who's cashing in on keeping migrants out?

Smugglers [1, 2, 3]

$17.5 billion

estimated smuggler profits on routes to Europe, 2000-15

$30,000

paid to smugglers, in cash, by Australian officials to push a boat of asylum-seekers back to Indonesia

agents and new technology; Europe for its part has largely mimicked the US, seeking to 'seal' borders since the early days of Schengen in the 1990s.

I surveyed the tragic, and sometimes absurd, results of the EU's security response to unwanted migration in my book *Illegality, Inc.* At the six-metre-tall fences that encircle Spain's small North African enclaves of Ceuta and Melilla, border guards proudly showed me the advanced machinery installed to halt undocumented migrants, yet admitted the barriers were rather 'useless'. After all, undocumented Africans kept clambering across the barbed-wired barriers—or else diverted towards more dangerous sea routes.

In West Africa, I followed local police on the patrols they carry out on Europe's behalf, hearing about their frustrated attempts—despite the new gadgetry at their disposal—to monitor thousands of kilometres of desert sands and coastlines.

In such sites, I came to see how Europe's security approach to 'halting migration' is failing spectacularly. Like the 'war on drugs', the 'fight against illegal migration' is what economists would call a 'supply-centric' effort. As a punitive attempt to cut off supply 'upstream', it fails to address demand—for safety and work, among refugees and migrants, or for labour, at destination countries. And it has brought immense 'negative externalities'—misery and chaos—without actually succeeding in its purported task of stopping migration.

Balloon Effect

As in the drug wars, migrant routes shift in response to crackdowns and fences, generating displacement effects not just within regions, but increasingly on a global scale, too. Evidence suggests that West Africans have moved on from Spain to Italy and Syrians from Italy to Greece; that Australia's 'no boats' policy may have contributed to the 'boat people' dramas on the Andaman Sea; and that Afghans have turned away from Israel and Australia to head instead towards Europe.[1,2]

Each shift forces migrants to take bigger risks along more dangerous routes, meaning more recourse to smugglers—but also more demand for border security. As refugees change direction, Balkan states build new barriers to keep them out; and when people keep drowning in the Mediterranean, politicians launch a military operation targeting smugglers' boats, or push Turkey to boost patrols. In this way, the failure of controls has perversely fed a market for ever more controls.

> *Europe's security approach to 'halting migration' is failing spectacularly*

'Migration is something that will never stop,' one frustrated Spanish Civil Guard told me, even as he showed me the latest surveillance systems rolled out for his coastlines. His assessment rang all too true from the Europe of 2015. Despite huge sums spent on border security, arrivals surpassed 800,000 in 2015 and some 3,500 people died trying.

The Winners

But while the 'fight against illegal migration' may be failing, it is proving a great success for those groups that stand to gain. These groups—which jointly make up what I call an 'illegality industry'—include the defence contractors providing the hardware; private-security companies that increasingly handle deportation and detention; border guards and military forces with bolstered status and resources; even the 'non-profit' sector which, along with international organizations, often collaborates with

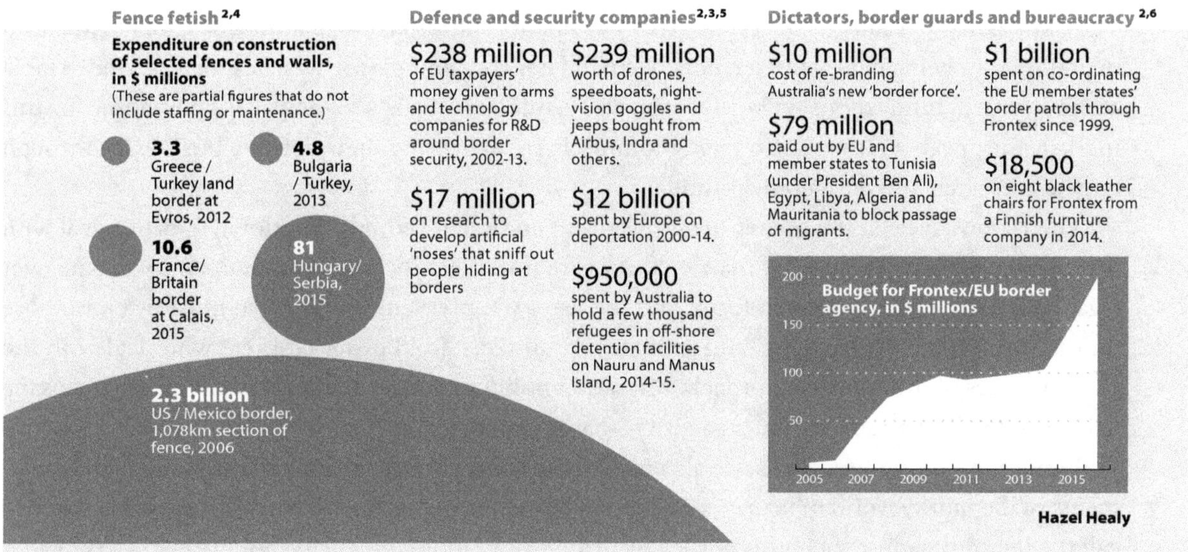

Sources for facts above:

1. Regional Mixed Migration Secretariat nin.tl/BeyondDefinitions
2. The Money Trails themigrantsfiles.com
3. Amnesty International nin.tl/Turnbacks
4. ABC News nin.tl/ABCFactCheck
5. *The Sydney Morning Herald* nin.tl/10MillionSplash
6. The Bureau of Investigative Journalism nin.tl/FrontexChaos

the security response; and neighbouring 'partner' countries, some of whom have turned the West's anxieties about the threat of migration into a bargaining chip, as seen in Morocco, Libya and Turkey.

Western governments can also extract political capital by appearing to 'do something' about the big, amorphous phenomenon of migration without damaging their economies, which depend on it. They achieve this, in part, by focusing controls on those people arriving by land and sea, and not on the air routes by which most irregular migrants in fact arrive (namely those who overstay their visas).

If these are the winners, the losers include almost everyone else: taxpayers footing the bill and the rational policymakers who find their arguments marginalized; the border communities hit by needless chaos and the rescuers who pick up the pieces after desperate crossings; and of course, people on the move, who suffer or perish in larger numbers, as seen from the Mediterranean to Arizona.

The 'illegality industry' not only *benefits* from an obsession with border security, it also generates its own demand. This is actively fed by its paymasters, the politicians. For those on the hunt for votes, the border is an almost endless 'natural resource' around which fears of foreign dangers—migrants, terrorists, diseases—can be easily mobilized.

Demand goes Global

The most extreme result can be seen in Arizona, where controls keep expanding despite net Mexican migration now being in negative territory. Demand has also gone global, as states such as Saudi Arabia adopt Western 'innovations' in border security. While Arizona is a principal shop window for this market, European states are also trying to muscle in, bolstering their defence businesses through targeted research and development funds.

The vicious cycle at the border means we need an urgent rethink. A rational effort to deal with migration via policy tools other than security is required. Politicians need to open up debate over legal pathways, labour market reform, and the ways we intervene abroad. We must listen to those on the frontlines—the migrants and refugees, volunteers and border workers who deal with the consequences of the security approach. Migration politics need to de-escalate, giving way to a sane debate on the limitations of border security—based on evidence.

Besides these long-term goals, we also need more transparency, audits and parliamentary assessments of the murky world of taxpayer-funded investments in border security. The time has come to call the illegality industry's bluff: 'Border security' brings more insecurity, not greater safety. And it does so at a great human and financial cost that has so far escaped serious political scrutiny.

UNIT I: CRITICAL THINKING QUESTIONS

1. Considering the strengths and weaknesses of the Marshall Project, are there others one could add? Explain any observable patterns.
2. Constitutional law is the foundation behind substantive law. Explain substantive law and its connection to human rights.
3. Describe the interaction of the changing role of criminal law with the procedural rights for human rights law.
4. Identify the goals and objectives of the Justice Index. Explain how this index may improve the CJS.
5. Explain the prison industrial complex. How do economic and demographic factors, racial profiling, and police policy influence it?
6. How is organized crime in Mexico affecting immigration to the United States? Explain your reasoning.
7. How does "border security" increase insecurity yet does not provide greater safety? What evidence does the reading provide?

   Overall

   Using only the information in this unit, how would you describe the CJS in the United States to someone from another country?

UNIT II

The Police

Unit Introduction

This unit begins by revisiting the history of tension between the police and its citizens. Today's riots and social movements are like those in the 1960s and 1970s. There were many groups protesting inequality, oppression, and discrimination and advocating for civil rights. Some of these groups were peaceful, while others embraced the use of violence. The Symbionese Liberation Army was one of these violent organizations which called for the death of police officers, deemed as the agents of the oppressors (Reading 2.1). This hatred against the police is further explored in the next reading which points out that racism is one of the factors institutionalized in the CJS which has allowed abusive police practices against people of color. Police abuses have led to the eruption of riots from Watts to Ferguson (Reading 2.2).

Many scholars and practitioners have noted that the police organizational culture is characterized by an "etiquette" of police brutality and hegemonic masculinity (Readings 2.3, 2.4, and 2.5). One method implemented to decrease the excessive use of force and increase accountability has been the use of body cams (Reading 2.6). On the other hand, other technological advancements have been scrutinized for violating the rights of citizens. For example, the Chicago police department has a history of using illegal surveillance tactics against civil rights activists, violating their right to peaceful protest, as well as their privacy (Reading 2.7). The final reading of the unit further investigates the organizational culture of the police as a site of gendered action, characterized by hegemonic masculinity and discrimination (Reading 2.8).

READING 2.1

Unhinged Hatred of the Police

It Has a Long, Sordid History

By Joshua Gelernter

The murdering of policemen to protest alleged police targeting of black people is not a new phenomenon. Nor are chants like "Pigs in a blanket, fry 'em like bacon," which featured at a Black Lives Matter protest in August. In the 1960s and '70s, the Black Panthers and the Black Liberation Army chanted "No more pigs in our community" and "Off the pigs," and between them they murdered 15 or 20 policemen. Killing policemen has always been at the top of the left-wing terrorist agenda. Policemen were part and parcel of the "fascist insect" the Symbionese Liberation Army called for murdering in its mission statement: "Death to the fascist insect that preys upon the life of the people." Most of us have forgotten the Symbionese Liberation Army; they didn't have the Black Panthers' PR or staying power. But September 18 was the 40th anniversary of the arrest of Patty Hearst, an event worth revisiting.

FBI wanted poster for Patty Hearst and other SLA fugitives

In March 1973, a black radical named Donald DeFreeze escaped from Soledad Prison in California, where he had been serving a sentence for armed robbery. He changed his name to Cinque Mtume—Cinque, for Joseph Cinqué, who led the revolt on the slave ship *Amistad,* and Mtume, from the Swahili for "prophet." He hooked up with a radical feminist named Patricia Soltysik, and together they founded the Symbionese Liberation Army, with DeFreeze as "general field marshal."

Police were a focus from the outset. That November, the SLA took their first "direct action": They murdered an education reformer named

Marcus Foster—Oakland, California's first black school superintendent—because they believed he planned to bring police into the Oakland schools. (They were wrong.) Foster was killed as he came out of a school board meeting. (Foster's deputy, Robert Blackburn, was shot, too; he was seriously injured, but survived.)

In February 1974, Patricia Hearst was a 19-year-old living in nearby Berkeley. She was a target for the SLA because she was a granddaughter of capitalist magnate William Randolph Hearst, and because she happened to live quite close to the SLA's headquarters. On February 4, the SLA burst into her apartment, beat her unconscious, and tossed her into the trunk of a car; they took her to an SLA hideout, where she was bound, blindfolded, and locked in a closet. She was kept in the closet for the better part of six weeks. After failing to trade their hostage for Superintendent Foster's murderers, the SLA began giving Hearst brief respites from the darkness of her blindfold and closet, in the form of a flashlight and leftist political manifestoes to read. DeFreeze repeatedly threatened to kill her, so—as Hearst put it in her memoir—"I accommodated my thoughts to coincide with theirs." In late March, Patty agreed to join the Symbionese Liberation Army; her blindfold was removed, and she was given the name Tania, a reference to Che Guevara's comrade-in-arms "Tania the Guerrilla." Then she was raped by DeFreeze and one of his lieutenants, William Wolfe.

On April 3, the SLA released an audiotape of Patty Hearst addressing her parents: "Mom, Dad," said Patty, "tell the poor and oppressed people of this nation what the corporate state is about to do. Warn black and poor people that they are about to be murdered down to the last man, woman, and child. … I have been given the choice of one, being released in a safe area, or two, joining the forces of the Symbionese Liberation Army and fighting for my freedom and the freedom of all oppressed people. I have chosen to stay and fight."

Over the next months, Patty accompanied the SLA in robbing the Hibernia Bank and committing various petty and less petty crimes. In May, six Symbionese members were killed in a police shootout in Los Angeles, prompting the SLA to release another tape narrated by Patty. She described her relationships with the dead terrorists, among them "Fahizah," who, said Patty, "taught me to shoot first and make sure the pig is dead before splitting."

As it happened, neither Nancy "Fahizah" Perry nor her comrades succeeded in shooting any policemen the day they were killed. Over the next year, the SLA tried several times to make up for that disappointment by building bombs with which to murder policemen. On August 21, 1975, two bombs (which Hearst had evidently helped assemble) were placed under two LAPD cars and rigged to explode when policemen got in and started driving. Neither went off. Three weeks later, Patty Hearst was captured, and the SLA began its slow drift into obscurity (though the last Symbionese fugitive wouldn't be arrested till 2002).

After 20 months of hardcore leftism, Patty Hearst weighed just 87 pounds and was found to have lost 18 IQ points. One of the court-appointed psychiatrists described her as a "low-affect zombie." Not yet having become the pinup girl for Stockholm syndrome, Hearst was rather unfairly sentenced to seven years in prison. After 22 months, her sentence was commuted by Jimmy Carter. (Bill Clinton pardoned her in 2001.)

Long before Occupy Cleveland members tried to blow up a bridge over the Cuyahoga Valley, the Symbionese Liberation Army had already pledged to destroy "all forms and institutions of Racism, Sexism, Ageism, Capitalism, Fascism, Individualism, Possessiveness, Competitiveness and all other such institutions that have made and sustained capitalism." And long before a Texas sheriff blamed the "dangerous rhetoric" of the Black Lives Matter movement for the "execution style" murder of one of his deputies, the Symbionese Liberation Army, the Black Liberation Army, the Black Panthers, and the Weathermen were already murdering policemen, and non-policemen, bombing police cars and police stations, and protesting the injustice of the American justice system.

That isn't to say that the Occupy and Black Lives Matter movements are terrorist organizations. They're not. But, as the saying goes, forgotten history tends to repeat itself. Anyone who coddles protesters calling for the murder of policemen or rationalizes their catchy chants or pretends they don't exist should keep that in mind.

READING 2.2

From Watts to Ferguson

The Riot is Still the 'Language of the Unheard'

By Rick Perlstein

It usually started with the police.

In July of 1964, barely hours after the close of the Republican National Convention that nominated Barry Goldwater, 15-year-old James "Little Jimmy" Powell was shot to death by an off-duty cop in an apartment building vestibule on East 76th Street in New York. Just as in the shooting of 25-year-old Kajieme Powell this past August 19 in St. Louis, the officer claimed that the victim had charged him with a knife, though eyewitnesses denied that. A bystander cried, "Come on, shoot another nigger!" Within hours, Harlem was ablaze.

That was the first in the wave of apocalyptic racial riots that swept American cities in the 1960s. Later that week, in Rochester, New York, the fires started after cops roughed up the very woman who'd called them in to break up a rowdy, drunken party. The next summer, in Watts, Los Angeles, the most famous of the 1960s riots kicked off after police hit people with batons at the scene of a drunk-driving arrest. In 1966, in Chicago, it began when cops turned off a fire hydrant in which kids were frolicking on the third straight day of 90-degree heat. In 1967, the most tumultuous year, the first riot came after cops in Newark beat a cabdriver because they thought he was a Black Muslim.

The parallels with this summer's uprising in Ferguson, Missouri, following the shooting of Michael Brown, an unarmed 18-year-old, are undeniable. In the 1960s, neighborhoods or cities that were overwhelmingly black were patrolled by police forces that were overwhelmingly white. The same is true in Ferguson today, where the force has an atrocious history of racial profiling: According to annual reporting from the office of the Missouri Attorney General, in a city that is about 30 percent white, 92.7 percent of those that police arrested in 2013 were black. Michael Brown's shooter, Darren Wilson, learned his policing on a force in nearby Jennings, Missouri, that was so corrupt and racist (a cop once kicked a woman in the stomach when she told him she couldn't move her van because it didn't run) it had to be shut down. Blatant racism, too, was a pattern in forces where police abuses set off riots in the 1960s. Los Angeles cops were led by William H. Parker, who coined the phrase "thin blue line"—as in, the cops were a thin blue line between chaos and civilization. Parker

Rick Perlstein, "From Watts to Ferguson," *In These Times*, vol. 38, no. 10, pp. 24-27, 29.

A state police officer restrains a man during the riot in Rochester, New York, in late July 1964.

liked to recruit white officers from the Mississippi Delta. Parker explained the origin of the Watts riots to an investigating commission: "One person threw a rock and then, like monkeys in a zoo, others started throwing rocks." His patrolmen, meanwhile, would begin tours of the ghetto with a ritual cry taken from a cigarette commercial, "LSMFT"—"Lucky Strike Means Fine Tobacco." Only, for them, the letters stood for "Let's Shoot a Motherfucker Tonight."

In Chicago, a Ku Klux Klan cell operated inside the force, stockpiling its very own arsenal (which included hand grenades). The San Francisco precinct responsible for patrolling Hunters Point, a black neighborhood that rioted in 1966 after cops shot a black 17-year-old, displayed a photo of a KKK imperial wizard on its bulletin board.

In cities like Cleveland, when it came to black neighborhoods, police simply refused to police; though when blacks dared enter white space, they were policed with an Old Testament vengeance—like the time a bus-station porter was beaten on and off in jail for four days, and made to bark like a dog, for the crime of sitting on the floor of the bus station after a tiring shift. The U.S. Commission on Civil Rights convened hearings on the situation after Cleveland suffered one of the worst riots in 1966, which began one hot night outside a tavern where the white owner posted a sign reading "NO WATER FOR NIGGERS," and bar employees patrolled its perimeter with shotguns. What did they find? Cops collaborating with pimps; "it has got to the place whereby a man's wife or daughter is not safe to walk the streets," an African-American minister testified. The police chief said he was for capital punishment "to keep the Negroes in line."

In Ferguson, police racism is built in, institutionalized in the town's business model of using revenue from fines to pay its bills (and in the process, turning some residents into unemployable criminals). The encounter with Ferguson's fierce justice system, if you are black, works like this: You have an overwhelming chance of being cited or arrested by police, for doing little or nothing that is wrong. A report from the legal group ArchCity Defenders found that in 2013, "the Ferguson Municipal Court disposed 24,532 warrants and 12,018 cases, or about three warrants and 1.5 cases per household," an incredibly high rate. Then you are likely to face a fine you cannot afford to pay—ArchCity Defenders calculates that the average fine is $275—or a summons to a court that is rigged against you showing up on time. "The bench routinely starts hearing cases 30 minutes before the appointed time and then locks the doors to the building as early as five minutes after the official hour, a practice that could easily lead a defendant arriving even slightly late to receive an additional charge for failure to appear," reads the report. Thus, you might end up in jail—with a criminal record that frequently bars employment.

Protesters are pushed back by police on August 19, in Ferguson, Missouri.

That Kafkaesque sense of futility explains some of the frustration that boiled over in Ferguson with the shooting of Michael Brown. But that's only one half of it. The other part is political.

Ferguson's six-person city council has only one black member. It's been much discussed that the dearth of African-American political representation has been helped along by what has been described as the apathy of black voters there, only 1.78 percent of whom turned out from one of the city's black townships in a recent municipal election. But reporters on the ground in Ferguson—and possibly the justice Department—should be looking at whether the powers that be have been practicing the sort of dark arts of malapportionment that disenfranchised other municipalities with sizable black populations in the past. Boston, for example, was able to defy a 1963 state law demanding school integration for nearly a decade by electing its school board "at large," instead of by district. And prior to its 1967 riot, Newark's Mayor Hugh Addonizio practiced a form of "urban renewal" that had a political twist: By building high-rises downtown, he was able to break up geographic concentrations of blacks, to ensure they would have no political power base.

Black Fergusonians have shown that they will vote when they have something to vote for and know that their vote will count. Seventy-six percent of them turned out in November 2012, when Missouri was a key swing state for Barack Obama's reelection. When it comes to local elections, they might just be making the rational decision that a hike to the polls is a waste of time. Even that one black council member, Dwayne James, has baffled observers by remaining mum in the face of the single issue now galvanizing his constituency, Michael Brown's killing. He's said only, "Our city charter provides that our mayor is the spokesperson for the city." I don't want to be unfair to James—I don't know his motives—but such quiescence recalls the behavior of Chicago's "Silent Six": the six African-American alderman, during the 1960s heyday of the Cook County Democratic Organization, who were so in thrall to Mayor Richard J. Daley that they didn't even support a proposed anti-housing-discrimination ordinance. (In response, wags dubbed the one alderman who forcefully advocated anti-discrimation, Leon Despres—who was white—the city's "only black alderman.")

Then as now, the national political context matters. Mainstream white liberal politicians of the 1960s, flummoxed that blacks would be rising up at the very moment when so much was "being done for them" (of course, the 1964 Civil Rights Act and the 1965 Voting Rights Act only affected the South) began making strikingly radical connections. Sen. Robert F. Kennedy said, "There is no point in telling Negroes to obey the law. To many Negroes, the law is the enemy." Vice President Hubert Humphrey predicted that unless slum conditions improved, and quick, there would be "open violence in every major city and county in America." He added a note of empathy, saying that if he lived in one of those slums, "I think you'd have more trouble than you have had already, because I've got enough spark left in me to lead a mighty good revolt."

The only building in Ferguson that fell to arson was a single QuikTrip store. Compare this to Watts in 1965, which created a third of a billion dollars in property damage.

Conservatives didn't want to hear it—and pivoted off such pronouncements to fuel a backlash. Rep. Howard Smith of Virginia replied to Humphrey, "The vice president will bear a grave responsibility in blood and lives if he tries to provoke minority group members to riot for rent supplements." During a 1966 debate over an open housing bill, Sen. Sam Ervin of North Carolina said, "The record shows that the more laws that are passed in the nation on the national, state and local levels, the more rioting and looting we have."

That soon became the conservative, and even the centrist, consensus: Laws to ameliorate misery, not the misery itself, were the problem. The bill failed—the first civil rights package not to become law in three years. Then, in 1967, a new Congress filled with freshly elected right-wingers, borne aloft on the backlash against civil rights, debated a modest federal outlay for rodent control in the slums. It was derided as the "civil rats" bill. The debate became an occasion for mockery: grown men guffawing about "rat patronage," "rat bureaucracies" and a "high commissioner of rats." Rep. Martha Griffiths, a Michigan Democrat, tried to shut them up: "If you're going to spend $79 billion to kill off a few Vietcong, I'd spend $40 million to kill off the most devastating enemy that man has ever had."

Her argument failed. The bill was slapped down. The next year, 1968, following the assassination of Martin Luther King, Jr., saw the deadliest riots of all. In light of all that, an answer to the mystery is clear: Why would people, no matter how angry, burn down what are, after all, their own neighborhoods? Because they feel so dispossessed that their neighborhoods don't seem like their own at all.

The Fire This Time

But history is the study of change as well as of continuity. And there are striking differences between the disturbances in Ferguson and those in Los Angeles, Chicago, Newark, Detroit, and all the rest more than 45 years ago. For one, what we saw in Ferguson was much less bloody. Violence and property damage were more rumor than reality. An early photo of what looked like someone throwing a Molotov cocktail turned out to be of a man throwing a steaming tear gas canister back at the police. Despite the rhetoric of the Right—*New York Post* columnist Linda Chavez called Attorney General Eric Holder "Eric the Arsonist" for daring to observe that as a black man, he understood black Fergusonians' mistrust of police—the one building that fell to arson was a QuikTrip store. Compare this to Watts in 1965, which created a third of a billion dollars in property damage, or the Chicago riot in 1968, which left two straight miles of Madison Street in ruins.

Tear gas rains down on a woman kneeling in the street after a demonstration in Ferguson on August 17.

One difference between then and now, for good or ill: The 1960s had a set of black self-appointed leaders who made a political virtue of arson and looting. In 1967, Student Non-Violent Coordinating Committee Chair H. Rap Brown visited the racially tense city of Cambridge, Maryland, stood on a street corner, and cried, "Detroit exploded, Newark exploded, Harlem exploded! It's time for Cambridge to explode!" He pointed to a dilapidated school down the street: "You should have burned that school a long time ago!" So, promptly, his listeners did.

Stokely Carmichael became a virtual riot circuit rider, tooling through Atlanta telling milling throngs it was time to "tear this city up" (they did), and announcing, "In Cleveland, they're building stores with no windows. I don't know what they think they'll accomplish. It just means we have to move from Molotov cocktails to dynamite."

A then-militant named Julius Lester—now a rabbi and children's book author—praised the work of a sniper in a city 13 miles down I-70 from Ferguson for cutting down what Lester termed "known enemies of the black community." This, he said, was a "move from self-defense to aggressive action," just like what the Vietcong were doing. Posing as a wartime guerrilla strategist, he wrote, "What is happening in East St. Louis points up once again the advantage of medium-sized cities, leaving Saigon, Danang and other large cities for the last." Despite the perfervid pornoviolent fantasies of Tea Partiers, no one's saying anything like that now.

Another difference: Despite the awful, inexcusable responses of law enforcement now, what is happening is the palest shadow of the response of law enforcement then.

Take Newark. After the first wave of looting and arson, the state police were sent in. Alongside the local police, they commenced, as documented by a brave investigative reporter named Ron Porambo in a 1971 book called *No Cause for Indictment,* a veritable turkey shoot. First they shot and killed a 45-year-old mother searching for one of her children; then a 28-year-old former basketball star who was shot shortly after advising his companions to submit quietly to police; then a young man shot in the back while running from a liquor store. Nine were killed by the end of the first day. That went on and on for six days, including one group cut down by police who fired into the milling crowd even as the men began waving their undershirts like white flags.

The death toll from these acts of official terror in Newark was 25. Newark's white residents, meanwhile, set up armed patrols at the perimeters of their neighborhoods, promising to shoot anyone who might "spill over onto white ground." No one was ever indicted in these deaths; hence the title of Porambo's numbing, classic book. (Two attempts on Porambo's life followed its publication.) A similar massacre by police, National Guardsmen and white vigilantes unfolded in Detroit a week and a half later, precipitated when police raided an afterhours bar that was operating illegally. The official death toll was 43.

Then, such white terrorists were protected by their anonymity. Perhaps it is because these protections are all but impossible in the era of cell phone cameras and social media that no one else has died in Ferguson. The whole world is watching, in a way that was impossible then, and the media is less able to filter events. In 1967, CBS executives decided not to run a wrenching dispatch from the funeral of a beloved 72-year-old victim in Newark, Isaac "Uncle Daddy" Harrison, fearing a sympathetic portrait of "rioters" would be far too controversial. Now, such a funeral would be a YouTube sensation and Uncle Daddy a household name. Similarly, far too many eyes are on the street for even a tepid *ur*-establishmentarian Democrat like Gov. Jay Nixon of Missouri to get away with a pro-police affirmation like the one offered by New Jersey's Democratic Gov. Richard Hughes, a close ally of President Lyndon Johnson, after Newark: "I felt a thrill of pride in the way our state police and National Guard have conducted themselves."

From Riots to Mobilization

By 1969, the urban riots all but stopped. With a handful of notable exceptions over the years—Miami's Liberty City in 1980, Los Angeles after the Rodney King verdict in 1992, Cincinnati in 2001—police violence no longer automatically sparks flare-ups. In recent years, there have been many, many police shootings of innocents: Think of Amadou Diallo in New York in 1999, or Oscar Grant in Oakland in 2009, whose shooting by BART transit cops inspired the movie *Fruitvale Station.* None inspired the level of uprising of the 1960s, or that we saw in Ferguson this year. So what explains the hiatus—and what made Ferguson et al the exceptions?

It certainly isn't that slums stopped being miserable places. In 1967, a presidential commission led by Illinois Gov. Otto Kerner investigated the roots of riots. In the words of the Kerner Commission Report's famous preface, America would have to stop being "two societies, one black, one white—separate and unequal." That didn't happen. Slums stayed, and grew worse, but they also stopped burning.

In his 2011 book, *Why Don't American Cities Burn,* the historian Michael Katz offers one explanation: The riots in the 1960s came in a context of cities undergoing radical transitions in political geography as they absorbed African Americans who migrated north for (often nonexistent) jobs after World War II. Disorganized, disenfranchised African-American communities were crowded into slums, with miserable results. Riots were signs of the strain of "transitioning" cities. But by the 1970s, when rioting all but stopped, white flight was so advanced that cities like Detroit were almost entirely black, and most neighborhoods were either all black or all white, without the attendant turf battles that frequently drove riots as well. The cities and neighborhoods that proved the exception between then and now more resemble that 1960s pattern: Liberty City was unsettled by ethnic rivalries between blacks and Cubans, and blacks in Los Angeles felt economically displaced by Korean immigrants. So, in fact, does Ferguson, which over the last 25 years has shifted from three-quarters white to predominantly black. In that sense it looks a lot like Newark or Detroit in 1967.

Garry Wills' 1968 book *The Second Civil War: Arming for Armageddon* offers another piece of the puzzle. One of its chapters profiled a policing expert who schooled Wills incisively on police tactics: how to cordon off disturbances where they begin and contain their spread; how to de-escalate violence with less-than-lethal technology and tactics; how white politicians and police officials could build trust on the street. And indeed, as the experience of New York City seemed to have shown, trust worked. In 1965, the year after that first riot in Harlem, John Lindsay was elected mayor. Facing a simmering neighborhood disturbance in a "transitioning" Brooklyn neighborhood, his police commissioner ordered cops to "keep their billies on their belts and their guns in their holsters." Lindsay himself, famously—it made it onto an episode of *Mad Men*—walked the streets of Harlem himself after King's assassination, calming nerves, assuring residents of official concern.

Police forces, for a time, seemed generally to be becoming more professionalized, less corrupt. In 1970, Lindsay, inspired by the publicity surrounding Frank Serpico's brave witness, empaneled the Knapp Commission, which thoroughly reorganized New York's rotten police. Elsewhere, cities acted on another of the Kerner Commission's less dramatic recommendations: Hire police forces that looked more like the cities they patrolled. The influence of Stokely Carmichael, ironically, helped. Genuine black power came to cities like Gary, Indiana, Cleveland and Detroit, which elected their first black mayors. Affirmative action in the workplace helped create at least some sense of African-American buy-in with the power structure. The impetus for diversity came almost entirely, as the political scientist John David Skrentny demonstrated in his classic 1996 book, *The Ironies of Affirmative Action,* from corporate executives who sought "To Prevent a Chain of Super-Watts"—the title of a 1968 article in the *Harvard Business Review,* which read: "If the businessman does not accept his rightful role as leader in the push for the goals of the 'Great Society,' we will be increasingly smothered by a growing welfare state ridden with riots and arson and spreading slums largely unchecked by the proliferating programs for the unemployed poor."

In all our cities, the poor blacks left behind by white flight are terrorized by our increasingly horrifying modern police state, with its full complement of surveillance, incarceration, and all the nihilistic violence that ensues.

That means that some of the things that stopped riots then are the kind of things that are being systematically undone now. (And the cities where riots *have* taken place in the interim—Miami, Los Angeles, Cincinnati—are the places where either police forces or city governments reformed the least.) What "businessman" now worries about his role in creating a great society? What cop, in our militarized, knock-kneed post-9/11 society, wants to keep his billy on his belt and his gun in his holster? (Think of all those terrifying images of the shock troops in Ferguson, instinctually drawing their military-grade rifles in their Robocop gear on women holding babes in arms.) Then there is the fact that cops, marinated in the same reactionary political culture as the rest of the country, watch Fox News, too. That San Francisco precinct house that sacralized a KKK imperial wizard in 1966? Think, today, of Officer Dan Page of St. Louis, who became famous for shoving a CNN reporter on live broadcast from Ferguson, and was later revealed to have recorded a speech in which he ranted about "rag heads" and the "four sodomites on the Supreme Court."

And of course, in all our cities, the poor blacks left behind by white flight are terrorized by our increasingly horrifying modern police state, with its full complement of surveillance, incarceration, and all the nihilistic violence that ensues. "It's good that we don't have mass civil violence," Michael Katz concluded, in an interview with *The Atlantic's* CityLab website. "But the question is: Why don't we have more political mobilization?" Blame the hopeless nihilism. Blame politics.

Sociologists in the 1960s, reaching for an explanation of why cities were burning, often spoke of the problem of "rising expectations." It wasn't that the times were especially miserable for blacks, or even that the neighborhoods that rioted were the most uninhabitable ones. Watts was a neighborhood of neat bungalows and well-tended lawns. Detroit was one of the biggest beneficiaries of Great Society largesse. But, in a time of dynamic change and an expanding sense of social possibility, the frustrations that *were* all too palpable—police forces that acted like occupying armies and municipal governments that wouldn't give them the time of day—became all the more the focus of rage, precisely because they felt so cruelly vestigial. Rioting, paradoxically, was at least partially an act of faith: At least we can do *something* to get their attention. Or, as Martin Luther King, Jr. famously put it, "A riot is the language of the unheard."

So in that sense, Ferguson feels like a sort of welcome blast from that past: a place where hopes whetted by a black president who seemed to promise so much more than what he could deliver were dashed; where lingering racial boundaries in an "integrated" city are still the site of everyday contestation; and where, because of all that, the everyday humiliations of dispossession and disenfranchisement burn, and burn, and burn. At least Black Ferguson *has* expectations. Maybe the rest of us should take some solace from that. Let the political mobilization begin.

READING 2.3

The Etiquette of Police Brutality

A Handy Guide to Confronting Unarmed Citizens

By Rion Amalcar Scott

Go ahead. Smack him one. He expects it so it would be rude not to. Besides, look at him giving you a dehumanizing stare.[3] How dare he look at you in that manner? He thinks he's better than you. Approach in such a way that makes you look huge, immense—a living blue wall of silence.[4] But be loud. Put this guy down before he even starts. Grab him from behind. Maybe use the baton. Don't be swayed by his screams and pleas of innocence. As a matter of fact, don't hear them at all. Be deaf to his cries. Innocence doesn't really matter here, anyway.[5] Sort it out later. Don't be inhibited with the violence—punches, kicks, strangulation holds,[6] baton blows, Tasers[7] and so on. Don't worry, the state has your back. Make up any excuse you want. It doesn't need to sound good. As a matter of fact, it would be insulting to make it sound too plausible. Say something like: "He was looking at us all leery and then he raised his hands. We had to throw him on the ground, smash his face to the concrete, knock his teeth out and put him in a chokehold.[8] It's important to neutralize the threat." Toss it off without thinking. Fuck it, say: "He was dancing funny and I found that threatening so I was forced to jab him in the ribs." The state has your back. No matter what you say, your superiors, the courts, everybody will nod and mumble: "Seems legit." Yell racial epithets.[9] Shoot wildly.[10] At least 40 shots if unarmed.[11] More might be better.[12] It's only polite to flex your authority every once in a while.[13] Let the world know how tough you are. The standard charge is resisting arrest. Assaulting an officer. Pile up any ol' charge. What does it matter? To make the people feel safe and whole you have to break[14] one or two every once in a while so they know your power is both awesome[15] and nearly completely unchecked.[16]

[1]Inspiration for this piece came from a short story collection called, *Modern Manners For Your Inner Demons* by Tara Laskowski. The work is structured like an etiquette book except each piece of advice covers how to properly comport yourself while doing something wicked such as homicide, adultery or arson. [2]I go back and forth with this satirical piece—or "mockery" as I call it ("humor piece;" "satirical piece," such clunky terms)—wondering if it's at all successful. It was written from

Rion Amalcar Scott, "The Etiquette of Police Brutality," *The Crisis*, vol. 122, no. 1, pp. 12-17.

a place of pretty raw anger and frankly, terror, after reading about a succession of police harassment and brutality cases, mostly involving Black and Brown "suspects."

Many of these incidents featured graphic and disturbing video of the assaults taking place. Sometimes I was brave enough to watch.

The public has been filming and broadcasting egregious acts of police violence since the 1990s when a motorist filmed Los Angeles police brutalizing Rodney King. Now that most of us carry video cameras in our pockets, such footage is nearly a weekly occurrence. This has done much to inspire the outrage of the public, but has seemed to do little to stem the tide of police abuse or even to ensure the type of decisive and swift punishment that would make police think twice about physically assaulting citizens.

One possible thin silver lining is a study done by Rialto, Calif. police that ran from February 2012 to July 2013. A group of officers wore tiny video cameras while interacting with citizens. According to the *New York Times,* the video cameras resulted in a 60 percent drop in the use of force and an 88 percent drop in complaints against officers.

[3]According to *CBS Miami,* Miami-Dade Police choked a 14-year-old boy on Memorial Day 2013 because he watched them with what police described as "dehumanizing stares."

[4]It's often said that a universal and morally bankrupt admonishment against "snitching" in poor Black communities enables crime in these neighborhoods, but when was the last time you heard of police informing on one another? As the rapper Immortal Technique said, "They never snitch on themselves, but they want you to snitch on you." An important question that's rarely asked in these debates is why would anyone want to report crimes to people who have a reputation for brutalizing them?

[5]In Sept. 2000 in Prince Georges County, Md.—the county I currently live in with my wife and son (in fact, this occurred in the very neighborhood I once lived)—Prince Jones, a man who had committed no crime, began his last stand. Undercover Prince Georges County narcotics officer, Cpl. Carlton B. Jones (no relation) followed Prince roughly 30 miles to Fairfax, Va. (coincidentally, the county where I went to school in the mid to late aughts) in an unmarked SUV and shot his car 16 times, killing him in the process. Police say they were trailing a suspect in the theft of an officer's gun and Prince's car resembled a car driven by the suspect.

Prince, a Howard University student (the university I hold an undergraduate degree from—as a matter of fact, I, too, was a Howard student at this time) nearing graduation, was unarmed.

Cpl. Jones claims Prince rammed his car and refused to stand down when he announced he was an officer, (though he admitted to showing no badge). Witnesses dispute this claim however, saying that Prince's car was not moving when Cpl. Jones fired his weapon. Despite killing Prince Jones, Cpl. Carlton Jones faced no criminal charges. (Sources: Washington Post; Washington Monthly).

[6]On Thursday July 17, 2014, police in Staten Island approached 43-year old Eric Garner, a 400-pound asthmatic, purportedly to arrest him for selling loose cigarettes. Garner had reportedly just broken up a fight. Video recorded by a bystander shows Garner protesting frequent harassment:

"Every time you see me you want to mess with me. It stops today… I'm minding my business, officer. Why don't you just leave me alone?" Four officers surround Garner and wrestle him to the ground. One deploys a chokehold, a use of force specifically banned by NYPD regulations. Despite video evidence, police claim a chokehold was not used on Garner. While an officer shoves Garner's head to the sidewalk, he repeatedly cries, "I can't breathe. I can't breathe." And those are his final words.

According to CBS Miami, Miami-Dade Police choked a 14-year-old boy on Memorial Day 2013 because he watched them with what police described as "dehumanizing stares."

[7]When Oakland transit officer Johannes Mehserle pulled his revolver, shooting and killing Oscar Grant while he lay handcuffed and face down, he claimed to have been reaching for his Taser. For killing Grant, Mehserle served less than a year in prison.

In 2007, after a video of a University of Florida student being tasered by campus police made the rounds on the Internet, "Don't tase me, bro!" became a late-aughts punchline, but the incident that inspired it, a young man being tasered by police for aggressively asking a politician a question during an open forum, is a chilling, abusive and reckless display of police power.

[8]From the *New York Daily News:* "The NYPD prohibited the use of chokeholds in 1993. The city's independent police watchdog has substantiated 10 chokehold cases filed against cops since 2009, but little has happened to the officers involved, records show.

"In one of the cases, the cop accused of putting a person in a chokehold lost up to 10 vacation days, records from the Civilian Complaint Review Board show.

"In two cases, the department declined to discipline the officers, and in three cases, cops received 'instructions,' or retraining. In another case, the cop retired before he could be disciplined, and the three remaining cases are pending, the records show."

[9]According to the *New York Times,* in 2011 the government intercepted a phone call in which NYPD officer Michael Daragjati bragged about falsely arresting a suspect. In regards to the young man, Daragjati said: "Fried another nigger." Even more horrifying: Also in 2011, a retired Marine, Kenneth Chamberlain, Sr., 68, inadvertently called police to his White Plains home when he accidently activated his medical alert bracelet. The response of police—this is not in dispute—was to ignore Chamberlain's request that they leave, call him a *nigger* and fatally shoot him. (Sources: *New York Times; New York Daily News*).

[10]In 2013, the NYPD shot a disturbed, unarmed man and two innocent bystanders. The man, Glenn Broadnax, caused a commotion by jumping into traffic. The wounded Broadnax was then charged with assault for the bullet wounds suffered by the bystanders under the theory that his actions caused the police shooting to occur. An attorney for one of the wounded bystanders speaking to the New York Times: "It's an incredibly unfortunate use of prosecutorial discretion to be prosecuting a man who didn't even injure my client. It's the police who injured my client."

The NYPD (again) in 2012 shot nine innocent bystanders during a confrontation with a gunman in Times Square. All nine bystanders were struck by bullets from police weapons. NYPD Commissioner Raymond Kelly on the shooting: "I believe it was handled well." (Source: FoxNews.com)

While searching for alleged cop killer Christopher Dorner in February 2013, the LAPD shot at trucks that were said to resemble Dorner's on two separate occasions. In the first incident, police fired on two Hispanic women—a mother and her 47-year old daughter as they delivered newspapers early in the morning. A bullet ripped through the back of 71-year old Emma Hernandez. Somehow this incident resulted in no fatalities despite the fact that police fired more than 100 rounds.

Later that day, police opened fire on a truck driven by a White male, David Perdue, a surfer on his way to the beach. In that instance, police rammed Purdue's truck before shooting at it. Perdue was not hit and prosecutors determined the use of force was reasonable. Domer, who died in a cabin fire police claimed to not have intentionally set, was a Black male. (Source: Christian Science Monitor)

Richard Pryor on California police in 1973: "They accidentally shoot more niggas out here than any place in the world. Every time you pick up the paper: nigga accidentally shot in the ass. How do you accidentally shoot a nigga six times in the chest? 'Well, my gun fell and just went crazy.'"

[11]Forty-one police shots took the life of Amadou Diallo in the infamous 1999 shooting in the Bronx. He was armed only with a wallet.

[12]In 2006, 50 police shots took the life of Sean Bell in Queens, N.Y. the morning he was to marry. He, too, was unarmed.

[13]The examples of police brutality used in this piece are all relatively current, which implies that this is a recent problem. That is certainly not the case. Worldwide, police and excessive police force have historically been tools of the state used against the disenfranchised and dispossessed to make sure they don't get too loud in their cries against their disenfranchisement and dispossession. As the rapper Boots Riley notes: "You never seen a police break up a strike by hitting the boss with his baton pipe."

It was police, for example, who held the fire hoses that mowed down civil rights protestors in the 1960s.

Huey P. Newton and Bobby Seale formed the Black Panther Party for Self-Defense in Oakland as a response to police harassment in 1966. Even then it was a long-standing community problem. The group's initial program was an armed patrol to evaluate the behavior of the police. Government suppression of the Party was codified in the COINTELPRO program (see FBI documents here), a wave of law enforcement intimidation and force unprecedented in its cruelty, lawlessness and violence. Chicago police murdered the Deputy Chairman of the Illinois Black Panther Party, Fred Hampton, in a police raid while he slept (drugged by infiltrators) on Dec. 4, 1968. Police fired nearly 100 rounds at the Illinois Panthers while the Panthers fired only one.

[14]Richard Pryor on the police from *Wanted/Richard Pryor Live in Concert* (1978): "Two grab your legs, one grab your head—they go, snap! 'Oh, shit he broke. Can you break 'em? Does it say so in the manual? Let's check. Yep, page 8, you can break a nigger.'"

[15]A 2014 American Civil Liberties Union report (*War Comes Home: The Excessive Militarization of American Policing*) details the increased militarization of police departments around the United States. SWAT teams armed with military weaponry, vehicles and equipment handed down from our decade long Middle East (mis)adventures are being deployed in American cities for fairly routine operations. Just outside of Atlanta in 2014, police raided a house in search of a small stash of drugs. They carried M16s and upon entering tossed a flashbang grenade that landed in a crib next to a sleeping toddler. The child suffered a hole in his chest and possible permanent brain damage. The suspect police were looking for was not in the home at the time and did not even live there, according to the toddler's mother, who wrote about the incident for *Salon.com.*

The family moved to Atlanta, a town that is no stranger to police raids gone astray. In 2006, police there invaded the home of 92-year-old Kathryn Johnston, shooting her dead in the process. After police found no drugs in her house they planted three bags of marijuana. The paperwork that served as the basis for the "no knock warrant"—which alleged that an informant purchased drugs at Johnston's home—turned out to be based on falsified evidence (Source: *CNN.com*).

[16]In many of the above cases, such as the Chamberlain case, police were cleared of any wrongdoing or faced relatively light or unspecified punishments, a situation that I imagine leaves police feeling comfortable in deploying any act of violence in their toolbox, no matter how reckless, if it leaves them standing when all the smoke from the gunfire has cleared. However, for much of the populace, that knot in their chests when a squad car sidles up next to them in traffic is the twinge of sheer terror.

READING 2.4

Spotlight on Police Culture

Seeing The Red Flags of Organizational Cultures Gone Wrong

By Mary Eleanor Wickersham

Takeaways

- Managers face more than fiscal liability when their law enforcement agencies are out of control; a broken trust with the public is even more damaging in the long term.
- Real change in policing organizations must derive from changes in the organizational culture.
- Managers must recognize and address the warning signs of a dysfunctional culture that reflects an "us vs. them" mentality.

National news coverage of alleged police misconduct has grabbed the nation's attention and had a direct impact on local government managers. The serious and long-term impact of police misconduct is the broken trust between residents and law enforcement organizations that occurs when negative perceptions of police values are reinforced by allegations of unnecessary use of force. And to this is added the potential fiscal liability of police wrongdoing.

The Wall Street Journal reported in July 2015 that the top 10 cities with the largest police departments had paid nearly $250 million in police misconduct cases in 2014 alone. Smaller cities are not exempt either.

The city manager of Inkster, Michigan, reported that his city—population less than 25,000—would have to levy additional taxes to fund a $1.4 million 2015 misconduct settlement. The long-term cost of the broken relationship between residents and law enforcement only grows as trust further erodes.

According to an April 2015 ABC News report, law enforcement agencies are seeing a decline in applicants, and recruitment is down by as much as 90 percent in some cities as policing has lost some of its allure. This tarnish is due at least in part to low pay, high stress, and heavy workloads, but

Mary Eleanor Wickersham, "Spotlight on Police Culture," *PM: Public Management*, vol. 98, no. 2, pp. 14-16, 18.

negative stereotyping of officers is increasingly a factor, according to police recruiters cited by ABC News.

"The significant improvements made in police-community relations over the last 25 years seem to have eroded," says Cedric Alexander, immediate past president of the National Organization of Black Law Enforcement Executives and chief of police, DeKalb County, Georgia. "This strain—not just with minorities but now with the larger community—has grown along with the perception of overzealous policing, a phenomenon largely driven not by data but by citizen documentation of incidents by cellphone and video and sharing on social media."

All too often, police and residents find themselves in a standoff in which neither side comes out the winner.

How did those appointed to serve and protect become perceived enemies of a significant proportion of the population, specifically minorities and those of color, in so many American communities?

Part of the answer lies in the organizational culture that has developed in many policing organizations, where cultural assumptions reinforce the "them-versus-us" attitude apparent since the Los Angeles Rampart neighborhood police scandal in the late 1990s.

Eye on Organizational Culture

Just as individuals have habits of thinking called schema, organizational culture is essentially a corporate schemata. Through workplace experience, employees often develop assumptions about organizational expectations. As values are shared, employee behaviors adapt to meet those expectations and over time, the organization develops its own distinctive culture.

In policing organizations, assumptions that derive from the culture are often passed along through more experienced officers, who effectively show new hires "how it's done around here." Although discretionary decision making is an integral part of policing, the individual's behaviors and responses in discretionary action will slowly adjust to meet the expectations of the organization itself.

Policing operations can be high-risk enterprises. It is vital for public managers to look carefully at the organizational culture of their policing agencies to determine the existence of any warning signs, which may require a review of the values of the policing entity and, in some cases, the local government itself. Here are nine warning signs:

Fear of reporting wrongdoing due to lack of trust. Timely and mandatory reporting of wrongdoing must be a condition of employment in all law enforcement agencies. When there is a lack of trust in the system, when employees believe there will be retaliation, and when they think reporting has no value, they are less likely to report. Without opportunities to address problems that are identified through reporting, there is no opportunity for correction, and rule breaking may be interpreted as the norm.

The unwritten "Blue Wall of Silence" in police departments may stem from a culture of stress driven by the public, the hierarchy, and internal investigations. Having a safe route for reporting can help change this dynamic.

Failure to adequately address ethical violations. In his classic 2005 article in *The Princeton Review*, "The Cognitive and Social Psychology of Contagious Organizational Corruption," author John Darley makes two important points about where organizations go wrong. First, he subscribes to the "bad barrel" theory, not the "bad apple theory."

Policing agencies rightly spend much time looking at the backgrounds of their potential employees, but even good people placed in bad situations can do wrong, especially when such actions go unpunished or are accepted. Darley says that when organizations fail to adequately address ethical violations, others are more likely to perform the same actions.

What is tolerated is repeated, a process he describes as "entrainment." Before long, an ethical organization can turn into a corrupt one.

Too much rigidity and too little humanity. Professor Rosemary O'Leary reminded readers of her 2006 book *The Ethics of Dissent* that rule-driven organizations can tend to make employees "go around the rules." While most police organizations are hierarchal, there must be opportunities for employees to make and learn from mistakes, to explore alternative ideas for handling difficult situations, and to offer creative solutions to problems.

Getting officer feedback is essential. Law enforcement organizations where rules are perceived as unfair or prejudicial to a certain class of employees and those where rules are not justified or explained can also lead to rule bending and, ultimately, to rule breaking.

Policing agencies rightly spend much time looking at the backgrounds of their potential employees, but even good people placed in a bad situation can do wrong, especially when such actions go unpunished or are accepted.

Lack of training. Training for officers often fails to address discretionary decision making, focusing more on hard skills like legal procedure, shooting guns, self-defense, and driving. The recent, large number of police shootings of unarmed victims provides an indication of the haste with which some officers draw their weapons.

Some law enforcement agencies are now using videos with changing scenarios that let officers practice discretionary action, after which they and their supervisors can critique decisions. "Ethical practice is not simply a matter of knowing and following a set of rules," explain authors Terrance Johnson and Raymond Cox in a 2004 article published in *Public Integrity*. "It also requires the use of discretion and making split-second judgments."

"Rules are not enough in such situations," the authors write. "What should be taught is a "framework for decision making that fosters ethical decisions. ..."

Organizations in which the end justifies the means. In 1995 in a book chapter in *The Legacy of Anomie Theory*, author Deborah Cohen explains that unethical and criminal behavior is the natural outcome of a society in which "the end justifies the means." When organizational goals are unattainable or when performance expectations are unrealistic, employees may interpret those demands as an excuse for rule bending or breaking.

Organizational wrongdoing is often the result of a misplaced emphasis on performance measurement in lieu of the core mission of the agency. Police departments that set quotas and have competitions for arrests, convictions, or traffic stops, may, in the eyes of employees, be effectively sanctioning rule breaking to achieve goals.

Absence of leadership focus and insistence on ethical behaviors. Author Tim Hallett wrote in *Sociological Theory* in 2003 that leaders have the power to "define the situation." Defining the culture does not happen overnight, but a focus on ethical actions and public service must come from the top and be consistent.

Empowering employees, providing consistent supervision and discipline, and supporting employees through mentorship are key actions for organizations that desire to build an ethical culture. When managers complain about the cost or time away from work for ethics training, so will the employees. When leaders tacitly accept or ignore even covert prejudice, such attitudes may spread. Johnson and Cox explain that "[t]he culture of being above the law ends only when leaders enforce rules against corrupt behavior and then recognize right behavior."

When the workforce does not mirror the citizenry. A well-established principle in public management is that the bureaucracy should, relatively speaking, look much like the public it serves where gender and race are concerned. The theory holds that inclusion of minority groups should help ensure that their ideas, feelings, issues, and concerns are recognized in government.

There is an old saw that says that people tend to hire people who look like themselves. It's easy for local governments to get into the trap of hiring someone recommended by or related to a fellow employee or depending for recruitment on the same tired methods, thereby limiting the field of candidates.

Broad recruitment efforts with an emphasis on a diverse workforce that is similar to the constituency served can help avoid problems like those in Ferguson, Missouri, but only if the workforce is given the opportunity to share its opinions and concerns.

"Us-vs.-them" mentality. Widespread corruption in some police departments is, according to Johnson and Cox, due in part to training that creates an us-vs.-them mentality that is deeply inculcated into the organizational culture from academy through service.

The spate of well-publicized police brutality and misuse-of-force allegations and convictions has exacerbated this us-vs.-them feeling in the law enforcement community. When the public responds and police departments go on the defensive, they are more likely to shift into "protect our own" mode, which can further erode an ethical culture.

Johnson and Cox believe that leaders can change the culture by integrating the organization's ethical vision and goals into training, especially training in decision-making. They write: "As long as police see controlling the 'enemy' as the first priority, the ideals of serving the community, of saving the weak from those who would use intimidation, and of the badge as an image of public confidence will not be adopted."

Negative outward symbols of the organizational culture. The militarization of many U.S. police departments has served as a symbol to some residents that the police have ultimate power and control. Part of this culture change has been driven by reductions in military force, leading to more surplus equipment, but in part, symbolic changes in dress and demeanor of officers have been driven internally and copied across communities.

"Imagery is important," writes Radley Balko in a May 18, 2015, *Washington Post* story. "It's an indication of how the police see themselves, how they see the community they serve, and how they perceive their relationship with that community. And all of that in turn affects how the community views the police."

Regaining footing as public servants can start with a shift toward becoming a part of the community, not just community enforcers.

Changing the Culture

Baltimore, Maryland, spent $5.7 million in police misconduct lawsuits and related costs between 2011 and September 2014. Though one might assume that the department had been properly chastened and reformed, the death of Baltimore resident Freddie Gray led in 2015 to a $6.4 million settlement with Gray's family.

Departments routinely credit this type of problem to a few rogue cops or to a situation that got out of control. The officers who chained Freddie Gray in the back of the police van were doing what other cops in Baltimore had done without critique. That sort of ingrained culture is hard to change, but it is possible, and cultural change is essential for long-lasting transformation.

As law Professor Barbara Armacost put it in a 2003 *George Washington Law Review* article: "Real reform requires police organizations to accept collective responsibility, not only for heroism, but for police brutality and corruption as well."

James Q. Wilson's and George Kelling's "Broken Windows Theory," which suggests that strictly controlling minor disorders and vandalism can reduce more serious crime, has fallen out of favor as an overly aggressive model that has resulted in some of the disconnect between police departments and those they serve. But author Kelling still has good advice for departments to help them evolve into highly ethical organizations:

- "Emphasize police adherence to a process (application of knowledge, skills, and values), rather than any predictable outcome, because outcomes of police interventions are often wildly unpredictable regardless of officers' skills, intent, and values.
- "Establish accountability standards that identify competent and excellent performance, violations of organizational rules, and incompetent or uncaring work, including performance within organizational rules."

Policing is not easy. Officers come out of their academies with a high degree of discretionary power while experiencing high stress to get it right in situations they have never before experienced. Compound this highly charged atmosphere with an altered public perception of police in their communities, and departments are likely to grow more insular. There is the potential for the "Blue Wall of Silence" to become a fortress of silence.

Local government managers have an opportunity to create and support change in police departments out of touch with their communities, changes that will ultimately benefit communities that no longer trust the police. It's time to get this right, but that means a frank assessment of the strengths and weaknesses of the culture.

READING 2.5

The Gender of Police Violence

By Nikki Jones

"Bye, sexy."

A teenaged boy launched the comment in my direction from just a few feet away. We'd just been sitting at a table together for about an hour, at a weekly meeting for young men in the neighborhood. I was stunned by the young man's transgression, but, as many women are conditioned to do, I didn't respond. Instead, I let the inappropriate comment hang in the air as I left the room.

Like most American women, I have been the target of uninvited comments like this one in the past. The regularity with which such intrusions are directed at women in public space recently inspired its own hashtag, #YouOkSis. The co-creators of the online campaign, Feminista Jones and @BlackGirlDanger, hoped the use of the hashtag would break the silence surrounding the experiences of black women and girls with street harassment. "I wanted to center our voices," said Feminista Jones in an interview published in the *Atlantic*, "because I feel like black women's voices are not always amplified. And I feel it's my responsibility to do that." Another recent online effort is #SayHerName, which was inspired by the activism of the Black Youth Project 100 and allies like the African American Policy Forum, a group that published a report called "Say Her Name: Resisting Police Brutality Against Black Women." This report seeks to amplify and center the experiences of black women and girls in local and national debates about police violence and reforms.

#YouOkSis and #SayHerName are modern-day campaigns made possible by the technological advances of the twenty-first century and fueled by the power of Black Twitter. Yet the efforts to understand violence as a continuum that includes black women, who also confront police violence and are disproportionately affected by various forms of violence against women, are a throwback to an unfinished black feminist project, one that Kimberlé Crenshaw and Andrea J. Ritchie address in the #SayHerName report: "Black women have consistently played a leadership role in struggles against state violence—from the Underground Railroad to the anti-lynching movement to the current Black Lives Matter campaign—yet the forms of victimization they face at the hands of police are consistently left out of social movement demands."

#SayHerName and #YouOkSis challenge the legacy of excluding black women and girls from conversations about violence in the black community. In doing so, these online efforts and their on-the-ground actions document the painful and liberating stories of black women and girls. The parallel movements also run the risk, however, of once again presenting these experiences as distinct and competing, rather than parts of a larger whole. Yet it is crucial for the safety of black men and black women to see structural violence and interpersonal violence, police violence and street harassment, as interconnected.

The "bye, sexy," farewell followed a discussion of police aggression. The discussion took place at a weekly meeting in a public housing complex in San Francisco's Lower Fillmore neighborhood. I lived there for more than two years while researching a new book. Lincoln, an African American man and father figure to several local teens, led the group. (Names in this article have been changed to protect the identities of those involved.) The weekly discussions helped participants process difficult events in the neighborhood, including arrests. On this night, the group was grappling with a recent arrest in the neighborhood. As Lincoln tells it, the incident began when the police got a call that a black man wearing a white T-shirt—a description broad enough to fit every young man in the room—had a gun. When the police arrived, they arrested a man known to the group but, it appears from the conversation, not known for his involvement in street violence. The police handled the man roughly, handcuffing him and slamming him to the ground before throwing him in the back of the police car.

Some of the boys at the meeting saw the arrest; they are saddened and frustrated. I join Lincoln's efforts to help the boys make sense of the incident, asking them how they felt after witnessing the arrest. One boy says that it makes you feel like you want to hurt the police. Lincoln reminds the boys that they can't hurt the police and returns to my original question. He asks the group again to talk about their *feelings*. One of the younger boys, about twelve years old, answers, saying that the arrest of the man makes him feel like it is racist, like the police do not like black people. They deliberately go after the older black men, he says, so that soon just young boys like them are going to be left on the property, and then they will need a pass to get on housing-complex property. I ask whether after witnessing the arrest they feel like the police are there to protect them. They say no, adding that the police do not care if somebody gets shot. When I question how it makes them feel about power, one boy says he feels like he has no power. I ask the group what they can do if they have no power. Stay out of trouble, do well in school, one boy suggests. Pressing, I ask, what else? The usually boisterous group falls silent.

Shortly after this conversation, I said my goodbyes to the group. I had an early flight the next day. I rose from the table and made my way to the door. As I placed my hand on the door's handle, one of the young men from the group—a young man who had always treated me with deference and respect—lofted the loud farewell into the air: "Bye, sexy." I knew my silence would not be the end of it. I was sure that Lincoln would scold the young man for his lack of respect—a lesson that he sometimes punctuated with a swift jab to a boy's chest.

No Haiti No Orleans **by Michael Massenburg. In his work, Massenburg explores issues class, race and culture "in an attempt to engage the subjects through representational, psychological, and spiritual perspectives."**

I was frustrated by the boy's outburst, but in that moment I also understood the young man's actions with a clarity that I'd never had before. Although young, he understood the fragility of his masculinity and had already learned that his effort to repair an injury to his budding manhood required a female body. Yet, I also understood that "bye, sexy" was more than an adolescent's jocular attempt to reassert his manhood. Our conversation was so powerful, so revealing, because it made visible the *origin* of the threat to the young man's sense of manhood and developing sense of self. The threat wasn't me or my body or my status position, as women who are the targets of uninvited comments in public are often encouraged to believe. Rather, the source of the young man's sense of powerlessness was, as the group conversation made clear, his own marginality and the seemingly arbitrary and all-controlling actions of the police in his neighborhood. His comment was not just a desperate grasp at a semblance of power and control over his social world after having his sense of power*less*ness laid bare before me. It was an attempt to *escape his own vulnerability*—a vulnerability that women and girls know well. If he hadn't made such an effort, then he would have had to settle in with an unsettling social fact: that he is embedded in a set of power relations that make him more like a woman or a girl than he'd like to admit.

The experiences of black women and girls with street harassment, and of black men and boys with police aggression, are both similar and interconnected. The experiences are far more similar than competing discourses around police violence and violence against black women suggest. Police violence and street harassment reveal a *shared* vulnerability to dominance and violence. Both forms of violence are gendered violence. Routine practices that come along with contact with the criminal justice system force black men into submissiveness. In effect, poor black men are subjugated in a way that mirrors the street harassment of black women: they become bodies that can be accessed, penetrated, and controlled at will and without recourse. The emotional impact of such encounters lingers long after the encounter ends, as is often the case when women are subjected to uninvited comments or physical aggression in public.

After another boys' group meeting, for instance, the boys finish the plates of food that are provided at each meeting and, one by one or in pairs, begin to trickle out of the meeting area. As they leave, they are confronted with a familiar scene. Two police cars have pulled into the parking lot near the meeting room's door. The activity draws the group outside en masse. Once outside, Lincoln takes a stand near the four officers who have arrived on the scene. Lincoln says that the officers are claiming that three of the boys attending the meeting broke into a resident's home. He says the boys were in the room the whole time. A small group of kids, who appeared to be between the ages of eight and eleven, gather around the officers. Lincoln orders the kids to run along. The older boys in the group walk away on their own, spreading out like water on pavement as they make their way across the street and away from the officers.

I hear Larry's voice rise from the crowd of observers. Larry is Lincoln's son. A senior in high school, he's been studying for the state-mandated exit exam. I've provided some support for him along the way. A few weeks earlier, at the end of an emergency tenants' meeting called to address a wave of evictions affecting the housing complex's residents, Larry shared a recent encounter with the police. He had been picked up and taken to the local station and "strip-searched," he said. He looked disheartened, frustrated, and somewhat defeated as he shared his experience.

The strip search Larry references is a routine practice in law enforcement and corrections. During the invasive search, a male suspect like Larry is coerced to bend over, spread his buttocks and manipulate his genitalia (or have it done by an officer) to show that he is not carrying contraband or weapons in or on his body. Invasive body searches can also take place on the street. Any failure to comply with an officer's direction would be seen as resistance and met with coercive force. The largely hidden nature of this invasive practice mirrors black women's experience with sexual violence as a form of social control.

"Not tonight, not tonight," Larry repeats in a monotone chant. "Ya'll ain't taking me in tonight," he says, bouncing on his toes like a boxer getting ready for a match. "You're not going to strip-search me. That's illegal."

Larry makes his way over to my place in the small crowd. He continues to bounce and chant as we watch what's going on from behind the railing that separates the entrance from the parking lot. Larry raises his voice and begins to yell in the direction of the officers. I turn to him to get his attention. In a low, soft tone I encourage him to calm down. He pauses for a moment.

"It's frustrating," he says, "they can come up in here, take me to the station, strip-search me, and I can't do anything back to them." I tell him that I understand, but that the way to get back at them is by taking and passing his exit exam. "You're trying to go somewhere," I say. I encourage him not to court the police into disrupting his path. He takes in my suggestion before retreating back into the crowd of bystanders.

It's not uncommon for bystanders to launch accusations at officers from the outskirts of a confrontation. But I was struck by the specificity of Larry's accusation: "you're not going to strip-search me, that's illegal." His accusation made public what was an otherwise private and intimate violation he had experienced at the hands of the police. As with the efforts of #YouOkSis and #SayHerName, he is challenging a routine but degrading experience. In doing so, he also challenges the idea that such practices are a natural or normal condition of social life for young black men. Like the supporters of #YouOkSis and #SayHerName, Larry's efforts to break the silence surrounding his experience also open him up to the potential for harsher forms of aggression, including the possibility of lethal violence at the hands of the police—a threat from which I hoped to insulate him by redirecting his frustration.

The omnipresent threat of sexual violence operates to keep women and girls (and other gendered outsiders) "in their place," Patricia Hill Collins writes in *Black Sexual Politics*. For black women, she says, the threat of violence acts as "an invisible cage of control." The penetration and expansion of law enforcement into the daily lives of young men is like an invisible cage, too. Reactions to these constraints can send ripples of aggression through a community; the aggression of the dramatic arrest that the boys witnessed eventually found its way to me. Yet, the hand that local policing efforts play in perpetuating aggression and violence in black communities, especially violence against black women at the hands of black men, is often made invisible. Disrupting the silence surrounding *this* relationship will require a broader analytical understanding of how violence moves through people's bodies and minds, landing on whoever is on the lower end of the social hierarchy.

That understanding won't emerge through competing discourses, but by acknowledging the similarities in the violence directed at black women and at black men, connecting concerns reflected in #YouOkSis and #SayHerName with recent debates over police violence. Such a conversation would not only make the necessary point that black women and girls are targets of police violence *too*, but would also reveal the striking similarity between men and boys' encounters with the police and women and girls' experience with street harassment and sexual violence. We should organize around a shared experience of vulnerability and challenge the acceptability of expressions of dominance *in any form* as a reaction to this vulnerability. To do so is the path to equality and justice, one that is liberating for black men and boys, black women and girls *at the same time*.

READING 2.6

Will the Widespread Use of Police Body Cameras Improve Police Accountability?

By Shira A. Scheindlin and Peter K. Manning

yes

People behave differently when they know they are being watched—and police are no exception.

As a trial judge, I have heard hundreds of cases involving charges of false arrest and excessive force by the police. All of these cases turn on credibility. The victim (assuming he or she is alive) tells the story from his or her perspective, and the police officers (often more than two) tell their story. The jury is left in the difficult and uncomfortable position of deciding which side is telling the truth and which side is providing false testimony.

One example makes the point. In a criminal case in Chicago, five police officers swore under oath that they pulled a suspect over after he failed to use a turn signal. One officer testified that when he asked the driver to produce his license and registration, he smelled marijuana and directed the suspect to leave the car and stand by the trunk as the vehicle was searched. During the search, officers found nearly a pound of marijuana in a backpack on the back seat of the car. Based on the discovery of the marijuana, the driver was arrested.

The suspect testified to a starkly different version of events. He swore that he used his turn signal, was never asked for his license and registration, and that the marijuana was not in a backpack on the back seat of the car, but was hidden under the seat. Then the suspect's lawyer got lucky. At the last minute, he subpoenaed and obtained a video that had been recorded automatically by the police car—which the police witnesses must have forgotten about. The video showed that immediately after being stopped, the suspect was removed from his car, frisked and handcuffed. The search of the car occurred after the arrest.

Shira A. Scheindlin and Peter K. Manning, "Will the Widespread Use of Police Body Cameras Improve Police Accountability? Yes," *Americas Quarterly*, vol. 9, no. 2, pp. 24-27.

The judge found that all five officers had lied and engaged in "outrageous conduct." She called it a conspiracy to lie, and suppressed both the arrest and the fruits of the search. Without that video, it would have been hard for a judge to find that five police officers had lied under oath while a guy caught with a pound of marijuana had told the truth.

But that is exactly what happened.

Officers wearing body cameras will be less aggressive and more respectful when they interact with the community.

The point should be clear: people behave differently when they know they are being watched, and police are no exception. Officers wearing body cameras will be less aggressive and more respectful when they interact with members of the community. They will also be more reluctant to use force unless it is necessary to protect themselves and the public. While body-worn police cameras may not be a panacea, they will not only lead to a reduction in the use of unnecessary or excessive force by police officers, but will also be beneficial for both the police and the community.

Evidence supporting this belief comes from jurisdictions in which experiments with the use of body-worn cameras have produced encouraging data. In one such jurisdiction—Rialto, California—after the police force had worn body cameras for a full year, citizen complaints against police declined by 60 percent. Other jurisdictions that have implemented body cameras have seen similar results. In Mesa, Arizona, for example, use-of-force complaints decreased by 75 percent for officers using cameras in a pilot program.[1] In Nampa, Idaho, they dropped by 24 percent.[2]

Another important statistic from the Rialto study is the number of incidents that resulted in the use of force by an officer, which dropped by 88 percent after the use of body cameras. Officers who were not equipped with cameras were twice as likely to use force as officers who were. Even more tellingly, when officers wore cameras, every incident of physical contact was initiated by a member of the public, but in the absence of cameras, 29 percent of the incidents involving physical force were initiated by the officer.[3]

Such studies have taken on increased significance in the wake of controversy over the deaths of several African Americans at the hands of police over the past year. This includes Michael Brown, an unarmed teenager who was shot by an officer in Ferguson, Missouri, and Eric Garner in Staten Island, New York, who died after being placed in a chokehold by a police officer. President Barack Obama and Attorney General Eric Holder have called for greater use of body-worn cameras by police officers. But even before these incidents, I concluded that such cameras could play a role in curtailing abuses of the long-standing police practice in New York of stopping and frisking young men—most of them African American—on suspicion of criminal behavior. As part of my August 2013 ruling in *Floyd v. City of New York* that the disproportional use of stop and frisk constituted a pattern of racial profiling and violated the U.S. Constitution, I ordered the New York City Police Department to conduct a trial in selected precincts requiring officers to wear body cameras.

The use of body cameras will also protect police officers. No longer will a person be able to claim that a police officer punched or kicked him without cause, when in fact it was that person who initiated the encounter by threatening or attacking the police officer. The contemporaneous record of what occurred should make it clear whether the officer was justified in using force. Everyone has a right to act in self defense. A video presents an unbiased account of the events. It has no motive to lie and no stake in the outcome. It merely records the event as it happens. If a police officer acts lawfully, then he should not be wrongly accused, forced to defend himself and risk a punishment he does not deserve. The camera will provide his defense.

There are some drawbacks to the use of body cameras—such as privacy concerns for both officers and the citizens they encounter, the storage of data capturing images of innocent people, the possible tampering with the images, and the accuracy of the images (with issues relating to lighting, lens clarity, movement, and angles). However, there is far more benefit than harm associated with their use. Once people know their actions are being recorded, their behavior changes. I am confident the widespread use of body cameras will reduce the amount of excessive force by police officers and will improve their relationships with the citizens they encounter and protect.

Given existing technologies, we should have the best evidence available at our fingertips. And speaking of fingers, millions of fingerprints are kept on file in case the police need to identify a suspect. Today, DNA databases are also available to law enforcement. Everyone agrees that DNA should be collected so long as storage and access are both carefully regulated. There is no reason that contemporaneous recordings of police encounters should not be treated the same way.

Notes

1. Michael D. White, "Police Officer Body-Worn Cameras: Assessing the Evidence," Washington, DC: Office of Community Oriented Policing Services, <ojpdiagnosticcenter.org/sites/default/files/spotlight/download/Police%20Officer%20Body-Worn%20Cameras.pdf> (accessed April 13, 2015).

2. Brian Morrin, "Police body camera: A watchful eye that doesn't lie," KBOI2.com, April 29, 2014, <www.kboi2.com/news/local/A-police-body-camera-A-watchful-eye-that-doesnt-lie-257002171.html> (accessed April 13, 2015).

3. Michael D. White, "Police Officer Body-Worn Cameras: Assessing the Evidence," Washington, DC: Office of Community Oriented Policing Services, <ojpdiagnosticcenter.org/sites/default/files/spotlight/download/Police%20Officer%20Body-Worn%20Cameras.pdf> (accessed April 13, 2015).

no

New technologies won't change police behavior unless there's a corresponding change in law enforcement culture.

Information technology is shaped by the organization that uses it. It is also shaped by the practices of the people who use it in their work. New kinds of information technology, or ways of processing work-related information, are thought to make work routines more efficient. In police work—just as in the work of doctors, lawyers and engineers—there is a persistent wish to cut through the complexity and get to the "heart of the problem" with a practical solution.

I would call it the "silver bullet fantasy." The arguments for police body cameras fall into that category.

Police officers are pragmatic. They seek the simplest, quickest and most effective technology to perform their jobs. At the same time, they value their freedom from close supervision and are wary of "big brother." These basic elements of law enforcement culture suggest we should be skeptical about whether the introduction of body-worn cameras will effectively address the concerns many critics have had—especially since the deaths of unarmed civilians in Ferguson, Missouri, Staten Island, New York, and elsewhere—about the lack of police accountability.

A historical perspective puts this in context. Since the late nineteenth century, politicians and police supervisors have sought to apply information technology (IT) to their work in order to improve response times and increase transparency. Consider, for example, the call box, the radio, the two-way radio, the computer-based dispatch, and the now widespread use of social media by police departments to inform citizens of their activities. More recently, cameras have been placed in patrol cars and closed-circuit technology video devices have been installed in more public spaces.

But often, IT is more about the efficient management of information systems than about enhancing the quality of police work. By tradition and legal precedent, policing is a secret and protected craft. In many respects, judges and prosecutors are quite happy not to know what "processes" ensued prior to any matter brought to their attention.

Let's be clear. Observational research of police officers interacting with citizens reveals that force beyond kicking, punching and pushing is not frequent.[1] But the nature of the job makes unexpected violent episodes likely. Police are protected, sanctioned and even rewarded by having these uses of force—including lethal force—overlooked by law and tradition.[2] Can we expect these uncertain, unexpected responses to be reduced or altered simply by being recorded? The technologies of any occupation are modified by the occupational culture, and the premise that a technology always reconfigures work in the expected way is false.

It should surprise no one that when cameras or other devices are used to monitor patrol officers, they have responded by turning off cameras and microphones, by "forgetting" to turn them on or to insert fresh tapes, by changing the camera angle, and by deleting strips of images. Officers have also failed to replace tapes and have taped over previous recordings by reusing tapes. Departments amplify these practices by failing to properly supervise the processing of data. Even if there are rules about keeping cameras and microphones on, supervising officers may not regularly view and monitor the tapes, check officers' use of them, maintain records of taping, or sanction officers who do not follow policies and procedures.[3]

These actions are forms of resistance to new IT, and they are rooted in the occupational culture of patrol officers. Any new surveillance technology is viewed with ambivalence. Although it could be argued that recordings of the officers' words and actions protect the officer in internal investigations, civil suits or criminal charges, they could also reveal the everyday brutalities and incivilities that research has shown are routinely employed in policing in this country.[4]

It has been proposed that miniature cameras worn on the uniform will increase accountability. This claim has no empirical basis. There has been little systematic research on the question. Police typically announce the success of innovations before they are evaluated. The police position generally is, "Why would we do it if we did not think it would improve things?" So, this begs the question: What would accountability-based body cameras mean?

There are two kinds of accountability: an in-advance definition of what is expected, and an after-the-fact justification for the decisions made. In policing, organizational accountability of either kind is an empty illusion because law enforcement is a profoundly conservative, stable and ossified institution. It has survived the community policing movement with little or no change in training, deployment, rewards systems, or management. The closest thing to true organizational accountability might be when the federal government places a department under a consent order for a specific pattern of abuses—for example, the Consent Decree Regarding the New Orleans Police Department in 2012.[5] But even with such oversight, the same structure, supervision, training, rules, regulations, and protective mandate—the tacit agreement between society and the police that gives police latitude to define how best to do their jobs—remain unchanged.[6]

It has been proposed that miniature cameras worn on the uniform will increase accountability. This claim has no empirical basis.

Consider why holding individual officers accountable in any case is problematic. The organizational structure gives officers significant discretion on patrol, and leaves them unsupervised with respect to when, how, why, and to what end they intervene in an incident. They are required after the fact to justify their actions—if they were known to the organization. But many actions are not recorded, or are labeled "action taken." The tacit assumption within the police hierarchy is that you cannot easily judge individual decisions because "you had to be there" to understand.

This ideology makes investigations, and holding individual officers accountable, very difficult in practice.

Let us assume that there are few, if any, changes in the police organization except for the introduction of body cameras. If cameras are used, one might ask about the processing, use and management of the incredible number of hours of data that would be generated. How will they view, code, store, analyze, and apply these data? If you trust the police, you trust their words and deeds—it's a contract.

The hope is that body cameras or statements by commissioners or chiefs regarding changes in policy will transform practices. But there is little evidence that top-down management policies or local and state legal rulings change police practices. Since supervision, training, rewards, and practices have not changed, what evidence is there to suggest that a camera on an officer's lapel will change behavior?

Notes

1. Geoffrey P. Alpert and Roger G. Dunham, *Understanding Police Use of Force: Officers, Suspects, and Reciprocity* (Cambridge: Cambridge University Press, 2004), 2.

2. Egon Bittner, *The Functions of the Police in Modern Society: A Review of Background Factors, Current Practices, and Possible Role Models* (Maryland: National Institute of Mental Health Center for Studies of Crime and Delinquency, 1970), 45.

3. Jennifer J. Dierickx, "Why camera cars do not fix the problem: a study of technology use and racial profiling" (PhD diss., Wayne State University, 2008).

4. Peter K. Manning, *Police Work: The Social Organization of Policing* (Cambridge: MIT Press, 1977), 41.

5. United States of America v. New Orleans, Consent Decree Regarding the New Orleans Police Department (2012).

6. See William Terrill, "Police Coercion," 260–279; and Ronald Weitzer, "Police Race Relations," 339–361 in Michael D. Reisig and Robert J. Kane, eds., *The Oxford Handbook of Police and Policing* (New York: Oxford University Press, 2014).

READING 2.7

Who Do You Protect, Who Do You Surveil?

By Joel Handley

On Black Friday, 2014, the biggest shopping day of the year, hundreds of protesters marched to Wicker Park, a trendy neighborhood on Chicago's northwest side. It was the third stop in a day-long march from one commercial district to the next: starting at downtown's Magnificent Mile, then heading north to an Apple Store, then west. Four days after the grand jury decision not to indict Ferguson police officer Darren Wilson in the killing of Michael Brown, the event was part of a nationwide action decrying complacent consumerism in the face of a national tragedy. Wicker Park's retail epicenter seemed an appropriate place to go.

A Chicago police officer, however, couldn't figure out the route. He took to his radio and called in a request to the local "fusion center," the Chicago Police Department (CPD) intelligence hub.

"One of the girls, she's kind of an organizer here, she's been on her phone a lot. You guys picking up any information, uh, where they're going, possibly?" the officer asked.

"Yeah, we're keeping an eye on it."

The conversation was quick, but when the audio from the call leaked online, activists saw proof of something they'd long suspected: Chicago police were tracking their cell phones, using a controversial new technology.

The StingRay—both a brand name and a generic term—is a suitcase-sized device that acts as a wiretap for the wireless age. But while a wiretap monitors a single line, a stingray acts like a roving cell phone tower, vacuuming in data from all nearby phones, tablets and other wireless devices. This includes call history and current and previous locations. Enhanced stingrays can also record and eavesdrop on phone calls.

An assortment of add-ons are now available: The FishHawk listens in on calls; the Harpoon broadens the StingRay's range; the AmberJack antenna helps pinpoint individual phones; the KingFish analyzes call patterns, doing in one stroke what might have taken Detective Lester Freamon an entire season of *The Wire* to accomplish.

U.S. military and intelligence agencies developed stingray technology in the 1990s, and police departments began using it as early as 2003. Before receiving StingRays, police departments must sign non-disclosure agreements. It wasn't until 2011, when the FBI presented information gathered from a stingray in court, that domestic use of the devices came to public attention. Civil liberties groups immediately sounded the alarm.

The ACLU says stingrays violate privacy rights because they capture information from every phone in the vicinity, not just a suspect's. There are also concerns regarding Fourth Amendment restrictions on unreasonable search and seizure, since stingrays can penetrate the walls of a home and track a person's movements even while inside.

The ACLU has identified at least 48 state and local law enforcement agencies that are using stingrays. While the Harris Corporation, maker of the StingRay brand device, assured the FCC the devices were for emergency use only (because they interfere with cell networks), the few available examples of their deployment show they are used for routine police work—and to spy on peaceful activists.

On November 12, 2003, for example, police in Miami-Dade, Florida, sought "retroactive authorization" from the county for the "emergency" purchase of a stingray on November 1. It was used to monitor protests at the Free Trade Area of the Americas Conference, according to a purchase request released to the ACLU.

In addition to its neverending covert obsession with activists, since its founding in 1855 the chicago police department has never given up its day-to-day focus on the poor and working class.

Police departments have striven to keep the details of their stingray use under wraps. The Chicago Police Department denied owning the devices until April 2014, after local activist Freddy Martinez filed a Freedom of Information Act (FOIA) request. In response to that and subsequent requests from Martinez, CPD admitted it has owned stingray devices since 2005 and has purchased upgrades, antennae and software at a total cost of at least $640,000—but has not disclosed how or when the devices are used.

Stingrays are part of a post-9/11 push by the federal government to step up local police departments' intelligence-gathering and coordination. Since 9/11, the Department of Homeland Security (DHS) has given more than $34 billion to local law enforcement, in part for high-tech surveillance gear like stingrays and facial recognition systems. Seventy-eight DHS-funded fusion centers, where police officers work side by side with federal agents, have sprung up across the country, and 18,000 departments and agencies swap reports daily.

The Chicago Police Department has led the way in the new surveillance age. A six-month investigation by *In These Times* indicates CPD is using its new tools to target poor communities of color and peaceful activists organizing against the city's power-holders.

New Tech, Same Policing

Policing in Chicago has changed little since the department was founded in 1855. When the old "police force" (a group of part-time constables) couldn't put down a construction workers' strike, the city's business class pushed the city government to fund a professional police department. CPD was tasked with shielding the well-to-do downtown residents from the surrounding rabble. Officers targeted the poorest immigrant group at the time: the Irish. In *The Rise of the Chicago Police Department,* Sam Mitrani writes that while Irish Chicagoans made up only one-fifth of the city's population, they accounted for two-thirds of arrests in the first six months of CPD's existence. "While the police investigated a small number of serious crimes, the bulk of their activity consisted of patrolling the everyday activity of the immigrant working class," Mitrani writes.

They also attempted to keep a lid on growing working-class unrest (which would erupt in the Haymarket affair in 1886). As early as May 1867, officers were monitoring rallies for the eight-hour workday. Police listened to soapbox speeches, infiltrated meetings, arrested speakers, intimidated strikers and shot demonstrators.

In the 20th century, various CPD intelligence units—known collectively as the Red Squad—broadened their target lists from labor unions and anarchists to, over time, Communists, black radicals, neighborhood organizations and New Left groups. Frank Donner, in *Protectors of Privilege: Red Squads and Police Repression in Urban America,* writes that officers stole mailing lists, burglarized homes and maintained files on hundreds of thousands of Chicagoans. One small community organization was infiltrated "apparently ... because it opposed a cross-town expressway." CPD launched its first effort at high-tech surveillance in the 1960s, using telephoto cameras to document the faces of protesters and rioters.

In 1982, a class action lawsuit quelled such abuses when a federal judge imposed a consent decree on the city of Chicago that prohibited "investigative activity … that is directed toward First Amendment conduct."

However, playing on fear of black gangs and terrorism, Mayor Richard M. Daley convinced a federal court to ease the rules in 2001. The following year, undercover police infiltrated meetings of the American Friends Service Committee, a Quaker organization. In 2009, a judge dissolved the consent decree in full. In other words, at a time when CPD was testing out a new fusion center and an arsenal of high-tech surveillance gadgets such as stingrays, it was freed from the oversight that protected Chicagoans from investigation for exercising the First Amendment. Police could again conduct secret surveillance, so long as they filled out a brief "First Amendment worksheet" and received departmental approval.

Whom they chose to surveil was in keeping with the department's long history. In addition to its covert obsession with activists, the department has never given up its day-to-day focus on the poor and working class. Today, black residents make up the city's racial group, and an analysis of 2010 arrest rates conducted by *In These Times* shows that 72 percent of all CPD arrests were of African Americans (most frequently for alleged drug violations). Blacks comprise only one-third of the city's population. Similarly, an ACLU of Illinois report released in March found that black Chicagoans were subject to 72 percent of "stop and frisks."

Malkia Cyril, the founder and executive director of the Center for Media Justice, wrote in a recent *Huffington Post* op-ed that "indiscriminate and covert collection of private data expedites, expands and entrenches" such discriminatory policing.

CPD Meets Big Data

In 2003, the Chicago Police Department introduced Police Observation Devices, or POD cameras—30 large blue-and-white boxes mounted on poles—with the aim of filming open-air drug markets. In March 2005, the city trumpeted the program's first success. Camera operators had spotted hand-to-hand drug transactions and notified a gang unit, which arrested three alleged West Side dealers.

Despite this slow start, CPD tech wunderkind Ron Huberman, the founder of the program, touted the cameras as "the future of crime fighting." Giving a tour of the control center to a *Wired* magazine writer in 2005, Huberman showed off the cameras, becoming agitated when he spotted what he thought was a drug deal. "You see that guy? … He's pitching dope—you can tell. Fucker," Huberman is quoted as saying. They zoom in on the suspect ("so tight I can see the wisps of a mustache," the writer says) and see him holding a brown bag and money. Huberman threatens to call in a bust then and there, but relents, saving the footage to use another day.

KNOWN COSTS OF CPD'S HIGH-TECH SURVEILLANCE

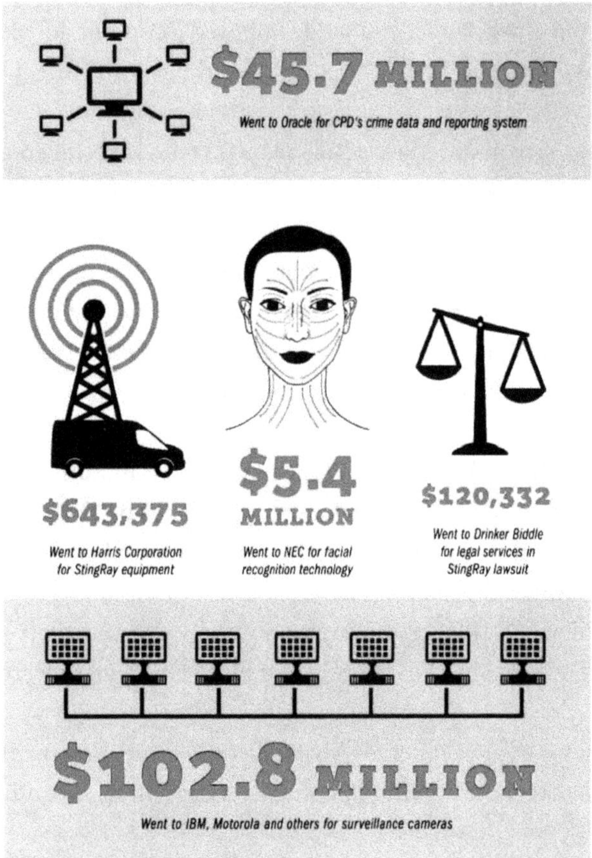

Evidently inspired by the program even before the first arrests, in 2004 Mayor Daley announced the creation of Operation Virtual Shield. In the downtown business district, 250 new cameras would be equipped with algorithms that could flag someone's behavior as suspicious and alert the police.

These cameras proved a modest beginning to what would become the "most extensive and integrated" surveillance network in the country, according to former DHS Secretary Michael Chertoff. Funded by tens of millions of dollars in DHS grants, Chicago's network has expanded to include cameras in more than 1,000 private businesses that have granted access to the city, plus 7,000 cameras in public schools and 3,200 on Chicago Housing Authority property. (Notably, 84.9 percent of the city's public-school students and 93 percent of CHA households are black or Latino.) Another 23,000 cameras have been installed in Chicago Transit Authority stations, buses and trains.

By 2011, the last time CPD released complete stats, the number of POD cameras had swelled to more than 1,200. Of the 632 POD addresses currently listed on CPD's website, more than 90 percent are in communities of color, primarily in the city's low-income South and West Sides.

When CPD boasted in 2013 that the surveillance network had led to 4,500 arrests in a four-year span, Adam Schwartz, an ACLU attorney in Illinois, noted that this was less than 1 percent of all arrests. Numerous studies have shown that video cameras don't reduce violent crime and do little to curb property crime. Given this, the ACLU wonders why Chicagoans should give up so much privacy, noting that the cameras' zoom functions allow operators to closely watch targets and peer into cars and windows.

Meanwhile, in 2005, the department secretly bought its first stingray equipment, taking advantage of an Illinois law allowing police to make purchases outside the normal budgetary and procurement processes by using seized drug money. Between 2009 and 2014, CPD acquired multiple upgrades to its original devices, as well as AmberJack and KingFish attachments.

While it was buying stingrays, CPD introduced automatic license plate readers (ALPRs) with some fanfare. In 2006, Police Superintendent Phil Cline unveiled to the *Chicago Sun-Times* a "futuristic squad car" outfitted with an ALPR that could scan 3,600 plates per hour, automatically cataloging the date, time and GPS location in a central database. Police would be alerted if their car's scanner caught a plate on a "hot list" of wanted vehicles. A 2007 CPD report explained that the ALPR-equipped cars were sent to high-crime neighborhoods, as well as "demonstrations and numerous special events throughout the city."

Today, of CPD's 25 ALPR-equipped squad cars, 22 are assigned to police districts and patrol areas with majority non-white populations. The five majority white districts share three of the cars. The department has also installed plate-scanning software in its POD cameras.

The cameras automatically send license-plate scans to a police database, which officers can check whenever they're curious about where a certain car has traveled. The CPD also subscribes to a private ALPR database that lets it run plates against more than 3 billion records.

This retention of data is what most worries the ACLU's Schwartz: "If you have hundreds of ALPRs around your city capturing hundreds of license plates every hour ... you can punch in somebody's license plate number and see where they've been, or after the fact, you can punch in the location of a protest three years ago and see who was there."

The Return of the Red Squad?

Chicago's $1 million fusion center, opened in 2008, is staffed with rotating agents from the FBI, DHS and Drug Enforcement Agency, among others. They have access to a stream of data from 911 calls, mug shots, video feeds and police reports. The center got a makeover in 2014, with new wall-to-wall monitors piping in the feeds from the city's surveillance camera network. Granted a tour in June 2014, NBC Chicago reported that if surveillance cameras recognize a target, a matching mug shot and criminal history appear on a monitor, suggesting that the fusion center runs advanced facial recognition software. CPD never responded to an *In These Times* request for a visit.

Elsewhere, fusion centers have taken their counterterrorism mandate as license to surveil Muslims. A document trove released to the ACLU in Northern California in 2013 shows that fear of Middle Eastern men animates many of the "suspicious activity reports" broadcast from California fusion centers. Samples include "Suspicious ME [Middle Eastern] Males Buy Several Large Pallets of Water," and "Two middle eastern looking males taking photographs of Folsom Dam."

There have been no such accounts in Chicago. However, its fusion center appears typical of a trend identified in a 2012 U.S. Senate report: Many fusion centers have lost track of their counterterrorism directive. Chicago police are directed to notify the fusion center of "*any* significant or newsworthy

A CPD officer videotapes protesters gathered at the Homan Square police facility on February 27.

event within the city" (emphasis in original). Of the more than 30 events listed as examples, most are run-of-the-mill policing. One, however, stands out: Police are directed to report "information concerning strikes, labor-management incidents or union controversies or the possibility thereof." CPD has yet to respond to a November 2014 *In These Times* FOIA request asking for examples of reports coded under this category.

It's clear that the center keeps a close eye on labor actions once they spill into the streets, along with all other protests and marches. In "private sector homeland security briefings," the fusion center and CPD assemble impressive lists of upcoming rallies and actions. It then sends the schedule out to downtown office building managers and security teams. One such briefing from August 2013 lists six upcoming events, including an anti-drone protest, rallies for women's rights and animal liberation, protests against banks and Boeing headquarters, and a march on City Hall "to stop police crimes." The list is sandwiched between news of global violence—Egyptian police killed in an ambush, a Missoula bomb scare—and "significant dates" that tend heavily toward terrorism, such as the five-year anniversary of a suicide bombing in Pakistan. A disclaimer on the briefing "recognizes that Americans have constitutionally protected rights to assemble."

How police and fusion center staffers get the protest information isn't clear—whether through protest permits, infiltrators, stingrays, scouring of social media sites or some combination thereof,

Jackson Potter, a staff coordinator for the Chicago Teachers Union (CTU), tells *In These Times* that both police and school board members regularly comment on things that are discussed in closed-door union meetings before they're made public, though he thinks this is likely a function of moles cultivated by the school board, not police infiltrators. In 2012, the union expelled "for life" a CTU delegate whom FOIA requests revealed to be an informant for the school board, just as the union was preparing for a major strike.

> *Chicago police officers are directed to report to the city's fusion center any 'information concerning strikes, labor-management incidents or union controversies or the possibility thereof.'*

Potter stresses that the union has a good relationship with the city police, which he chalks up to working-class solidarity. But he says he's not naive about being targeted and suspects the police have files on many of the active CTU members and their community partners. He says that when the union applies for protest permits, officers will sometimes say, "We were wondering when you were going to call about this."

Once the police arrive at a protest, they make no secret of some of their surveillance activities. Chicago attorney Jerry Boyle recalls that police "had the full-blown operation going" at a thousands-strong Take Back Chicago rally on October 10, 2011, where Occupy Chicago, unions and grassroots groups gathered to highlight the many ways big banks had devastated the city. Surveillance vans, undercover officers and handheld cameras were all deployed, says Boyle, a long-time legal observer for the National Lawyers Guild.

At protests and political events across the city, including the CTU picket lines in 2012 and recent demonstrations against police torture (after the *Guardian* revealed abuses at a Chicago police detention facility known as Homan Square), CPD officers routinely point cameras at crowds, sometimes shoving them in protesters' faces. Babur Balos, a Chicago organizer, sees the cameras as intimidation. He jokes, "I think they're running empty cameras." CPD used that tactic in the 1960s.

The question remains: Is CPD using covert high-tech surveillance—stingrays, ALPRs—to investigate activists? Since the lifting of the consent decree in 2009, CPD intelligence units have conducted at least six "intelligence gathering" investigations into First Amendment-protected activities (one launched several months before the decree officially ended), according to documents released in March to the *Chicago Reader*. The redacted documents show that police utilized "electronic surveillance" and "undercover methods" against Occupy Chicago and protesters of the 2012 NATO Summit in Chicago. Another "intelligence gathering" mission began on November 7, 2014, two days after a protest against police brutality at CPD headquarters and as the Black Lives Matter movement was gaining steam in Chicago.

There's no specification as to what "electronic surveillance" means, but given the indication that CPD used a stingray at the Black Friday protest in 2014 and its admission of deploying ALPRs at demonstrations in 2007, it could very well be using this gear to surveil activists. At the height of the 20th century Red Squad, officers wrote down license plate numbers outside meeting spots and protest sites, and stole mailing lists to map social connections. Today, a stingray deployed at the edge of an event, or an ALPR-equipped squad car circling through a union hall parking lot, could replace much of that legwork.

In the past, officers would use this type of information to harass activists, tip off employers and landlords to the activities of their workers and tenants, and create massive police files. Without court oversight, the only things preventing a return to such practices are the personalities of CPD officials and the professional standards to which they hold themselves.

Keep It Like a Secret

In These Times submitted 11 FOIA requests in November 2014 on a variety of CPD high-tech surveillance activities. After requesting extensions, the department has given partial answers to three of the 11 requests. Revised requests have yet to receive a response. The outstanding requests include files on individual activists, video footage from demonstrations and audits of officers abusing department computer systems.

Despite its apparent reluctance to disclose details of its spying, CPD actively promotes an image as an eager adopter of technology. In 2013, Chicago police claimed to have made the country's first facial recognition technology (FRT)-assisted arrest, capturing a phone thief's face on a train station camera and matching it to previous mug shots. However, in response to FOIA requests from *In These Times* and tech website The Verge, CPD said a search of records since 2013 turned up no reference to facial recognition technology. The Verge reports that the suspected phone thief's arrest report did not mention FRT and his public defender was led to believe his client was identified in a police lineup.

To be fair, when it comes to disclosing its use of high-tech surveillance, CPD is a bit damned if it does, damned if it doesn't: subject to FOIA lawsuits if it withholds information, but under duress from federal agencies and technology manufacturers to stay mum.

In December 2014, for example, the FBI and Harris—the defense contractor that manufactures StingRay—supported the CPD's motion to the Cook County Circuit Court to dismiss Martinez's FOIA lawsuit. The FBI argued that the release of information on StingRay would violate the Homeland Security Act and other federal laws, while Harris claimed that its proprietary trade secrets would be compromised.

The affidavits also noted the penalties CPD would face if it caved. Harris said that a release of its manuals or guides "would make it difficult for Harris to continue providing equipment." Bradley Morrison, head of the FBI's technology tracking unit, wrote a sterner admonition, claiming that disclosing details about StingRay could violate the International Traffic in Arms Regulations, "a felony punishable by up to 20 years imprisonment and up to $1 million per occurrence."

Documents released in the course of the lawsuit suggest that CPD is not just hiding stingrays from the public, but also from judges, through an arcane trick police have used elsewhere across the country. Police can ask a judge for a "pen register" court order to obtain a phone's incoming and outgoing call information from a cell phone company. In Washington, Florida and Maryland, court cases have shown that police routinely seek pen register court orders to request information that—unbeknownst to the judges—they've already procured, or plan to procure, via stingrays, thus covering up stingray use while securing nominal authorization.

Since July 2013, the Chicago Police Department has applied for at least 14 court orders that Sgt. Jack Costa wrote in an affidavit he "understood to authorize the use of" stingrays. The department refuses to produce these court orders, citing a federal law that allows pen register orders to be sealed.

Despite having obtained the court orders, CPD claimed in a February response to another FOIA request that it had not used stingrays in the previous five months (a time span that includes the suspected police eavesdropping on the 2014 Black Friday march).

Privacy's Defenders

As technologies proliferate, location privacy has become a paramount concern to the ACLU and civil liberties groups such as the Electronic Frontier Foundation (EFF). Both stingrays and ALPRs, through their abilities to track historical and real-time location data, can violate location privacy, which the EFF considers a human right. Even the International Association of Chiefs of Police—a professional organization originally founded by Chicago police to track and detain fugitives—has raised concerns about the privacy problems posed by new technology.

Regulation efforts are taking shape, such as a pending Illinois Senate bill drafted by the ACLU that would limit police use of ALPRs to open investigations and limit the data retention period to 30 days. Similar efforts to force police to obtain search warrants to use stingrays have gained ground in a handful of states.

But even with regulation of high-tech surveillance, the question, chanted often at police officers during street protests, still stands: "Who do you protect? Who do you serve?"

According to Sam Mitrani, when leftist movements in the 19th century and mid-20th century realized that police were not working in their interests, huge mobilizations won concessions. More immigrants were hired to the force, and some of the worst civil rights violations were curbed. With a new movement for police reform and accountability swelling today, Mitrani says, "The more people who stand up and fight, the more demands they can make, the better off everyone will be."

READING 2.8

Gender and Policing

Critical Issues and Analyses

By Susan L. Miller and Emily Bonistall

> U got some brass balls, girl ... u r my hero!!! (message on a social networking site, Facebook, where a fan page was set up to commemorate civilian police officer Kimberly Munley's quick action to shoot the gunman at Fort Hood, November 2009)

Introduction

Have female officers come a long way in the male world of policing? Since women's entrance into this occupation in the 1880s, their acceptance into the working environment and their performance assessments are issues examined and debated with great interest. Reactions to the female police officer who ended the Fort Hood massacre in 2009 ranged from calling her a "mighty mouse" to describing her performance as "amazing and aggressive" (Simon & Spellman, 2009). The majority of the leading news stories mentioned little about her as a *female* police officer, focusing instead on her bravery and quick action under fire. However, this inattention to sex and gender contrasts vividly with female officers' continued experience of resistance to their presence and barriers to advancement, which exist in policing both in the United States and abroad (for some studies of women and policing abroad see Brown & Heidensohn, 2000; Natarajan, 2008; Sun & Wasileski, 2010).

Research on women officers' performance has been conducted only in the last 40 years, with most of it concerned with gender differences that could affect citizen safety or the ability of female officers to possess and use the qualities of authority and strength that many think are necessary in the police role. This chapter reviews and raises some of the central issues relevant to a critical criminological approach to gender and policing. We explore several topics, beginning with a quick introduction to gender and institutions that leads to an investigation about what we know about police performance and behavior. Next, we look at one of the most contentious issues related to police responses, that of how police handle crimes of intimate partner violence. Finally, we examine how diversity in policing affects both the subculture of policing and the communities in which police serve.

Policing as a "Male" Institution and Site of Gendered Action

Despite inroads into policing by women, law enforcement remains one of the most male-dominated and masculine occupations. Similar to other male-dominated professions such as firefighting and the military, research reveals the gendered nature of organizations and how these structures shape the behavior of men and women so that their responses and the responses to them by others are also conditioned by gender role expectations (Acker, 1990; Connell, 1987; Martin & Jurik 1996, 2007; Messerschmidt, 1993; West & Zimmerman, 1987). The sociological term "doing gender" describes the activity of practicing such behavior. It characterizes an interactive social process through which assumptions about power, sexuality, and role expectations shape reactions to men and women (see Martin & Jurik, 1996, 2007). "Doing gender" goes far beyond the social identity of being a man or a woman; it involves "the activity of managing situated conduct in light of normative conceptions, attitudes, and activities appropriate to one's sex category" (West & Zimmerman, 1987, p. 127). "Doing gender" reflects differences in how persons are treated and overseen within organizations, such that "advantage and disadvantage, exploitation and control, action and emotion, meaning and identity, are patterned through and in terms of a distinction between male and female, masculine and feminine" (Acker, 1990, p. 146). Policing, as a masculine organization, assumes that there are "socially gendered perceptual, interactional, and micro-political activities that cast particular pursuits as expressions of masculine and feminine 'natures'" (West & Zimmerman, 1987, p. 126). The issue is *not* one of not all women possessing these traits (or of *all* men not having at least some of them), but that these entrenched gender-role stereotypes and assumptions have been used to exclude women from becoming fully participating, vested police officers with job roles and responsibilities similar to those of their male counterparts. Although men of color share male gender privilege, women of color and/or men and women who identify as gay, lesbian, bisexual, and transgender (GLBT) are not as easily accepted by the dominant group. For instance, Susan Martin's (1994) work on women in policing suggests that not only sexism but also racism further divides police officers, with men of color and white men ending up more closely aligned because of shared masculinist assumptions of male power. Women of color, however, remain separated from both white men and white women as well as from men of color. Officers' sexual identity is another area in which dynamics may be altered and masculine–feminine polarities may be realigned.

Despite changes made since the 1970s in assigning women police officers to routine patrol activities, the division of labor within the force remains segregated as women remain under-represented in upper-level management, thus reproducing the gendered power relations that exist in society at large.

Much of this disparity reflects the fact that police work is still viewed by police themselves and the public as a masculine pursuit best characterized by aggressive macho crime fighting. Messerschmidt (1993) contends that:

> [w]ithin police agencies, men's power is deemed an authentic and acceptable part of social relations. This legitimacy of the power by men in police work adorns them with greater authority ... Police work is defined culturally as an activity only "masculine men" can accomplish.
>
> *(p. 175)*

Accepting women as police officers who are equal to men challenges the masculine association with police work: "if women can do it, the value of the practice as a means for exhibiting masculinity is called into question" (Messerschmidt, 1993, p. 175).

Certainly, women's numbers have increased from the 1975 statistics which revealed that women constituted 2.2 percent of sworn personnel in municipal departments (Martin, 1980). Although women are still under-represented in policing, their numbers continue to climb, especially in certain federal law enforcement agencies and if one looks at representation by gender/race/ethnicity in municipal policing. Looking beyond the patrol officer level, however, shows that police supervisory and management positions remain still very gendered today, despite growth in the number of women as sworn personnel. For instance, women accounted for 11.3 percent of sworn municipal officers in 2003 and 16 percent of federal officers in 2004. In terms of racial or ethnic composition, women and men of color made up 23.6 percent of full-time local police officers in 2003, and one-third of federal officers in 2004. In Sheriff's offices, women were about 13 percent of officers in 2003 and racial and ethnic minorities were 18 percent of full-time sworn personnel (Office of Justice Programs, n.d.). With the current law enforcement emphasis on fighting terrorism, it will be interesting to see how this focus affects recruitment and retention of both women and/or racial/ethnic minorities.

Gender and Police Performance

As the quintessential police officer evokes an image of a macho white heterosexual male who is as comfortable with exercising authority and physical use of force as he is uncomfortable with exercising feminine behaviors of caretaking and comforting, outsiders to the occupation face multiple levels of individual and institutional discrimination. Historically, male officers argued against women's inclusion once women wanted to undertake patrol work because of perceived differences in women's physical strength and ability to command authority and respect from offenders and citizens (and other males in the police subculture). Since the 1970s, empirical analyses of female officers demonstrate that, in arrest situations, women use less force than their male counterparts (Garner & Maxwell, 2002; Schuck & Rabe-Hemp, 2005). Given that the bulk of police work entails routine service and order maintenance calls rather than aggressive crime fighting, it raised the question about how much importance should be attached to women's use of force. Although police officers must be prepared to use coercive force during any situation (Bittner, 1970), there is room for alternative policing abilities and skills.

A recent study examined seven big city police agencies to determine how likely women are to be involved in problems of excessive force, vis-à-vis their male counterparts. It used measurements of citizen complaints, sustained allegations, and civil liability payouts, finding that women officers are dramatically under-represented in excessive force incidents (Lonsway et al., 2002). In statistical terms, as women constitute 12.7 percent of sworn officers in large police organizations, they would account for 12.7 percent of citizen complaints, sustained allegations, and payouts for lawsuits. Yet only 5 percent of the citizen complaints for excessive force and 2 percent of the sustained allegations of excessive force in large police agencies involved female officers (Lonsway et al., 2002). Only 6 percent of the civil liability payouts in court judgments and settlements for use of excessive force were attributed to women. In dollar terms, for the Los Angeles Police Department (LAPD), $63.4 million was paid in judgments or settlements in civil liability suits involving excessive force by men compared with $2.8 million for judgments or settlements involving women during the same time period (Lonsway et al., 2002). Not only are women less likely to engage in excessive force, but also hiring additional women may reduce these kinds of problems in police departments. When one looks at sexual assault and molestation allegations in LAPD, the male officer payout was over $8 million, while the female officer payout was zero (Lonsway et al., 2002). Women officers receive more favorable evaluations and fewer complaints from citizens than their male counterparts, perhaps reflecting better communications skills used to finesse cooperation from community members and to garner their trust (Lonsway et al., 2002).

Clearly, gender exerts an impact on how police officers use force, although less empirical work has been conducted that assesses gender differences in other routine police activities. Because of different socialization experiences, some gender scholars contend that men and women will bring different skills and talents to policing. Drawing on Carol Gilligan's (1982) social psychological work, which suggests that women have a unique feminine approach and world view that emphasizes care and connection and is guided by empathy, female police officers may bring better interpersonal communication skills and a deeper contextual understanding of situations to police work. In contrast, men prioritize bureaucratic efficiency and objectivity, which could lead male police officers to see situations as either right or wrong and act with less helping behaviors towards citizens. One way to gauge gender differences and police models is to examine how male and female officers do their work within a community policing context as this model introduces a more contextualized and personalized policing operation.

Community policing, which began to be adopted by departments in the late 1980s nationwide, challenges the masculinized ethos by prioritizing connections and cooperation between police officers and community members in addressing crime and other social problems. Thus, although the goals of community policing are similar to those of traditional policing (e.g. fighting crime through deterrence and apprehension), the ways in which it is carried out vary tremendously. No longer is the aloof, crime control-oriented professional appropriate in community policing; rather, a more informal, relational, and conciliatory style of policing is encouraged. Roles that were previously denigrated as feminine, and too "soft" or emotional for "real" police work, have become the ideal qualities for community police officers to possess. Although both men and women can achieve this style, women may be more likely to be comfortable with this policing model given differences in gender role socializations and experiences. At the same time, however, women's support for community policing models might undermine their credibility as physically competent and efficient crime fighters. Although much research suggests that women bring different styles and skills to their law enforcement responsibilities, it may be that the police occupation is too entrenched in its crime-fighting ideology to embrace broader structural changes that challenge the macho culture. Given this, the inability to "bend granite" (Guyot, 1979) may be most pronounced when evaluating job performances of male and female officers in a community policing context. Women officers who excel at interpersonal communication skills and at improving community relations between police and citizens may be dismissed as performing skills innate to women's nature, in comparison with men who do the same thing and are evaluated as "supermen" because these skills seem less "natural" for male officers to possess (Miller, 1999; Miller & Hodge, 2004, p. 39).

In brief, community policing models emphasize social work activities that are absent from the more traditional methods of policing. Indeed, as Miller (1999) asserts, "[The] image of the ideal community police officer has a social-work orientation, a style that traditionally has been beyond the purview of acceptable policing" (p. 5). With its emphasis on connections between police and their constituents, community policing reintroduces feminine constructs that have been traditionally devalued by the hypermasculine police culture inherent in a crime control model of policing (Miller, 1999). Since women's entrance into policing, they were viewed as unfit for the male job of "crime fighting," but tolerated in "softer" assignments involving interpersonal communication skills and informal conflict resolution tactics such as handling women, children, and typewriters (Appier, 1998; Milton, 1972; Schulz, 1995). Community policing challenges these assumptions by elevating "feminine" skills such as empathy, caring, and connection that historically were unacceptable to the male culture of traditional policing (Miller, 1999). Therefore, for community policing to succeed, these denigrated skills must be repackaged so that adherents of traditional policing do not sabotage its potential for success. It is ironic that stereotypically feminine traits that once were used to exclude women from participating in patrol work, or to separate "real cops" from "office cops," have been resurrected. However, the success of this resurrection, and with it community policing, depends on reshaping the unacceptable traits associated with femininity into acceptable traits associated with masculinity and "real police work," so that "both men and women are able to deploy skills and talents in the ostensibly gender-neutral realm of community policing" (Miller, 1999, p. 95). Indeed, it may be necessary for recruitment strategies to target candidates from more diverse backgrounds, such as nursing, education, and social work (Harrington & Lonsway, 2004).

Miller's (1999) study also revealed that efforts were made by (mostly male) officers to routinely challenge efforts that appeared to reflect "feminine" versions of police work. Male officers often asserted their masculinity by emphasizing the connection of their roles as community police officers to traditional methods of law enforcement. Male officers were also more likely to point out the "macho" work that they had been involved in prior to becoming a community police officer. For example, Miller (1999) found that male officers were eager to tell the researchers about their experiences with units historically viewed as elite and dangerous (e.g. SWAT teams, drug and gang squads, undercover details, and hostage negotiation teams). Moreover, Miller discovered that male officers, unlike female officers, were quick to proclaim their heterosexual identities: "The male Neighborhood POs deliberately wove some mention of their heterosexual status into the interviews and fieldwork, usually offering information about their female dating partners, wives, and children" (p. 106). Although female officers did not assert their sexual identities in the same manner as men, they were also concerned with their image as community police officers. Because women are oftentimes perceived as "nurturers" and expected to be more emotional than men, the female officers were averse to being essentialized as "perfect" for community policing. Therefore, as the above discussion illustrates, for community policing models to be effective, and for both male and female officers to be comfortable in these roles, it is important that efforts be made to gender neutralize community police work and performance evaluation standards (Herbert, 2001; Miller & Hodge, 2004). In this new era of increased attention to domestic threats, a critical criminological perspective can guide how police can encourage community connections to challenge biased policing and help to frame a more collaborative approach to problem-solving.

Police Responses to Intimate Partner Violence

Although intimate partner violence (IPV) was historically regarded as a private family matter, the emergence of mandatory and preferred arrest policies in the 1980s has thrust IPV from the private sphere to the public realm. Following the perception that IPV was private and not considered a criminal incident, police officers called to the scene of IPV would mediate and/or separate the couple. The battered women's movement of the 1970s and 1980s challenged the inaction by the criminal justice system to IPV, and, fueled by the victims' rights movement, the women's movement, and civil liability suits against police, were successful in demonstrating that police failed to protect victims. With the onset of mandatory arrest statutes, police officers have to or should arrest offenders if probable cause exists, regardless of whether the violence occurred in the officer's presence and/or whether the victim prefers that no arrest be made. This policy was launched by the ground-breaking Minneapolis Domestic Violence Experiment conducted by Sherman and Berk in 1984, which found that arrest was more effective in deterring IPV than mediation and/or separation (Sherman & Berk, 1984). Most jurisdictions modified their arrest practices, replacing them with what are known as mandatory and preferred arrest policies (Miller, 2004). Arrest policies have continued to stay at the focus of research, although replication studies yielded inconsistent findings with results revealing that the effect of arrest on subsequent IPV varied for different groups depending on the perceived cost of arrest (Dunford, Huizinga, & Elliot, 1990; Hirschel, Hutchison, Dean, Kelley, & Pesackis, 1991; Pate & Hamilton, 1992), and, in fact, Sherman (1992) distanced himself from his original support of mandatory arrest policies.

Despite pro-arrest policies, officers continue to hold a great deal of discretion in responding to IPV calls (Buzawa & Buzawa, 2003; Miller, 2000). Studying police responses to IPV in the context of race, gender, police experience, age, injury, and pro-arrest policies is the center of the critical criminologist's research. The norms of the department, in addition to the policies, influence police response, as indicated by Finn, Blackwell, Stalans, Studdard, and Dugan (2004). Officers who thought their department policy would support dual arrest acted upon those beliefs and arrested both individuals. Those officers in the study who believed that their department was supportive of primary aggressor policies were more likely to arrest only the husband (Finn et al., 2004). Outside of the department, the norms and values of the community also influence police response (Buzawa, Austin, & Buzawa, 1995). Police response to IPV may also vary based on victim preference; Buzawa and Austin (1993) highly recommend that police officers follow the preference of the victim in order to avoid victim dissatisfaction with the police. Including these various contextual factors in critical criminological research will help to illuminate the influences of structural inequality on police response to IPV.

A recent quantitative investigation expands on the influence of officer gender in response to IPV, specifically whether female officers respond to domestic violence differently from male officers (Sun, 2007). Using variables from the Project on Policing Neighborhoods data (see Mastrofski et al., 1998), Sun's research explored police officers' supportive and controlling actions when responding to citizens involved in domestic violence incidents. Sun (2007) questions whether the discretion used by male and female police officers reflects gendered assumptions that women are more nurturing and thus would use fewer control actions in a IPV situation and instead provide more supportive actions vis-à-vis their male officer counterparts. Findings from this study suggest that female officers "do masculinity" but also "do femininity," indicating that, although female and male officers did not differ significantly in exerting control actions, the female officers were more likely than their male counterparts to provide supportive actions to the victim. Qualitative research that explores how male and female officers "do gender" when responding to IPV calls within a community policing area reveals that the gender of an officer matters less than the relationship that develops and is maintained between the neighborhood officer and residents (Miller, 1999). These findings indicate the importance of expanding officers' repertoire of skills. Although increasing the numbers of female officers is one approach that some have suggested to capitalize on women's interpersonal communication skills, this assumes that these traits are innately feminine and female; departments then run the risk of "essentializing" women, meaning that they mistakenly believe that *all* women will act the same and, conversely, that *all* men will respond with opposing action, which is not the case. Training to broaden the repertoire of skills and response to IPV—and reward "feminine" performance—will be fruitful for both men and women in policing. Supervisors must support different roles of and actions by their officers.

As with many new policies, unintended consequences often arise. The shift to favoring mandatory or pro-arrest for IPV represented an effort to deter batterers and hold them accountable for their violence as well as to empower victims by supporting their arrest preferences and moving away from a trivialization of IPV. As critical criminologists aim to challenge the effects of structural inequality found within the criminal justice system, IPV becomes an arena to do just that as it becomes increasingly apparent that, following the enactment of mandatory arrest statutes, an increased number of women have been arrested for IPV, either as the sole perpetrator or in the context of a dual arrest (DeLeon-Granados, Wells, & Binsbacher, 2006; Feder & Henning, 2005; Hirschel, Buzawa, Pattavina, Faggiani, & Reuland, 2007; Miller, 2005; Muftić, Bouffard, & Bouffard, 2007). Although women do use force in various situations, within the context of domestic or intimate partner violence, women tend to use self-defensive force, not pre-emptive aggressive force. If one is only counting "use of force" without a contextual understanding of under what circumstances that force was used, arrest statistics can be misleading and show that men and women are equally violent.

Given that mandatory arrest statutes are written in a gender-neutral manner, on the face of it, anyone who uses force can be subject to an arrest. This fails to take into account the motivation, context, and result of violence. One way that police departments have responded to this criticism is to enact primary aggressor laws, which are laws that help ensure that police officers distinguish between offensive and defensive injuries when arresting during an IPV call (Hirschel & Buzawa, 2002), in addition to examining a woman's violent action within the context of ongoing abuse (Dasgupta, 1999, 2002; Hamberger, 2005; Kimmel, 2002; Miller, 2005; Osthoff, 2002; Swan et al., 2008).

Primary aggressor laws do not solve everything. Responding police officers may still treat the woman as the primary aggressor as women tend to remember each violent incident (Dasgupta, 1999; Kimmel, 2002) and more readily admit to their use of violence (Dobash, Dobash, Cavanaugh, & Lewis, 1998). Additionally, women who are still experiencing emotional trauma from the battering situation may appear less credible than men who may be better able to describe the preceding events to their benefit (Miller, 2005). Criminalizing women for taking actions in self-defense may have many negative consequences, including denial of safe housing in a shelter, loss of custody of children, economic hardship, and unwillingness to call police in the future (Hirschel & Buzawa, 2002).

Although the criminal justice system continues to progress with new policies intended to protect IPV victims, researchers must watch with a critical eye for these unintended consequences. Issues of gender within the police force, variation in officer response to IPV that takes into account the contextual factors of the situation, and the implications of (even unintended) dual-arrest policies should continue to be studied. In doing so, the field of critical criminology and feminist criminology will push scholars in the direction that recognizes the structure of gender and racial inequality within society and how social institutions such as the police perpetuate such inequalities.

Diversity and Policing

Policing is an occupation that is also sexualized as ideals of heterosexual masculinity inform practices and social interactions within policing. Critical criminologists need to be cognizant of how officers manage multiple identities of sexual orientation, race/ethnicity, and gender within a homophobic and male-dominated police force. Additionally, attention should remain focused on the way that women officers are kept on the periphery of the police working environment based on these characteristics. Critical criminologists need to use an intersectionality approach to studying these issues as gender discrimination is compounded by issues of race/ethnicity and sexual orientation. In fact, research suggests that homosexuals are the social group most disliked by police (Burke, 1994) and other research documents the frequency with which police are identified by victims as perpetrators of the violence against lesbian and gay citizens (see Comstock, 1991). Such beliefs persist despite empirical evidence that lesbians and gay men perform police work as well as heterosexuals (Hiatt & Hargrave, 1994). This climate of intolerance reflects lingering biases in the law: it is still legal to deny housing and employment on the basis of sexual orientation in federal jurisdictions. More recent research explores the role that police play in responding to crimes committed against the GLBT community (Wolff & Cokely, 2007). Based on a content analysis of almost 2,000 incident reports collected by a Minnesota GLBT advocacy group, researchers found that, although law enforcement conduct has improved, negative responses and actions of police outnumbered positive ones (Wolff & Cokely, 2007). Although positive change is heartening, taken altogether it is clear that there is a continued need for training and educating police regarding issues facing citizens from the GLBT and other disenfranchised communities.

Sexual harassment also continues to plague police departments. Although gender discrimination is less overt now than when women joined the police force, Gossett and Williams (1998) found that two-thirds of the women police officers in their sample experienced discrimination from their supervisors, peers, and citizens ranging from inappropriate comments and behaviors to not taking them seriously based on their gender. A more recent study of 804 female officers from 35 countries in Europe and the American continents revealed that 77 percent reported sexual harassment by male colleagues (Brown & Heidensohn, 2000). Gender discrimination is compounded by the sexualized nature of the police environment, where sexual harassment is rampant in many forms, including unwanted touching, attempted forced sexual intercourse from supervisors, derogatory comments regarding their sexuality or gender, and various forms of joking (Hunt, 1984; Martin, 1980, 1990; Sugden, 2005; Young, 1991). This sexualized workplace maintains women as "others" in the police environment (Cockburn, 1991; Swerdlow, 1989). Indeed, lesbian officers report that it was harder to break into the male world of policing than the heterosexual world of policing, because of the intractability of the "good ol' boys' network," and the lesbian officers felt a common bond with heterosexual women in combating sexism on the force (Miller, Forest, & Jurik, 2003). Similarly, Heidensohn's (1994) research found that female officers ranked dealing with harassment by their male colleagues as more of an issue than dealing with violence while on patrol.

Whereas female officers must deal with gender discrimination, black women, specifically, are situated uniquely. White women are often "protected" by the white male officers who see them as little sisters and they are more likely to land coveted positions over black women (Martin, 1990). Black women not only experience gender discrimination, but also are treated according to racial stereotypes (Belknap & Shelley, 1992; Martin, 1994; Price, Sokoloff, & Kuleshnyka, 1992; Texeira, 2002; Wordon, 1993), which adds another layer of discrimination in the policing environment. Often their experiences of sexual harassment are "racialized sexual harassment" in which the harassment may be due to their gender, race, or both (Texeira, 2002). Other research exploring black and Asian female officers and their experiences of discrimination found that they suffered more kinds of and more severe harassment and discrimination than their white women counterparts (Holder, Nee, & Ellis, 2000). Research in the health field shows that female police officers were more bothered by sexual harassment than male officers, and that "more bothered" victims reported more mental and physical health problems (de Haas, Timmerman, & Hoing, 2009; see also Cantisano, Dominguez, & Depolo, 2009; Sbraga & O'Donohue, 2000); this finding suggests that the consequences of sexual harassment may be more detrimental to females who appraise sexual harassment as bothersome.

Thus, the sexualized nature of the police environment is one of heterosexual masculinity that perpetuates and exacerbates both homophobia and sexism within the police force. Problems in the workplace may be intensified for GLBT officers, who must decide whether to openly declare their sexual identity and risk degradation and discrimination by their colleagues (Miller et al., 2003), thus adding another layer of oppression to existing gender and/or race/ethnicity issues. Critical criminologists should use an intersectionality approach when studying diversity within the police environment to account for this multi-faceted discrimination of gender, race/ethnicity, and sexual orientation.

Conclusion

Hegemonic masculinity is neither stable nor complete, but reacts to changes in history and social context. Using the context of the post-9/11 world's focus on the danger of and protection against terrorism, Messner (2007) shows how displays of compassion and care get subordinated to toughness, strength, and decisiveness. In valorizing this more dominant form of masculinity, connection and context are eclipsed and what becomes the "exemplar of manhood" (p. 463) rejects the central efforts of the women's movement to ensure that equality and respect are assured in working environments. As shown in this chapter, challenges to this traditional kind of masculinity encompass the voices of women, people of color, the GLBT community, and men who do not wield such masculine power and privilege. Through changes in police practice, such as the move to more community-based policing in addition to continued change and research surrounding approaches to combating IPV, law enforcement officers are ideally situated to respond with greater efficacy and skill to the diverse and enduring problems they face. Continued resistance to non-traditional officers may reflect more about what change symbolizes than about performance indicators (Herbert, 2001). In other words, if women (or lesbians or gay men or people of color) can do the job as well as men, men's resistance is an attempt to preserve the myth that police work is a job for men only (Hunt, 1984). Clearly, this chapter demonstrates that people and institutions can accommodate or sabotage "outsiders" who dare to find a place within traditionally male domains such as policing. Critical criminologists must be aware of the implications of such actions and resistance, and continue to explore how police performance and behavior affect and are affected by an intersectionality approach to core law enforcement issues.

Even as crime rates have remained relatively stable or even decreased, the public perception is that threats to our nation's security are spiraling out of control. This concern develops specific directions to help shape empirical work, policy, and practice. Moving forward, critical criminologists first need to remain cognizant of efforts to shore up homeland security at the expense of jeopardizing the ideological goal and practice of community policing. Changing from a philosophy that invites diverse communities to be invested in quality policing to a suspiciousness of diversity and an emphasis on traditional crime control practices will derail the progress that has been accomplished. Mona Danner's (1998) research on the unintended consequences of the war on crime reveals a decrease in state assistance to women and children and a decrease in the employment of women in these social welfare jobs as the nation focused on building (and paying for) new prisons, and it is not out of the question that similar funding and ideological practices will change in the name of national security. Second, Jonathan Simon (2007) argues that the war on crime has given more power to the state to invade our schools, families, workplaces, and communities. An agenda for empirical research and policy-making must include a challenge to the "culture of fear" that Simon documents, especially as it manifests in police policy and practices. Finally, in this time of vociferous debate about immigration and the role of law enforcement, critical criminologists also will be involved with the increased vulnerability of women who are victims and afraid to call the police for help because of their undocumented status.

References

Acker, J. (1990). Hierarchies, jobs and bodies: A theory of gendered organizations. *Gender & Society, 4*, 139–158.

Appier, J. (1998). *Policing women: The sexual politics of law enforcement and the LAPD.* Philadelphia: Temple University Press.

Belknap, J., & Shelley, J. K. (1992). The new lone ranger: Policewomen on patrol. *American Journal of Police, 12*, 47–75.

Bittner, E. (1970). *The functions of police in modern society: A review of the background factors, current practices, and possible role models.* Bethesda, MD: NIMH.

Brown, J. M., & Heidensohn, F. (2000). *Gender and policing: Comparative perspectives.* New York: St. Martin's Press.

Burke, M. E. (1994). *Coming out of the blue: British police officers talk about their lives in "the job" as lesbians, gays and bisexuals.* London: Cassell.

Buzawa, E., & Austin, T. (1993). Determining police response to domestic violence victims: The role of victim preference. *American Behavioral Scientist, 36*, 610–623.

Buzawa, E., Austin, T., & Buzawa, C. (1995). Responding to crimes of violence against women: Gender differences versus organizational imperatives. *Crime and Delinquency, 41*, 443–466.

Buzawa, E., & Buzawa, C. (2003). *Domestic violence: The criminal justice response.* Thousand Oaks, CA: Sage.

Cantisano, G. T., Dominguez, J. F. M., & Depolo, M. (2008). Perceived sexual harassment at work: Meta-analysis and structural model of antecedents and consequences. *Spanish Journal of Psychology, 11*, 207–218.

Cockburn, C. (1991). *In the way of women: Men's resistance to sex equality in organizations.* Ithaca, NY: ILR Press.

Comstock, G. D. (1991). *Violence against lesbians and gay men.* New York: Columbia University Press.

Connell, R. W. (1987). *Gender and power: Society, the person and sexual politics.* Stanford, CA: Stanford University Press.

Danner, M. J. E. (1998). Three strikes and it's women who are out: The hidden consequences for women of criminal justice police reforms. In S. L. Miller (Ed.), *Crime control and women: Feminist implications of criminal justice policy* (pp. 1–14). Thousand Oaks, CA: Sage.

Dasgupta, S. D. (1999). Just like men? A critical review of violence by women. In M. F. Shephard & E. L. Pence (Eds.), *Coordinating community response to domestic violence: Lessons from Duluth and beyond* (pp. 195–222). Thousand Oaks, CA: Sage.

Dasgupta, S. D. (2002). A framework for understanding women's use of nonlethal violence in intimate heterosexual relationships. *Violence against Women, 8*(11), 1364–1389.

de Haas, S., Timmerman, G., & Hoing, M. (2009). Sexual harassment and health among male and female police officers. *Journal of Occupational Health Psychology, 14*, 4.

DeLeon-Granados, W., Wells, W., & Binsbacher, R. (2006). Arresting developments trends in female arrests for domestic violence and proposed explanations. *Violence against Women, 12*, 355–371.

Dobash, R. E., Dobash, R. P., Cavanaugh, K., & Lewis, R. (1998). Separate and intersecting realities: A comparison of men's and women's accounts of violence against women. *Violence against Women, 4*(4), 382–414.

Dunford, F., Huizinga, D., & Elliot, D. (1990). Role of arrest in domestic assault: The Omaha police experiment. *Criminology, 28*, 183–206.

Feder, L., & Henning, K. (2005). A comparison of male and female dually arrested domestic violence offenders. *Violence and Victims, 20*, 153–171.

Finn, M., Blackwell, B., Stalans, L., Studdard, S., & Dugan, L. (2004). Dual arrest decisions in domestic violence cases: The influence of departmental policies. *Crime and Delinquency, 50*, 565–589.

Garner, J. H., & Maxwell, C. D. (2002). *Understanding the prevalence and severity of force used by and against the police.* Rockville, MD: NIJ.

Gilligan, C. (1982). *In a different voice.* Cambridge, MA: Harvard University Press.

Gossett, J. L., & Williams, J. E. (1998). Perceived discrimination among women law enforcement. *Women & Criminal Justice, 10*(1), 53–75.

Guyot, D. (1979). Bending granite: Attempts to change the rank structure of American police departments. *Journal of Police Science and Administration, 7*(3), 253–284.

Hamberger, L. K. (2005). Men's and women's use of intimate partner violence in clinical samples: Toward a gender sensitive analysis. *Violence and Victims, 20*(2), 131–151.

Harrington, P., & Lonsway, K. A. (2004). Current barriers and future promise for women in policing. In B. R. Price & N. J. Sokoloff (Eds.), *The criminal justice system and women: Offenders, prisoners, victims, & workers* (pp. 495–510). New York: McGraw-Hill.

Heidensohn, F. (1994). We can handle it out here: Women officers in Britain and the USA and the policing of public order. *Policing and Society, 4*(4), 293–303.

Herbert, S. (2001). "Hard charger" or "station queen"? Policing and the masculinist state. *Gender, Place and Culture, 8*(1), 55–71.

Hiatt, D., & Hargrave, G. E. (1994). Psychological assessment of gay and lesbian law enforcement applicants. *Journal of Personality Assessment, 63*, 80–88.

Hirschel, D., & Buzawa, E. (2002). Understanding the context of dual arrest with directions for future research. *Violence against Women, 8*(12), 1449–1473.

Hirschel, D., Buzawa, E., Pattavina, A., Faggiani, D., & Reuland, M. (2007). Explaining the prevalence, context, and consequences of dual arrest in intimate partner cases (NCJ 218355). Washington, DC: U.S. Department of Justice.

Hirschel, J., Hutchison, I., Dean, C., Kelley, J., & Pesackis, C. (1991). Charlotte spouse assault replication project: Final report. Washington, DC: National Institute of Justice.

Holder, K. A., Nee, C., & Ellis, T. (2000). Triple jeopardy? Black and Asian women police officers' experiences of discrimination. *International Journal of Police Science and Management, 3*(1), 68–87.

Hunt, J. (1984). The development of rapport through negotiation of gender in field work among police. *Human Organization, 43*, 283–296.

Kimmel, M. S. (2002). Gender symmetry in domestic violence: A substantive and methodological research review. *Violence against Women, 8*(11), 1336–1367.

Lonsway, K., Wood, M., Fickling, M., de Leon, A., Moore, M., Harrington, P., Smeal, E., & Sillar, K. (2002). *Men, women, and police excessive force: A tale of two genders.* Los Angeles: National Center for Women and Policing.

Martin, S. E. (1980). *Breaking and entering: Policewomen on patrol.* Berkeley: University of California Press.

Martin, S. E. (1990). *On the move: The status of women in policing.* Washington, DC: Police Foundation.

Martin, S. E. (1994). "Outsider within" the stationhouse: The impact of race and gender on black women police. *Social Problems, 41*, 383–400.

Martin, S. E., & Jurik, N. C. (1996). *Doing justice, doing gender: Women in law and criminal justice occupations.* Thousand Oaks, CA: Sage.

Martin, S. E., & Jurik, N. C. (2007). *Doing justice, doing gender: Women in legal and criminal justice occupations* (2nd edn.). Thousand Oaks, CA: Sage.

Mastrofski, S., Parks, R., Reiss, A., Worden R., DeJong, C., & Snipes, J. (1998). *Systematic observation of public police: Applying field research methods to policy issues.* Washington, DC: National Institute of Justice.

Messerschmidt, J. (1993). *Masculinities and crime.* Lanham, MD: Rowman & Littlefield.

Messner, M. A. (2007). The masculinity of the Governator: Muscle and compassion in American politics. *Gender & Society, 21*(4), 461–480.

Miller, N. (2004). *Domestic violence: A review of state legislation defining police and prosecution duties and powers.* Alexandria, VA: Institute for Law and Justice. Available at http://www.ilj.org/publications/DV_Legislation-3.pdf (accessed May 13, 2009).

Miller, S. L. (1999). *Gender and community policing: Walking the talk.* Boston: Northeastern University Press.

Miller, S. L. (2000). Arrest policies for domestic violence and their implications for battered women. In R. Muraskin (Ed.), *It's a crime: Women and justice* (pp. 287–310). Upper Saddle River, NJ: Prentice Hall.

Miller, S. L. (2005). *Victims as offenders: The paradox of women's violence in relationships.* New Brunswick, NJ: Rutgers University Press.

Miller, S. L., Forest, K. B., & Jurik, N. C. (2003). Diversity in blue: Job and gender issues among lesbian and gay police officers. *Men & Masculinities, 5*(4), 355–385.

Miller, S. L., & Hodge, J. (2004). Rethinking gender and community policing: Cultural obstacles and policy issues. *Law Enforcement Executive Forum, 4*(4), 39–49.

Milton, C. (1972). *Women in policing.* Washington, DC: Police Foundation.

Muftić, L. R., Bouffard, J. A., & Bouffard, L. A. (2007). An exploratory study of women arrested for intimate partner violence: Violent women or violent resistance? *Journal of Interpersonal Violence, 22*, 753–774.

Natarajan, M. (2008). *Women police in a changing society: Back door to equality.* Burlington, VT: Ashgate.

Office of Justice Programs (n.d.) Law enforcement. Bureau of Justice Statistics (BJS). Available at http://bjs.ojp.usdoj.gov/index.cfm?ty=tp&tid=7 (accessed July 3, 2011).

Osthoff, S. (2002). But, Gertrude, I beg to differ, a hit is not a hit is not a hit: When battered women are arrested for assaulting their partners. *Violence against Women, 8*(12), 1521–1544.

Pate, A., & Hamilton, E. (1992). Formal and informal deterrents to domestic violence: The Dade County spouse assault experiment. *American Sociological Review, 57*, 691–697.

Price, B. R., Sokoloff, N. J., & Kuleshnyka, I. (1992). A study of black and white police in an urban police department. *Justice Professional, 6*, 68–85.

Sbraga, T. P., & O'Donohue, W. (2000). Sexual harassment. *Annual Review of Sex Research, 11*, 258–285.

Schuck, A. M., & Rabe-Hemp, C. (2005). Women police: The use of force by and against female officers. *Journal of Women and Criminal Justice, 16*, 91–117.

Schulz, D. M. (1995). *From social worker to crimefighter: Women in United States municipal policing.* Westport, CT: Praeger.

Sherman, L. W. (1992). *Policing domestic violence: Experiments and dilemmas.* New York: Free Press.

Sherman, L. W., & Berk, R. A. (1984). The specific deterrent effects of arrest for domestic assault. *American Sociological Review, 49*(2), 261–272.

Simon, J. (2007). *Governing through crime: How the war on crime transformed American democracy and created a culture of fear.* New York: Oxford.

Simon, M., & Spellman, J. (2009). "Tough woman" cop hailed Fort Hood hero. CNN. Available at http://articles.cnn.com/2009-11-06/justice/fort.hood.munley_1_kimberly-munley-fort-hood-police-officer?_s=PM:CRIME (accessed July 3, 2011).

Sugden, N. (2005). Disruptive bodies: Women performing policing. Ph.D. dissertation. Charles Stuart University, Queensland, Australia.

Sun, I. Y. (2007). Policing domestic violence: Does officer gender matter? *Journal of Criminal Justice, 35*, 581–595.

Sun, I., & Wasileski, G. (2010). Gender differences in occupational attitudes among Slovak police. *International Criminal Justice Review, 20*, 248–264.

Swan, S. C., Gambone, L. J., Caldwell, J. E., Sullivan, T. P., & Snow, D. L. (2008). A review of research on women's use of violence with male intimate partners. *Violence and Victims, 23*(3), 301–314.

Swerdlow, M. (1989). Men's accommodations to women entering a nontraditional occupation: A case of rapid transit operatives. *Gender & Society, 3*, 373–387.

Texeira, M. T. (2002). "Who protects and serves me?" A case study of sexual harassment of African American women in one U.S. law enforcement agency. *Gender & Society, 16*(4), 524–545.

West, C., & Zimmerman, D. H. (1987). Doing gender. *Gender & Society, 1*, 125–151.

Wolff, K. B., & Cokely, C. L. (2007). "To protect and to serve?": An exploration of police conduct in relation to the gay, lesbian, bisexual, and transgender community. *Sexuality and Culture, 11*, 1–23.

Wordon, A. P. (1993). The attitudes of women and men in policing: Testing conventional and contemporary wisdom. *Criminology, 31*, 203–242.

Young, M. (1991). *An inside job: Policing and police culture in Britain.* Oxford: Clarendon Press.

UNIT II: CRITICAL THINKING QUESTIONS

1. Describe the purpose and objectives of the Symbionese Liberation Army. Explain how its goals became compromised.
2. What is institutionalized racism? Do you agree that institutionalized racism is an issue? Why or why not?
3. Identify the common "scenario" in cases of police brutality. Explain how and why a police force is used as a tool of the state.
4. Explain the development of the police organizational culture. Describe how police misconduct affects the relationship between police and non-police community members.
5. Describe how police violence and street harassment reveals a shared vulnerability to dominance and violence for African American males and females. Explain the how structural violence affects interpersonal violence.
6. Identify the pros and cons for the use of body cams. Describe the main goal and objective for the use of information technology in police work.
7. Explain how the Chicago police department has violated the rights of citizens involved in protests.
8. Describe what is meant by gendered action. Explain how gender is perceived within the police system. Identify the positives and negatives of gender as related to policing.

   Overall

   Using only the information in this unit, how would you describe the police in the United States to someone from another country?

UNIT III

The Judicial System

Unit Introduction

Unit Three, The Judicial System, begins with the acknowledgement that there is "a racial bias in the enforcement of its laws." With that in mind, researchers examine if race affects the sentencing outcomes between appointed judges versus elected judges (Reading 3.1). A major issue the courts face is the excessive number of cases that need to be processed in a timely manner. The judicial system has had to adapt and incorporate innovative technological programs to manage the overburdened legal system (Reading 3.2). The courts are also inundated with domestic violence cases which present unique challenges in processing. Although policies have changed to decrease discretion and increase convictions, courts have legal cultures which affect prosecution negatively, especially when dealing with intimate partner violence (Reading 3.3).

The judicial system has had to respond to the many challenges it faces by creating specialty courts to manage populations with distinct characteristics. Veterans and juvenile offenders have benefited from these initiatives, which are driven by a restorative justice framework. For veterans, the transition from military to civilian life is challenging, with an overrepresentation of non-violent felony offenders and substance abuse (Readings 3.4 and 3.5). Finally, because a significant percentage of individuals who appear in general trial courts suffer from a mental health problem, specialty courts have been developed to address those who need treatment rather than incarceration (Reading 3.6).

READING 3.1

How Judges Respond to the Racial Composition of Their Constituencies

By Rey Hernández-Julián and Aleksandar Tomic

Introduction

That race matters in the courtroom comes as no surprise. The relationships between the defendant's race and both the probability of incarceration and the length of sentence have been thoroughly examined. Further, the race of the judge can also affect the defendant's outcome. Our paper tackles a new question that, to our knowledge, remains absent from the literature: how the racial composition of the defendant's community is related to the incarceration or sentence of a defendant. In particular, whether a minority defendant's outcome can be predicted by the percentage of the population of the judicial district is of his or her own race. We also examine whether this relationship depends on the manner of judicial selection: is an elected judge more sensitive to his constituents' race than an appointed judge?

We estimate the relationship described above by regressing the length of a defendant's sentence on the percent of a district's population that is of the defendant's race. Since some judges are elected and others are appointed, we estimate the regression separately for the two groups. We argue that elected judges should be particularly responsive to the racial composition of their population; appointed judges should not respond as strongly, and provide an adequate comparison group. Appointed judges are generally selected state-wide and report to the state government, and as such they should be less sensitive to local characteristics.

Although we estimate the regression above for defendants of all races, we focus on African American defendants, where we expect the relationship to be strongest. Discrimination has historically been most prevalent against African Americans (DiIulio, 1994). They are over-represented in the courts and the prisons. For example, in our sample 52 percent of cases when judge is appointed, and 44 percent of cases in front of an elected judge are against an African American defendant. African Americans are over-represented in prison population as well. According to the 2012 prions count,

Rey Hernández-Julián and Aleksandar Tomic, "How Judges Respond to the Racial Composition of Their Constituencies," *Journal of Legal, Ethical and Regulatory Issues*, vol. 17, no. 2, pp. 115-127.

conducted by the Bureau of Justice Statistics, African Americans accounted for 38 percent of inmates in state prisons (Carson and Golinelli, 2013). At the same time, African Americans account for only 13% of US population (Bureau of Census, 2013).

We use data from the *State Court Processing Statistics 1990, 1992, 1994, 1996, and 1998: Felony Defendants in Large Urban Counties.* The data include adjudication and case information on all filings that take place in the month of May of the recorded year. We combine these data with Shepherd's (2002) demographic information for each county, which includes the number of arrests by category of crime and racial composition. A county's method of judicial selection is publicly available American Judicature Society's "Judicial Selection in the States: Appellate and General Jurisdiction Courts" (2004).

We estimate a two-stage Heckman regression, where the first stage estimates the probability of the defendant becoming incarcerated, while the second stage estimates the length of the defendant's sentence, which is the most common treatment in the literature (Bushway and Piehl, 2001). Both stages control for the characteristics of the case and of the defendant. The first stage, in addition, controls for additional variables of the defendant's status, as well as the degree to which local jails are overcrowded.

We find that African Americans facing an elected judge receive shorter sentences as the percentage of the African American population in their district rises. The probability of incarceration, however, is unaffected. When we estimate the same regression for only appointed judges, we find no statistical significance on the coefficient on the percentage of the electorate that is African American. There is also no association when the defendants are white or of other races. We believe that our finding supports the hypothesis that judicial selection has real consequences upon the outcomes of judicial proceedings. Since elected judges give shorter sentences as the percentage of the population that is black increases, we believe that direct election punishes discrimination more strongly than appointment. Our finding is particularly important because the magnitude of the relationship is large: a unit increase in the percentage that is African American diminishes the sentence by 0.435 of a month (or about 13 days). A one standard deviation increase in the percentage of a jurisdiction's population that is African American would decrease a defendant's sentence by almost 6 months.

Background

The Leadership Conference on Civil Rights reports that "criminal laws ... are enforced in a manner that is massively and pervasively biased" (Welch and Angulo, 2000). If the US suffers from racial bias in the enforcement of its laws, that bias could stem from several sources. Dozens of papers analyze the effect of the defendant's race, while others look at the race of the judge (Daly and Tonry (1997), Wolfgand and Riedel (1973), Mustard (2001), and Schazenbach (2005)) or the race of the victim (Glaeser and Sacerdote (2003)). Other papers have studied the differences in the sentencing behavior of elected and appointed judges and regulators (Besley and Coate (2000), and Fields, Klein, and Sfridis

(1997)). Our paper goes beyond the existing research by combining these literatures and focusing on the differential effect of community demographics on appointed and elected judges.

Mustard (2001) focuses on ethnic and gender disparities in sentencing at the federal level. He finds that, after controlling for most case characteristics, blacks, males, and defendants with lower levels of education and income are more likely to be incarcerated and to receive longer sentences in the federal courts. Like most researchers, Mustard is unable to distinguish between the possibility of discrimination due to the judge's discretion from other systematic causes for the discrepancies. For example, drug laws at the federal level (and in most states) prescribe tougher sentences for crack cocaine than for powder cocaine. If blacks are more likely to be involved with crack, then they will receive systematically higher sentences without the presence of discrimination in judges or voters. Mustard (2001) does not assert that he finds discrimination due to the difficulty in separating its effects from those of unobservable characteristics.

Schazenbach (2005) uses data on federal judges, which are all appointed, to see how sentencing varies with the characteristics of the judge and the judge's district, and finds that the "judges' race and sex have little influence on prison sentences in general but do affect racial and sex disparities." Schazenbach (2005) additional contribution is a thorough surveys on the literature on race and sentencing, a literature which overlooks one particular factor. Although the effects of the judge's and the defendant's races have been examined extensively, no previous research has studied the relationship between the method of judicial selection combined with the characteristics of the jurisdiction and sentencing.

We take advantage of the variation in the judicial selection system—some judges are appointed, while others are elected—to answer these questions. An elected judge does not have the luxury to ignore the preferences of the local community. If an elected judge responds to the preferences of his electors, then one would expect the disparate treatment of minorities to decrease as the population share of the defendant's minority increases. Since the judges are elected locally, they are directly accountable to their constituents. Minority voters are likely to be more sensitive to and stronger in their opposition against discrimination against their own group, thus, the higher the percentage of voters that belong to the discriminated group, the lower the elected judge's ability to discriminate and keep his seat. But, this is a double-edged sword. If judges do not have taste for discrimination, but the majority of county electorate does, an elected judge may feel pressure to engage in disparate treatment. An appointed judge may certainly discriminate, but he should be less responsive to the characteristics and preferences of the local community. This study contributes to the literature by answering whether the form of judicial selection matters to a minority defendant, where the bias in sentencing is coming from, and how the racial composition of the community affects the bias.

A so far unstated assumption of this study is that judges have some ability to exercise discretion in sentencing. We feel comfortable with this assumption as previous research "has consistently established that when judges have discretion, they indulge personal policy preferences to some extent"

(Schazenbach, 2005). For instance, Bushway and Piehl (2001) state that "African Americans have 20 percent longer sentences than whites, on average, holding constant age, gender, and recommended sentence length from the guidelines." Most of this variation stems from the fact that African Americans are more likely to be sentenced for crimes that leave more room for discretion by the judge.

Methodology and Data

The decision to incarcerate, like the decision to work, operates on two margins: first there is the decision on whether to incarcerate, followed by the decision on for how long. The estimation strategy will follow that pioneered by Heckman (1976) in the context of the work decision. The first-stage regression estimates the incarceration decision:

$$incarceration_{ijt} = \beta X_{ijt} + \delta percentageofpopulationofdefendant'srace_{jt} + \mu Z_{ijt} + \varepsilon_{ijt} \quad (1)$$

where the subscript i denotes a defendant facing a judge in a trial, j denotes the judicial district, and t denotes the year of the trial. The second stage estimates the following:

$$lengthofsentense_{ijt} = \alpha + \phi X_{ijt} + \theta percentageofpopulationofdefendant'srace_{jt} + \tau(\hat{\lambda}) + \varepsilon_{ijt}. \quad (2)$$

The lambda-hat is the inverse Mills ratio on the predicted probability of being incarcerated estimated from the first stage regression. The vector Z in the first stage includes the required additional factors that enter into the incarceration decision but can be excluded from the sentence length estimation: whether the defendant is a fugitive, on parole, on probation, on bail, and whether the jails are overcrowded. A defendant captured when on parole, probation or bale will almost certainly be incarcerated, independently of the crime, so these factors will be good predictors in the first stage, though not necessary in the second. The β and ϕ are the coefficients on the control variables in X_{ijt} describing the case and the defendant: the gender and age of the defendant, whether the defendant is a minor, whether the defendant pleads guilty, whether the defendant has prior convictions and how many, the nature of the crime, whether the defendant was in custody when he committed the crime, who represented the defendant in court, and fixed effects for the year and state of the crime.

The coefficients of most interest are δ and θ which estimate the effect of the percentage of the population of the defendant's race on the probability of incarceration and length of sentence. The political pressure on the judge to give a lighter sentence could increase as the percentage of a district's population that is of the defendant's race increases. If that is the case, both δ and θ will be positive and significant. Elected judges are directly accountable to the population and should respond to this pressure more strongly than appointed judges, who are accountable to a legislature. To compare elected and appointed judges, both equations are estimated separately by the form of judicial selection.[1]

We also estimate the regression separately for African Americans, for white defendants, and for all others. This allows us to estimate whether the effect of the percentage of the population is unique to African Americans, or whether it is true for all racial groups. African Americans are over-represented both in our sample and in the prison system. As a result, they have a stronger interest in becoming familiar with judges and their behavior, and in punishing those judges who are unfair.

We collect data on case characteristics, defendant characteristics, judicial selection system, and basic demographics. The data on court cases come from the Third Inter-University Consortium for Political and Social Research (ICPSR) Edition of Bureau of Justice Statistics' dataset, *State Court Processing Statistics 1990, 1992, 1994, 1996, and 1998: Felony Defendants in Large Urban Counties.* The file contains 72,602 observations on felony defendants in 54 of the nation's 75 most populous counties. These counties account for around a third of U.S. population and about a half of all crime in the U.S. The 75 counties were divided according to the number of filings; all of the most active counties were chosen, and additional counties were chosen based on the frequency of filings. The data samples counties to accommodate the full range of variation in the frequency of filings, and the data are weighted accordingly. The data include all filings that take place in the month of May of the recorded year. The filings represent all filings for the month of May of each year, and also include adjudication and case information. The sentences are measured in months and range from zero for those not given any jail time to 1440 for those given a life sentence.

Shepherd (2002) provides demographic information for each county, which includes the number of arrests by category of crime and racial composition. The data on judicial selection come from American Judicature Society's publication titled "Judicial Selection in the States Appellate and General Jurisdiction Courts." The courts in the dataset are all general jurisdiction courts; they are criminal courts and the first ones to hear the case.

The summary statistics for the data are presented in Table 3.1.1. The number of observations used in the regressions is lower because of missing adjudication information or missing data on jail populations in Hawaii. A plurality of the defendants are black (49 percent) followed by white (37 percent). Among the remaining cases 69 percent resulted in conviction, of which 93 percent were pleaded. Only 1 percent of cases ended in an acquittal, while 27 percent of the cases were dismissed. Roughly 39 percent of defendants are incarcerated (about half of those convicted), and the average sentence is around 30 months. Counties with elected judges have higher mean population of blacks, and elected judges handle more black defendants.

Results

Table 3.1.2 presents regressions, separately by elected and appointed judges, for defendants of all races. The control variables show that being charged with more crimes increases the probability of incarceration, as does being older, for both elected and appointed judges. Minors and females are less

Table 3.1.1: Summary Statistics

	Elected				Appointed			
	mean	std. Dev.	min.	max	mean	std. Dev.	min.	max
demographics								
percent pop. black	22.39	12.87	1.83	53.39	17.65	15.24	0.82	66.61
percent pop. white	61.09	17.19	18.73	91.63	63.99	18.97	18.73	95.41
arrest charge								
murder	0.005	0.071	0	1	0.007	0.085	0	1
rape	0.015	0.120	0	1	0.015	0.123	0	1
robbery	0.075	0.263	0	1	0.075	0.263	0	1
assault	0.118	0.323	0	1	0.124	0.330	0	1
oth. violent	0.039	0.193	0	1	0.030	0.170	0	1
burglary	0.089	0.284	0	1	0.105	0.306	0	1
theft	0.120	0.325	0	1	0.125	0.331	0	1
oth. property	0.117	0.322	0	1	0.096	0.295	0	1
drug trafick.	0.142	0.349	0	1	0.212	0.409	0	1
oth. drug	0.189	0.392	0	1	0.130	0.336	0	1
weapon	0.033	0.179	0	1	0.031	0.172	0	1
driving	0.025	0.156	0	1	0.028	0.164	0	1
oth. public	0.033	0.179	0	1	0.022	0.147	0	1
conviction charge								
murder	0.002	0.049	0	1	0.004	0.059	0	1
rape	0.006	0.076	0	1	0.006	0.080	0	1
robbery	0.024	0.153	0	1	0.042	0.201	0	1
assault	0.022	0.148	0	1	0.054	0.227	0	1
oth. violent	0.017	0.131	0	1	0.023	0.151	0	1
burglary	0.041	0.198	0	1	0.068	0.251	0	1
theft	0.057	0.231	0	1	0.082	0.275	0	1
oth. property	0.056	0.231	0	1	0.063	0.243	0	1
drug trafick	0.073	0.260	0	1	0.147	0.354	0	1
oth. drug	0.092	0.289	0	1	0.108	0.311	0	1
weapon	0.018	0.134	0	1	0.026	0.161	0	1
driving	0.014	0.119	0	1	0.022	0.147	0	1
oth. public	0.015	0.120	0	1	0.016	0.124	0	1
unkwn. fel.	0.002	0.041	0	1	0.005	0.069	0	1
race of the defendant								
white	0.341	0.474	0	1	0.406	0.491	0	1

black	0.522	0.500	0	1		0.443	0.497	0	1
hispanic	0.180	0.384	0	1		0.224	0.417	0	1
asian	0.011	0.104	0	1		0.019	0.135	0	1
other	0.003	0.057	0	1		0.005	0.071	0	1
N	30,184					30,812			

likely to be incarcerated, but when incarcerated, are treated no differently. A guilty plea, as expected, will increase the probability of incarceration, but will result in a lower sentence. Having no prior convictions benefits the defendant in the first stage, with no clear benefit in sentencing. Elected and appointed judges respond differently to whether jails are overcrowded.

The variable of most interest is in the first row, the percentage of the district's population that is of the defendant's race. This variable is significant, but of a magnitude with little economic importance, only in the first stage regression for appointed judges. There is no evidence of a relationship between the percentage of a district's population that is of a defendant's race and the length of that defendant's sentence. This result, however, could depend on the fact that this regression includes defendants of all races.

Table 3.1.3 estimates the same regression in Table 3.1.2, but only for African American defendants. The variable of interest is now the percentage of the district's population that is African American. Although this variable has no effect on the probability of incarceration, the length of the sentence is reduced significantly when the district's population becomes more African American. A one percent increase in the African American population is related to a 0.435 month, or 13 day, reduction in the defendant's sentence. A one standard deviation increase in the percentage of population that is African American, 12.87 percent, is related to a substantial decrease in the defendant's sentence: 5.7 months or 168 days.

The following panel presents evidence that our result is driven by elected judges and the different incentives that they face. Among appointed judges, there is no association between the composition of the population and the race of the defendant. Elected judges, more directly subject to the preferences of their district, are more likely to respond to the racial characteristics of their constituencies when facing an African American defendant. An appointed judge is not accountable to the local communities, and as a result is unresponsive to its composition.

We test whether the finding on African Americans defendants extends to other racial sub-samples. We present estimates from regressions on white defendants, separately for elected and appointed judges, in Table 3.1.4. The results show that the percentage of the population that is white has no effect, at conventional levels of significance, on the length of sentence for elected or appointed judges. Table 3.1.5 aggregates all other racial groups and the percentage of the districts' populations that is neither African American nor white. In these regressions, the population has no significant relationship to the defendant's outcome.

Table 3.1.2: All Defendants

	Elected Judges		Appointed Judges	
	Stage 1	**Stage 2**	**Stage 1**	**Stage 2**
	Incarceration	**Length of Sentence**	**Incarceration**	**Length of Sentence**
% of district of defendant's race	0	0.011	−0.001	0.005
	(0.15)	(0.41)	(5.92)**	(0.15)
Number of charges	0.016	1.724	0.015	1.689
	(5.35)**	(3.15)**	(5.85)**	(2.60)**
Age	0.011	0.072	0.01	0.298
	(4.77)**	(0.19)	(4.78)**	(0.42)
Age squared	0	0	0	−0.001
	(5.01)**	(0.06)	(4.79)**	(0.12)
Under 18	−0.053	−0.317	−0.095	−1.437
	(2.38)*	(0.05)	(4.04)**	(0.25)
Female	−0.069	−1.708	−0.064	−2.191
	(6.10)**	(1.41)	(7.08)**	(1.92)
Pleaded Guilty	0.549	−53.113	0.446	−60.136
	(60.98)**	(7.53)**	(38.77)**	(7.08)**
No prior convictions	−0.167	0.311	−0.165	−4.885
	(13.00)**	(0.14)	(15.97)**	(2.89)**
Jails overcrowded	−0.149		0.146	
	(7.36)**		(6.60)**	
On probation	0.081		0.076	
	(7.27)**		(6.65)**	
On parole	0.13		0.14	
	(8.02)**		(7.71)**	
Arrested on Bail	0.043		0.05	
	(3.10)**		(3.57)**	
Fugitive	0.15		0.031	
	(6.75)**		(1.16)	
Constant		95.996		100.619
		(5.14)**		(4.32)**
Observations	27,242	26,323	29,088	28,194

Includes controls for the crime, legal representation, state, and year of crime | Robust z statistics in parentheses | * significant at 5%; ** significant at 1%

Table 3.1.3: African American Defendants

	Elected Judges		Appointed Judges	
	Stage 1	Stage 2	Stage 1	Stage 2
	Incarceration	Length of Sentence	Incarceration	Length of Sentence
% of district African Amer.	0	−0.435	0.001	−0.145
	(0.55)	(3.51)**	(0.95)	(0.77)
Number of charges	0.017	1.341	0.021	2.066
	(3.93)**	(1-62)	(5.17)**	(1.79)
Age	0.013	0.02	0.012	0.904
	(4.28)**	(0.03)	(3.62)**	(1.28)
Age squared	0	0.001	0	−0.015
	(4.31)**	(0.14)	(3.29)**	(1.68)
Under 18	−0.008	1.723	−0.084	−11.004
	(0.30)	(0.18)	(2.66)**	(1.34)
Female	−0.085	−0.297	−0.091	−3.355
	(5.06)**	(0.11)	(5.68)**	(1.30)
Pleaded Guilty	0.51	−65.958	0.485	−56.254
	(42.60)**	(6.04)**	(30.92)**	(5.14)**
No prior convictions	−0.168	6.548	−0.177	−2.012
	(10.43)**	(1.74)	(12.24)**	(0.73)
Jails overcrowded	−0.127		0.162	
	(4.22)**		(4.84)**	
On probation	0.09		0.068	
	(5.96)**		(4.18)**	
On parole	0.129		0.135	
	(6.54)**		(5.66)**	
Arrested on Bail	0.035		0.02	
	(2.06)*		(1.10)	
Fugitive	0.164		0.027	
	(6.25)**		(0.77)	
Constant		122.266		74.61
		(5.08)**		(3.28)**
Observations	14,784	14,243	13,466	13,012

Includes controls for the crime, legal representation, state, and year of crime | Robust z statistics in parentheses | * significant at 5%; ** significant at 1%

Table 3.1.4: White Defendants

	Elected Judges		Appointed Judges	
	Stage 1	Stage 2	Stage 1	Stage 2
	Incarceration	Length of Sentence	Incarceration	Length of Sentence
% of district of white	0.001	−0.106	−0.002	0.293
	(2.13)*	(1.19)	(4.28)**	(1.91)
Number of charges	0.013	2.295	0.009	2.81
	(2.78)**	(2.37)*	(3.11)**	(2.15)*
Age	0.01	−0.514	0.008	1.215
	(2.88)**	(0.77)	(2.62)**	(1.37)
Age squared	0	0.007	0	−0.014
	(3.12)**	(0.73)	(2.83)**	(1.01)
Under 18	−0.121	−0.616	−0.086	13.576
	(3.07)**	(0.06)	(2.17)*	(1.56)
Female	−0.045	−3.601	−0.044	−1.218
	(2.69)**	(3.25)**	(3.71)**	(0.81)
Pleaded Guilty	0.565	−36.468	0.368	−61.625
	(37.00)**	(3.85)**	(20.54)**	(4.55)**
No prior convictions	−0.159	−5.022	−0.137	−3.976
	(7.59)**	(1.46)	(8.41)**	(1.54)
Jails overcrowded	−0.172		0.176	
	(5.43)**		(5.30)**	
On probation	0.063		0.09	
	(3.40)**		(4.99)**	
On parole	0.175		0.175	
	(5.60)**		(5.46)**	
Arrested on Bail	0.083		0.072	
	(3.32)**		(3.00)**	
Fugitive	0.13		0.023	
	(2.99)**		(0.53)	
Constant		121.802		−0.466
		(2.37)*		(0.02)
Observations	9,622	9,357	11,935	11,599

Includes controls for the crime, legal representation, state, and year of crime | Robust z statistics in parentheses | * significant at 5%; ** significant at 1%

Table 3.1.5: All Other Defendants

	Elected Judges		Appointed Judges	
	Stage 1	**Stage 2**	**Stage 1**	**Stage 2**
	Incarceration	**Length of Sentence**	**Incarceration**	**Length of Sentence**
% of district of other	−0.001	−0.003	−0.002	0.037
	(0.48)	(0.05)	(1−72)	(0.13)
Number of charges	0.015	0.372	0.016	0.201
	(1.82)	(1.01)	(2.93)**	(0.30)
Age	0.004	0.725	0.01	−1.046
	(0.76)	(3.05)**	(2.03)*	(0.50)
Age squared	0	−0.009	0	0.024
	(0.80)	(2.89)**	(2.38)*	(0.70)
Under 18	−0.024	5.953	−0.168	−5.749
	(0.34)	(0.77)	(2.59)**	(0.71)
Female	0.009	−0.931	−0.035	−4.859
	(0.40)	(0.93)	(2.69)**	(2.56)*
Pleaded Guilty	0.699	−10.319	0.533	−76.289
	(23.33)**	(1.27)	(15.34)**	(2.68)**
No prior convictions	−0.157	−2.902	−0.154	−11.289
	(4.01)**	(2.27)*	(5.51)**	(2.56)*
Jails overcrowded	0.091		0.084	
	(2.84)**		(3.04)**	
On probation	0.053		0.086	
	(1.00)		(1.90)	
On parole	0.064		0.129	
	(1.13)		(3.10)**	
Arrested on Bail	0.135		0.084	
	(1.40)		(1.06)	
Fugitive	−0.102		0.029	
	(1.87)		(0.50)	
Constant		−14.214		124.782
		(1.77)		(2.04)*
Observations	3,752	2,723	4,207	4,096

Includes controls for the crime, legal representation, state, and year of crime | Robust z statistics in parentheses | * significant at 5%; ** significant at 1%

Policy Implications and Conclusion

When a black defendant faces an elected judge, he is significantly better off in a community where there are more blacks is negatively related to the length of his sentence. This relationship is present only when judge is elected, as appointed judges are, unsurprisingly, not responsive to the racial composition of their judicial district. The fact that elected and appointed judges behave differently suggests that the longer sentences of black defendants cannot be explained by a bias that exists in the law or the usual factors. Judicial selection and population characteristics matter as well. The disparities between races in sentencing will be greatest in counties with elected judiciary and an extremely low share of blacks in county population.

If one believes that identical crimes should be given comparable sentences, the results of this study will be discouraging. Punishment clearly depends on more than the nature of the crime. That said, these findings could be useful in improving access to a fair trial. An African American defendant facing an elected judge in a district where the population is overwhelmingly not African American could use these results as part of an argument in a request for a change of venue. Areas where African Americans are the minority could also consider selecting their judges through appointment, rather than elections, to decrease the probability of race affecting the outcome.

Note

We would like to thank Scott Baier. Robert Blewett. Angela Dills, William Dougan, Jahn Hakes, Dan Rees, Raymond Sauer, Joanna Shepherd, and Robert Tollison.

1. An alternate for of estimation, using a triple interaction of a racial identifier, percentage of the population of the defendant's race, and a dummy for elected judges, delivers results consistent with those presented.

References

American Judicature Society. 2004. "Judicial Selection in the States: Appellate and General Jurisdiction Courts." Available online: http://www.ajs.org/js/materials.htm.

Besley, T. & Coate, S. 2000 "Elected versus Appointed Regulators: Theory and Evidence." NBER working paper #7579.

Bushway, S. & A. Morris Piehl. 2001. "Judging Judicial Discretion: Legal Factors and Racial Discrimination in Sentencing," *Law & Society-Review,* v. 35, pp. 733–64.

Bureau of Census, 2013. "USA QuickFacts" retrieved from http://quickfacts.census.gov/qfd/states/00000.html on October 26, 2013.

Carson, E. A. & Golinelli, D. 2013. "Prisoners in 2012-Advance Counts." Bureau of Justice Statistics.

Daly, K. & Tonry, M. 1997. "Gender, Race, and Sentencing" *Crime and Justice,* v. 22, pp. 201–252.

Fields. J. A., Klein, L. S., & Sfiridis, J. M. 1997. "A Market Based Evaluation of the Election versus Appointment of Regulatory Commissioners," *Public Choice,* v. 92. pp. 337–351.

Glaeser E. L. & Sacerdote, B. 2003. Sentencing in Homicide Cases and the Role of Vengeance." *The Journal of Legal Studies,* v. 32, pp. 363–382.

Hall, M. G. 1995. "Justices as Representatives: Elections and Judicial Politics in the American States," *American Politics Quarterly,* v. 75, pp. 136–51.

Hanssen, F. A. 1999. "The Effect of Judicial Institutions on Uncertainty and the Rate of Litigation: The Election Versus Appointment of State Judges," *The Journal of Legal Studies,* v. 28, pp. 205–32.

Heckman, J. (1976) "The Common Structure of Statistical Models of Truncation, Sample Selection and Limited Dependent Variables and a Simple Estimator for Such Models." *Annals of Economic and Social Measurement,* v. 5, pp. 475–492.

Helland, E. & Tabarrok, A. 1999. "Court Politics: The Political Economy of Tort Awards." *Journal of Law and Economics XLII.* pp. 157–188.

Helland, E. & Tabarrok, A. 2002. "The Effect of Electoral Institutions on Tort Awards." *American Law and Economics Review.* v. 4, pp. 341–370.

Helland, E. & Tabarrok, A. 2003. "Race, Poverty, and American Tort Awards: Evidence form Three Datasets." *Journal of Legal Studies* v. 32, pp. 27–58.

Jensen, J. M. & Beyle, T. 2003. "Of Footnotes, Missing Data, and Lessons for 50-State Data Collection: The Gubernatorial Campaign Finance Project, 1977–2001," *State Politics and Policy Quarterly* v. 3, pp. 203–14. Data are available at http://www.unc.edu/~beyle/guber.html.

Mustard, D. B. 2001. "Racial, Ethnic, and Gender Disparities in Sentencing: Evidence from the U.S. Federal Courts." *Journal of Law and Economics,* v. 44, pp. 285–314.

Schazenbach, M. 2005. "Racial and Sex Disparities in Prison Sentences: The Effect of District-Level Judicial Demographics." *Journal of Legal Studies,* v. 34, pp. 57–92.

Shepherd, J. 2002. "Fear of the First Strike: The Full Deterrent Effect of California's Two- and Three-Strikes Legislation." *Journal of Legal Studies,* v. 31, pp. 159–201.

Tomic, A. 2006. "Incarceration and Sentencing Differences between Appointed and Elected Judges." Working Paper.

U.S. Dept. of Justice, Bureau of Justice Statistics. 2002. "State Court Processing Statistics, 1990, 1992, 1994, 1996, AND 1998: Felony Defendants in Large Urban Counties" [Computer file]. Conducted by Pretrial Services Resource Center, 2001. Third edition distributed by the Inter-university Consortium for Political and Social Research, Ann Arbor, MI.

Welch, R. H. & Angulo, C. T. 2000., "Justice on Trial: Racial Disparities in the American Criminal Justice System," *Leadership Conference on Civil Rights,* Washington, DC, p. 7.

Wolfgang M. E. & Riedel, M. 1973. "Race, Judicial Discretion, and the Death Penalty" *Annals of the American Academy of Political and Social Science,* v. 407. pp. 119–133.

READING 3.2

Workflow Software Solutions

Document Management, e-Filing and Beyond ... Into the Cloud

By Bill Schiffner

Just about every court system today utilizes some sort of document workflow process. Whether that process is limited to a single individual or multiple people, a series of steps is completed to formulate the workflow process. Document workflow can consist of an invoice, order processing, email, snail mail, or other document, and it occurs every single day in every single business. Once the realization occurs regarding how often document workflow occurs each day, systems administrators begin to consider ways to improve and streamline the document workflow process to maximize time and cost savings. Records and document management are at the heart of most courts' business processes. These two elements are directly related; document management focus on how courts obtain/acquire documents while records management focuses on care and storage after acquisition.

Scott Bade, president at ImageSoft, Inc. says, "Courts are struggling to compete for precious IT resources and are turning to the Cloud for faster deployments, lower costs and higher functionality. Courts, like commercial markets, are realizing that they cannot afford to be in the software development business. Twenty sixteen will be the year of the Cloud in courts with products like Office365 leading the way."

"Using technology effectively is key for many aspects of a successful document management workflow including speeding juror processing and management as well as facilitating a positive juror experience, for example," adds Tessa Prophet, marketing specialist at Jury Systems Inc.

More Integrated Solutions

Phil Hatton, vice president, Justice Solutions Manager at Xerox Government Systems, LLC, says integration of these systems is the key for a more streamlined workflow. "Our Xerox court case management solutions include an integrated content management component within our base offerings

Bill Schiffner, "Workflow Software Solutions: Document Management, e-Filing and Beyond... Into the Cloud," *Courts Today*, vol. 14, no. 1, pp. 18, 20-24.

or our CMS solutions can be easily integrated with a court-selected third party content management system. With our Xerox AgileCourt solution, the Apache Jackrabbit repository is included and our Xerox Contexte solution comes complete with built-in database content management functionality," he reports.

Going Mobile

Gary Dower, president at Judicial Systems Inc., points out that courts have long been able to capture digital images of documents by scanning paper documents and extracting specific data elements in the process. He says that Judicial Systems, Inc. has provided document management with Advanced Data Extraction to court jurisdictions nationally as a component of its Jury Management System for more than 20 years.

"Today's mobile devices are taking the inputting of information to a new level by repurposing their built-in cameras for use as content-entry tool," Dower explains. "Image capture from any device and from anywhere will grow to become essential. In the future, scanning and inputting documents while sitting by a traditional scanner will not cut it by itself. Image capture will now need to include the use of mobile devices such as smartphones and tablets with built-in cameras. We already see a huge application for this with mobile banking and check processing."

"Judicial Systems' Document Management System coupled with the functionality of mJuror, the texting component of Judicial Systems' JMS, now adds tremendous value to the Document Management process," he adds.

"The public is trending towards mobile first services, utilizing desktop and web services, secondly. Judicial Systems integration between its Document Management System and its mJuror Texting System will insure that jurisdictions are ready to accept the eventual mobile first business strategy regarding Document Imaging and Management while providing citizens a quality mobile experience," Dower concludes.

E-Filing Capabilities Continue to Grow

E-Filing software is another area that is on the rise. The solution provides a secure, easy-to-use electronic filing system that streamlines and manages the two-way flow of information among attorneys, clerks, court personnel, and judges.

Sue Humphreys, Court View's director, Industry Solutions, notes, "As e-filing solutions gain steam, we're seeing a real shift where clerks are more involved in facilitating and quality-checks rather than heads-down data entry. That's a great thing for caseflow overall. And with e-filing standards in place, we'll soon start seeing even greater mobility—filings, alerts, updates—all on your smart device from wherever you happen to be."

"E-filing creates a tipping point to creating an electronic court, "agrees Michael Kleiman, director of marketing for Tyler's Courts & Justice Division. "Once filings come into the system as electronic documents it becomes much easier to create electronic case files and automated processes. Integration between e-Filing, and case and document management allow courts to save money, free up space, and be more responsive to constituents," he adds.

Document Classification

"Document classification is at the heart of any system that captures and stores documents. E-filing attempts to place the responsibility of coding on the submitter, however in the majority of cases, court clerk staff still inspect documents and correct docket codes to reflect what local understanding of the document is," says Henry Sal, president at Computing System Innovations. "We've taken some of our technology and it has allowed us to redact privacy information and create iclassify. IClassify for Courts upgrades court docketing workflows by replacing manual efforts with machine learning technology that includes both linguistics and semantics," he adds.

Here's a look at some of the latest document management and e-Filing software solutions for the courts:

Mobile Management Solutions

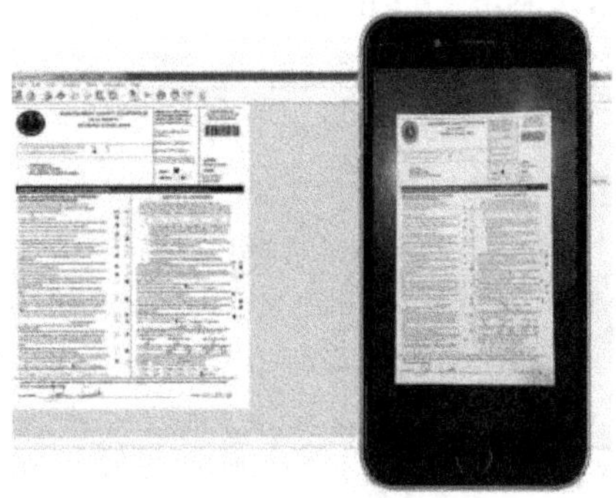

Judicial Systems' Document Management System coupled with the functionality of mJuror, the texting component of Judicial Systems' JMS, now is reported to add tremendous value to the Document Management Process. Document images and content may now be entered into the document workflow within the JMS by the use of smartphones/tablets rather than by document scanners alone. Potential jurors may take picture of a Qualification Questionnaire, Medical Affidavit, etc., with their smartphone and text the picture to mJuror, which, in conjunction with the Document Imaging System, verify that the form is complete and acceptable. Once the document is accepted, the potential juror will be notified via text.

www.judicialsystems.com, 1.800.205.4068

Pretrial Management

TRIBRIDGE

With strict guidelines in place for processing and preparing defendants for trial, Tribridge Pretrial360 provides the technology necessary for probation, parole and court users to easily and securely enter and track data. It's also optimized for information sharing and improving accountability to enhance public safety. Built on Microsoft Dynamics CRM, these solutions allow for more informed decision-making at each phase in the pretrial process, from first contact with law enforcement through adjudication. Three distinct modules focus on different areas of Pretrial Management: Defendant Management, Supervision Case Management, and Risk Assessments to help jurisdictions move from resource-based to risk-based bail decision-making process.

www.tribridge.com, 1.877.744.1360

Digital Solutions

ImageSoft delivers a unique integrated digital solution for both courts and prosecutors that runs in the Cloud. The ImageSoft JusticeTech solution provides Dynamic Case Management (CMS), Enterprise Content Management (ECM), and the TrueFiling e-filing platform in a single hosted platform at an affordable subscription price. The solution supports all major case types and for criminal cases it offers complete digital integration of law enforcement, the prosecutor, and the court.

www.imagesoftinc.com, 1.888.315.3901

Virtual Court Records

CourtView's JusticeFiling System is a Launchpad for virtual court records. Whatever the source—attorneys, pro se, other agencies, or a judge—JusticeFiling lets you receive, review, route, accept, associate, and store documents efficiently and according to your rules and flow. The filer portal provides quick access to personal queues and status updates, with automatic notifications as filings progress. JusticeFiling easily integrates with CourtView's ShowCase iDMS or third-party document systems. Whether they are incoming or outgoing, documents are always available online to those with access permission. DMS security controls who can markup/annotate or edit documents and which document versions or "layers" are viewable by whom.

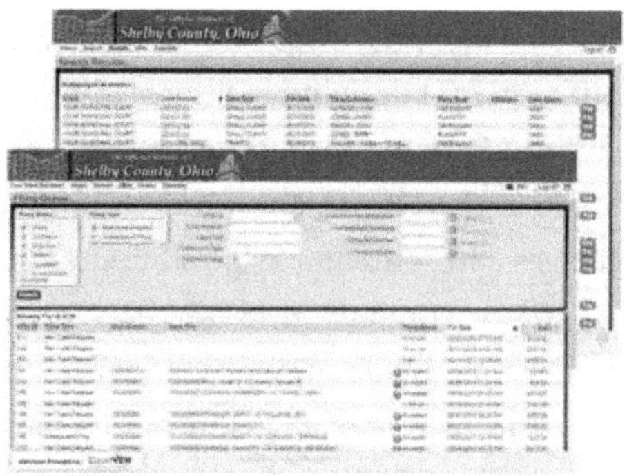

JusticeFiling queues are configurable by filer type and easily accessible through online portals

www.courtview.com, 1.800.406.4333

Optical Character Recognition

Odyssey provides tight integration between e-filing and case management, including document management. This generates efficiencies by creating electronic queues for accepting and routing filings. Optical Character Recognition (OCR) capabilities enable users to search electronically filed documents for words and phrases. Odyssey File & Serve is the solution of choice for 11 statewide e-filing implementations, and Odyssey Case Manager is being used in more than 600 counties.

www.tylertech.com, 1.800.431.5776

Web Portal for E-Filing

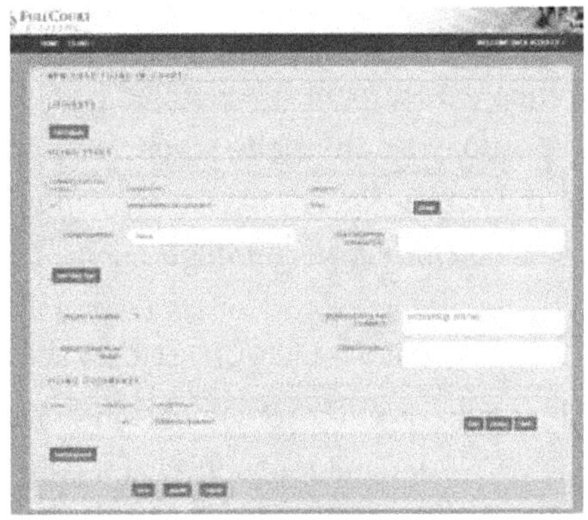

FullCourt e-filing provides a web portal for filing documents with the court electronically, creating cases from the filings, and providing notices to filers and parties to the case. Payment of filing fees is fully integrated through its ePayment solution, CitePayUSA and provides for seamless recording of financial transactions with the court case management system, FullCourt Enterprise. Once filings are submitted, clerks can review and process all filings within Full Court Enterprise.

www.justicesystems.com, 505.883.3987

Content Management Functionality

The Xerox AgileCourt solution's Apache Jackrabbit repository is included in the Xerox Contexte solution. It comes complete with built-in database content management functionality. Both solutions can effectively manage all types of required content (audio files, video clips, documents, fingerprint, photographs, etc.). If desired, the court can automatically store documents generated from within either CMS, store scanned documents or store electronically filed documents within the Apache Jackrabbit repository using our built-in database content management functionality.

http://xerox.com/justice, 1.877.414.2676

Management Solutions

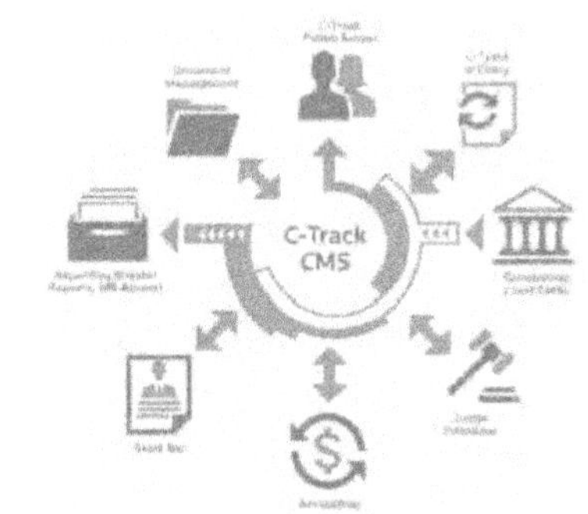

Thomson Reuters is committed to provide customers with unrivaled solutions that integrate content, expertise and technologies, the firm says. C-Track CMS delivers just that, offering courts customizable management solutions configured to how a court functions. Their suite of programs features the next generation of document management and e-filing solutions.

www.thomsonreuters.com, 1.877.923.7800

Web-Based Management Solution

ECourt provides a document management system as well as scanning, indexing and storage of paper-based and electronic documents. All documents, regardless of file formats (scanned images and electronic files such as PDF, Word, Excel, PowerPoint, Visio, text, audio, video), are easily stored, managed, and retrieved from within eCourt for a single, centrally managed repository that has the necessary security and automation features to support the business. When a document is generated by eCourt, it is automatically associated to the case and saved to the repository. Additionally, when the user has to provide edits prior to saving the document and sending it, they can upload it to eCourt using the Microsoft Word ribbon tool bar and all revisions are saved.

www.journaltechnologies.com, 1.877.587.8927

Document Management System

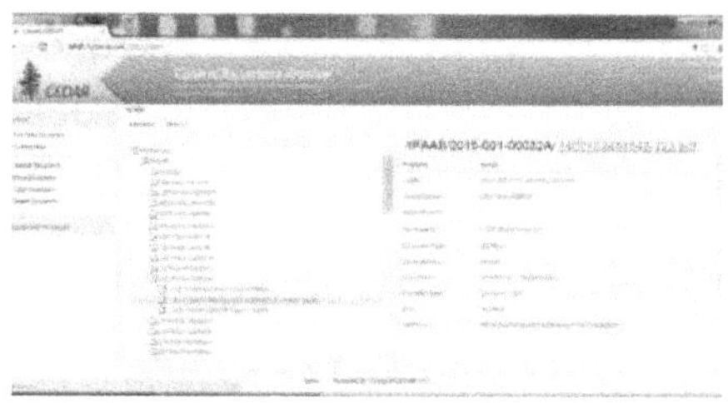

The Tybera CEDAR Document Management System (DMS) is designed specifically for courts. Many courts are moving away from full-featured DMS systems because of the high cost. The cost to license and maintain most DMS systems is based on the number of users or interactive connections. When an e-filing system is connected to a DMS, each account actively using the system requires one of the interactive connections. The more attorneys, Pro Se filers, and court employees using the system, the more connections to the DMS are mandatory.

www.tybera.com, 801.226.2746

Document Classification

IClassify for Courts improves court docketing workflows by replacing manual efforts with machine learning technology which includes both linguistics and semantics. It is the examination of language form, language meaning, and language in context. IClassify is actually able to resolve the ambiguity of expressions and the relationship of words in a body of text. This greatly improves the precision of document classification and at the same time allows distinguishing between important and irrelevant features in text.

www.csisoft.com, 407.598.1825

Jury Solutions

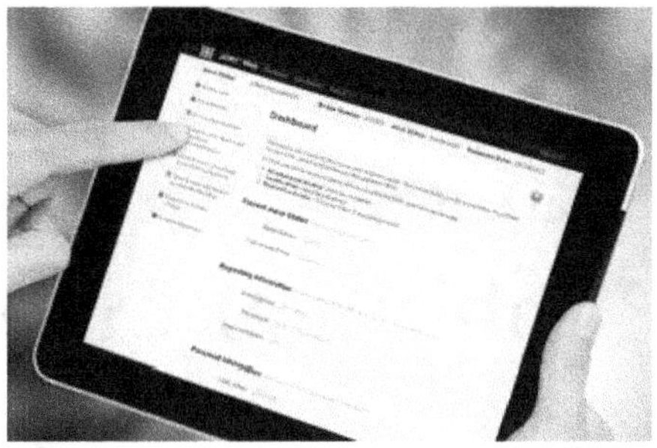

With its suite of JURY+ Solutions, the entire jury process is easier for both jury staff as well as prospective jurors. Jurors may use JURY+ Web Solution to go online to qualify/disqualify themselves, request a postponement, or update information. Once submitted, it is archived in the core JMS, JURY+ Web Generation. If jurors prefer to mail in their paperwork, JURY+ Imaging Solution allows specific data fields to be extracted from the form and updated into the database based on the court's rules. Information is indexed with the juror's record and retained in our searchable document archive.

www.jurysystems.com, 1.800.222.6974

ID Shield

Extract Systems developed the ID Shield to meet the specific demands of government and public organizations to automatically capture and redact information from their recorded documents. ID Shield removes sensitive data from electronic or paper-based content permanently and securely. The system's technology was designed to seamlessly integrate with all case management systems and other workflow solutions.

www.extractsystems.com, 608.821.6520

READING 3.3

Domestic Violence and the Problem of Courts

By Kathleen Erin Currul-Dykeman

Challenges to the Identification and Prosecution of Domestic Violence

Domestic violence crimes face a myriad of legal and social barriers to effective case processing. Crimes between intimates were rarely handled by the criminal justice system until the 1980s. Seen as a private family matter, batterers were routinely told to "cool off" or "take a walk" when confronted by a police officer who responded for assistance. These responses are no longer accepted as adequate. Mandated arrest and prosecution policies have been enacted and victim services have increased. However, domestic violence crimes still persist and our nation's courts still struggle with handling them.

Prior to the late 1970s, all but 14 states required police officers to witness a violent misdemeanor prior to making a warrantless arrest (Buzawa & Buzawa, 1996). Starting in the mid-1980s, legal changes were made to arrest requirements. These statutory changes followed the Sherman and Berk (1984) Minneapolis Domestic Violence Experiment (MDVE). Sherman and Berk first studied the deterrent impact of arrest on domestic violence offenders. In their study, offenders were randomly assigned to three groups: 1) mediation; 2) arrest; 3) an order to cool off and leave the premises. Sherman and Berk found that the batterers who were arrested were the least likely to recidivate. Soon thereafter, states began to enact exceptions to the misdemeanor arrest laws for domestic violence cases. Often called mandated arrest policies, police officers were told that the preferred response to an allegation of abuse between domestic partners was arrest, and that this could be based on probable cause. These arrest laws, if uniformly applied, were intended to hold more batterers accountable. By 1992, 47 states and the District of Columbia enacted statutes authorizing arrest in domestic violence misdemeanor cases (Buzawa & Buzawa, 1996). Fourteen of these 47 states mandated arrest when the officer concluded that a crime involved domestic violence (Buzawa & Buzawa, 1996). Replication studies have yielded mixed results. Evaluation studies were conducted in: Minneapolis, Minnesota; Metro-Dade County, Florida; Colorado Springs, Colorado; Milwaukee, Wisconsin; Charlotte, North Carolina; and Omaha, Nebraska. These studies attempted to replicate the findings of the Sherman and Berk's (1984) study. Overall, it was found that while arrest did initially deter reoffending among employed men, it did not have the same impact among the unemployed men sampled, and in the long run, battering increased (Buzawa & Buzawa, 1992, 1996; Schmidt & Sherman, 1998; Stark, 1998; Zorza, 1998).

By the early 1990s, twenty one states and the District of Columbia had adopted mandatory or quasi mandatory arrest policies (Buzawa & Buzawa, 2003). Despite the movement toward mandating arrest, only a fraction of all domestic violence crimes actually result in an arrest. There are many possible explanations for this discrepancy. Women are less likely to call the police when the defendant is known to them (Bachman, 1998; Franklin, 2010; Tjaden & Thoennes, 2000). When they do contact the police, arrest is unlikely. In a sample of women residing in a shelter, Coulter, Kuehnle, Byers, and Alfonso (1999) found that more than half of the women contacted the police, but less than one-quarter of the offenders were arrested. Additionally, Smith (2001) found that the presence of physical injury did not lead to a higher arrest rate. In a study where more than 60 percent of cases involved physical injury to the victim, only 28 percent resulted in arrest (Smith, 2001). Other studies have published arrest rates that include 29 percent (Bourg & Stock, 1993), 33 percent (Mignon & Holmes, 1995), 34 percent (Buzawa & Hoatling, 2000), and 36 percent (Robinson & Chandek, 2000) respectively. Indeed, arrest for domestic violence crimes still only occurs in one-third of all reported cases. This is because police officers have great discretion when they respond to a scene and can still decide not to take any official action.

Arrest is only the first step in the criminal justice process. In order for the mandatory arrest policies to affect domestic violence case processing, the remainder of the criminal justice system must support the policy and be prepared to follow through (Buzawa & Buzawa, 2003). Prosecutors have discretion in how they choose to handle these cases in the courts. Public pressure for increased prosecution of domestic violence cases rose after the adoption of mandated arrest policies (Rebovich, 1996). In response to such pressure, prosecutors often chose to either dismiss cases early in the process or to adopt a method for prosecution that could be successful without the victim's cooperation (Cahn, 1992). In response, "no-drop" policies were implemented by many jurisdictions in attempt to change the way that cases are handled by prosecutors (Lerman, 1981). Under these policies, the victim's role as a witness in the case is emphasized rather than her being treated as the complainant. The prosecution attempts to prosecute the defendant with or without the consent of the victim. This rationale relies on the concept that domestic violence is not just a crime against a person but is a crime against the public order of the state.

Subsequent to the adoption of mandated arrest and prosecution policies, statistics revealed low rates of prosecution in domestic violence cases (Ames & Dunham, 2002; Messing, 2010). Early estimates reported that less than 10 percent of misdemeanor cases were prosecuted under the newly adopted policies (Fagan, 1989; Ford 1993; Schmidt & Steury, 1989; Sherman, 1992). Dutton (1995) reported that obtaining convictions and sentencing defendants were even rarer. Still, Robbins (1999) found that no-drop policies have been "the single most effective method for getting domestic violence charges to stick" (p. 217). Several more recent studies have found that victims report that they perceive these policies as being disempowering, entrapping, and coercive (Ford, 2003; McDermott & Garofalo, 2004; Messing, 2010; Mills, 1999, 2003). Stark (2004) found that even though these policies have flaws, there is still evidence that they help reduce the biases shown toward victims by law police officers and prosecutors on the basis of their race, history, and social class (Stark, 2004).

The unique nature of domestic violence cases could be blamed for their frequent dismissals and low conviction rates. These crimes often take place in private locations, with only the defendant and victim present. The private nature of the crime results in an absence of independent witnesses. Since the possibility of victim corroboration is absent, the cases often rely on victim credibility alone. It has been found that this reliance often leads to dismissals and low conviction rates (Hirschel & Hutchinson, 2001, Jordan, 2011). Adding to this problem, victims of domestic violence are often unwilling to testify against their batterers. Studies have shown that victims are reluctant to cooperate in the prosecution of these cases for a host of social reasons (Buzawa, 2003). Financial dependence on the batterer makes proceeding with the criminal justice process difficult (Fagan, 1996; Wolf, 2013). Victims are often afraid that incarceration could result from conviction, and they fear being unable to support themselves and their children in the absence of the batterer (Fagan, 1996; Wolf, 2013). Social isolation is another important factor. Often times, victims of domestic violence become isolated from their extended families and friends. When victims are dependent on the batterer for both financial and social support, losing him can be terrifying. Bennett, Goodman, and Dutton (1999) found that lack of social support by families and friends and the severity of abuse added to victims' reluctance to prosecute. Confusion and frustration with the process, fear of the batterer, and internal conflict about incarcerating the batterer were also found to play a role (Bennett et al., 1999).

To compound these problems, when victims do cooperate with the criminal justice system they are often threatened or physically harmed by the offender (Fischer & Rose, 1995). Indeed, several studies have shown that the primary barrier to victims' seeking redress through the criminal justice system is fear of retaliation by the offenders (Ferraro, 1997; Mears, Carlson, Holden, & Harris, 2001; Zoellner, Feeny, Alvarez, & Watlington, 2000). Studies have shown that among batterers who were arrested for domestic violence, 27 percent re-battered prior to trial (Ford & Regoli, 1998). Consequently, victims of domestic violence often seek rehabilitation for the batterer or desire that the charges be dropped (Bennett, Goodman, & Dutton, 1999; Wolf, 2013). This could pose a problem for prosecutors who work in jurisdictions with discretion limiting no-drop policies. However, in reality, research has shown that even in jurisdictions with explicit no-drop policies, informal case screening processes take place that alleviate having to prosecute a "weak" case. For example, in the San Diego City District Attorney's Office, the prosecutors refused to proceed against one-third of all domestic violence cases because without a cooperating witness, criminal conviction would have been impossible given the lack of independent corroborating evidence (Hartman, 1999). Additionally, "taking iffy misdemeanors to trial ... is seen as wasteful, not ethical" (Hartman, 1999, p. 74).

Additionally, victims who have cooperated with the criminal justice system have often found their dealings to be humiliating and degrading. Due to the relationship between victim and batterer, victims' lives and pasts are often involved in the public court case. "The defense has a great deal more ammunition available to discredit the victim's testimony during trial." (Hartley, 2003, p. 415) Consequently, the themes of domestic violence trials often focus more on the victim's blame in the incident than on traditional defense strategies (Colb, 2001; Scheppele, 1992). A victim's psychiatric history, dependence on drugs or alcohol, and even the status of the custody of her children can all be used to discredit her. Such humiliating information alone could deter a victim's participation in the process. It has been found that the victims' continued exposure to and interaction with criminal justice agents affects their ability to identify themselves as credible victims (Dunn, 2001). Being a victim can be viewed as a "complex interactional process" where court community members continually make assessments and evaluations of victims' worth (Dunn, 2001, p. 289). When victims do not present themselves in an ideal manner, they are regarded and treated in a more culpable manner which could then be internalized and have negative consequences (Kennedy & Sacco, 1998, p. 14).

The existence of a relationship between the defendant and victim also leads domestic violence cases to be seen as weak and more difficult to prosecute. Decisions to prosecute cases often hinge on whether a relationship exists between the victim and defendant (Albonetti, 1987; Simon, 1996; Stanko, 1988). Spohn, Beichner, and Davis-Frenzel (2001) found that cases were less likely to be prosecuted when they involved a victim and defendant who were in a relationship, than when the incident happened between strangers. Prior relationships with the defendant raise questions about the legitimacy of the victims' account of the facts and may lead the victims to refuse to cooperate as the case moves forward (Myers & Hagan, 1979). Kingsnorth, MacIntosh, and Wentworth (2002) assessed the impact of prior relationship and victim characteristics on criminal justice proceedings by tracking 467 sexual assault cases through the Sacramento County Courthouse, from arraignment to sentencing. Among other things, they found that crimes involving strangers were almost twice as likely to go to trial, 33.9 percent versus 18.2 percent (Kingsnorth, MacIntosh, & Wentworth, 2002). Additionally, victims having a prior relationship with the defendant on average reduced the sentence length by 35 months (Kingsnorth, MacIntosh, & Wentworth, 2002). Similarly, each victim characteristic viewed as negative by the judge reduced the sentence by 17 months (Kingsnorth, Macintosh, & Wentworth, 2002). This supports other studies that have found that when a victim demonstrated "nontraditional" behavior, the defendant received a shorter prison sentence (LaFree, 1989; Spears

& Spohn, 1997). Examples of nontraditional behaviors include risk-taking behavior (hitchhiking, using alcohol and drugs), reputation for sexual promiscuity, and previous criminal records. Thus, there is a great focus on the victim, her cooperation, demeanor, behavior, and ultimately credibility when processing cases between individuals who have or have had a relationship.

While mandated arrest and prosecution policies affect the daily business of the courts, discretion remains. Court workgroup members' attitudes toward domestic violence cases affect the manner in which they choose to handle them. Indeed, research has shown that prosecutors' and judges' attitudes have not changed in accordance with policy regarding the processing of domestic violence cases. A survey of prosecutors revealed that their attitudes in being assigned domestic violence cases ranged from "apathetic to disdainful" (Rebovich, 1996, p. 176). These negative views were due to prosecutors' expectations that victims would be uncooperative, and a general misunderstanding of what legal options were available for prosecution (Ford & Regoli, 1993; Williams, 1976). Even when victims want the abuser pursued by courts, prosecutors have often found the victims to be unreliable witnesses (Buzawa & Austin, 1993; Erez & Belknap, 1998, Franklin, 2010). Prosecutors' and other court officials' perceptions that domestic violence cases were trivial or difficult to prosecute successfully contributed to their negative attitudes when dealing with them (Rebovich, 1996). Hartman and Belknap (2003) talked to 62 judges, prosecutors, and public defenders that routinely processed domestic violence cases. They found that the respondents routinely emphasized victim cooperation as being influential on case processing decisions. The respondents also described their domestic violence cases as "frustrating" and "unique" in terms of victims' behaviors (Hartman & Belknap, 2003, p. 370). Court personnel did not report seeking alternative methods for processing cases and only seemed to focus on victim participation (or lack thereof). Most recently, Belknap, Hartman, and Lippen (2010) found that prosecutors' time and investment in domestic violence cases was scarce. They found that the prosecutors blamed the victims' lack of cooperation for their high dismissal rates, but also found that the prosecutors were not routinely making efforts to contact their victims prior to disposition. The researchers blamed a "serious structural problem" within the prosecutors' office that precluded meaningful prosecution of domestic violence cases due to extremely high caseloads (Belknap, Hartman, & Lippen, 2010, p. 275). What remains unclear is whether the local legal culture of these courts had some impact on these prosecutors' inability to meaningfully prosecute these cases. The findings about judicial attitudes toward domestic violence have also been troubling. Studies have shown that judges attempt to dissuade victims from pursuing charges against their batterer (Zora, 1992). Ptacek (1999) observed judicial demeanor during restraining order hearings and also conducted in-person interviews of judges in two courthouses. Like prosecutors, judges often assumed that domestic violence victims were in some way to blame for their abuse. Ptacek noted that judges often blamed the victims for using the court system as a way to litigate a "family squabbling" (Ptacek, 1999; Welch, 1994).

The negative perceptions of victims shared by prosecutors and judges impact how they view domestic violence cases in general. After repeated interactions with victims and each other, norms pertaining to domestic violence cases develop and become part of the local legal culture of the courthouse. Due to the perceptions of the court workgroup members, domestic violence cases may be characterized as weak, have low priority status, and result in dismissals. As stated previously, domestic violence cases depend on victim credibility and the existence of independent corroborating evidence. This is a tricky combination of subjective judgments about victims and objective evidentiary requirements. How the court community has come to evaluate domestic violence cases precludes the majority of them from being fully pursued. Regardless of statutory changes, unless judges, prosecutors, and defense attorneys recognize the disjuncture between how they evaluate case strength and the reality of how domestic violence crimes transpire, these crimes will continue to be handled leniently.

The Court Community Response to Domestic Violence

The local legal culture that exists in courts contributes to the lenient treatment that domestic violence cases receive. Until this study, the court community literature has not been utilized to help frame inquiries about the challenges of processing domestic violence cases. Previous studies have looked at the case processing decisions made by individual judges, prosecutors, and defense attorneys. There is no literature, however, that looks at how the community that forms between these court workgroup members might impact the processing of domestic violence cases. The court community literature offers a possible explanation as to why the processing of domestic violence cases: their reputation within the community, their low priority status, and their high dismissal rates; may be more a product of culture than of law. While each subsequent chapter provides a detailed review of the relevant literature on court communities, a brief overview of the main features of the court community that relate to the processing of domestic violence is provided here.

Court Norms and Culture

Communities of key court actors develop in all of our courts across the country, each with its own unique local legal culture. A court's local legal culture is comprised of internalized norms, traditions, and values that are shared through informal communication networks (Eisenstein, Flemming, and Nardulli, 1988). Court workgroup members are comprised of judges, prosecutors and defense attorneys. Many of them appear day in and day out in the same court house and develop relationships with one another. These individuals are known by the literature as repeat players (Galanter, 1974). In order to get through the business of the day it is important to learn "how things are done" in a particular court (Kritzer and Zemans, 1993, 537). Interdependence is developed between its members. This means that court workgroup members depend on each other to efficiently work through their cases (Eisenstein, Flemming, & Nardulli, 1999). This interdependence is possible because court workgroup members share beliefs about how cases should be processed and resolved in their court. When the courts are busy and the dockets are full, being able to rely on each other and having shared knowledge helps to achieve the goals of the court more efficiently. Occasionally, an attorney will appear in a court in a limited fashion. He is called a one shooter (Galanter, 1974). Being a one shooter will impact the attorneys' abilities to effectively handle their cases because they may not know the rules of that court. Attorneys who have lower perceived status and power (due to lack of experience or to being part of the community for only a limited time) will also cause impact their influence in a court.

Case Typifications

Dependent on the court's local legal culture, court work group members typify cases as strong or weak. They use their informal shared understanding of how to evaluate a case which is based on a combination of social and legal factors (Beichner & Spohn, 2012; Myers and Hagan, 1979). This will impact how attorneys prioritize their work; allocate resources, and their resulting sentencing recommendations. Weak case typifications are based in part on the stereotypes court workgroup members have internalized. They can lead the court community to conclude that certain cases are not serious. Domestic violence cases have historically suffered from weak case typification. How the local legal culture of the specialized session impacted this process and the conclusion that were drawn from their case typifications is discussed further in Chapter 4.

Going Rates

A set of informal rules is established and adopted by group members as to the value of a case (Chen, 2013; Ulmer, 1995). As cases are typified as strong and weak, court workgroup members come to agree on what an appropriate sentence is for the case type. This varies by court and is influenced by a number of factors (court congestion, perceived seriousness of other cases, judicial inclinations). In time, court workgroup members agree to what an appropriate sentence for a case should be or what that case is "worth." This process is based on the norms that have been internalized by court workgroup members and is a result of the typification process. It is helpful and necessary for court workgroup members to agree in this manner for the courts are overburdened with cases. Since most traditional courts share the goal of efficiency, agreeing to the appropriate going rate helps to move cases along (Walker, 2001). Additionally, attorneys who do not go along with the going rate may suffer from informal sanctions and be viewed as "boat rockers" by other attorneys. Going rates are communicated informally between court workgroup members when they interact with one another.

The Interaction of Law and Culture

As previously stated, a strong sense of tradition is a characteristic of court communities. Court communities, like other complex organizations, have "shared pasts" because they engage in similar types of transactions on a day-to-day basis (Chen, 2013; Ulmer, 1995). The relationship between these members and the rules that they agree to live by has been found to be as influential in criminal case processing as the formal laws and policies held by the state (Dixon, 1995; Eisenstein et al., 1977, 1988, 1992). Indeed, they may be more influential in certain circumstances. Ulmer and Kramer (1998) looked at formal sentencing guidelines within the organizational context of the court community and found that court workgroup members used the formal guidelines "dependent on their local relationships, activities, and informal decisions making criteria" within the context of the court community (Ulmer & Kramer, 1998, p. 248). The result is that case outcomes will vary depending on where a case is adjudicated, regardless of a normative legal standard. Likewise, Engen and Steen (2000) found a pattern of charge manipulation being exercised by the prosecutors in response to a change in the sentencing guidelines which would have changed their pre-conceived notions of how certain case types should be dealt with inside that court house. Thus, several researchers have found that, despite the formal rules of the sentencing guidelines, the informal norms that have developed between court workgroup members allow them to make exceptions, circumvent the law, or differ in how they apply these formal rules (Chen, 2013; Knapp, 1987; Loftin & McDowell, 1981; Miethe, 1987). In many of these studies, prosecutors changed their charging decisions in order to accomplish what the court community had long regarded as the appropriate sentence and/or going rate for that crime type, independent of sentencing guidelines.

While discretion-limiting policy changes have been adopted across the country, they have had a limited impact on the processing of domestic violence cases. More individuals are being arrested and processed than twenty years ago, but still, most of those cases are dismissed. A recent study found that about half of the domestic violence cases analyzed resulted in dismissal (Belknap, Hartman, & Lippen, 2010). Looking to the court community for a possible explanation for the problem in processing domestic violence cases may be the answer. Domestic violence cases may finish last in traditional courts whose local legal cultures are characterized by an overburdened docket, scarce resources, and varied cases. This, coupled with a primary goal to efficiently process cases, makes domestic violence cases a good target for quick dismissals. Chapter 6 more fully explores how this culture/law paradigm impacts the processing of domestic violence cases in a specialized and traditional court.

Problem Solving Courts: An Answer to the Problem of Criminally Prosecuting Domestic Violence Cases?

A specialized court model, which evaluated and valued domestic violence cases differently, could change how the cases are processed. Since the 1990s, "problem solving courts" have been developed to address specialized concerns (Mirchandani, 2005). Different examples include drugs courts, community courts, mental health courts, and domestic violence courts. These courts were created not only to address the individual troubles presented by certain cases but also to address the broader social problems of society. They operate within the constraints of the larger criminal court system but have the opportunity to create their own unique local legal cultures. Norms, goals, and priorities could potentially vary within these models. This could have an impact on the processing of domestic violence cases if the court community that processes them changes its evaluation and treatment of these cases. Domestic violence courts are not as widespread as other types of specialized courts. According to Fagan & Dorf (2003) there was 1,091 drug courts nationwide compared to only 300 domestic violence courts (Keilitz, 2000).

Berman and Feinblatt (2001) at the New York-based Center for Court Innovation (CCI) identified six attributes that make specialized courts different from their traditional counter parts: 1) focus on case outcomes rather than processing alone; 2) judicial monitoring or having the judge monitor the case after adjudication; 3) informed decision-making or dedicated resources to target and deal with the problem at hand; 4) collaboration between community agents and criminal justice agents or within the criminal justice community itself; 5) nontraditional practices or employing different innovative ways that better serve the community as a whole; 6) systematic changes or widespread changes to the administration of justice in general.

Similar to other specialized courts, domestic violence courts can focus on the social problem of intimate partner violence. They typically try to help and protect victims of domestic violence but also closely monitor and aid the defendants in an effort to help end the cycle of violence. A specialized domestic violence court would coordinate the efforts of "medical, social service, and treatment providers and establish special procedures and alternative sentencing options to promote more effective outcomes" (Ostrom, 2003, p. 105).

References

Albonetti, C. A. (1987). Prosecutorial discretion: The effects of uncertainty. *Law and Society Review, 21*(2), 291–313.

Ames, K., & Dunham, L. (2002). Asymptotic justice: Probation as a criminal justice response to intimate partner violence. Violence against Women, 8(1), 6–34.

Bachman, R. (1998). The factors related to rape reporting behavior and arrest: New evidence from the National Crime Victimization Survey. Criminal Justice and Behavior, 25(1), 8–29.

Beichner, D., & Spohn, C. (2012). Modeling the effects of victim behavior and moral character on prosecutors' charging decisions in sexual assault cases. Violence and victims, 27(1), 3–24.

Belknap, J., Hartman, J. L., & Lippen, V. L. (2010). Misdemeanor domestic violence cases in the courts, In Venessa Garcia & Janice Clifford (Eds.) Female victims of crime: Reality reconsidered (pp. 259–278). Columbus, OH: Prentice Hall.

Bennett, L., Goodman, L., & Dutton, M. A. (1999). Systemic obstacles to the criminal prosecution of a battering partner. Journal of Interpersonal Violence, 14(7), 761–772.

Berman, G., & Feinblatt, J. (2001). Problem solving courts: A brief primer. Law and Policy, 23(2), 125–140.

Bourg, S., & Stock, H. V. (1994). A review of domestic violence statistics in a police department using a pro-arrest policy: Are pro-arrest policies enough? Journal of Family Violence, 9, 177–189.

Buzawa, E. S., & Austin, T. (1993). Determining police response to domestic violence victims: The role of victim preference. American Behavioral Scientist, 36(5), 610–623.

Buzawa, E. S., & Buzawa, C. G. (1996). Domestic violence: The criminal justice response (2nd ed.). Thousand Oaks, CA: Sage.

Buzawa, E. S., & Buzawa, C. G. (2003). Domestic violence: The criminal justice response (3rd ed.). Thousand Oaks, CA: Sage.

Buzawa, E. S., & Hotaling, G. (2000). The police response to domestic violence calls for assistance in three Massachusetts towns: Final report. Washington, DC: National Institute of Justice.

Cahn, N. (1992). Innovative approaches to the prosecution of domestic violence crimes: An overview. In E. S. Buzawa & C. G. Buzawa (Eds.), Domestic violence: The criminal justice response (pp. 161–180). Thousand Oaks, CA: Sage Publications.

Chen, E. Y. (2013). Is All Punishment Local? The Effects of Jurisdictional Context on Sentence Length. Social Science Quarterly.

Colb, S. F. (2001) Who-dunnit versus what was done: When to admit character evidence in criminal trials. North Carolina Law Review, 79, 939.

Coulter, M. L., Kuehnle, K., Byers, R., & Alfonso, M. (1999). Police-reporting behavior and victim-police interactions as described by women in a domestic shelter. Journal of Interpersonal Violence, 14(12), 1290–1298.

Dixon, J. (1995). The organizational context of criminal sentencing. American Journal of Sociology, 100(5), 1157–1198.

Dorf, M., & Fagan, J. (2003, Fall). Problem solving courts: From innovation to institutionalization. American Criminal Law Review. 40(4), 1501–1511.

Dunn, J. L. (2001). Innocence lost: Accomplishing victimization in intimate stalking cases. Symbolic Interaction, 24(3), 285–313.

Dutton, D. G. (1995). The batterer: A psychological profile (with Susan K. Golant). New York: Basic Books.

Eisenstein, J., & Jacob, H. (1977). Felony justice: An organizational analysis of criminal courts. Boston, MA: Little Brown.

Eisenstein, J., Flemming, R., & Nardulli, P. (1999). The contours of justice: Communities and their courts. Boston, MA: Little Brown.

Engen, R., & Steen, S. (2000). The power to punish: Discretion and sentencing reform in the war on drugs. American Journal of Sociology, 105(5), 1357–1395.

Erez, E., & Belknap, J. (1998). In their own words: Battered women's assessment of the criminal processing system's responses. Violence and Victims, 13(3), 251–268.

Fagan, J. A. (1989). Cessation of family violence: Deterrence and dissuasion. *Crime and Justice*, 11, 377–425.

Fagan, J. A. (1996). The criminalization of domestic violence: Promises and limits. NIJ Research Report. Washington, DC: National Institute of Justice.

Ferraro, K. J. (1997). Battered women: Strategies for survival. In A. Carderelli (Ed.), Violence among intimate partners: Patterns, causes, and effects (pp. 124–140). New York: MacMillan.

Fischer, K., & Rose, M. (1995). When "enough is enough": Battered women's decision making around court orders of protection, Crime and Delinquency, 41, 414–428.

Ford, D. A. (1993). The Indianapolis domestic violence prosecution experiment: Final report submitted to the National Institute of Justice. Washington, DC: U.S. Department of Justice.

Ford, D. A. (2003). Coercing victim participation in domestic violence prosecutions. Journal of Interpersonal Violence, 18(6), 669–684.

Ford, D. A., & Regoli, M. J. (1993). The criminal prosecution of wife assaulters: Process, problems, and effects. In N. Zoe Hilton (Ed.), *Legal responses to wife assault: Current trends and evaluation.* Newbury Park, CA: Sage.

Franklin, E. (2010). When Domestic Violence and Sex-Based Discrimination Collide: Civil Rights Approaches to Combating Domestic Violence and its Aftermath. DePaul J. Soc. Just., 4, 335.

Galanter, M. (1974). Why the "haves" come out ahead: Speculations on the limits of legal change. Law and Society Review, 9(1), 95–160.

Hartley, C. (2003). A therapeutic jurisprudence approach to the trial process in domestic violence felony trials. Violence against Women, 9(4), 410–437.

Hartman, H. H. (1999). Aggressive prosecution requires money, not more mandates. Domestic Violence Report. Kingston, NJ: Civic Research Institute.

Hartman, J., & Belknap, J. (2003). Beyond the gatekeepers. Criminal Justice and Behavior, 30(3), 349–373.

Hirschel, D., & Hutchinson, I. (2001). The relative effects of offense, offender, and victim variables on the decision to prosecute domestic violence cases. Violence against Women, 7(1), 46–59.

Jordan, J. (2011). Professional Discretion and the Use of Restorative Justice Programs in Appropriate Domestic Violence Cases: An Effective Innovation. Chap. J. Crim. Just., 2, 129.

Keilitz, S. L. (2000). Specialized domestic violence case management: A national survey. Williamsburg, VA: National Center for State Courts.

Kennedy, L. W., & Sacco, V. F. (1998). Crime victims in context. Los Angeles, CA: Roxbury Publishing.

Kingsnorth, R. F., MacIntosh, R. C., & Wentworth, J. (2002). Sexual assault: The role of prior relationships and victim characteristics in case processing. Justice Quarterly, 16(2), 275–301.

Knapp, J. (1988). The impact of children witnessing violence. Pediatrics Clinics of North America, 45(2), 355–364.

Kritzer, H. M., & Zemans, F. K. (1993). Local legal culture and the control of litigation. Law and Society Review, 27(3), 535.

LaFree, G. (1980). The effect of sexual stratification by race on official reaction to rape. American Sociological Review, 45, 842–854.

Lerman, L. (1981). Prosecution of spouse abuse innovations in criminal justice response. Washington, DC: Center for Women Policy Studies.

Loftin, C., & McDowell, D. (1981). "One with a gun gets you two": Mandatory sentencing and firearms sentencing in Detroit. Annals of the American Academy of Political and Social Science, 455(1), 150–167.

McDermott, M. J., & Garofalo, J. (2004). When advocacy for domestic violence victims backfires: Types and sources of victim disempowerment. Violence Against Women, 10(11), pp. 1245–1266.

Mears, D. P., Carlson, M. J., Holden, G., & Harris, S. D. (2001). Reducing domestic violence revictimization: The effect of individual and contextual factors and types of legal intervention. Journal of Interpersonal Violence, 16, 1260–1283.

Messing, J. T. (2010). Evidence-based prosecution of intimate partner violence in the post-Crawford era: a single-city study of the factors leading to prosecution. Crime & Delinquency.

Miethe, T. (1987). Charging and plea bargaining practices under determinate sentencing: An investigation of the hydraulic displacement of discretion. Criminology, 78(1), 155–176.

Mignon, S. I., & Holmes, W. M. (1995). Police response to mandated arrest laws. Crime and Delinquency, 41(4), 430–442.

Mills, L. (1999). Killing her softly: Intimate abuse and the violence of state intervention. Harvard Law Review, 113, 550.

Mills, L. (2003). Insult to injury: Rethinking our response to domestic violence. Princeton, NJ: Princeton University Press.

Mirchandani, R. (2005). What's so special about specialized courts? The state and social change in Salt Lake City's domestic violence court. Law and Society Review 39(2), 379–418.

Myers, M., & Hagan, J. (1979). Private and public trouble: Prosecutors and the allocation of court resources. Social Problems, 26, 439–452.

Nardulli, P., Eisenstein, J., & Flemming, R., (1988). The tenors of justice: Criminal courts and the guilty plea process. Boston, MA: Little Brown.

Ostrom, B. J. (2003). Domestic violence courts. Criminology and Public Policy, 3(1), 105–108.

Ptacek, J. (1999). Battered women in the courtroom: The power of judicial response. Boston, MA: Northeastern University Press.

Rebovich, D. J. (1996). Prosecution responses to domestic violence: Results of a survey of large jurisdictions. In E. S. Buzawa & C. G. Buzawa (Eds.), Do arrests and restraining orders work? (pp. 176–191). Thousand Oaks, CA: Sage.

Robbins, K. (1999). No-drop prosecution of domestic violence: Just good policy, or equal protection mandate? Stanford Law Review, 52, 205–233.

Robinson, A., & Chandek, M. (2000). The domestic violence arrest decision: Examining demographics, attitudinal and situational variables. Crime and Delinquency, 46(1), 18–37.

Scheppele, K. L. (1992). "Just the facts ma'am": Sexualized violence, evidentiary habits and the revision of truth. New York Law School Law Review, 37, 123.

Schmidt, J., & Hochstetler Steury, E. (1989). Prosecutorial discretion in filing charges in domestic violence cases. Criminology, 27(3), 487–510.

Sherman, L. W., & Berk, R. A. (1984). The specific deterrent effects of arrest for domestic assault. *American Sociological Review, 49*, 261–272.

Sherman, L. W. (1992). Policing domestic violence: Experiments and dilemmas. New York: Free Press.

Simon, L. (1996). The effect of the victim-offender relationship on the sentence length of violent offenders. Journal of Crime and Justice, 19, 129–148.

Smith, A. (2001). Domestic violence laws: The voices of battered women. Violence and Victims, 16(1), 91–111.

Spears, J. W., & Spohn, C. C. (1997). The effect of evidence factors and victim characteristics on prosecutors' charging decisions in sexual assault cases. Justice Quarterly, 14(3), 501–524.

Spohn, C. C., Beichner, D., & Davis-Frenzel, E. (2001). Prosecutorial justifications for sexual assault case rejection: Guarding the "gateway to justice." Social Problems, 48(2), 206–235.

Stanko, E. A. (1988). Fear of crime and the myth of the safe home: A feminist critique of criminology. In Ylloe, K. and Bogard, M. (Eds.), Feminist perspectives on wife abuse (pp. 75–88). London: Sage.

Stark, E. (2004). Insults, injury, and injustice. Violence Against Women, 10(11), 1302–1330.

Tjaden P., & Thoennes, N. (2000). Extent, nature, and consequences of intimate partner violence: Findings from the National Violence Against Women Survey. Washington, DC: U.S. Department of Justice. Publication No. NCJ 181867.

Ulmer, J. T. (1995). The organization and consequences of social pasts in criminal courts. Sociological Quarterly, 36, 587–605.

Ulmer, J. T., & Kramer, J. H. (1998). The use of transformation of formal decision making criteria: Sentencing guidelines, organizational contexts, and case processing strategies. Social Problems, 45(2), 48.

Walker, S. (2001). Sense and nonsense about crime and drugs (5th ed.). Belmont, CA:Wadsworth.

Welch, C., & Fuller, J. R. (2013). American Criminal Courts: Legal Process and Social Context. Access Online via Elsevier.

Williams, K. M. (1976). The effects of victim characteristics on the disposition of violent crimes. In W. F. McDonald (Ed.), Criminal justice and the victim (pp. 55). Beverly Hills: Sage.

Wolff, N. (2013). Domestic Violence Courts: The Case of Lady Justice Meets the Serpents of the Caduceus. In Problem Solving Courts (pp. 83–112). Springer New York.

Zoellner, L. A., Feeny, N. C., Alvarez, J., & Watlington, C. (2000). Factors associated with completion of restraining order process in female victims of partner violence. Journal of Interpersonal Violence, 56(3), 1081–1099.

Zora, J. (1992). The criminal law of misdemeanor domestic violence, 1970–1990. Journal of Criminal Law and Criminology, 83(1), 46–72.

READING 3.4

Veterans Courts and Diversion Alternatives

By Bradley Schaffer

Veterans courts and diversion concepts are a growing therapeutic jurisprudence trend in the United States. These new judicial approaches are challenging the traditional roles of judges, courts, corrections, county sheriffs, and Department of Veterans Affairs (VA) staff while affording unique alternatives and sanctions. These courts are a special docket within the court system and target veterans charged with nonviolent felony offenses. All these parties are collaborating in this effort to address the needs of military veterans who commit various crimes in order to deal with the aftermath of military service. These courts address the needs of all veterans ready, willing, and able to abide by the court sanctions and make the necessary changes in their lives. The need for intervention, services, and treatment related to their military service has drastically increased in the last several years, especially with the impact of the Operation Iraqi Freedom (OIF) and Operation Enduring Freedom (OEF) wars amid a turbulent economy.

The ongoing OIF/OEF wars have yielded many veterans who are returning with incidences of substance abuse, domestic violence, post-traumatic stress disorder (PTSD), traumatic brain injury (TBI), unemployment, depression, suicidal ideations, fear of redeployment, and

Bradley Schaffer, "Veterans Courts and Diversion Alternatives," *American Jails*, vol. 23, no. 6, pp. 21-22, 24.

related issues. The war's unpopularity and the prospect of a draft have resulted in enlistment standards being relaxed over the past few years. This has allowed recruitment of those with criminal records, commonly referred to as the moral waiver process. Like those of the Vietnam War, many veterans encounter the criminal justice system (CJS) post-deployment or post-discharge and need a treatment alternative versus incarceration. Veterans in this country appear to be overrepresented when it comes to psychosocial problems such as substance abuse, driving under the influence (DUI), higher rates of unemployment, assaults, intimate partner violence (IPV), family conflicts, homelessness episodes, suicides, PTSD, and other problems. Tragically, some studies report that veterans, in general, are twice as likely to commit suicide. Another study (Wortzel, 2009) also suggests that veterans in jails and prisons face an increased risk of suicide. Most veterans have more violent offenses, are usually first-time offenders and honorably discharged (Noonan, 2007). Recent 2009 U.S. Department of Labor unemployment statistics revealed that veterans have a higher unemployment rate than nonveterans. The combination of these issues, along with studies and statistics, all point the timeliness and urgency of utilizing veterans courts and diversion programs.

Legislation

Currently, the Services, Education, and Rehabilitation for Veterans' (SERV) Act, also known as S3379 is pending approval (*www.govtrack.us/congress/bill.xpd?bill=s111-902*). This legislation will significantly aid the veterans in our community who emerge in the criminal justice system with co-occurring mental health and substance abuse disorders. The SERVE Act would authorize funds to go to the Office of National Drug Control Policy for the development and implementation of veterans' treatment courts or to enhance operational drug courts to serve veterans. The grants would be administered by the Department of Justice in consultation with the VA. This is a new and challenging nexus of VA, courts, and corrections staff.

Veterans Courts: When and Where

In 2008, the first veterans court was initiated in Buffalo, New York, by Judge Robert Russell. Since this court began, veterans courts have opened in Orange and Santa Clara counties in California; Tulsa, Oklahoma; Rochester, New York; and Anchorage, Alaska. Most are seeing in excess of 100 veterans per month. New courts are being considered in Phoenix, Arizona; Edwardsville, Illinois; Colorado Springs, Colorado; Las Vegas, Nevada; southern Oregon; and Pittsburgh, Philadelphia, and Erie, Pennsylvania. Their successes will lead to others being developed. The SERV Act would enhance and hopefully sustain these efforts to help spread the veterans court trend across the country.

Generally, the key ingredients of these veterans court and diversion programs are:

- Local county court and/or magistrate jurisdiction.

- A reliable mechanism to verify a veteran's status.
- Court liaison to interface with the VA.
- Development and implementation through partnership between court system, corrections, VA, and other advocate parties.
- Treatment, mentoring, monitoring, advocacy, and support.
- Availability to all veterans from all periods of service.

Diversion Example

The author facilitated an Incarcerated Veterans Outreach Program (IVOP) and the Domestic Relations Clinic (DRC) at the VA in Cincinnati, OH, from 2002 to 2008. Both the IVOP and DRC were diversion and justice-related. The DRC is a 13-week domestic violence prevention program that was approved by the Ohio Department of Rehabilitation and Corrections (ODRC) and Adult Parole Authority (APA) for reentry.

The program targeted veterans having anger and domestic violence problems. Nearly 1,000 veterans were screened for IPV in the DRC. Veterans that successfully completed (56.8%) the program were less likely to repeat (27.6%) the offense. This outcome partially represents what the veterans courts are striving for with all offenders. Hence, this type of program offers an aspect of the problems that are encountered and is a commensurate fit into the veterans court equation. Within the VA system, only Bay Pines and Tampa, Florida; Albuquerque, New Mexico; Cincinnati, Ohio; Buffalo, New York; Tacoma, Washington; and Boston, Massachusetts, have IPV services. The latter are focal studies on IPV and PTSD.

In traditional courts, an offender is sentenced if found guilty. Alternative courts offer qualified participants an opportunity to participate in court-supervised, community-based treatment in lieu of typical criminal sanctions. Some studies on drug courts have shown a lower recidivism rate and cost savings than traditional court approaches. All parties in these courts (e.g., judges, prosecutors, law enforcement, probation officers, substance abuse counselors, therapists, community, advocates, mentors, and families) work together toward a holistic outcome that focuses on recovery and support rather than incarceration.

Studies have shown that as many as half of the troops returning from OEF/OIF suffer PTSD and other disorders, and mental health is the second most-treated ailment for returning veterans in the VA system. However, some question the necessity of separate veterans courts, the stigma of being a veteran, and the underlying theme of culpability in the veteran's offense. Is there a connection between their service and crime?

Veterans have generally committed nonviolent offenses such as DUI, drug possession, theft, domestic violence, and assaults. Veterans who agree to stay clean and sober, take urine screens, obtain

Box 3.4.1 Website Launched for Veterans' Treatment Courts

This past Veterans Day, the National Association of Drug Court Professionals launched the new Veterans' Treatment Court Clearinghouse, the Nation's only comprehensive site currently on the Internet dedicated solely to news and information about Veterans' Treatment Courts.

The clearinghouse offers sections for downloadable resources, important studies and statistics, information on how courts can work with the U.S. Department of Veterans Affairs, updates on national and local legislation, and national and local media coverage.

To access the Veterans' Treatment Court Clearinghouse, visit *www.nadcp.org/learn/veterans-treatment-court-clearinghouse.*

mental health or addiction counseling, and so forth will get their lives back on track. Generally, both the court and VA staff meet with the veterans routinely for case management and progress. Some court systems even assign a mentor or adviser to support the veterans recovery and monitor progress. Once the veteran completes the requirements, charges can be reduced or cases dismissed and/or expunged, if they fail to comply, they risk facing their original criminal charges and could be sentenced to jail and/or prison time.

Summary

Not all veterans commit crimes. However, the transition from military to civilian life is challenging and these individuals cope in many different ways whether exposed to combat or not. Some will isolate themselves and/or turn to substance abuse, domestic violence, assault, etc., trying to cope with their experiences in the war. As for the courts, VA, and military systems, they are overburdened and lack sufficient resources to meet the needs of those suffering from PTSD, readjustment, and other psychological issues. This places veterans at-risk for a host of problems. As in prior armed conflicts, today's veterans also face the growing stigma of war. Many may think getting help is weak, but it takes strength to ask for help. As indicated by the veteran court bench practice and diversion trends, veterans who are involved in a collective, holistic, and multisystem program have a chance to get their lives back in order. Hence, veterans courts and diversion programs are viable options that also warrant chances to survive and thrive.

References

Noonan, M. E. (2007). *Veterans in State and Federal Prison, 2004.* Washington, DC: U.S. Department of Justice, Bureau of Justice Statistics Special Report.

Schaffer, B., & Seals, C. (2008, Fall). Jailed rural veterans: VA/county jail & sheriff reentry outreach collaboration. *Sheriff.* 31–32.

Wortzel, H. S., Binswanger, I. A., Anderson, C. A., & Adler, L. E. (2009). Suicide among incarcerated veterans, *Journal of American Academy of Psychiatry and the Law,* 37: 82–91.

READING 3.5

Juvenile Court and CTE

Partnering for Education and Justice

By Sheila D. J. Calloway

Many years ago when I was working as a criminal defense attorney, I never imagined my professional experience could be relevant to the school system. As I moved up in my career—from attorney to Juvenile Court magistrate and then to Juvenile Court judge of Nashville, Tennessee—I still did not see a place for myself in the world of education. The courtroom was an easy fit for me ... but the classroom?

But then I had the chance to work with the Academy of Law at Cane Ridge High School in Nashville, and a light began to shine. I realized that it is imperative that legal professionals, and Juvenile Court officials in particular, play an active role in the education of our youth. We should not sit back and wait for youth to come to Juvenile Court to learn about juvenile justice, but rather we needed to bring Juvenile Court into schools.

My Introduction to CTE Programs

One day I received an unexpected e-mail from a fellow lawyer who knew that I, as Juvenile Court magistrate, had a passion for the well-being of our youth. He wanted to talk to me about a new venture—the chance to work with youth outside the courtroom. He invited me to join the Human and Public Service Partnership Council, which is managed by the Nashville Chamber of Commerce. The Council was designed to assist Metropolitan Nashville Public Schools (MNPS) officials with providing real-world business experiences to youth in the school system. The Council would also give leaders in the human and public services business/industry an occasion to become involved in the education of our youth.

Although I agreed to participate, I wasn't completely sold on the concept. I was not sure what the role of the court system should or could be within the school system. Nor was I convinced that bringing business partners into the school was even a good idea. After all, I never remembered

Sheila D. J. Calloway, "Juvenile Court And CTE: Partnering For Education And Justice," *Techniques*, vol. 91, no. 2, pp. 21-23.

working with an attorney or a judge, or any other business leader, when I was in class in high school. Could this type of experience really have a positive effect on a young person's education?

It took only a couple of months for me to begin to see the picture come into focus. Sitting at the table with school leaders, principals, teachers and other business and industry stakeholders, it became clear that this was more than a good idea—it could become an integral component of a well-rounded education. The concepts we discussed could bring a new learning technique to the students. It would mean more than just having an occasional guest speaker on "career day;" it meant engaging experts in business to help the schools develop methods to enhance the workforce in our community. It would also allow business experts to advise schools on the types of classes and information students need in order to succeed in the current business climate.

As I became more involved with the Partnership Council, my passion for connecting the legal profession and education continued to grow. I began to see how the Juvenile Court's work with the school system could improve the educational curriculum for students, while also increasing my personal knowledge about Nashville's youth so that I could serve more effectively as a judicial officer. So when the chance came for Juvenile Court to partner directly with a Nashville high school, I jumped at the opportunity. Cane Ridge High School was looking for business partners to help develop their Academy of Law. It was a perfect match.

As part of the Academy of Law Advisory Board, Juvenile Court would work directly with the school, principals, law teachers and students; recommend classes that would be beneficial for students interested in entering the field of law; and work inside the school on a regular basis to expose youth to the field of law and educate them about concepts of justice.

History of Youth Courts

Around the same time that I began to volunteer with Cane Ridge High School's Academy of Law, the Tennessee Bar Association (TBA) expressed interest in revamping a youth justice program in Nashville. According to Denise Bentley, the Youth Court coordinator for TBA, "[Y]outh justice programs are peer-driven, family-focused juvenile delinquency intervention programs that are used as local juvenile diversion programs supported by adults."

Across the nation, these programs are referred to as "youth court, teen court, peer court, student court and youth peer panel" (Global Youth Justice, n.d.). According to the report, "Youth Cases for Youth Courts (2007), there are more than 1,150 youth courts in 49 states and the District of Columbia. The programs are evidence-based models recommended by the U.S. Department of Justice, Office of Juvenile Justice and Delinquency Prevention.

There are many reasons jurisdictions find youth justice programs appealing. According to Bentley, these programs:

- Serve as an education, prevention and early juvenile intervention program.

- Provide a way to hold juvenile offenders accountable.
- Offer a means for educating youth on the legal and judicial system.
- Contribute to a meaningful forum for youth to build competencies and practice and enhance skills.
- Offer an avenue for youth to provide service for and build ties to their own local communities.
- Are among the least expensive juvenile justice intervention programs, given the strong volunteer support from youth and adults.

As I learned more about these programs, it became clear to me that the benefits of bringing youth court back to Nashville would be invaluable.

Although there had once been a youth court program in Nashville, it had been inactive for several years. At the same time, Bentley was witness to the success of youth courts throughout Tennessee, but not within Nashville. There were nearly 2,000 cases going through various youth court programs with less than a 6 percent recidivism rate (the percentage of youth who later reoffended after completing youth court) in the state (Bentley, 2015). The Tennessee legislature expressly approved the youth court program through various statutes.

The Intersection of Youth Court and CTE

And in no time the pieces started coming together. As I met with Bentley about the benefits of youth courts, and as I continued to work with the Academy of Law at Cane Ridge, it became clear that merging the two could be a wonderful way to bring a CTE program to the students. As a result, we decided to design part of the curriculum for students in the Academy of Law around a youth court:

- The students would learn about court processes and the court system while conducting actual court proceedings.
- Juvenile Court would have the opportunity to use restorative justice practices to determine the results in selected delinquency cases.
- The schools would develop a system of internally dealing with students who made mistakes, but who deserved a second chance.
- Together, the system could grow in a positive way while the students had a meaningful learning experience.

We had several meetings with MNPS officials, Cane Ridge leadership and Juvenile Court leaders. Together we developed an educational pathway that would allow junior and senior students to serve as officials in various aspects of the courtroom, e. g., defense attorney, prosecuting attorney, clerk, court officer, case manager and juror; an adult attorney would serve as the judge. We asked local attorneys to serve as mentors for the student attorneys, and the students would receive training from attorneys and officials of Juvenile Court to learn the court processes. They would also receive education and training in restorative justice. It was the perfect CTE moment.

The Benefits of Partnership

Since the swearing-in of the first student participants of the Cane Ridge Restorative Court (as named by the students) in 2011, youth court has expanded to three additional high schools in the Nashville area—Antioch High School, McGavock High School and Whites Creek High School. Each school has made the Youth Court program an important part of the learning process for the student participants. Across the board—for Juvenile Court, the school system and the students—we have seen great benefits from the program.

Most importantly, having youth courts in the schools allows an opportunity for Juvenile Court to use the principles of restorative justice. The premise behind restorative justice is to give victims an occasion to participate in the justice process, while showing offenders the harm caused by and the impact of their actions. Restorative justice gives offenders a means to build upon their strengths and competencies. It also helps the public by making individual victims, the community and the offenders all valuable stakeholders in the justice process (Godwin, 2001). The process of youth court is directly in line with these restorative justice practices.

For the schools, youth courts equip the teachers and leadership with an additional tool to educate students about the law and the justice system. According to Eric Haines, youth court sponsor at Antioch High School, youth court fits well within the school's CTE goals. "The ultimate goal of our small learning community's educational format used at Antioch High School is to provide students with more real-world learning opportunities, and the Youth Court program has been extremely effective in providing such opportunities."

Youth court has also had a positive effect on the students who participate in the program, including the respondents who have had their cases heard by the court. Many of the students who have served in youth court have now decided they want to pursue careers in criminal justice. One parent told Haines that her daughter changed her major in college to begin working toward a career in law based on her experience in youth court.

In the recent article "In Nashville's Youth Courts, a True Jury of Peers" that ran in The Tennessean, student Demetré Ridley discussed his experience in the youth court at Whites Creek High School. He said that his first encounter with youth court was as an offender. After his court proceeding, however, he felt confident that he could have done a better job arguing his case. He now serves as a defense attorney in youth court (Barchenger, 2015). He is just one of many students who have gained confidence and developed professional competencies through youth court.

Building on the Momentum

Through the commitment of MNPS, the Nashville Chamber of Commerce, TBA and the Juvenile Court system, we are excited to continue supplying students with real-world experiences in the field of law in new and innovative ways. By bringing private industry, the court system and the schools together to work toward the common goal of high-quality CTE, Nashville's youth courts have become a true model of restorative justice and a CTE program that is certain to change lives.

Sheila D. J. Calloway is a 1994 graduate of Vanderbilt Law School. Judge Calloway's vision for the Juvenile Court is to "promote positive potential, prevent problems, and pursue fairness and hope" for the children and families of Nashville. E-mail her at sheilacalloway@jis.nashville.org.

References

Barchenger, S. (2015, November 20). In Nashville's youth courts, a true jury of peers. The Tennessean. Retrieved from http://www.tennessean.com/story/news/crime/2015/11/20/nashvilles-youthcourts-true-jury-peers/75900820/

Bentley, D. (2015, March 31). Youth courts model restorative justice. Retrieved from http://www.tba.org/journal/youth-courts-model-restorative-justice

Fisher, M. E. (2007). Youth cases for youth courts: A guide to the typical offenses handled by youth courts. American Bar Association: Washington, DC. Retrieved from http://www.americanbar.org/content/dam/aba/migrated/2011_build/public_education/youthcases_youthcourts. Authcheckdam.pdf

Global Youth Justice. (n.d) Global youth justice: About and mission and vision. Retrieved from http://www.Globalyouthjustice.org/About_Us.html

Godwin, T. M. (2001). The role of restorative justice in teen courts: A preliminary look. American Probation and Parole Association: Lexington, KY. Retrieved from http://www.globalyouthjustice.org/uploads/The_Role_of_Restorative_Justice.PDF

READING 3.6

Mental Health Courts Try to Impose Treatment

By Anonymous

A mental health court in nearby Upper Marlboro, Md., is just one of a growing number across the U.S., according to the *Washington Post.* More than half of U.S. jail and prison inmates—more than 1.2 million people—reported symptoms of mental illness, said a 2006 federal study. That number had quadrupled since 1998, and other studies suggest that the number has continued to rise in recent years. About 300 jurisdictions have set up specialized dockets for judges who impose mental health treatment on some of society's most troubled residents. They are charged with assault, theft, arson, trespassing, harassment, stalking, and other crimes short of homicide. Their mental illness is often part of a tapestry of problems that might include drug addiction or other issues that increase their risk of violence.

The courts operate in different ways from state to state. The one in Upper Marlboro handles only misdemeanor cases. Defendants must agree to participate, and after that, the judge can make mental health treatment a condition of pretrial release or probation. The goal is to restore healthier, more stable people to a community that is ultimately safer for the time, tax dollars and energy spent. The reality is that challenges are inherent in trying to impose the order of the judicial system on the most disordered of minds—in asking someone with a serious mental illness to handle court dates, therapy appointments, medication, and other logistics of a decentralized and often inadequate mental-health-care system. As Judge Patrice Lewis of Prince George's County, Md., said one day after a particularly difficult session: "Sometimes I don't know who can solve all of these problems. Maybe no one can."

Washington Post

UNIT III: CRITICAL THINKING QUESTIONS

1. Describe the differences between appointed and elected judges. Explain how the racial composition of the community affects appointed and elected judges in their sentencing.
2. Discuss the implementation of document management software in the judicial system. Address the types of assistance the software provides for practitioners in the court setting. Indicate how the use of document management software impacts defendants.
3. Identify the challenges in the identification and prosecution of domestic violence cases. Explain how these challenges can be addressed.
4. Explain why veteran courts are created. Identify the key elements of veteran courts.
5. Describe the objectives/goals of restorative justice. Explain why youth courts are appealing as a positive step in juvenile justice.
6. Explain the need for mental health courts. Describe how they are being used.

   Overall

   Using only the information in this unit, how would you describe the judicial system in the United States to someone from another country?

UNIT IV

Punishment and Corrections

Unit Introduction

Unit 4 on Punishment and Corrections examines the crisis of mass incarceration, as well as policies and resources, to structural factors of the prison industrial complex and its corruption. It begins with an examination of criminal justice policies which perpetuate criminal behavior and do not prevent recidivism. CJS scholars and practitioners offer various solutions such as the creation of new legislation aimed at redefining practices hindering the rehabilitation and reintegration of offenders to society (Reading 4.1). Prison overcrowding is another problem of fiscal concern for states, requiring alternative sentencing strategies to decrease inmate populations (Reading 4.2).

Another area of growth is the ever-growing participation of women in corrections as professionals and leaders. The change of demographics in the CJS profession has required a response with gender-focused resources to assist the working relationships of staff and supervisors (Readings 4.3 and 4.4).

Tough-on-crime policies have contributed to the crisis of mass incarceration and prison overcrowding. However, these tough-on-crime policies have disproportionately targeted people of color. To understand the growth of the prison industrial complex, we have to study the socioeconomic conditions which have driven the war on the poor, the war on drugs, and the criminalization of migration (Reading 4.5).

The growth of the private prison industry is plagued with corruption. Investigative journalism has uncovered state policies and practices facilitating criminal violations (Reading 4.6). Another source for corruption is "crony capitalism," which provides incentives for the private prison industry. The incentives provided to the private sector have allowed abusive financial practices leading to the rise of the prison population, and therefore more profit (Reading 4.7). Aside from economic corruption, human rights violations have been a concern for both female and male inmates who have been raped while in custody. The final reading of this unit provides a historical overview which forced the CJS to undergo legislative reform to address sexual violence in the prisons. In 2003 the Prison Rape Elimination Act was passed (Reading 4.8).

READING 4.1

Redefining the Criminal Justice System

By Phyllis Back

Historically, the judicial system, law enforcement, and corrections have each had separate goals and visions for achieving the united mission of safety and justice within the criminal justice community. Today, it appears that these goals have hindered the original intent or purpose of those goals. Progressing into the second decade of the 21st century, the criminal justice system has realized that to achieve its ultimate mission—public safety—for its citizens, it must be united in redefining its goals and visions. This approach requires a profound across-the-board collaboration in a manner that thus far has not been broached.

The contemporary criminal justice system must respond in a proactive rather than a reactive manner to provide both the necessary and immediate sanctions for the convicted, and at the same time ensure that victims' needs are addressed respectfully. One way to achieve this is to implement a program for the sole purpose of sharing information about all new arrests. This information includes:

- Family history and background
- Delinquent offenses
- Previous encounters with the law
- Prior convictions
- Probation or parole mandates
- Work history
- Education
- Stable living conditions

The strategy is to share this information during an inmate's entire involvement with the criminal justice system. For the data program assessment, an offender would be evaluated annually and a

Phyllis Back, "Redefining the Criminal Justice System," *American Jails*, vol. 26, no. 6, pp. 8-10, 12-14.

continuum of care established and shared with every participating agency—beginning at pretrial, following through to the completion of any mandated requirements of post-release sentencing. All information pertaining to treatment interventions, including an offender's progress and failure with his or her treatment plans, is entered into the data program. If an offender relapses or reoffends, the data are updated and the continuum is reestablished to help redirect as needed.

Legislative Approaches

The criminal justice system needs legislative support for sentencing practices such as habilitation, rehabilitation, restoration, and reintegration. Criminal sanctions that lack intervention and prevention strategies are not a deterrent from future criminal activity. Creating laws that mark people as criminals for the remainder of their lives denies former inmates the opportunities available to other citizens.

To address these issues, legislators and officials established the Public Safety Performance Project (PSPP) in 2006. The focus of PSPP is not only to allow ex-offenders to return to the community as productive members of society, but also to improve public safety. (See "Public Safety Performance Project.")

If laws continue to limit offenders' opportunities for employment (including self-employment), education, and housing, the criminal justice system is only fostering further criminal behavior. As mentioned, laws should not be debilitative; otherwise, the interests of public safety are ultimately defeated. Policymakers of the 21st century must re-examine the purpose and outcomes of such laws. Possible affirmative actions include:

- Providing restricted driver's licenses to ex-offenders. Relying on a friend or family member or even public transportation is not always an effective option. Aside from the fact that public transportation is limited in many areas, it is unavailable in most rural regions. An ex-offender's probation or parole is violated when he or she fails to appear on time for a meeting, and many employers require that employees have reliable transportation.
- Allow criminal justice agencies access to the juvenile records (treatment) of adult offenders. Although expunging a juvenile's record once a teenager reaches legal adulthood is currently part of the justice system, it is detrimental to the intervention and rehabilitation methods of the now-young adult who is still involved with the adult criminal justice system.
- Establish local reentry courts in every local jurisdiction. Reentry courts prevent a probation violator's case from becoming backlogged in the court system by providing swift and immediate sanctions for technical violations. Reentry courts also provide an alternative to jail while inmates await a preliminary hearing. Such alternatives allow ex-offenders to remain at home, stay employed, and continue to provide income to support their families.
- Establish reentry probation officers (RPOs) in every local jurisdiction. RPOs provide stringent but realistic requirements for ex-offenders as part of a pre-release transition plan tailored to individual needs. RPOs collect information about an offender's specific needs

(such as medical, mental, and disability services) and help direct that individual to the appropriate resources. In addition, RPOs work with employers, educational institutions, and public housing authorities, thereby helping ex-offenders obtain employment, work to achieve a high school or general education diploma, and secure stable living conditions. RPOs also engage family members in an ex-offenders' reentry plans before release.

- Remove criminal convictions from any records visible to employers and financial and educational institutions if an ex-offender has successfully completed reentry probation; been established in the community (i.e., obtained housing and employment); paid all debts to the courts, community, and victims; and not lapsed into criminal behavior for six years. This enables former inmates to seek employment that increases financial stability. Ex-offenders could perform tasks currently prohibited by law, and apply for credit to buy a home, receive a personal loan, or become self-employed. In addition, they could apply for Federal grants to pursue a college education.
- Change current stipulations that legally prohibit ex-offenders from securing a home in public housing. Public housing (Section 8) regulations are currently too stringent, and in many cases are the only affordable housing option available to ex-offenders. Many ex-offenders' families also live in public housing developments, and for some it is the only viable option after losing their primary financial contributor because of incarceration. Future public housing options should distinguish between violent and nonviolent ex-offenders.
- Review policies and procedures that determine whether a crime is a felony or a misdemeanor, and which degree. The classification process for felony and misdemeanor crimes should be given in-depth consideration and review because many nonviolent crimes are considered felonies on the first or second offense.

Some States are now proactively working to correct legislative decisions to enable ex-offenders opportunities that were previously unachievable. New Hampshire, a State commonly known for having a low crime rate in comparison with other States, enacted Senate Bill 500 (SB 500) on June 30, 2010. The goal of this bill is to reduce recidivism among probation violators and reduce taxpayer spending on correctional costs. "SB 500 will accomplish the following:

- Focus supervision on high-risk offenders by reducing the length of supervision for low-risk offenders.
- Enable probation officers to employ short, swift jail sanctions for minor probation violations, when permitted by judges at sentencing.
- Establish a seven-day residential intermediate sanction for minor parole violators and a designated 90-day parole revocation facility to re-engage parole violators in treatment and with supervision.
- Ensure that everyone leaving prison receives at least nine months of supervision.
- Require nonviolent offenders to serve no more than 120 percent of their minimum sentence.
- Furthermore, New Hampshire's policy changes are projected to generate savings that could be reinvested in drug treatment, mental health services, and rapid drug testing—three areas to which the State currently allocates no State funding to the community through the

Department of Corrections. The majority of individuals in prison and jail have either mental health or addiction disorders (or both), which has been associated with homelessness, joblessness, family dysfunction, crime, and recidivism" Justice Center, The Council of State Governments |CSG], 2010).

Chief Justice John Broderick further states,

> Without available State funds for drug tests, intermediate sanctions to quickly respond to minor violations, or contracted drug treatment in the community, probation and parole officers have few tools beyond revocation. This law will make a difference not only in terms of public safety outcomes, but also in families restored and lives saved. (Justice Center, CSG, 2010)

SB 500 is a landmark bill that comes to the forefront not because of the need to find ways to reduce correctional populations, but as a byproduct of serious Federal, State, and local budget cuts that have produced a ripple effect across the Nation. Nonetheless, other States (including those with a much higher crime rate, such as California and Florida) might consider following New Hampshire's proactive lead in response to a national concern.

Law Enforcement

Following the events of the terrorist attacks on September 11, 2001, every level of law enforcement realized how extremely detrimental it was not to share information with other agencies. Today, law enforcement has made great strides not only in ensuring that current data are shared interdepartmentally, but also that they are collaborating on new information-sharing strategies.

The accomplishments of multijurisdictional agencies have created an awareness of how the incorporation of community-oriented policing (COP) programs is not only necessary but extremely effective. COP programs have successfully brought members of a community together in a united mission for public safety.

> Community-oriented policing is defined as collaboration between the police and the community that identifies and solves community problems. Ideally, such collaboration helps develop better relationships and mutual understanding between police officers and community members, which in turn helps in solving community problems. (RAND Organization, 2003, p. vii)

COP programs create an awareness of the diverse needs within a community, thus enabling law enforcement to better understand and respond to individual and group needs of the citizens by using a proactive approach. These programs actively engage citizens and create relationships with sectors of the community, such as minorities and juveniles, who may have an inaccurate perception of police officers. From their earliest origin in the early 1960s, COP programs have made great strides in building relationships between law enforcement and the communities they serve. The creation of these relationships has:

> *... restorative justice continues to gain support as a realistic and rational intervention.*

- Communicated a department's goals and interest in its citizens.
- Broken down barriers such as racial disparity.
- Protected property.
- Provided a broader understanding to meet the needs of victims.
- Reduced the number of violent crimes.
- Improved public safety overall through problem solving.

In addition, partnering with other groups or individuals in the private sector is a contemporary and proactive method of crime prevention that has true potential for improvements and continues to provide public safety. This method has also proven to be a successful business venture because it allows law enforcement executives, command staff, and departmental managers to redirect the resources that would otherwise be consumed by these logistical tasks.

There also are positive consequences for the courts. For example, the backlog of court dockets would be reduced, thus giving prosecutors, district attorneys, and courts the opportunity to focus more on criminal cases and better meet victims' needs. It would also ensure that sentencing goals are imposed to meet both traditional and contemporary theories of jurisprudence. Ultimately, the greater the success of crime prevention and intervention programs like COP programs, the greater the public safety will become for an entire community.

Criminal Sentencing

Although violent crime rates have decreased over the past two decades, the public's view is seriously distorted, largely because of the media perspective that criminal justice is too lenient and stiffer sentences should be imposed.

The criminal justice system needs to revise its methodology of retribution to improve public safety and the outcomes of the criminal justice system. No longer can warehousing inmates be considered an appropriate and stand-alone resolution through retribution. For the 21st century, rehabilitation, restoration, and reintegration must replace the criminal justice theory of retribution. Future forms of retribution must be derived from research that holistically evaluates the short- and long-term outcomes of the goals and mission of the criminal justice system. The results of such research, new approaches, and insights, will be based on broad evidence-based decision making, beginning with law enforcement and permeating the judicial system and correctional facilities, and extending into the post-release support systems for offenders (Schmalleger, 2012).

Future restorative justice practices will require politicians to educate their constituents about how current sentencing practices have failed and how an over-inflated issue can be corrected. Among a growing number of correctional policymakers and practitioners, victim advocates, court officials, and law enforcement officials, restorative justice continues to gain support as a realistic and rational intervention.

At its best, restorative justice truly represents a unique way of responding to crime through more active involvement of crime victims and the community. It goes far beyond the traditional liberal and conservative positions of the past by identifying underlying truths and joint interests of all of those concerned about crime policy in a democratic society. (Umbreit, n.d)

Although a relatively new concept for sentencing goals, restorative justice equally advances the contemporary and future criminal justice goals of merit as they apply to evolving values in the criminal justice system.

Corrections

Although violent crime rates have decreased, incarceration rates have tripled over the last 30 years. Because of this, an extraordinary amount of tax revenue is consumed by the criminal justice system. Public agencies and political entities are only now recognizing the necessity of increasing public awareness. To successfully accomplish this, it has become necessary to collaborate with the media. This may be done by:

- Creating a variety of public service announcements to educate the community about the criminal justice system and its struggles to provide successful longterm results for public safety. Information on the action recourse plan of the criminal system should be included.
- Covering nonprofit, for-profit, local, and State meetings that discuss sentencing alternatives and their success rate compared with current practices.
- Interviewing criminal justice officials from all levels about their goals for improved public safety, how they plan to improve tax revenue expenditures, and how ineffective traditional sentencing practices will be upgraded. In addition, officials can discuss changes to their goals and mission, what approaches need to be taken, why the success of offender reintegration programs is so vitally important to future generations, and overall anticipated results for public safety.

It may come as no surprise that the general public has no comprehension of corrections and how it correlates with the goals and mission statements of most correctional facilities. The characteristics of corrections are defined as:

- Something that is substituted or proposed for what is wrong or inaccurate; emendation.
- The act of correcting.

- Punishment intended to reform, improve, or rehabilitate; chastisement; reproof.
- Usually, corrections. The various methods, as incarceration, parole, and probation, by which society deals with convicted offenders.
- A quantity applied or other adjustment made in order to increase accuracy, as in the use of an instrument or the solution of a problem. *(Dictionary.com,* 2011) Commonly, the terminology in almost any correctional facility's mission statement discusses the responsibility to:
- Confine an awaiting or convicted offender.
- Ensure public safety.
- Provide adequate access to medical and mental health services.
- Provide treatment through habilitation, rehabilitation, education, and job training.
- Provide reintegration programming to return an offender to the community having gained new skill sets, and assistance with having identified appropriate support systems in the community to facilitate the transition from incarceration and the ability to live as a productive citizen.

All of these goals exemplify the actual definition of corrections and incorporate the purposes of sentencing. However, the way correctional agencies translate and carry out these goals can be as varied as the levels of jails and prisons within the criminal justice system. In the 21st century, the ultimate goal of law enforcement, courts, and corrections should be the successful reintegration of offenders into the community.

To realize the maximum potential of reintegration, reentry programming must be incorporated into the final phase of the sentence of every offender sentenced to a term of no less than six months of confinement, because removal from society for this amount of time significantly breaks down or destroys any pro-social relationships in the community that the former offender had. Studies have shown that criminal sentences of more than two years of incarceration have a negative impact on prisoners when they are released and return home. Consequently, the incapacitation sanction without reintegration services inadvertently increases the risk of recidivism or the likelihood of ex-offenders committing a new crime.

It is important for both the public and the criminal justice system to acknowledge that few if any people choose to live a life of crime. In most cases, engaging in crime is the consequence of an offender's environment. A large percentage of offenders live in lower socioeconomic conditions. Also, it is no surprise that for these offenders to survive or compete with peers, they engage in criminal behavior. Once incarcerated, offenders become even more disadvantaged because they are further denied socially acceptable options to establish prosocial relationships, gain employment that provides income above the living wage, and assist with familial responsibilities. Reintegration through reentry programming during incarceration not only provides an opportunity for offenders to reconnect with these aspects of life, but it can also introduce positive resources and tools to which an offender has not previously been exposed.

Reentry and the benefits of offender reintegration were introduced and defined by President Bush in his 2004 State of the Union Address: "If prisoners released back into society can't find work, or a home, or help, they are much more likely to commit crime" (Bush, 2004).

Continuing to support offender reentry programs, the Obama administration has appropriated Federal funding for reintegration initiatives for State and local governments. These initiatives will develop strategies instrumental to creating partnerships with a variety of other social service agencies. Reentry programming strives to provide the education and training that society has thus far failed to provide. As reentry programming is further researched and improved, revised versions will incorporate essentially every sector of society associated with effectively reintegrating an ex-offender into his or her community.

Understanding that successful reentry programs cannot be achieved solely by experts in the criminal justice field, a massive collaboration of social welfare agencies and community officials across the United States must continue to provide effective reentry programming to inmates both pre- and post-release from jails and prisons. These programs are research based and validated by theory. Because the long-term goal of inmate reentry programs is their continuation beyond release, they will continue to be integral to improving public safety that is both cost effective and reduces tax expenditures.

As previously noted, crime prevention through offender reentry programming must be research-based and community-specific. Thus, it should be understood that not all communities have the same resources or need to fight crime and reduce recidivism rates. Various types of crime affect communities with different demographic variables to different degrees. To create successful programs for offenders, all of these variables should be considered.

> Programs are typically developed on the basis of the current understanding of the dynamic risk factors associated with recidivism, the typical needs of offenders, and the challenges they encounter upon their release from prison. Programs vary according to the recidivism risk factors and the type of social integration challenges they are designed to address. Many programs focus on specific challenges confronting offenders, such as the correction of cognitive thinking errors, addiction, drug abuse, codependency, or unemployment. Likewise, many offender reintegration programs have been designed to deal with specific categories of offenders, such as chronic offenders, drug addicted offenders, young offenders, mentally ill offenders, or dangerous sexual offenders. (Griffiths, Dandurand, & Murdoch, 2010, p. 6)

Reentry programming is prevention through intensive intervention. Therefore, the possibility of future success for reentry programs to accomplish their goals of reintegration and productive citizenship must rely on supporting partnerships between:

- The entire criminal justice community.

Box 4.1.1 Public Safety Performance Project

PSPP helps States advance fiscally sound, research-based policies and practices in sentencing and corrections that protect public safety, hold offenders accountable and control corrections costs. The project carries out these objectives by:

- Helping States collect and analyze data—who is admitted to their prisons, how long they stay, who returns—and the implications of corrections practices for public safety and State budgets.
- Improving States' understanding of how their existing policies, practices, and outcomes for dealing with criminal offenders compare to those of other States; and encouraging States to use the best research available to advance reforms that will reduce crime and recidivism, and deliver a solid return on taxpayers' investments.

PSPP also helps State officials and others share state-of-the-art knowledge and ideas through policy forums; public opinion surveys; multi-State meetings; national, regional and State-level meetings; and online information.

Source: The Pew Charitable Trusts Organization. *Sentencing and corrections.* Retrieved from www.pewtrusts.org/our_work_detail.aspx?id=356

- Legislative bodies at the local level.
- State and Federal governments.
- Social welfare agencies.
- The community workforce.
- Educational institutions.
- An offender's family (familial or extended), friends, and religious organizations.
- The community at large.

Conclusion

Public safety is a concern for every citizen in the United States. It is, however, the responsibility of our government to establish laws, statues, and ordinances that respond to such concerns and provide appropriate safety nets via our Nation's criminal justice system. Legislation proposed to improve public safety in the 21st century should be responsive to research that supports long-term success, and consideration must be given to all productive and/or consequential outcomes that would either promote or diminish the effects on society. Once such laws are codified, established courts, law enforcement, and corrections agencies at all levels should work to enforce them. These branches of the criminal justice system must actively engage the collaborative involvement of all sectors of society associated with the public welfare (public and private) and the community at large. Once these partnerships have joined forces, the entire criminal justice system will see improvements in crime reduction through intervention and prevention and realize a significant cost savings that would otherwise be spent on a stumbling criminal justice system that mirrors today's faltering situational status.

References

Bush, G. W. (2004, January 20). *2004 State of the Union Address* (White Paper). Retrieved from http://www.americanrhetoric.com/speeches/stateoftheunion2004.htm

Griffiths, C. T. Dandurand, Y., & Murdoch, D. (2010, September 13). *The social reintegration of offenders and crime prevention* (Research Report). Retrieved from www.public-safety.gc.ca/res/cp/res/soc-reint-eng.aspx#s2

Justice Center, The Council of State Governments. (2010). *New Hampshire enacts law to reduce recidivism and generate savings.* Retrieved from www.nationalreentryresourcecenter.org/announcements/new-hampshire-enacts-law-to-reduce-recidivism-and-generate-savings

RAND Organization. (2003). *The police responsibility to community-oriented policing in a diverse society* (Policy Brief). Los Angeles, CA: RAND.

Schmalleger, F. (2011). *Criminal justice today: An introductory text for the 21st century* (11th ed.). Upper Saddle River, NY: Pearson Education.

Umbreit, M. (n.d). *Restorative justice.* Retrieved from http://law.jrank.org/pages/1954/Restorative-Justice.html

READING 4.2

The Budget Case for Criminal Justice Reform

By David R. Eichenthal

In response to prison overcrowding, California has turned to county governments to assume the burden of housing tens of thousands of offenders who would otherwise be in state prison. If other states that are in fiscal distress and have overcrowded prisons follow California's lead and turn to local governments to pay for and manage the continued reliance on incarceration as a crime reduction strategy, county and other local governments would face real operational and fiscal challenges. This situation could also provide the impetus for decreasing national incarceration rates, if it leads local governments to implement fundamental reforms in criminal justice systems. Budget officials need to be an important part of that discussion, given the potential cost to local government.

To the extent that local governments pay for and manage incarceration as a crime reduction strategy, local government budget officials need to be an important part of the discussion.

Growth in the U.S. Jail Population

The number of adult inmates in local jails at year end quadrupled to a high of 777,852 in 2008 from 182,288 in 1980. This trend has begun to reverse—nationally, year-end adult population in jails dropped by 2.2 percent and 1.5 percent, respectively, in 2009 and 2010.

To the extent that the jail population is driven by crime and activity in the criminal justice system, it would appear that population reductions should have begun some time ago. In the 1980s and early 1990s, the crack epidemic drove U.S. crime rates to new highs, and government at the federal, state,

David R. Eichenthal, "The Budget Case for Criminal Justice Reform," *Government Finance Review*, vol. 28, no. 2, pp. 61-64.

and local levels responded with new investments in law enforcement capacity. Between 1980 and 1990, arrests increased nationally by 35.9 percent, and the adult jail population increased by 121 percent.[1]

For the last 20 years, though, both violent and property crime have been declining in the United States, 30.7 percent and 24.7 percent, respectively, between 1995 and 2010.[2] Arrest activity is also down, by 13.2 percent to an estimated 13.1 million in 2010, from 15.1 million in 1995.

During the same period, the average daily jail population rose to 748,552 from 509,828. In 2010, 61.1 percent of inmates in a local jail at mid-year had not been convicted of a crime, up from 56 percent in 1995.[3] The overall jail population increased by half over the last 15 years and the number of sentenced inmates increased by approximately one-third, but the number of individuals in jail pre-trial increased by nearly two-thirds.

The Growing Costs

Jails cost money to build and operate. Between 1995 and 2010, the operating capacity of jails in the United States increased to 866,782 from 545,763, or by 321,019 new jail beds at the local level. Assuming a cost of $75,000 per bed to build, this increase in capacity would have cost local governments more than $24 billion over the last 15 years.[4]

Annual local government spending on jails has increased at a faster rate than overall spending or state spending on corrections. Between 1995 and 2009, total local spending on corrections operations nationally increased to $24.9 billion from $10.7 billion.[5] (These data may understate the increase in spending, as costs might be higher when fully accounting for debt service, pension, and retiree health benefits.)

The Implications of California's Realignment

In May 2011, the U.S. Supreme Court upheld a federal court order requiring the State of California to release 30,000 inmates—approximately 20 percent of its inmate population—from the state prison system over the next two years.[6] In April 2011, the state enacted the first of a series of budgetary and statutory actions designed to effect a "realignment" of its current correction system, and California defendants convicted of non-serious, non-violent, non-sexual felonies were to be housed in county jail facilities rather than state prisons, as of October 2011. In addition, counties would be responsible for those defendants when they were released on parole.[7]

This ruling will result in significant changes in the population and operation of county jail facilities throughout the nation's largest state. While California will provide local governments with up to $1 billion in aid by fiscal 2014 for implementing the corrections realignment, that amount represents nowhere near the cost of building capacity for and housing 30,000 inmates who would have previously entered the state prison system.[8]

California counties might respond in various ways. If county governments rely on incarceration, they will need to increase jail capacity. On the other hand, local prosecutors and judges, subject to the ballot box views of local taxpayers, might respond by reducing the number of offenders prosecuted for "non-non-non" offenses and increasing the numbers of offenders charged with felonies that are still eligible for state time. To manage the jail population in a more cost-effective way, local prosecutors and judges could also work to use more alternatives to incarceration. Finally, the increase in convicted inmates in county systems might compel local criminal justice systems to reduce the number of offenders who are currently held in jails pre-trial.

While realignment is causing California counties to start addressing these questions, local governments throughout the nation face the same essential choice: either better manage jail populations or continue to expend increasing amounts of local tax dollars on housing offenders.

Differences in Local Trends

The continued growth in the national jail population has not been uniform, and neither has the recent decline. As the Bureau of Justice Statistics noted in its most recent survey of jails, six jail systems—Los Angeles County, California; Maricopa County, Arizona; Orange County, California; Philadelphia, Pennsylvania; Fresno County, California; and Harris County, Texas—accounted for half of the net national decline in average daily jail population between mid-2009 and 2010.[9]

An analysis of the average daily population and population for the 20 U.S. local jurisdictions with the most inmates in jail reflects wide differences. In 2010, these jurisdictions had an average of 29.75 inmates for every 10,000 residents. San Diego, California, had 15.66 inmates per 10,000 residents, the lowest rate, and Shelby County, Tennessee, had 62.16 inmates per 10,000 residents.

During the last decade, the incarceration rate decreased in 13 of the 20 jurisdictions, led by declines of 20 percent or more in Orange County, Florida; Miami-Dade County, Florida; and Santa Clara County, California. Of the seven counties with the greatest increases in incarceration rates, the incarceration rates in four counties—Philadelphia; Jacksonville, Florida (in Duval County); Sacramento County, California; and Baltimore County, Maryland—grew nearly 20 percent.

The four local jurisdictions with the greatest declines in incarceration rates all experienced declines in average daily population as well. These declines appear to be the result of reductions in crime, at least in part:

- In Orange County, Florida, the two largest police agencies—the Orlando Police Department and the Orange County Sheriff—reported declines in violent crime of 28.8 and 27.7 percent, respectively, during the last decade. Property crime also declined by 5.9 percent and 41.3 percent, respectively, for the two jurisdictions.
- In Miami Dade County, the Metro Dade Police Department and the Miami Police Department

reported declines of 38 percent and 36.7 percent, respectively, in violent crime, and 34.8 and 34.8 percent, respectively, in property crime.

- New York City's record reductions in crime continued through the decade as the average daily population in the city jails also continued to decline. Violent crime was down by 38.8 percent, and property crime was down by 33.2 percent.
- In Santa Clara County, California, the San Jose Police Department—the largest police force in the county—reported a 30.2 percent decline in violent crime, but a 27.2 percent increase in property crime.

Not every local jurisdiction that experienced a reduction in crime, however, was able to convert that into a reduction in either its jail population or incarceration rate. Of the six counties where both population and incarceration rate increased—Philadelphia, Jacksonville, Sacramento, Baltimore, Harris, and Orange County, California—three had significant reductions in crime.

New York's Story

Between 1995 and 2010, New York City's average daily jail population declined by 28.3 percent, to 13,049 from 18,200. During the same period, New York experienced record-breaking reductions in overall crime.

Beyond the public safety and justice benefits, New York has experienced a crime reduction dividend. Having fewer inmates allowed the city to reduce its Correction Department staff by 13.2 percent (or almost 1,600 lull-time equivalent positions), while overall city staffing increased by 18.7 percent.[10] Between fiscal 1995 and 2009, the city's overall operating budget spending increased by 90.6 percent. During the same period, the operating cost for the Correction Department increased by just 27.3 percent. if Correction Department spending had increased at the same rate as overall city spending, rather than at the national average for the same period, it would have increased the cost of local government by $561 million per year.

Strategies For Reductions

A number of strategies exist for reducing the jail population and achieving a criminal justice dividend, and local government budget officials can play a critical role in assessing these strategies.

Reduce Crime. Reductions in the crime rate do not always lead to reductions in the jail population, but it can be an important first step; less crime should ultimately lead to fewer arrests. While crime is down nationally, some jurisdictions have failed to follow national trends: crime rates have either remained steady or, in some cases, increased. In these jurisdictions, efforts to reduce jail population must complement an overall crime reduction strategy.

Early Diversion. Not every criminal offense needs to result in an actual arrest, with processing and short-term stays in jail. Just as every individual stopped for a traffic offense need not be arrested, people who commit other low-level criminal offenses could receive a citation and a court date rather than being arrested and processed through the local jail.

Efficient Early Case Processing. For those individuals who are arrested and booked, it becomes essential that the processing of their criminal case proceed expeditiously. A timely first court appearance can reduce the length of jail stay by allowing for early disposition of the case or pre-trial release.

Early Plea Agreements. Most criminal cases do not go to trial and instead are disposed of by dismissals or pleas. Moreover, most guilty pleas do not result in incarceration—instead, they usually result in some form of alternative, through a formal program, probation, or a fine. Thus, the sooner in the process that prosecutors, defendants, and the court can arrive at an appropriate disposition and punishment, the less time defendants will spend in jail waiting.

Alternatives to Bail or Bond. More reasonable bail or bond might be the single most important step that jurisdictions can take to reduce the jail population—especially the fastest-growing part of the jail population. Bail reform is hardly a new idea. Fifty years ago, the Vera Institute of Justice's Manhattan Bail Project demonstrated that carefully weighing a defendant's ties to the community would allow for an accurate prediction of which defendants posed little to no risk of flight prior to trial.

Non-Jail Sanctions. The available sanctions other than incarceration can affect both the number of pre-trial detainees and defendants convicted of misdemeanors. The extent to which prosecutors can offer sentences other than jail as part of a plea negotiation affects the willingness of defendants to plead guilty early in a case. The availability of alternative sanctions for defendants who would otherwise be sentenced to jail time (as opposed to those who would ordinarily receive probation anyway) also reduces the convicted population.

Court Case Processing. Most judges—and for that matter, most prosecutors and defense attorneys—focus relatively little attention on the speed or efficiency of court cases: instead, their principal concern is to do justice and to zealously represent the interests of their clients. Yet, especially for those defendants who are in jail awaiting trial, all parties should have an interest in speedy justice. More efficient and timely scheduling of hearings, motions, and discovery can all help speed the processing of a case and reduce the amount of time that some inmates spend in local jails.

Reducing Recidivism. One of the most important strategies for reducing crime and reducing the jail population is to lower the number of offenders being released from prison from re-offending. While half of all prisoners released from state prisons return to prison within three years, an even greater number are re-arrested. As a result, reducing recidivism can have an even greater fiscal impact on local jail population than on the state prison population.

Conclusions

If more states start turning to local governments to pay for and manage incarceration as a crime reduction strategy, local government budget officials will need to be an important part of the discussion. The ability to accurately project costs and fiscal benefits can tip the balance in local policy debates.

Notes

1. Howard Snyder, "Arrests in the United States, 1980-2009," U.S. Department of Justice, Bureau of Justice Statistics, September 2011; see, also, arrest data at www.ucrdatatool.gov.

2. Throughout the article, data on arrests and crime are from Synder 2011, www.ucrdatatool.gov and Crime in the United States 2010 at www.fbi.gov/about-us/cjis/ucr/crime-in-the-u.s/2010/crime-in-the-u.s.-2010.

3. Throughout the article, data on jail populations are from the following sources: Todd Minton, "Jail Inmates at Midyear 2010—Statistical Tables," U.S. Department of Justice, Bureau of Justice Statistics, Revised June 28, 2011, Darrell Gilliard and Allen Beck, "Prison and Jail Inmates at Midyear 1996," U.S. Department of Justice, Bureau of Justice Statistics, January 1997; Darrell Gilliard, "Correctional Populations in the United States, 1995," U.S. Department of Justice. Bureau of Justice Statistics accessed at http://bjs.ojp.usdoj.gov/content/pub/pdf/cpius952.pdf. Data for 2010 include all jail inmates at midyear, including the estimated 1 percent of the jail population who were juveniles. Data for 1995 do not include juveniles.

4. The cost of construction varies widely; $75,000 is an example of potential cost.

5. U.S. Census Bureau, Annual Surveys of State and Local Government Finances available at www.census.gov/govs/estimate/.

6. *Brown v. Plata,* 131 S. Ct. 1910 (2011) available at www.supremecourt.gov/opinions/10pdf/09-1233.pdf.

7. Dean Misczynski, "Rethinking the State-Local Relationship: Corrections," Public Policy Institute of California, August 2011 available at www.ppic.org/content/pubs/report/R_811DMR.pdf.

8. Misczynski.

9. Minton 2011.

10. Historical data on spending and personnel were obtained from the New York City Independent Budget Office through its online data files in the Fiscal History section of its website at http://www.ibo.nyc.ny.us/.

READING 4.3

Gender-Focused Resources

For Criminal Justice and Corrections Practitioners

By Stevyn Fogg

The terms "gender-responsive," "gender-specific," and "gender-informed" are slowly becoming a daily part of the lexicon of the criminal justice and corrections fields. This evolution has been long in coming for a variety of reasons. The primary impetus has been the rapid increase and involvement of women and girls in the criminal and juvenile justice systems. This issue of American Jails contains articles introducing gender-specific topics, examining gender-responsive strategies and practices, and providing summaries of supportive solutions. This initial article provides an overview of available gender-informed resources applicable to corrections professionals and practitioners, researchers, law enforcement, and institutional and community supervision staff.

The focus on women in corrections emerged early in the 1970s on the tail end of the civil and women's rights movements. The 1971 National Conference on Corrections included a presentation on "The Special Problems of Female Offenders," advising that an improved understanding of women and their criminal conduct had important implications for managing and treating female offenders. Of particular interest came these key recommendations from Dr. Edith Flynn (1971):

- "Develop crime prevention and diversion programmes to screen socio-medical problems (i.e., addiction, alcoholism) from criminal prosecution."
- "Maximise alternatives to incarceration."
- "Develop suitable prison programmes but follow recommended patterns of community-based programmes (i.e., restore community and family ties; use community resources;

Stevyn Fogg, "Gender-focused Resources: For Criminal Justice and Corrections Practitioners," *American Jails*, vol. 27, no. 6, pp. 55-57, 59.

create educational/vocational programmes to develop self-sufficiency, self-respect and fully functioning community members; reduce the line of distinction between community and institutions; normalise institutional environment; and pursue regionally located facilities)."
- "Conduct research to combat the dearth of information on women offenders."

Since then, there has been growth in research specific to women, which has resulted in reports on State and local initiatives, evidence-based models and assessment tools, training curricula, and technical assistance covering topics such as classification and assessment, case management, treatment and interventions, trauma-informed care, women's physical and mental health, transition and reentry, the use of restraints, sexual safety, women and violence, correctional environments, program assessment, and offender management and supervision.

The National Institute of Corrections (NIC) received its first request for technical assistance related to women in 1977. NIC has since led national efforts to strengthen the research on women offenders and was instrumental in supporting the development of gender-informed risk and needs assessment tools (e.g., the Women's Risk and Needs Assessment [WRNA], Gender-Informed Practice Assessment [GIPA], and the Women Offender Case Management Model [WOCMM]). NIC has also hosted conferences and training events focused on women at various stages of their involvement in the criminal justice system, produced myriad documents on gender-responsive approaches to managing women offenders, provided assistance to numerous State and local agencies working with justice-involved women, established a Federal Resource Center for Children of Prisoners, and produced a National Directory of Programs for Women with Criminal Justice Involvement in collaboration with the Women's Prison Association. Additional information and resources are available on their website, *http://nicic.gov/WomenOffenders.*

Center for Effective Public Policy

One of the organizations with which NIC has had a long history is the Center for Effective Public Policy (the Center), a nonprofit organization first incorporated in Pennsylvania in 1981. The Center has advanced the field on the issue of gender responsiveness in the criminal justice system and built capacity by working effectively with criminal justice practitioners to integrate emerging knowledge and best practices for more than two decades. In addition to their expertise in evidence-based practices, Center efforts have resulted in the development of tools and publications for practitioners, professional meetings and training events, assistance to leaders in assessing their policies and practices against the research, and supporting jurisdictions as they implement new strategies.

Between 2008 and 2011, Center staff coordinated the work of an advisory group of experts to complete the design and pilot testing of an NIC-sponsored women offender policy and practice assessment protocol called the Gender-Informed Practice Assessment (GIPA). GIPA was developed to assess environments and practices within correctional facilities for women. The tool is helpful in serving as a gap analysis of current institutional practices specific to women, supporting quality assurance processes, and providing the feedback necessary to improve current programs and other aspects of the facility (e.g., staffing, culture, services).

National Resource Center on Justice Involved Women

Since 2010, the Center has administered the National Resource Center on Justice Involved Women (NRCJIW) (*www.cjinvolvedwomen.org*), funded by the U.S. Department of Justice (DOJ), Office of Justice Programs, Bureau of Justice Assistance, in partnership with NIC. The NRCJIW supports and enhances the capacities, strategies, and skills of State and local criminal justice agencies in their efforts to manage women offenders in an evidence-based and gender-informed manner with the ultimate goal of reduced recidivism and increased successful outcomes with women involved in the criminal justice system. This support comes in the form of targeted training and technical assistance to State and local criminal justice agencies; the development of training curricula, policy briefs, and coaching packets to address gaps in knowledge and practice; and an information center to enrich practitioners' and policymakers' knowledge about working with women in the criminal justice system. A few key initiatives include:

- **Providing pretrial training and technical assistance to local jails and pretrial services agencies to help them implement gender-responsive approaches to pretrial screening and services.** As part of this project, currently in progress, NRCJIW staff demonstrate how gender-informed practices can be helpful in achieving better pretrial outcomes, provide training on using an evidence-based assessment tool, and help criminal justice agencies assess and engage resources that will meet the immediate and long-term needs of women offenders. Lessons learned will be chronicled in a future Toolkit publication.
- **Facilitating a meeting of the Task Force on the Use of Restraints on Pregnant Inmates.** In 2012, the Center brought together a diverse group of practitioners and stakeholders across the country to develop a best practices statement with regard to the use of restraints on pregnant women confined in correctional facilities. The Center worked collaboratively with the Substance Abuse Mental Health Services Administration's (SAMHSA) Center for Trauma-Informed Care to plan for and conduct this event, which culminated in a draft Best Practices statement. The American Jail Association has taken a lead role in this policy development effort, participating in both the National Symposium and serving on the Task Force. The Best Practices Statement is forthcoming from SAMHSA and the DOJ. This statement will provide jail and prison administrators with a set of principles and recommendations for developing and/or revising policy in this area.
- **Producing a number of practical documents for jails, prisons, community corrections, and other criminal justice agencies, including:**
  - *Using Jail Exit Surveys To Improve Community Responses to Women Offenders*, which describes the use of jail exit surveys as an effective data collection tool for creating a

picture of the characteristics of women in contact with local jails.

— *Systemic Criminal Justice Planning: Improving Responses to Women in Hamilton County, Ohio* and *Responding to Women Offenders: The Department of Women's Justice Services in Cook County, Illinois*, two briefs highlighting accomplishments and lessons learned from jurisdictions that have implemented gender-responsive strategies for women in jail settings.

— *Ten Truths that Matter When Working with Justice Involved Women*, a research brief that has become a resource to inform work with women offenders. This brief uses updated research to explain and describe the difference in pathways to crime and the criminal justice system for women and men offenders; how female inmates respond to institutional discipline, rules, and treatment interventions differently; and the low risk that women offenders pose to institutions and communities, among other important facts that influence effective practice in working with women offenders.

— *Responding to the Needs of Women Veterans Involved in the Criminal Justice System*, which provides criminal justice practitioners with information about the unique needs of female veterans and what is known about their involvement in the criminal justice system. It offers a gender- and trauma-informed approach that criminal justice practitioners can use to manage this population more effectively.

All of these resources are available on the NRCJIW website at *http://cjinvolvedwomen.org/resources*.

Resources on gender-responsive approaches, trauma-informed care, sexual safety, and risk/needs assessment are also available from NRCJIW's other partners:

- **CORE Associates** (*http://coreassociates.org/*) provides training and technical assistance in the assessment, development, implementation, and evaluation of gender-specific services/interventions to agencies, programs, institutions, and systems.
- **The Moss Group, Inc.** (*http://www.mossgroup.us/*) provides consultation, technical assistance, training, and tailored educational resources on correctional management and operations (including gender-responsive strategies; custodial sexual abuse in juvenile and adult settings; implementation of the Prison Rape Elimination Act [PREA] in consultation with the PREA Resource Center); and leadership, mentoring, and aligning organizational and facility culture and strategic planning.
- **Orbis Partners** (*www.orbispartners.com/females*), recognizing the need for gender-informed approaches to working with female offenders, developed such innovative tools as the Service Planning Instrument for Women (SPin-W); the NIC-sponsored Women Offender Case Management Model (WOCMM); and "Moving On," an evidence-based program developed for women at risk for criminal justice involvement.
- **SAMHSA's National Center for Trauma-Informed Care (NCTIC)** (*www.samhsa.gov/nctic/*) provides a technical assistance center dedicated to building awareness of trauma-informed care and promoting the implementation of trauma-informed practices in programs and services.

- **University of Cincinnati, School of Criminal Justice** (*www.uc.edu/womenoffenders.html*) has spearheaded research efforts to establish the Women's Risk and Needs Assessment (WRNA) and provides ongoing training and technical assistance on the implementation of risk/needs assessments for women offenders.
- **Women's Prison Association** (*www.wpaonline.org/*) is a service and advocacy organization committed to helping women with criminal justice histories realize new possibilities for themselves and their families. Through their jail- and prison-based programs, the Women's Prison Association provides direct assistance to approximately 2,500 women and their families each year.

Two pioneers in the field of gender-responsivity, Dr. Stephanie Covington and Dr. Barbara Bloom, lead another seminal resource, the Center for Gender and Justice (*www.centerforgenderandjustice.org*), which seeks to develop gender-responsive policies and practices for women and girls who are under criminal justice supervision. The Center for Gender and Justice is committed to research and the implementation of policies and programs that will encourage positive outcomes for this population.

Conclusion

Administrators and professionals working with women in local jail facilities and other criminal justice policymakers and practitioners will find all of these resources helpful in obtaining research, technical assistance, training, and guidance on becoming gender-informed.

Reference

Flynn, E. (1971). *The Special Problems of Female Offenders.* Paper presented at the National Conference on Corrections, December 6, Williamsburg, VA.

READING 4.4

Pennsylvania Empowers Women in Criminal Justice

By Shirley Moore Smeal, Susan Bensinger, and Susan McNaughton

No matter what state you work in, the criminal justice system has been long viewed as a male-dominated field. The general public, when thinking of correctional officers and superintendents or parole agents and prosecutors, often picture men in those positions. Several decades ago, that was an acceptable norm. However, today that norm is being challenged. While men continue to hold a majority of these positions, more women are stepping up and taking initiative to lead in these areas.

Within the Pennsylvania Department of Corrections (DOC), specifically, there are more than 16,000 dedicated employees who perform a multitude of job duties. A diverse group of individuals are tasked with providing public safety for the citizens of Pennsylvania as well as operating correctional facilities that provide humane incarceration while assisting inmates with skills to reintegrate into the community. While women first began assuming prison duties in the early 1980s, today they represent only 25 percent of the corrections workforce in Pennsylvania.

Why should citizens even care about this? Because women are beneficial to any field due to the fact that they look at issues and situations differently than men. Often, women are also great at multitasking and possess excellent communications skills. Women should be encouraged to step out of their comfort zones and perform jobs that traditionally have been filled by men.

Executive Women's Leadership Conference

Despite efforts of DOC officials during the past 12 years to provide employees with empowerment opportunities through annual symposiums, during tours of the facilities, interactions with staff and conversations with DOC Secretary John Wetzel, it became obvious to DOC officials that more was needed in order to support women specifically, not just in the field of corrections, but in the criminal justice system overall. In an effort to expand the DOC's work in this area, officials

Shirley Moore Smeal, Susan Bensinger, and Susan McNaughton, "Pennsylvania Empowers Women in Criminal Justice," *Corrections Today*, vol. 74, no. 6, pp. 25-27.

recently spearheaded the Executive Women's Leadership Conference where, for one day, women were encouraged to support each other, provide guidance and advice to each other, and pursue goals.

Inspired by the Association of Women Executives in Corrections' mission to provide leadership development for executive women, to support the career advancement of women in corrections and to promote informed discussion of correctional issues in an atmosphere of mutual respect,[1] the first Executive Women's Leadership Conference in Pennsylvania included participants from several state criminal justice agencies. It was important to the DOC that the conference provide an atmosphere of mutual respect where women believed they were valued and recognized for the significant role they play in public safety. Overall, the mission of the conference is to promote the professional and personal growth for DOC employees and to recognize and appreciate the department's diversity.

At the conference held on April 12, 2012, more than 200 women from the DOC. Pennsylvania Board of Probation and Parole, Pennsylvania Commission on Crime and Delinquency, Office of General Counsel and county prisons embarked together on a journey of self-awareness with the freedom to express the goals of future advancement and past accomplishments. Many attendees, having already attained executive levels, supported and advised one another to remain true to oneself. "Set goals, learn from others, both male and female, reach for the top, understand failures, expect roadblocks and be who you are" were messages setting the theme for the event.

During the conference, DOC Executive Deputy Secretary Shirley Moore Smeal spoke to attendees about her experiences working in the male-dominated field of corrections:

> I started my career as a clerk typist and have progressed through the ranks of purchasing agent, superintendent's assistant, unit manager, executive assistant, deputy superintendent, superintendent, regional deputy secretary and now executive deputy secretary. Regardless of the position held, one fundamental challenge remains—1 am female. It seems like yesterday that male officers 1 supervised very clearly let me know that working inside of a facility was no place for a woman and that my place was to be pregnant and in the home.

Moore Smeal also discussed effective leadership styles. "We are here to work side-by-side with our male counterparts," she said. "While celebrating our female staff and the many accomplishments made, we are looking to the future—understanding that each of you are to carry the message to your work site, to empower others around you. Build up and support your co-workers." Moore Smeal also stated that women each have a responsibility to mentor others to take her place. She emphasized that working in the male-dominated field of corrections is educational, challenging and rewarding.

Pennsylvania Gov. Tom Corbett, who made the conference a priority, fitting it into many appearances and obligations for that day, acknowledged that the female viewpoint is different than that of males. "Women approach a problem or situation differently than their male counterparts," he said.

He then cited a study conducted several years ago by a New Jersey management consulting firm that identified a number of characteristics that distinguish women leaders from men when it comes to qualities of leadership. Those characteristics are assertiveness, persuasiveness and flexibility, in addition, women are risk-takers, task-oriented, empathetic and offer strong interpersonal skills and genuine caring. Throughout his speech, Corbett emphasized his points by using his wife as an example, stating she is his best and truest sounding board. He spoke openly and honestly of the need to hire, not based on gender, but based on qualifications.

Leaders from across the country also attended and spoke to the attendees. Margaret Moore, Ph.D., assistant professor at the University of the District of Columbia and a DOC alumna, having served as the first female superintendent at a male facility and later deputy commissioner, gave advice to the conference attendees. "Model the way for your co-workers," Moore said. "Components of this concept include: show by actions, work side-by-side, be willing to do the same task, have a positive attitude, respect others, be proud and enthusiastic and be about 'we.' Make it a team effort,"

Representatives from a variety of criminal justice organizations gathered for a panel discussion, including the Office of Chief Counsel, the Pennsylvania Board of Probation and Parole, Berks County Prison, the State Correctional Institution at Rockview and the Moss Group. The discussion included questions regarding balancing professional and personal life. Attendees gave each other career strategies and advice on making oneself more promotable. The panel discussed being a female in a male-dominated career while remaining true to oneself, not emulating male traits. Although women are viewed as the caretakers, attendees advised each other to "take care of you—mind, body and soul."

Taking advantage of the time together, a working lunch was held so participants could hear from Pennsylvania Secretary of State Carol Aichele and her husband, Pennsylvania General Counsel Stephen Aichele. A true power couple working in state government, they used humor and a blunt charm that was endearing and informative. Carol Aichele talked about her decision to be a full-time mother but not necessarily a stay-at-home mother. She remained involved in her community by volunteering while making contacts in local government. When the time was right, she reentered the workforce full time. Stephen Aichele cultivated his career in private practice while always being involved with his wife's achievements. After the lunch, presenters held breakout sessions in intimate classroom settings that gave the women the opportunity to ask questions.

DOC Secretary John E. Wetzel wrapped up the day with expressions of enthusiasm. His drive and positive attitude was infectious and elevated the conference to an even higher level, stressing again that the DOC "will hire and promote based on ability not on anatomy." As the event concluded, each participant felt valued in her mission and the mission of the DOC. With clear direction to pay it forward and lift up others, to continue as a team and make every day a day of accomplishment, the women returned to their workplace confident in their ability to make the criminal justice system stronger.

This was not a one-time event, however. Officials are already planning to provide this opportunity to other women in criminal justice by expanding attendance at future conferences to include additional women from other Pennsylvania state agencies, "This is just the beginning of an important movement," Moore Smeal told attendees. "Stay tuned."

Note

1. Association of Women Executives in Corrections Mission Statement, Retrieved from www.awec.us.

READING 4.5

Unpacking the Crisis

Women of Color, Globalization, and the Prison-Industrial Complex

By Julia Sudbury

The emergence of a vibrant antiprison movement has brought attention to the crisis of mass incarceration in the United States. This crisis is a direct outgrowth of tough-on-crime policies that have lengthened prison sentences and widened the net of activities that U.S. society deals with through imprisonment. As more and more people have received longer sentences, federal and state governments have responded to the ensuing overcrowding by building more prisons and contracting with private prison firms for additional prison beds. Low-income women and girls of color have particularly felt the impacts of the exponential growth in the use of prisons and jails.[1] Since the 1980s, governments have withdrawn resources from community infrastructure and economic supports for low-income families, in part to fund costly law enforcement and prison budgets.[2] This shift in public spending priorities is one manifestation of a global process of economic restructuring. Faced with ever-shrinking options amid these social and economic transformations, women turn to survival strategies that are increasingly criminalized. Poverty, racism, gender violence, and sometimes addiction intersect to create a cycle of survival, criminalization, and repeated incarceration. At the same time, as mothers, grandmothers, and community activists, women in low-income communities of color bear the burden of supporting and advocating for loved ones who have been locked up and caring for their dependents.

To address the cycle of mass incarceration, activists, academics, and policy makers need to understand the socioeconomic conditions that lie at its root. Unpacking these root causes allows us to identify meaningful transformative possibilities for long-lasting change. Connecting these phenomena with global transformations enables us to identify commonalties with women's struggles for justice in other parts of the world and thus strengthen transnational feminist solidarities. This essay examines four interlocking factors that underlie the prison crisis. First, I examine the impacts of globalization and economic restructuring on low-income communities in the United States. The rise in low-waged casual labor and cutbacks in welfare, education, health care, and social provision all contribute to women's economic insecurity, leading to the use of criminalized survival strategies. Second, I explore the war on drugs, a set of policies and practices that are U.S. led but global in nature and that have led to an exponential rise in domestic and international imprisonment. Third, I explore the role of globalization in fueling migration from the global South, the criminalization of migration, and the growth in immigrant incarceration in the United States. Finally, I describe the emergence of the prison-industrial complex, a symbiotic relationship between corporate and governmental interests that has fueled prison expansion in the United States and increasingly around the world. As an activist-scholar, my writing aims to encourage the reader to live in the solution rather than simply dissect the problem. The second part of the essay discusses the antiprison movement. I explore the antiracist and feminist abolitionist visions developed by antiprison activists and describe steps toward a world without prisons. This section includes examples of contemporary abolitionist work in the United States and Canada. I hope that these examples may dismantle the apparent omnipotence of the prison-industrial complex and help inspire grassroots action.

The Problem

Economic Restructuring and the War on the Poor

The introduction of Reaganomics in the 1980s signaled the beginning of a lasting shift in U.S. economic policy.[3] Arguing that "small government"—a combination of reduced spending on social provision, reduced government restrictions on corporate profit-making, and tax cuts—was necessary to stimulate economic growth and stem unemployment, the Reagan administration gradually rolled back the supports and protections on which many working families relied. Despite the rhetoric of small government, Reagan dramatically increased government spending on the military and imprisonment. During the 1980s, both federal and state criminal justice budgets grew exponentially as prison populations swelled due to tough-on-crime legislation and the war on drugs.[4] This shift from welfare state to law-and-order state was not unique to the United States. In Britain, for example, Thatcherism pushed a laissez-faire government, the ascendance of the free market, privatization, union busting, and cutbacks to the welfare state. And like Reagan, Thatcher pursued a racialized war on crime that targeted low-income communities of color for surveillance and punishment.[5]

At a global level, these strategies can be seen as political responses to corporate economic restructuring. Since the 1970s, corporations have begun to separate their manufacturing and administrative components. By using new technological developments, corporate headquarters in advanced capitalist nations could manage manufacturing operations in locations where land and labor were cheaper. Corporations headquartered in the United States and Europe were quick to capitalize on the low-waged, nonunionized women workers in nations in Asia, Latin America, and the Caribbean, many of which were still struggling with the legacies of colonialism and underdevelopment. As manufacturing moved overseas, economies in advanced industrialized countries began to shift toward service industries and specialized management and technology. A segmented labor market emerged, consisting of highly paid, high-tech positions for highly educated workers and more numerous low-waged, nonunionized, and casual positions.[6] With well-paying unionized skilled trade jobs in decline, women and men in urban communities faced unemployment or dead-end jobs that did not pay enough to support a family. Cutbacks and trickle-down economics were a double-pronged tool that governments in advanced industrialized nations used to reduce the potential economic burden of a growing population that was surplus to the needs of global capital. And criminalization and warehousing were the weapons of choice for minimizing the potential for social unrest and dissent.[7]

During her reign, Thatcher coined the acronym TINA, There Is No Alternative, to describe the lasting shift in economic policy signaled by free trade and economic liberalization. Since the 1980s, even left-leaning parties have been unwilling or unable to turn the tide of neoliberalism.[8] The impact on low-income women and girls of color of three decades of neoliberal policies has been severe. A key aspect of the move toward "small government" has been the radical transformation of welfare. Welfare reform has targeted women of color, depicting them as "welfare queens," overly dependent on state handouts, and as irresponsible mothers. Although the rhetoric of welfare-to-work programs emphasized "tough love" to wean poor women, in particular mothers, off dependency and push them to build economic independence, the reality has been the ejection of numerous families from the welfare rolls into minimum-wage jobs.[9] Because economic restructuring has involved the creation of numerous casual, low-waged jobs that often lack health insurance and seldom pay enough to cover adequate child care as well as living expenses, the welfare-to-work policy has largely furthered the sedimentation of poor women of color into a permanent poverty trap.[10]

With social expenditure decreasing, criminalization has become the primary response to growing poverty. Women's poverty is criminalized in numerous ways. Women who turn to the street economy, sex work, petty theft, welfare "fraud," or other economic survival strategies in the face of declining incomes and few economic opportunities are frequently caught up in the revolving door of initially short and then lengthier jail times.[11] For poor young women of color, especially those who have escaped abusive homes, the courts have become the state's alternative to adequate social services, youth programming, and educational opportunities. Queer and transgendered youth and young people of color who have been in foster or institutional care are particularly likely to spend time in the juvenile-justice system and to "graduate" to adult prisons and jails.[12] The criminalization of poverty also occurs when women with mental illness, including many who live with post-traumatic symptoms from childhood and adult sexual trauma, come in conflict with the law, either through antisocial or violent behavior or through self-medication with illegal drugs.[13] The next section examines the primacy of the war on drugs in the prison boom of the past three decades.

Making Addiction a Crime: The War on Drugs

In 1973, the state of New York's Rockefeller drug laws ushered in a new era of punitive antidrug measures and a shift toward determinate sentencing, with fixed sentences related to the quantity of drugs involved, regardless of the individual's history or circumstances.[14] By the early 1980s, Reagan had formally announced the "war on drugs" as a government priority, and throughout the 1980s, the federal government pumped billions of dollars into combating the newly identified "enemy."[15] With federal initiatives led by the "drug czar" and dramatic media representations fueling public fears, states soon began introducing mandatory sentencing. As judges were compelled to hand down lengthy sentences, even when they believed that the defendant posed little threat to public safety, the number of women in prison and the length of time they spent inside grew exponentially throughout the 1980s and 1990s.

The war on drugs has been a major contributor to the U.S. imprisonment binge. It has also expanded the criminalization of people by race and gender, leading to sharp increases in the numbers of incarcerated African American women and Latinas.[16] Women come into contact with the war on drugs both as consumers of criminalized drugs and as low-level dealers and couriers or family members of participants in the drug industry. The war on drugs has coincided with the retrenchment of health services in general, and drug treatment facilities in particular. Increasingly, women of color who are struggling with drug addiction are processed through the criminal punishment system rather than through drug rehabilitation programs or services that offer support for underlying issues, such as mental illness and trauma. Rather than viewing a rise in drug use as a public health crisis requiring generous public funding of treatment centers, education programs, mental health facilities, and clean-and-sober living arrangements, the war on drugs identifies drug use as a threat to public safety and pumps funds into the arrest and incarceration of both users and suppliers of criminalized drugs.

In the 1990s, low-income African American communities were particularly hurt by the moral panic about crack cocaine, a cheaper, more accessible form of the drug than the powder form. The media presented the "crack epidemic" as a crisis that posed a far greater threat to public safety than did the drugs more commonly used by middle-class users, such as powder cocaine, heroin, and methamphetamine. In addition, although the majority of crack users are white, the use and retail marketing of the drug was depicted as a black phenomenon.[17] Thus, policing operations focused on low-income urban black communities, sweeping up female family members and users as well as women and men working as low-level dealers and distributors. In addition, defendants in trials involving crack continue to be subject to discriminatory sentencing practices whereby the penalty ratio for crack versus powder cocaine is one hundred to one. Thus, a woman in possession of only five grams of crack cocaine receives the same sentence as one who possesses five hundred grams of powder cocaine.[18] Kemba Smith's case (see chapter 68 in this volume) demonstrates the intersection of racial targeting, gender violence, and punitive drug laws. A young mother and college student, Kemba neither used nor dealt in drugs, yet she was punished for "conspiring" with her abusive boyfriend and sentenced to a 23.5-year mandatory minimum sentence. Kemba was subsequently granted clemency by President Clinton in his final days in office and has dedicated her life to working for the women sentenced in the war on drugs.

The war on drugs has also disproportionately affected Latino/a communities. In 1997, Latinas/os comprised 33 percent of people held for drug offenses in federal prisons.[19] Latino/a communities in the United States and in Latin American countries have been stereotyped by the media and government initiatives as "narcotraffickers."[20] Whereas African American communities are stereotyped as dealers and distributors, Latinos/as are largely depicted as traffickers who bring drugs across the border or as "illegal aliens" who live outside the law. Both sets of controlling images lead to disproportionate policing, arrests, and incarceration rates. Latinos/as are subject to overpolicing, random stops for suspected insurance and immigration violations, inadequate and inaccessible legal representation, and language barriers at every level of the criminal justice system. For Latinas, racial discrepancies and cultural barriers are exacerbated by gendered vulnerabilities. As Juanita Díaz-Cotto demonstrates in her study of Chicana "pintas," Latinas are likely to self-medicate with drugs and alcohol to deal with childhood and adult gender violence and abuse. Once arrested, Latinas are disadvantaged by their low status in patriarchally structured drug networks; they often lack the valuable information necessary for plea bargaining. Finally, Latinas are sometimes caught in law enforcement efforts to intercept their male family members and may be encouraged to take full responsibility for a crime in order to protect their menfolk.[21]

Latin American women are also vulnerable to criminalization and incarceration within the United States. The federal government wages a war on drugs both within and outside its borders. The U.S. strategy of destroying agricultural land to eradicate the coca crop, while failing to address demand for illegal drugs, promotes economic insecurity among rural communities, which are simultaneously suffering from the impact of free-trade agreements in the region.[22] In the context of foreign debt, structural adjustment, civil unrest, and U.S. interventions in Latin America, women face increasingly limited survival options. With the unabated demand for illegal drugs in the United States, acting as a courier or "mula" is one option available to women struggling to make ends meet. Once they cross into the United States and are interdicted at the border or in the airport, these women are treated as "traffickers" and consequently receive lengthy sentences disproportionate to their low-level involvement in the illegal drug industry. On completing their prison time, these women are deported to their countries of origin, with few resources to survive, and are thus forced back into the cycle of poverty and criminalization.

If we look only at the racial and ethnic makeup of women's prison populations, we overlook the impact of immigrant status. Latinas in U.S. prisons include women arrested when crossing the border, women who were living in the United States either as documented or undocumented immigrants before their arrest, and women who were born in the United States. The next section turns to the criminalization of migration and argues that Latina immigrants are the overlooked face of women's imprisonment in the United States.

Criminalizing Migration

Globalization creates the structural conditions for mass movements of women and men around the globe, leading immigrant rights activists to label migrants "the refugees of globalization."[23] In 2005, approximately 185 million, or one in thirty-three of the world's population were migrants, and nearly half that number were women.[24] Globalization and neoliberal economic policies drive women's migration in multiple ways. Women are particularly vulnerable to structural adjustment policies, often imposed on debt-laden developing nations by the International Monetary Fund. Like economic reforms in the United States, structural adjustment policies involve cutbacks in government spending on education, health care, and social provision. As women struggle to pay more for basics such as education, health care, water, and food, migration becomes a realistic alternative to extreme poverty and offers the opportunity to provide remittances that can support dependents. Women are also affected by food insecurity caused by free trade and the global integration of food production, processing, and sales.[25] With less access to growing their own food, women must work for transnational corporations or migrate if they are to meet family nutritional needs. Women who migrate to work in export-processing zones are also more likely to continue their migration journeys into the global North.

A key aspect of globalization is the selective control of national borders. Although free-trade agreements open borders to the flow of capital and enable free movement of a highly educated capitalist elite, they call for much stricter control of the movement of workers. As socioeconomic conditions at home drive outmigration from countries in Latin America, the Caribbean, Asia, and the Philippines, labor needs in U.S. agriculture and service industries draw workers across the border. Many women rely on family reunification provisions in immigration legislation or come on temporary work visas, but those who are ineligible are forced to rely on migrant "traffickers" who facilitate illegal entry into the country. Once these women are in the United States, racism, xenophobia, and anti-immigrant sentiment combine with lack of documentation to ensure that they are restricted to low-waged, casual, and nonunionized labor in the service sector, jobs as domestic caregivers, or work in the sex industry.

During the past three decades, the budget of the U.S. Citizenship and Immigration Services (USCIS, formerly the Immigration and Naturalization Service, or INS) has grown exponentially as U.S. immigration policy has become more punitive. Although the USCIS is also tasked with providing information and services to "new Americans," budget increases over the years have focused on enforcement and interdiction, with an emphasis on the U.S.-Mexico border. Increasingly, the goal of controlling migration has been conflated with that of controlling drug importation and crime, and it has been classified as a national security concern rather than a matter for economic policy. This emphasis in turn has led to closer integration of the USCIS, the Border Patrol, the Drug Enforcement Agency, the military, and the police.[26] Enforcement activities on the U.S.-Mexico border have become militarized operations, involving military technology, surveillance equipment, and tactics to trap undocumented migrants. Women are particularly affected by the militarization of the border because they are vulnerable to the sexual assault and harassment that is a documented characteristic of war zones.[27] These operations clearly demonstrate the racialization of immigration policy, with Latinos/as making up 90 percent of deportations.[28] The surveillance and policing of Latinos/as, who are racially profiled as potential "illegal aliens," ensures that a disproportionate number of Latino/a immigrants are picked up for other infractions, from drug possession to driving without a license. These frequent interactions with law enforcement lead to higher rates of arrest and incarceration.

Noncitizen immigrant women who are convicted of offenses other than immigration-related charges are labeled "criminal aliens" by the state. These women make up 27 percent of the federal prison population. In the state prison system, 80 percent of noncitizens are imprisoned in five states: Arizona, California, Florida, New York, and Texas.[29] The policing and criminalization of immigrant Latinas has therefore been an important factor in U.S. prison expansion in the past three decades and has become a feature of life in the border states in particular. The majority (over 60 percent) of incarcerated noncitizens are from Mexico, with women and men from Colombia, the Dominican Republic, Jamaica, and Cuba making up about one-fifth of the federal noncitizen population. When globalization, free trade, and neoliberalism in Latin America and the Caribbean intersect with xenophobic and racialized law enforcement in the United States, the result is the criminalization of migration and the growth of globalized prison populations.

Profiting from Punishment: The Rise of the Transnational Prison-Industrial Complex

Since the late 1990s, antiprison activists and scholars have adopted the concept of the "prison-industrial complex" to explain the complex web of overlapping interests that together have driven three decades of prison expansion. The concept derives from the "military-industrial complex," a term coined by President Dwight D. Eisenhower to describe the "conjunction of an immense military establishment and a large arms industry."[30] Making visible the corporate interests behind the Cold War arms buildup, Eisenhower called on "an alert and knowledgeable citizenry" to prevent this complex from exerting "unwarranted influence" over national policy. The term *prison-industrial complex* was first used by urban theorist Mike Davis in 1995 to describe a multibillion-dollar prison-building boom in California that, he argued, "rivals agribusiness as the dominant force in the life of rural California and competes with land developers as the chief seducer of legislators in Sacramento."[31] Conceptualizing prison expansion as the result of interlocking economic and political forces has enabled radical intellectuals to explain the apparently illogical willingness of politicians to continue to spend billions of dollars on a failed social policy despite evidence that the prison buildup has had no positive impact on public safety or the fear of crime.

The concept captures two related processes. The first is the transformation of prisoners into profits. In private prisons, criminalized and processed bodies are bought, sold, and traded. Federal and state governments pay private corporations a fee per prisoner per day, thus transforming the deprivation of a human being's freedom into a transaction that can be traded on the stock market. The majority of private prisons are designed, constructed, managed, and financed by multinational corporations. Thus, this form of private enterprise has integrated low-income communities of color into the global economy. Warehoused in megaprisons designed for economies of scale rather than rehabilitation, prisoners have become a commodity that is sold to governments, and ultimately to taxpayers, under the guise of "keeping us safe." And the corporations and their stakeholders that profit from these transactions in turn benefit from and actively promote criminal justice policies that guarantee rising rates of incarceration.[32]

The dramatic increase in the number of people sentenced to time behind bars has led to a prison-building boom in the United States, Canada, Latin America, parts of Europe, Australia, and elsewhere. Prison construction has also become denationalized. Today a prison in South Africa is likely to have been built by a U.S.-headquartered multinational corporation, or a prison in Chile may be constructed by a Chilean subsidiary of a French-headquartered multinational corporation. Prison expansion has generated a host of profit-making opportunities for both multinational and local construction firms, architecture firms, and manufacturers of security and telecommunications equipment, as well as for service industries, including real estate agents, banks, and restaurants. These profits flow whether the prison is ultimately operated by the state or by a private company. Imprisonment transforms immense sums of public money into private profits. These funds are then unavailable for expenditure on the public workers and facilities—from schools to rehabilitation centers—that support families and individuals in crisis before they can come into conflict with the law.

The second process that scholars have drawn to our attention is the cementing of the prison into local economies. For rural towns devastated by economic restructuring and free-trade competition, prisons seem to be a panacea for economic stagnation and population loss.[33] Amid the farm bankruptcies and factory closures caused by the rise of corporate agribusiness and the influx of foreign products, the jobs and construction contracts offered by new public or private prisons have pitted small towns against each other in bids to offer the most attractive package of tax breaks, cheap land, and other incentives. Politicians and business elites in rural towns in the United States and Canada have promoted prison construction as a form of economic development, touting prisons as a recession-proof and nonpolluting industry.[34] Ultimately, however, prison towns fail to reap the promised benefits and instead suffer from inflated real estate prices, high unemployment, and environmental degradation.[35]

Although the prison-industrial complex emerged in the United States, the past two decades have seen it become a transnational phenomenon. Punitive U.S. measures—including tough sentencing for troubled youth, three strikes, truth-in-sentencing policies, and mandatory minimums—have spread internationally.[36] As politicians around the world have pushed their own versions of U.S.-style tough-on-crime strategies, global prison populations have begun to rise inexorably. As a result, countries have again turned to the United States for an answer to the dilemma of how to lock more people away while minimizing the cost of growing prison populations. Mass warehousing in "no frills" superjails that may house over a thousand prisoners has increasingly become politicians' solution, fueling the growth of a transnational prison-industrial complex.

Envisioning a Solution: Women Imagine a World Without Prisons

The brutal impact of the prison-industrial complex on families and communities has led to the creation of a strong grassroots antiprison movement. This movement is made up of a plethora of organizations, campaign and lobby groups, activist collectives, nonprofits, prisoner associations, and student groups. These groups focus on a range of intertwined issues, including the war on drugs, police accountability, incarcerated women, LGBT (lesbian-gay-bisexual-transsexual) prisoners, political prisoners, private prisons, prison expansion, prison financing, the death penalty, juvenile justice, human rights violations in prisons, access to health care, control units, deaths in custody, post-9/11 harassment and detention of Muslims and Arab Americans, detentions in the war on terror, and the rights of undocumented and incarcerated immigrants.[37]

Although men make up over 90 percent of prison populations in the United States and globally, women, particularly women of color, play critical roles in antiprison movements. In the United States, activist-intellectuals and former prisoners such as Angela Y. Davis, Ruth Wilson Gilmore, Ramona Africa, Linda Evans, and Kemba Smith have played key roles in analyzing the prison-industrial complex, popularizing understanding of this analysis, and mobilizing opposition. As activists and mothers, women do much of the hard work of community organizing and providing support to prisoners and their families. Women activists have ensured the visibility of women prisoners and their issues through organizations such as the National Network for Women in Prison, the California Coalition for Women Prisoners, Justice Now, Free Battered Women, Legal Services for Prisoners with Children, and the Out of Control Lesbian Committee to Support Women Political Prisoners.

For diverse groups to become part of a collective movement, they must be unified by a common understanding of the problem and share a vision of the possible solutions. These radicalizing and life-affirming visions move us beyond a combative dualism, whereby we know only what we are against, to a place of constructive imagination, where we can begin to build the world we want to live in. For the antiprison movement, abolition is the key to a radical and profoundly transformative vision of social change. A number of organizations are promoting dialogue about abolition, discussing what it means and how it can translate into concrete action.[38] Justice Now is an Oakland, California–based organization that provides legal services for women prisoners and campaigns against women's imprisonment. The organization's Building a World Without Prisons campaign provides a forum for women in and out of prison to share abolitionist ideas and strategies. Informed by women's experiences of interpersonal violation and state violence, Justice Now's politics is feminist and abolitionist:

> As an organization that works with women in prison, we see that prisons are a form of violence against women, and that locking up men is not a solution to interpersonal violence in our communities. We are interested not only in challenging what we see happening in prisons, but also in building a different world—a world where all of us have affordable housing, food, healthcare, economic opportunity and freedom from both individual and state violence. This vision includes creating new ways to respond when people hurt each other, ways that no longer rely on violence and control.[39]

This feminist abolitionism grows out of the deep belief that a world without prisons can also be a world in which women are safe from interpersonal violence. It resists the antiviolence movement's tendency to assume that policing and prisons are an effective tool against male violence, but it also holds the antiprison movement accountable for finding alternative strategies to end violence and build safety.

For an abolitionist vision to offer anything meaningful to communities and individuals suffering from overpolicing, criminalization, and incarceration, it must be accompanied by practical actions that promise short- and medium-term successes as well as long-term transformation. Critical Resistance, founded in 1998 by a group of Bay Area activists including Angela Y. Davis, has played a critical role in coordinating gatherings where diverse organizations can generate alternatives to the prison-industrial complex. Critical Resistance describe abolition as:

> [a] political vision that seeks to eliminate the need for prisons, policing, and surveillance by creating sustainable alternatives to punishment and imprisonment. ... An abolitionist vision means that we must build models today that can represent how we want to live in the future. It means developing practical strategies for taking small steps that move us toward making our dreams real and that lead the average person to believe that things really could be different. It means living this vision in our daily lives.[40]

In this sense, prison abolitionists shoulder a dual burden of first, transforming people's consciousness so that they can believe that their own visions of a different world are possible; and second, taking practical steps to oppose the prison-industrial complex. Abolitionist work involves three steps that build on one another with the ultimate goal of "shrink[ing] the system into non-existence."[41]

The first is a moratorium: ending prison expansion. This step may call for raising public awareness of the cost of prisons to reduce public support for prison constriction and laws that increase prison populations. It may also require campaigns to prevent the construction of specific prisons or jails. For example, the Prisoner Justice Action Committee's 81 Reasons 2005 campaign asked Ontario residents to think of alternative ways of spending the $81.1 million (Canadian) that the provincial government planned to spend on a new youth "superjail" in Brampton, a suburb of Toronto.[42] The campaigners mobilized public concerns about spending cuts in other areas, including education, to create pressure on the provincial government to explore less expensive and punitive alternatives to incarceration for youth.

The second step is decarceration: shrinking the prison population. The most common approach is to target a specific prison population that the public sees as low risk and argue for an end to imprisonment of this population. For example, California's passage of Proposition 36, the Substance Abuse and Crime Prevention Act, in 2000 allows first and second-time nonviolent drug offenders charged with possession to receive substance abuse treatment instead of prison, and this measure channels approximately thirty-five thousand people into treatment annually.[43] Free Battered Women's (FBW's) campaign for the release of incarcerated survivors is another example of decarceration. The organization supports women imprisoned for killing an abuser, challenging their convictions by demonstrating how the battering led to the killing. In addition, FBW draws attention to the large proportion of women prisoners who have a history of intimate violence and challenges the state's use of imprisonment as its response to women's victimization. By revealing the connection between women incarcerated for defending themselves against a violent partner and the majority of women in prison, FBW promotes the decarceration of women at a massive scale.

The third strategy is abolition: building a world without prisons. As a strategy, abolition moves from opposition to construction. It aims to build "a world where all people have access to the material, educational, emotional, and spiritual resources necessary to be safe and thrive in our communities."[44] For Critical Resistance South, located in New Orleans, abolition means working in coalition with grassroots economic and racial justice organizations to build community empowerment and representation in the reconstruction of the city.[45] Because the war on drugs has played such a huge role in the boom in imprisonment, strategies to tackle substance abuse and addiction must play a critical role in any abolitionist vision. The recovery movement, a user-led mental health and addiction movement, offers an important alternative to the criminalization of drug and alcohol abuse.[46] Divesting of prisons and investing in sober-living houses, recovery programs, treatment centers, and women's wellness and mental health programs designed and run by and for women and men in recovery would promote healing from addiction and self-determination for affected individuals and communities. Promoting community recovery would also stem the demand for criminalized drugs, undermining the transnational drug industry and creating economic crises for rural communities around the world that cultivate coca and opium. Transforming the war on drugs through an abolitionist politics must therefore involve a commitment to global economic justice and the creation of alternative economic development opportunities for all communities involved in the drug trade.

Abolition also requires alternative strategies for dealing with interpersonal harms that threaten the safety of individuals from oppressed groups. For Justice Now, abolition means facilitating community conversations about collective strategies for tackling violence against women that do not rely on criminal punishment. For INCITE! Women of Color Against Violence, abolition means developing and disseminating "community accountability" politics and practices for progressive organizations run by people of color, so that gender abuse and violence in activist settings is neither brushed under the carpet nor dealt with using the criminal punishment model.[47] Through their activities, these organizations become a reflection of the world we want to live in, providing real safety based on justice and focusing on healing and transformation rather than punishment and imprisonment.

Notes

1. See Arthur T. Denzau's *Fiscal Policy Convergence from Reagan to Blair* (New York: Routledge, 2003) for a detailed overview of, and the legacies bequeathed by, Reaganomics and Thatcherism.

2. Although fewer women are imprisoned than men, women's imprisonment has grown at a faster rate than men's since the 1980s. Between 1986 and 1991, the number of people in state women's prisons increased 75 percent, versus a 53 percent increase for men. The trend continues, with women's prison populations increasing 4.8 percent in the twelve months to midyear 2006, versus a 2.7 percent increase for men. U.S. Department of Justice, Bureau of Justice Statistics, *Special Report: Women in Prison* (Washington, DC, 1994); U.S Department of Justice, Bureau of Justice Statistics, *Prison and Jail Inmates at Midyear 2006* (Washington, DC, 2007). African American women and Latinas are imprisoned at four times and twice the rate of white women, respectively, indicating that the prison boom has disproportionately affected women of color (U.S. Department of Justice, *Prison and Jail Inmates.*)

3. Rebecca Bohrman and Naomi Murakawa, "Remaking Big Government: Immigration and Crime Control in the United States," in *Global Lockdown: Race, Gender, and the Prison-Industrial Complex,* ed. J. Sudbury, 109–26. (New York: Routledge, 2005). The other major shift of public spending priorities has been from the welfare state to the global war on terror.

4. Ibid.

5. Julia Sudbury, "Transatlantic Visions: Resisting the Globalization of Mass Incarceration," *Social Justice* 27, no. 3 (Fall 2000): 133.

6. Saskia Sassen, *The Global City: New York, London, Tokyo* (Princeton, NJ: Princeton University Press, 2001).

7. Angela Y. Davis, "Race and Criminalization: Black Americans and the Punishment Industry," in *The Angela Y. Davis Reader*, ed. James Joy, 61–73 (Oxford: Blackwell Publishers, 1998).

8. Neoliberalism is a philosophy that views the unfettered market as the key to economic and social progress. Neoliberal policies include government cutbacks, privatization of state services, reduced governmental protection of workers and the environment, and the removal of trade barriers, in particular through international trade agreements such as the North American Free Trade Agreement and the Free Trade Area of the Americas. Antiglobalization activists and scholars view these developments as a recipe for corporate profit at the expense of marginalized communities. See Noam Chomsky, *Profit Over People: Neoliberalism and Global Order* (New York: Seven Stories, 1998).

9. National Women's Law Center, "Welfare Reform Should Help Women Striving to Support Their Families, Not Hold Them Back" (Washington, D.C.: National Women's Law Center, February 2003); www.nwlc.org.

10. Judith Goode, "From New Deal to Bad Deal: Racial and Political Implications of U.S. Welfare Reform," in *Western Welfare in Decline: Globalization and Women's Poverty*, ed. Catherine Kingfisher, 65–89 (Philadelphia: University of Pennsylvania Press, 2003).

11. Beth Richie, *Compelled to Crime: The Gender Entrapment of Battered Black Women* (New York: Routledge, 1995).

12. Beth Richie, "Queering Antiprison Work," in Sudbury, *Global Lockdown;* Dorothy Roberts, *Shattered Bonds: The Color of Child Welfare* (New York: Basic Civitas Books, 2002), 201–7.

13. Terry Kupers, *Prison Madness: The Mental Health Crisis Behind Bars and What We Must Do About It* (San Francisco: Jossey-Bass, 1999).

14. For example, anyone convicted of selling two ounces or possessing four ounces of narcotics would receive a sentence of fifteen years. Marc Mauer, "The Causes and Consequences of Prison Growth in the United States," in *Mass Imprisonment: Social Causes and Consequences,* ed. David Garland (London, Thousand Oaks: Sage Publications, 2001), 6.

15. The federal budget for the war on drugs grew from $1.5 billion in 1981 at the beginning of Reagan's term to $6.6 billion in 1989, and it hit $17 billion ten years later; ibid.

16. Stephanie Bush-Baskette, "The War on Drugs as a War on Black Women," in *Crime Control and Women,* ed. Susan Miller, 113–29 (Thousand Oaks, CA: Sage Publications, 1998); Juanita Díaz-Cotto, *Chicana Lives and Criminal Justice: Voices from El Barrio* (Austin: University of Texas Press, 2006).

17. Although the majority of crack users are white, nearly 90 percent of those convicted in federal court for crack-cocaine distribution are African American. U.S. Sentencing Commission, *Special Report to Congress: Cocaine and Federal Sentencing Policy* (Washington, DC, April 2007), 8.

18. Drug Policy Alliance 2001, "Crack/Cocaine Disparity"; www.drugpolicy.org.

19. Díaz-Cotto, *Chicana Lives and Criminal Justice,* 20.

20. Ibid.

21. Ibid.

22. Julia Sudbury, "Women of Color, Globalization, and the Politics of Incarceration," in *The Criminal Justice System and Women: Offenders, Prisoners, Victims, & Workers,* ed. Barbara Raffel Price and Natalie J. Sokoloff, 219–33 (New York: McGraw Hill, 2003).

23. National Network for Immigrant and Refugee Rights, "Excerpts from the Mexico City Report: Globalization, Immigration, and Militarization: A Dialogue between NGOs"; www.nnirr.org.

24. Estimate by United Nations Population Division, International Organization for Migration, *World Migration 2005: Costs and Benefits of International Migration;* www.iom.int.

25. Food and Agriculture Organization of the United Nations, *The State of Food Insecurity in the World 2004;* www.fao.org.

26. Bohrman and Murakawa, "Remaking Big Government."

27. Sylvanna Falcón, "'National Security' and the Violation of Women: Militarized Border Rape at the U.S.-Mexico Border," in *Color of Violence: The Incite! Anthology,* ed. Incite! Women of Color Against Violence (Boston: South End Press, 2006).

28. Bohrman and Murakawa, "Remaking Big Government," 112.

29. U.S. Government Accountability Office, *Information on Criminal Aliens Incarcerated in Federal and State Prisons and Local Jails* (Washington, DC, April 7, 2005); www.gao.gov.

30. Dwight D. Eisenhower, "Military-Industrial Complex Speech," Public Papers of the Presidents, Eisenhower 1961(Washington, DC: Office of the Federal Register), 1035–40.

31. Mike Davis, "Hell Factories in the Field: A Prison-Industrial Complex," *Nation,* February 20, 1995, 260.

32. For example, the Institute on Money in State Politics report identified evidence that legislators were introducing or voting favorably on bills that would benefit the private prison companies that had donated to their campaigns in Mississippi, Georgia, Florida, Oklahoma, and North Carolina during the 2000 election cycle. Edwin Bender, *A Contributing Influence: The Private-Prison Industry and Political Giving in the South* (Helena, MT: Institute on Money in State Politics, 2002), 4.

33. Ruthie Gilmore, *Golden Gulag: Prisons, Surplus, Crisis, and Opposition in Globalizing California* (Berkeley: University of California Press, 2007).

34. Geert Dhondt, "Big Prisons and Small Towns" (Amherst, MA: Center for Popular Economics, 2002).

35. Gilmore, *Golden Gulag.*

36. Sudbury, "Transatlantic Visions."

37. For an excellent list of over one hundred organizations, see the Prison Activist Resource Center's links page: www.prisonactivist.org.

38. These organizations include Critical Resistance, the Prison Moratorium Project, the Prison Activist Resource Center, Justice Now, the Prison Justice Action Committee (Toronto, Canada), and the International Conference on Penal Abolition.

39. Justice Now, "The VoicesProject: Building a World Without Prisons"; www.jnow.org.

40. Critical Resistance. "What Is Prison Abolition All About?" as reprinted in "Abolitionism: A British Perspective," www.alternatives2prison.ik.com/p_What_is_Abolition.ikml.

41. Ibid.

42. Prisoner Justice Action Committee, "The 81 Reasons Campaign Statement"; www.pjac.org.

43. Drug Policy Alliance, "California Proposition 36: Substance Abuse and Crime Prevention Act of 2000"; www.prop36.org.

44. Free Battered Women, "What We Believe: Our Vision & Guiding Principles"; http://freebat teredwomen.org.

45. Critical Resistance, "Hurricane Katrina Rebuilding and Relief"; www.criticalresistance.org.

46. The recovery movement includes twelve-step programs such as Alcoholics Anonymous and Narcotics Anonymous and a range of community-based recovery facilities. These programs are peer led and run, nonhierarchical and noncommercial.

47. INCITE! Women of Color Against Violence, *Gender Oppression, Abuse, Violence: Community Accountability within the People of Color Progressive Movement* (Seattle, WA, July 2005); www.incite-na tional.org.

READING 4.6

Correctional Corruption

Investigation Reveals Abuse in Florida's Private Prison Industry

By Chris Kirkham

The tip arrived the usual way: completely out of thin air.

I was on a routine call with a civil rights lawyer in Florida, on the lookout for stories about youth prisons run by private corporations. I had just written about a private juvenile facility in Mississippi that got slammed by the Justice Department for inhumane conditions, and I figured there was more to the story.

So I called David Utter, a renowned advocate with the Southern Poverty Law Center, to see what else he knew about juvenile justice in Mississippi. Not much, he admitted. But he knew a lot about Florida, which was about to fully outsource its juvenile prison system to private contractors.

I wondered who the main players were in Florida's growing market for juvenile corrections—one of the largest in the country. Utter mentioned a few names, but one stuck out: Youth Services International, run by an executive named James Slattery.

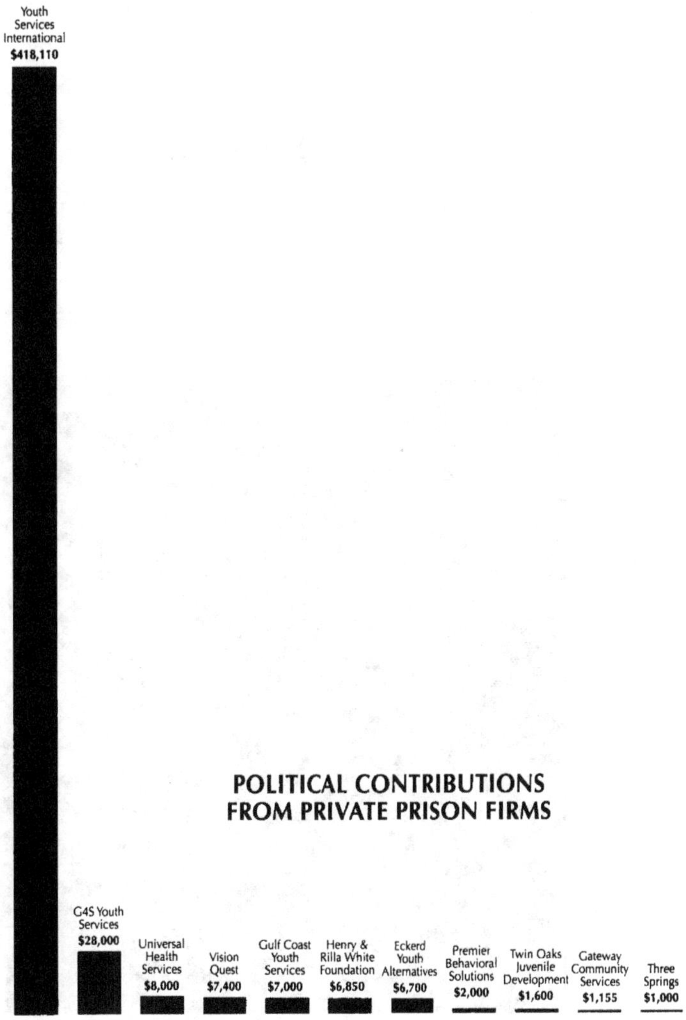

Political contributions in the state of Florida since 1998 from contractors who handled residential facilities for the Florida Department of Juvenile Justice. Source: Influence Explorer.

After running a few Nexis searches, I realized Slattery had been around for a long time, in the same industry, but he kept changing the names of his businesses.

As I asked around more, I realized this was a rich tale: A former New York City hotelier who rented rooms to released federal inmates found his way into the prison business and moved to Florida as the state rapidly embraced privatization in the 1990s. Trouble always seemed to follow his operations. A quick clip search revealed local stories and briefs about riots, escapes and abuse investigations.

One main question stuck out: How can a company with such history continue to receive tens of millions of dollars worth of contracts?

To get the answer, I needed to go forward on two distinct tracks.

First, I needed to find as many audits, inspections and other primary source materials as I could to document abuse through the years. Then I needed to understand Florida's juvenile prison contracting and oversight procedures, to determine how these past abuses went undetected.

Resistance on Records

I started by digging into Florida's inspection process. I requested basic data on assaults, escapes and other serious incidents at juvenile prisons across the state.

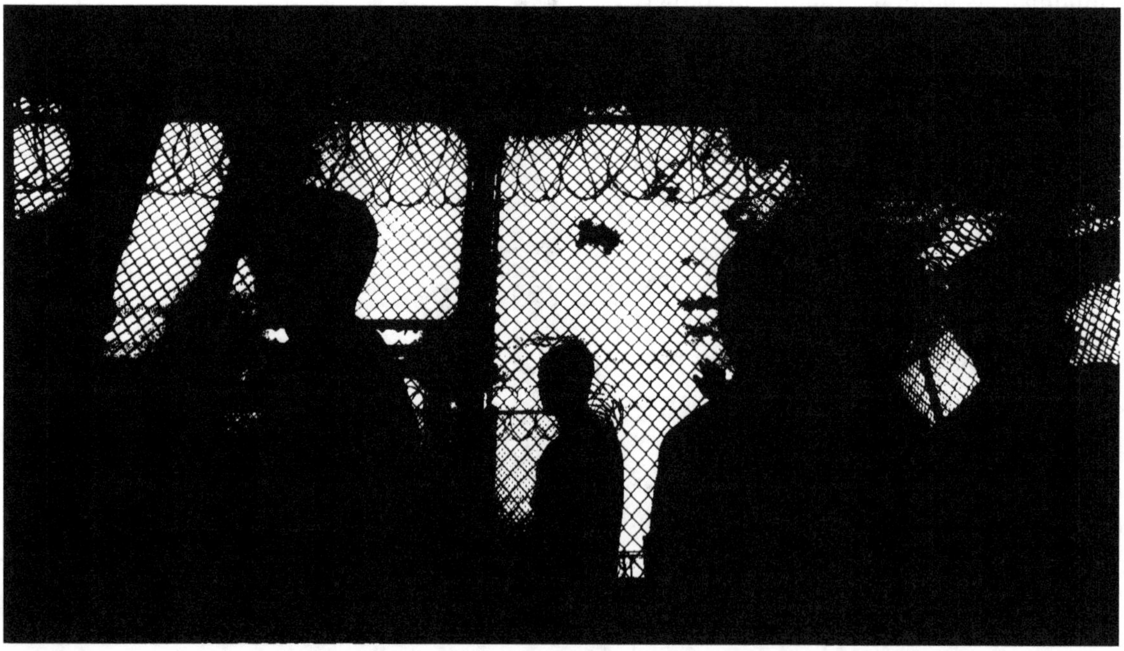

Youths wait in line to return to their dorms at the Pahokee Youth Development Center, a facility run by James F. Slattery's company in the late 1990s. Pahokee faced criticism for a high incidence of violence.

I had never worked extensively with any Florida agency, and I wasn't sure exactly how the state's oversight system worked. But I was certain the government would track such data in a comprehensive way. I was wrong.

My first red flag came just a few weeks into the investigation, when the state Department of Juvenile Justice sent me a cost estimate on the records: nearly $67,000. This struck me as an outrageous tab. I was certain that it was a tactic to chill the investigation, which piqued my curiosity even more.

I pushed back to clarify that I was looking for logs and master lists of these incidents—not every underlying report and document—but I continued to get resistance. The state public information officer handling my records request gave only vague updates on the process. One response made me think that it wasn't being honored as an official public records request: "I can't predict exactly when it will all be ready for delivery, but only after we are confident that it accurately portrays the whole, and not half, of the story."

I knew the state law, but I consulted with our in-house lawyer to get his take on the department's response. He agreed that the agency was violating the law and sent a strongly worded letter to get things back on track. From that point forward, I was in direct correspondence with the department's lawyers, not their communications staff, which made the process much more efficient.

But I still didn't have anything to show how the state tracks complaints and incidents of violence across its juvenile prison system. The department kept telling me there were no records responsive to my request. So I changed the conversation.

If the state has no such records, I replied, was I then correct in writing that the state has no way to track when violent incidents occur in its juvenile prison system? A few days later, they came through with the logs.

Still, I faced another hurdle: Those logs were simply listings of incidents, printouts generated from an internal tracking system used by the department. There was no way to distill the data into a spreadsheet for easy analysis. I told my editor, Peter Goodman, about the data difficulties, and he rightly recognized it as a key part of the story. If we built the database ourselves, we could shine light on trends that even the state wasn't aware of.

So I took five years worth of the incident report logs and built my own spreadsheet to do the analysis. I figured out which private contractors ran each facility, plugged in the data by hand and analyzed several categories of violent incidents.

The results showed that allegations of excessive force and incidents of youth injury at Youth Services International facilities were disproportionately high compared to other private providers, based on the size of each company's facilities in the state.

Decades of Neglect

As I was wrangling with the state of Florida over the data, I was also unearthing documents and inspection reports to get a sense of the conditions inside Slattery's facilities through the years.

Staying organized was essential: The company had a long history and at its peak was operating in more than a dozen states. I systematically requested documents from each state, starting with annual audits.

I also did clip searches in different parts of the country to determine if there had been references to escapes or other major disturbances at facilities owned by Slattery's company. Then I followed up to get specific incident reports or investigations related to those incidents. I kept track of those requests in a spreadsheet and created Google calendar alerts as a reminder to follow up on public records deadlines that had passed.

It was difficult to track down some of the documents that were more than 10 years old (even five years, in some cases). Many of the state juvenile justice agencies said they no longer had the records because the document retention periods had passed. In those instances, I sought out lawyers, advocates or state consultants who worked on the cases and might be familiar with the files. That was usually a goldmine.

To shine light on what was happening more recently in Florida, I used the facility addresses to seek logs of local police and emergency calls during the previous five years. I determined which cases seemed the most serious from the logs and requested the underlying police reports. Both the police reports and reports from the department's inspector general listed the names of YSI staffers whom I could look up to contact for more information.

Public defenders were also helpful sources in finding former employees and inmates. For years, several of the juvenile defenders in South Florida had been hearing complaints of abuse and lousy conditions from youths housed YSI facilities.

Yet they often lacked the authority—and time—to demand change.

Using those leads, I was able to create my own network of contacts who were familiar with the operations of YSI and the state Department of Juvenile Justice.

One of the most valuable resources was a former prison monitor with the Department of Juvenile Justice who called up the public defender's office in Broward County. He had been fired from DJJ after sounding alarms at a YSI facility nearly a decade before.

He turned out to be one of those rare gems, an insider who had been sitting on a trove of documents for years, just waiting for someone to listen to his story.

After spending an entire Sunday afternoon talking at his home in South Florida, he handed over hundreds of pages of documents for me to take back to New York and review. Those files became a road map for requesting other documents, helping me to learn the state's terminology for inspection records and other audits.

Faulty Background Checks

I was armed with documented evidence of abuse across many states, including one where a guard had fractured an inmate's elbow after the boy refused instructions to throw away a cup, according to incident reports. My last challenge was figuring out how the state of Florida kept signing contracts with the company.

To learn how the state picks juvenile prison operators, I needed to put myself in the shoes of a potential contractor. How much does the state investigate prior performance? And how does the state rank and evaluate contractors?

I requested the original proposals that YSI submitted for more than a dozen contracts over the last 10 years. Then I asked for the state's score sheets, known as "bid tabulations," to get a sense of what criteria the state used to rank competitors.

What I found was a system that relied primarily on promises from private prison contractors. The vast majority of a potential prison contractor's rating came from a written proposal.

YSI's proposals sounded fantastic, boasting of an "extensive and successful history" running juvenile facilities and an "excellent working relationship" with the state.

In reviewing the proposals, I noticed that YSI essentially used the same format and wording for every contract. Some proposals were carbon copies of earlier ones; the only differences were the address and the number of prison beds.

Tips

- **Social media is a godsend**. Linkedin and Facebook provided excellent avenues to identify company insiders. If you haven't already, attend a free Linkedin for journalists session, which will give you premium access to the site, opening up more distant networks.
- **Names beget names**. Scrub documents for references to specific employees or inspectors. Call all of them and ask all of them for more names. Former employees usually keep in touch with co-workers through the years.
- **Look for patterns**. For a company like Youth Services International, run by the same chief executive for nearly 25 years, it helps the narrative to identify common themes or patterns of incidents.
- **Use "no" to your advantage**. If a government agency denies the public records you request, use that as a lever to get what you want. When you are seeking common-sense data about an essential public service, you have the upper hand. If a government entity says such information doesn't exist, it raises bigger questions about how that agency does business.

Only about a quarter of the score dealt with past performance. In the case of YSI, a multi-state operation, Florida officials didn't examine records in other states. During one of the firm's most rapid periods of expansion in Florida, for example, the Justice Department was investigating a notoriously violent YSI facility in Maryland called the Charles H. Hickey Jr. School.

And just a few years earlier, in 2001, an 18-year-old died of pneumonia at a company boot camp in Texas following nine days of medical neglect. Investigative reports from state law enforcement detailed how a nurse forced the inmate to do push-ups in his own vomit.

Those out-of-state troubles never surfaced in Florida's review of YSI, nor would they today, according to the state's contracting procedures. Florida looks beyond its borders only when a contractor has no previous affiliation with the state.

From Documents to Design

Once the stories were written, I knew that we needed to do something different with the presentation. It would be a shame to have collected thousands of pages of documents and not allow readers to also engage with the material.

I had been using DocumentCloud throughout the reporting process to organize the large amounts of information coming in and take notes along the way. So I started talking with Andrei Scheinkman, our data editor, about ways to incorporate those notes into our design.

Rather than just link to a massive trove of documents, we could allow readers to interact in real time with specific primary source material. He was able to use the URLs from each annotation to link to interactive passages throughout the piece. It was a way of bulletproofing the story and adding an interactive feature to accompany the photos, timelines and interactive map we created.

Since publication in October, our investigation has prompted calls for reform from several key Florida senators. Lawmakers have requested troves of documents from the Department of Juvenile Justice to begin an investigation.

A Florida Senate panel in January held a hearing on the company and the state's juvenile justice oversight system. Several senators are drafting legislation to reform the state's juvenile prison contracting procedures, based on our findings.

Chris Kirkham is a business reporter at the Huffington Post in New York, where he has worked for three years covering the intersection of business and public policy. Previously he worked as an environmental and politics reporter at The Times-Picayune in New Orleans. A native of Texas, Chris attended the Medill School of Journalism at Northwestern University.

READING 4.7

Cage Complex

Why is America's Prison Population Soaring?

By Wendy McElroy

The United States leads the world, by a large margin, in the production of at least one thing: prisoners. We have 25 percent of the world's inmates, but just 5 percent of the world's population.

Where do they come from? Well, since the Anti-Drug Abuse Act of 1986, the number of American inmates has risen from approximately 300,000 to a currently estimated 2.3 million. This statistic points to the role of drug-related victimless "crime" in creating prisoners.

There are other sources. The "private prison complex" is a creation of crony capitalism through which privileged corporations are paid well for the "care" of inmates and for leasing out prison labor to other businesses.

Ten percent of American prisons are now "privately" operated, for-profit businesses. Between 1990 and 2010, the number of for-profit prisons rose 1600 percent, far outpacing the growth of

spirit of america/Shutterstock

Wendy McElroy, "Cage Complex: Why Is America's Prison Population Soaring?" *Freeman*, vol. 64, no. 2, pp. 14-16.

public ones or the population at large. The likelihood of being arrested is already higher in America than anywhere else in the world. That likelihood will rise if the financial incentives to imprison more people continue or increase.

"Private" Prisons Insult Real Privatization

Privatization involves a transfer of ownership and control from the State to a private entity; post offices and public lands are commonly used examples. In a free market, a privatized business competes for customer dollars without any legal advantages or other privileges. Under crony capitalism, the "privatized" business enjoys legal privileges and other advantages such as tax funding.

"Private" prisons are run by corporations to which government outsources the care of inmates. The corporation receives X tax dollars for each prisoner, quite apart from the actual cost of care. This builds in an incentive to skimp on services such as food and medical care. And, indeed, most prison contracts include a "low-crime tax" or "lockup quota." This system means taxpayers compensate the corporation for empty cells if the number of prisoners falls below a set quota. A recent report, "Criminal: How Lockup Quotas and 'Low-Crime Taxes' Guarantee Profits for Private Prison Corporations," found the average "occupancy guarantee" to be 90 percent; in four states, it is between 95 percent and 100 percent. Thus the "private" prison is guaranteed a tax-funded profit.

Prisoners' labor is also leased out to government agencies or to major corporations. Prison labor reportedly produces 100 percent of military helmets, shirts, pants, tents, bags, canteens, and a variety of other equipment. Prison labor makes circuit boards for IBM, Texas Instruments, and Dell. Many McDonald's uniforms are sewn by inmates. Other corporations—Microsoft, Victoria's Secret, Boeing, Motorola, Compaq, Revlon, and Kmart—also benefit from prison labor.

The "private" prison industry is *private* in the same sense that crony capitalism is *capitalist.* Namely, *not at all.* It is the antithesis of a truly private industry that competes in the free market, does not accept tax funds, and cannot compel labor. By contrast, the "private" prisons enjoy a monopoly over a service that is created by laws and sentencing policies. They receive tax money and preferential treatment. They exploit captive labor through circumstances similar to plantation slavery.

In an article titled "The Prison Industry in the United States: Big Business or a New Form of Slavery?" by Global Research, the authors describe the advantages of leasing prison labor.

> They don't have to worry about strikes or paying unemployment insurance, vacations or comp time. All of their workers are full-time, and never arrive late or are absent because of family problems; moreover, if they don't like the pay of 25 cents an hour and refuse to work, they are locked up in isolation cells. [Note: payment rates vary and are cited as high as $2 an hour.]

The beneficiaries of "private" prisons are the government entities that claim to save money through outsourcing, the politicians who facilitate the contracts, the "private" prison corporations, and the corporations who lease prison labor.

The victims of "private" prisons are the coerced workers and the true private sector, because the corporations that lease extremely cheap prison labor can undercut their competitors. The tractor-trailer division of Lufkin Industries in Texas provides a dramatic illustration. Its competitor, the Direct Trailer and Equipment Co., began to offer the same basic product for about $2,000 less than Lufkin. It could do so because it enjoyed both prison labor and state subsidies; for example, Direct Trailer paid a nominal fee ($1 a year) to use manufacturing facilities within the prison compound. Lufkin's division went out of business, laying off 150 people because they could not outcompete prison labor.

Incentives to Increase the Prison Population

Louisiana, too, is instructive. A *Times-Picayune* article, "Louisiana Is the World's Prison Capital," reported, "The state imprisons more of its people, per head, than any of its U.S. counterparts. First among Americans means first in the world. ... The hidden engine behind the state's well-oiled prison machine is cold, hard cash. A majority of Louisiana inmates are housed in for-profit facilities, which must be supplied with a constant influx of human beings or a $182 million industry will go bankrupt."

One in 86 adults in Louisiana is doing time. The article hints at the reason: the entanglement of State and crony enterprise.

> In a uniquely Louisiana twist, most prison entrepreneurs are rural sheriffs, who hold tremendous sway in remote parishes. ... A good portion of Louisiana law enforcement is financed with dollars legally skimmed off the top of prison operations. If the inmate count dips, sheriffs bleed money. Their constituents lose jobs. The prison lobby ensures this does not happen by thwarting nearly every reform that could result in fewer people behind bars.

These and similar incentives have created "the prison-industrial complex." In 2008, the human cost of the complex was starkly revealed in what was called the "kids for cash scandal." The private prison company Mid-Atlantic Youth Services Corp. ran juvenile facilities in Pennsylvania. Two judges were found guilty of pocketing $2.6 million for sending approximately 2,000 children to the facilities. Even first-time offenders were given harsh sentences for trivial offenses such as mocking a principal on social media. Several hundred of the judges' convictions were overturned. But expunging records could not help a traumatized child, a first-time offender, who committed suicide.

Corporations have a long history of providing specific services, such as food preparation, to prisons. This tradition stretches back to well before the drug war. During the early 1980s recession, prison overcrowding spiked and tax revenue declined, opening the door to expansion. In 1984, the Corrections Corporation of America (CCA) assumed total control of a Tennessee detention facility. This was the first such contract in the United States.

Prisons have continued to face the same dilemma: overcrowding, scarce funding, and employee cutbacks. The *Times-Picayune* describes Louisiana's response: "In the early 1990s, when the incarceration rate was half what it is now, Louisiana was at a crossroads." The state was court-ordered to correct overcrowding. There were two choices: fewer inmates or more prisons. The state chose the latter by "encouraging sheriffs to foot the construction bills in return for future profits. The financial incentives were so sweet, and the corrections jobs so sought after, that new prisons sprouted up all over rural Louisiana."

The inmate population has soared since.

Backlash

A backlash is underway and some opponents speak with powerful voices.

For example, labor unions decry prison work. The pressure is having an effect. Some states, like Nevada, are considering legislation to require "oversight and transparency" for "private" prisons. Other states have been shaken by reports of cost-cutting measures taken by private prison corporations. The ACLU reported on one such prison in Ohio:

> The compliance rating [with state standards] plummeted from the 97.3 percent compliance ... when publicly-owned to 66.7 percent. Auditors found outrageous violations like prisoners being forced to use plastic bags for defecation and cups for urination because they had no running water for toilets. Basic conditions were heinous, with black mold, standing water, and spoiled food found throughout the prison. ... The medical department is grossly understaffed and many prisoners go untreated.

Meanwhile, the private prison complex is entrenched. It wields lobbying clout, as do the corporations that lease prison labor.

The large "private" prison corporation, the Corrections Corporation of America, is unabashed about its plans. The 2010 CCA Annual Report stated, "We believe we have been successful in increasing the number of residents [prisoners] in our care and continue to pursue a number of initiatives intended to further increase our occupancy and revenue." Translated from corporate speak: They plan on nabbing many more people and locking them up.

Reform

A giant step toward reducing overcrowding and the perceived need for outsourcing prisons would be to stop arresting nonviolent "criminals." Another big step would be to require criminals who damage or steal property to pay restitution to their victims rather than be punished by incarceration.

Unfortunately, there is no profit to the State nor to crony corporations in those solutions. In the foreseeable future, the prison population of America will grow, with minor infractions drawing lengthy jail terms.

Police states are the mother of prison complexes. Whatever solutions arise will come from shining the harsh light of reality upon both.

READING 4.8

An Introduction to the Prison Rape Elimination Act

By Janet I. Warren and Shelly L. Jackson

Our research emerged in the context of a federal initiative to study and address the problem of prison rape among both male and female inmates. While initially overestimated in terms of prevalence, this national attention nonetheless spawned a number of research projects that cumulatively began to broaden and deepen our understanding of this complex aspect of prison life. Our research, which chose to encompass the full continuum of sexual behavior among incarcerated individuals, succeeded in identifying multi-layered predictive models for different types of sexual behavior across and within genders. The process by which we came to our study design, our experiences while implementing it, and the nature and significance of our findings represent the content of this book.

Historical Context of the Prison Rape Elimination Act (PREA)

The PREA legislation reflected a culmination of efforts that emerged both in the context of human rights advocacy, both inside and outside of Washington DC, and the legal thrust of the United States Supreme Court coupled with amendments to federal law concerning civil rights litigation by prisoners.

Human Rights Advocacy

With the passage of PREA in 2003, federal and state correctional institutions were required to engage seriously in activities designed to eliminate prison rape. Part of the impetus for the PREA legislation emerged in the context of human rights law and the ratification of two international treaties, the *International Covenant on Civil and Political Rights*, adopted in 1976, and the *Convention against Torture and Other Cruel, Inhumane and Degrading Treatment or Punishment*, adopted in 1987. Both of these declarations require the United States (US) to protect prisoners from sexual violence. Along with the *Universal Declaration of Human Rights* (1948), these statements define basic human rights, which include protection against cruel, degrading, or inhumane treatment or punishment along with the accessibility of individuals to remedies for the violation of these rights. The decision to address prison rape within this human rights perspective helped to separate the issue from the criminal arena and the specifics of the crimes for which these victims had been incarcerated. Vulnerability to infection with the AIDS virus further aligned the issue to the basic principle of human rights and the avoidance of a death sentence that had not been imposed by the court.

It was this human rights perspective that came to define the mission and purpose of Just Detention International (JDI), an organization established in 1980 by Russell Dan Smith. Smith, an inmate who had experienced a sexual assault in prison, began the grassroots organization, People Organized to Stop the Rape of Imprisoned Persons, to "deal with the problems of rape, sexual assault, sex slavery, and forced prostitution in the prison context" (http://www.justdetention.org/en/spr_history.aspx). Shortly thereafter, the organization was renamed Stop Prison Rape, and in 1994 was incorporated by Stephen Donaldson, who went on to serve as the President of the organization until his death.

In 1973, Stephen Donaldson was arrested for trespassing after participating in a prayer-in at the White House which was advocating for peace in Vietnam. Mr. Donaldson was a Quaker activist who refused to post a $10 bond on moral grounds and was sent to a Washington, DC jail. Mr. Donaldson was behind bars for two nights, during which time he was gang raped approximately 60 times by various inmates. When Mr. Donaldson was released, he became a prolific and committed activist, writing many editorials and appearing on national television before his death in 1996 from AIDS, believed to have been contracted as a result of his assaults in the Washington, DC jail.

After his death, the Stop Prison Rape staff was active in advocating for the passage of the Prison Rape Elimination Act, and after its passage, the implementation of its legislative mandates in a meaningful and effective manner. In 2008, the name of the organization was changed to Just Detention International. Currently located in Los Angeles, California, the organization identifies three core goals for its work: To ensure governmental accountability for prisoner rape, to transform ill-informed public attitudes about sexual assault in detention, and to promote access to resources for individuals who have experienced sexual assault while confined in a penal institution. It is currently active in advocating for protections of detainees in US immigration centers.

A second wave of human rights involvement emerged in 2001 when Michael Horowitz, Director of the Hudson Institute's Project for Civil Justice Reform and Project for International Religious Freedom, turned his attention to prison rape based upon his earlier work with the *International Religious Freedom Act* of 1998, followed by the *Victims of Trafficking and Violence Protection Act* of 2000. A human rights coalition had been formed to pass these two legislative mandates, and after completion of these advocacy endeavors, the question of "what next?" remained. According to Mr. Horowitz, he raised this question informally with Linda Chavez of the Center for Equal Opportunity, and a member of the coalition, and she replied "You know, prison rape has always troubled me." At that point, the coalition identified this as their next legislative goal and, based upon their prior experience, they began convening both conservative and liberal groups who had been working on prison rape, a group that collectively became known as the "Prison Rape Coalition." Initially made up of 18 members including a congressman, congressional aides, academic researchers, religious leaders for prison reform, a victim of prison rape, and a philanthropic CEO, the group gradually expanded to 58 members by the time the bill passed in 2003. The group sponsored congressional hearings, drafted legislation, and procured sponsorship from four congressmen (Michael Horowitz, personal communication, October 18, 2006). One commentator, who was central to the negotiations that transpired during this time period, observed that the swiftness with which the legislation obtained bipartisan support reflected a rather unexpected blending of concern about the conditions and rehabilitation of incarcerated individuals on the one hand, and an ideological commitment to eradicating homosexual behavior on the other (Bobby Vassar, personal communication, October 2, 2006).

Farmer v. Brennan (1994), United Supreme Court

Perhaps the most significant Supreme Court case relevant to prison rape litigation is *Farmer v. Brennan* (1994). Dee Farmer was a pre-operative transsexual who had undergone unsuccessful black market surgery to remove her testicles. At the time of her 20-year imprisonment for multiple counts of credit card fraud, she had a noticeable feminine appearance with silicone breast implants, hormone replacement therapy, and a manner of dress that was designed to portray a feminine appearance. Due to the rules concerning gender determinations and custody in the Federal Bureau of Prisons, she was sentenced to serve her time in an all-male prison.

On March 9, 1989, Ms. Farmer was transferred from the Federal Correctional Institute at Oxford, Wisconsin, to a maximum security penitentiary at Terre Haute, Indiana, after she was found guilty of ordering fruit baskets and flowers with a stolen credit card over the prison telephone. She was initially placed in administrative segregation but on March 23, 1989, she was released into general population based on earlier challenges she had made for pertinent medical treatment and safe housing that did not involve segregation. On April 1, 1989, Ms. Farmer was approached by another inmate "demanding" sexual intercourse with her. When she refused she was punched in the face, kicked, and raped at knife point with the assailant threatening to kill her if she reported it to prison officials. One week later, Ms. Farmer reported the incident to the prison and, acting without counsel, filed a complaint against the Federal Bureau of Prisons requesting transfer to a mixed gender facility and compensatory damages. The district court and the Court of Appeals for the Seventh Circuit granted the defendant's motion for summary judgment and Ms. Farmer acting pro se petitioned the Supreme Court successfully for certiorari.

In June of 1994, the Supreme Court ruled unanimously and unambiguously that prison officials had a duty under the Eighth Amendment to protect prisoners from harm at the hands of other prisoners.

The court applied the standard of "deliberate indifference" identified in cases involving medical care thus broadening the "malicious and sadistic" standard applied to prior cases of physical violence perpetrated by prison officials against prison inmates. The Supreme Court vacated the lower court decision and remanded Ms. Farmer's case with Justice Blackmun's statement that the court's decision "creates no new obstacles to prison inmates to overcome and sends a clear message to prison officials that their affirmative duty to provide for the safety of inmates is not to be taken lightly." In upholding this decision, the court accepted the argument that the Federal Bureau of Prisons was aware of Ms. Farmer's transsexual status and demonstrated deliberate indifference in not protecting her from this risk. It also made clear that prison officials could not escape liability merely by showing that they did not know that a specific inmate posed a risk to the specific plaintiff (see also *Wilson v. Wright*, 1998).

Prison Litigation Reform Act (1996)

A second legal impetus for the PREA legislation emerged in response to the passage of the Prison Litigation Reform Act (PLRA) in 1996. PLRA amended and supplemented the US Code that addressed civil rights litigation and *in forma pauperis* proceedings and was designed to "curtail the ability of prisoners to bring frivolous and malicious lawsuits." The number of prisoners filing civil rights lawsuits annually had risen from 8,235 in 1977 to more than 40,000 in 1996 (Maguire & Pestore, 1997). Advocates of the bill argued that "tying our courts in knots" was unnecessary and that the time and money the state expended defending against these frivolous lawsuits could be used instead to fight crime. Senators Robert Dole and Orrin Hatch were active in this debate and contributed to the publication in the *Congressional Record* that was entitled "Top 10 Frivolous Inmate Lawsuits Nationally." Included in this list were suits brought by prisoners because their ice cream had melted, they were forced to listen to the unit manager's country western music, their dessert cake had arrived "hacked up," they were served chunky instead of smooth peanut butter, they were making $21.00 an hour at work after being promised $29.40, they had to send packages by UPS rather than Federal Express, they were supplied with LA Gear sneakers instead of Converse, and they had been denied sex change operations while in prison (Puplava, 1997).

Critics of the law argued that PLRA made it more difficult for indigent inmates to file reasonable claims and to receive judgment on these claims. Within these parameters, two of the PLRA requirements were seen as particularly antithetical to the rights of individuals who are seeking to litigate allegations of coerced sex and rape. The PLRA (amended 1998) instructed federal district courts to dismiss all actions alleging mental suffering without any showing of prior physical injury (Taylor, 2000). Based upon this instruction, some courts determined that rape constitutes a physical injury (e.g., *Liner v. Goord*, 1999; *Noguera v. Hasty*, 2001; *Nunn v. Michigan Department of Corrections*, 1997), although the holdings provided little useful analysis, stating simply "the alleged sexual assaults qualify as physical injuries as a matter of common sense" (*Liner v. Goord*, 1999). Other courts have refused to find sexual assault a per se physical injury (*Kemner v. Hemphill*, 2002; *Hancock v. Payne*, 2006) (Golden,

2006). A second requirement of the PLRA mandated that all prison avenues for vetting grievances be exhausted by a prisoner before the civil action would be reviewed by the court, even if the prisoner was suing for damages and the grievance system did not provide damages (Columbia Human Rights Law Review, 2009). Criticism of this exhaustion requirement as it pertains to sexual assault in prison underscored the risk that some prisoners might take in documenting sexual assault within a prison environment, particularly when the accused perpetrator might be a correctional officer or member of the prison staff (Ribet, 2010).

The contradictions between these legal mandates, the one arguing for the protection of sexually assaulted prisoners based upon the Eighth Amendment of the US Constitution, and the other limiting inmates' ability to bring suit in federal court, created a legal tension that further contributed to a growing sense that prison rape was a specific and unique hazard of incarceration and one that should be addressed though a unique law and ongoing congressional oversight.

Brief Summary of the Prison Rape Elimination Act

The Prison Rape Reduction Act of 2003 (H.R. 1707) was originally introduced by Representatives Frank Wolf (R-VA10) and Bobby Scott (D-VA3) on April 19, 2003, to the House Committee on the Judiciary. On July 21, 2003, the renamed Prison Rape Elimination Act (S. 1435) passed the Senate with unanimous support after being introduced by Senator Jeff Sessions (R-Ala) and Senator Ted M. Kennedy (D-Mass). On April 22, 2003, H.R. 1765 was referred to the Subcommittee on Crime, Terrorism, and Homeland Security. Six weeks later, on September 4, 2003, the Honorable George W. Bush signed the legislation into law during a White House ceremony. The Act was authorized to spend $302 million over a five-year period to provide for the analysis of the incidence and effects of prison rape in federal, state, and local correctional institutions and to provide information, resources, recommendations, and funding intended to protect individuals from prison rape.

The rationale for the law derived from 13 assertions that were presented in PREA. These assertions included estimates that 13 percent of prison inmates were sexually assaulted in prison, often repeatedly; inmates who are young and who suffer from mental illness were at higher risk for sexual assault; prison rape undermined the public health by exposing inmates to HIV/AIDS, tuberculosis, and hepatitis C and B; prison rape brutalized inmates and made it more likely that they will be violent when they return to the community; the interracial nature of many prison sexual assaults exacerbated interracial tensions in the prisons and in the community; prison rape contributed to the rate of assaults and homicides against inmates and staff and contributed to the risk of insurrections and riots within institutions; victims of prison rape suffered severe psychological and physical effects that hindered their ability to reintegrate into their communities; the high rate of sexual assault within prisons involved actual and potential violations of the US Constitution as reflected in *Farmer v. Brennan* (1994); and the high incidence of prison rape undermined the effectiveness and efficiency of federal expenditures and the nature of interstate commerce. These assertions were presented in what appears to have been a good faith effort to identify the many ramifications of what was considered an epidemic of sexual violence in prison, although later research demonstrated that some of these assertions were in fact exaggerated and overly simplistic in the definition of the problem and its possible solutions.

Upon first review, the intent and goals of PREA were straightforward. Philosophically, it sought to further define the position of the US Supreme Court in *Farmer v. Brennan* (1994) in which the Court ruled that deliberate indifference to the substantial risk of sexual assault of incarcerated individuals violated the prisoners' rights under the Cruel and Unusual Punishment Clause of the Eighth Amendment of the US Constitution. It required the Bureau of Justice Statistics (BJS) to collect data on the incidence and prevalence of prison rape in a nationally representative manner that included at least a 10 percent random sample of all federal, state, and county prison inmates, mandated all facility administrators to participate in any data collection requests by BJS, and to provide BJS with access to the inmates under their legal custody. Programmatically, PREA sought to create a zero tolerance standard for the incidence of prison rape, to make prison rape prevention a top priority in each prison system, and to create national standards for the detection, prevention, reduction, and punishment of prison rape. These goals were strengthened by a possible reduction in federal subsidies of 5 percent per year if the standards eventually promulgated by the National Prison Rape Reduction Commission were not met and certified by the chief executive of each state. Taken as a whole, PREA suggested a clear-cut commitment to rape reduction and provided financial incentives for research and programming that were robust and convincing in their intent.

PREA has been conceptualized by some as the needed catalyst for changes in societal and institutional attitudes and responses to sexual assault in prison. It required the Attorney General to submit an annual report to Congress and to the Secretary of Health and Human Services on the activities being conducted pursuant to the law and to publish at the end of the study period a final rule adopting national standards for the detection, prevention, reduction, and punishment of prison rape. It appointed a nine member National Prison Rape Reduction Commission (hereafter referred to as the Commission) and provided the Commission full support in collecting information from various agencies and in conducting hearings pertaining to the appropriate means for classifying and assigning prisoners; investigating and resolving complaints of prison sexual assault; preserving physical and testimonial evidence of the investigation of prison rapes; addressing the acute trauma care of rape victims; developing educational and medical testing measures for reducing the incidence of HIV transmission; the training of correctional staff to better understand the significance of prison rape; protecting the confidentiality of prison rape complaints; and creating a system for reporting incidents of prison rape to ensure the impartial resolution of prison rape complaints. Finally, it created a Review Panel of Prison Rape situated within the National Institute of Justice to carry out public hearings each year concerning the operations of the three prisons with the highest incidence of prison rape, and the two prisons with the lowest incidence of prison rape, in each category of facilities to identify the characteristics of prison systems that are associated with different levels of prison rape.

The Contribution of Our Study to PREA Through Three Unique Areas of Inquiry

The purpose of our research, funded by the National Institute of Justice, was to begin the development of a risk classification scheme for use in men's and women's prisons to identify individuals at increased risk for sexual predation or victimization. It was our assumption that with this knowledge, prison officials would be better able to protect inmates from sexual victimization as required under PREA.

To realize this conceptually straightforward but empirically complex goal, we sought to extend the exceedingly small literature on prison rape in three distinct ways. First, as there were no existing sexual violence risk assessment measures, we chose to adapt violence risk assessment measures to study sexual violence in prison. This would also enable us to examine differences between violence and sexual violence risk markers among inmates. Second, we chose a study design that would allow us to directly examine gender differences in sexual behavior among male and female inmates. Finally, we chose to examine the continuum of sexual behavior among incarcerated individuals, thus allowing us to place sexual coercion in the broader context of sexual behavior in prison.

The Adaptation of Clinical Risk Assessment Measures

Clinical violence risk assessment is designed to identify relevant static and dynamic risk factors with interventions being designed to lower the impact of the dynamic factors, contain the static factors, and through these efforts lower the overall level of risk of the individual. We believed that the identification of these dynamic and static risk factors could not only improve classification but also assist in the identification of interventions that prisons might use to lower the level of risk among groups of offenders who were believed early in their prison careers to pose a higher than average risk for either sexual predation or sexual victimization. Our endeavor thus sought to identify the most empirically sound violence risk markers within the clinical violence risk literature, with a particular emphasis on sexual violence, and to explore the combination of factors that would produce risk models intended to inform correctional interventions and classification and management policies.

We believed that this type of study was timely given advances in the clinical assessment of violence risk that had occurred over the past decade and the development of structured clinical assessment instruments that were demonstrating good predictive power and relevance in assessing and managing violence in the community (Borum, Bartel, & Forth, 2002; Monahan et al., 2001; Webster, Douglas, Eaves, & Hart, 1997). We also believed that the field of clinical risk assessment could inform the correctional risk literature which up until this time had focused almost exclusively on the use of demographic, criminal history, and institutional variables to classify offenders and predict physical violence in correctional facilities among male inmates only (Gaes, Wallace, Gilman, Klein-Saffran, & Suppa, 2002; Wooldredge, 1994).

The Inclusion of Males and Females to Assess Gender Differences

As we developed our study design we decided to include an equal number of male and female inmates in our sample, despite this contradicting the significant disparities that exist in the number of males and females currently held in our state and federal prisons. We decided that this was important both to address rather implicit differences in gendered research on prison rape and to allow us to undertake an empirical analysis of the similarities and differences in the risk markers for the various types of sex as they occurred for both men and women.

Our review of the research regarding prison rape led us to the same conclusion as other researchers. Research on male sexual activity in prisons had primarily focused on sexual coercion whereas the research on female sexual activity in prisons had primarily focused on consensual sex (Hensley, Struckman-Johnson, & Eigenberg, 2000). Hensley et al. (2000) noted that as of 2000, only four studies had been conducted on consensual sex in male prisons. In contrast, from the earliest research (Otis, 1913), there has been a focus on consensual sexual activity among female inmates (Koscheski, Hensley, Wright, & Tewksbury, 2002), with studies of sexual coercion among female inmates appearing for the first time in the mid to late 1990s (see Struckman-Johnson, Struckman-Johnson, Rucker, Bumby, & Donaldson, 1996; Struckman-Johnson & Struckman-Johnson, 2002). As noted by Hensley et al. (2000), it was difficult to determine whether these differences in research orientation reflect reality or whether they reflect researchers' personal attitudes toward sex in prison. Whether males and females experience sex in prisons differently remained an empirical question that to our mind had not been answered.

The Integration of a Full Continuum of Sexual Behavior Observed in Prisons

The PREA legislation identified a forceful mandate to study coerced sexuality in prison. This initial perspective provided us with a clear definition of the illegal acts that we were studying and a pre-existent understanding of the destructive aftermath that could be anticipated particularly in a closed, enduring, and tightly controlled prison environment.

This traditional perspective on sexual assault and victimization, however, began to erode as we left the confines of our university offices and began to visit the many prisons that were to be the site of our data collection. Quickly the wardens and the inmates that were part of our pilot testing began to convey to us a sexual world inside each prison that was far more complex and multifaceted than our initial approach was prepared to handle. We found that there were significant rates of consensual sex occurring in both the male and female prisons, that bartered sex was occurring to obtain various kinds of commodities and psychological benefits, and that there was a small but significant number of rapes that occurred, largely as an expression of dominance and control, and which generally were not reported to the authorities. These were accompanied by a common understanding that retaliation would follow any type of reporting and that there were significant and longstanding effects associated with being labeled a "snitch" in the institution.

As we were encountering this new dimension of prison living, four publications appeared almost simultaneously that helped us appreciate the complexity of the behavior that we were seeking to understand. Smith (2006) published a law review article that explored the motivations that inmates had for being sexual in prison. She observed, "[n]ot withstanding the desire to think otherwise, individuals continue to have an affirmative interest in sexual expression even during institutionalization" (p. 204). Based upon this principle, she identified seven motivational themes that she felt contributed to this continuation of sexual desire including sex for pleasure, trade, freedom, transgression, procreation, safety, and love. Based upon this review, she concluded that sex was a basic drive that did not dissipate upon incarceration but rather reflected an integral but publically unacknowledged part of correctional life commonly recognized by inmates and prison staff alike.

Ristroph (2006) published another law review article in which she argued that distinctions between coerced and consensual sex in prison were sadly artificial and that only a third kind of sex could occur in these surroundings: sex that is "produced by the overwhelmingly coercive environment of prison, sex sought or agreed to under ambiguous circumstances, sex that may constitute prostitution or 'sexual extortion', or just a conflicted quest for a measure of safety in an inherently dangerous environment" (p. 157). Commenting on the prison subculture, she observed that each inmate is by the nature of the institution robbed of any sense of sexual privacy and is contained in an environment in which their body is monitored, restrained, and regulated. The institutional environment is also replete with hierarchical inequalities which spawn opportunities for the "have-nots" to perceive sex as a commodity that can be used to negotiate issues of procurement and safety. From this perspective, Ristroph argued that many inmates consented to sexual encounters not because of a fear of immediate or threatened violence but rather for money, drugs, food, comfort, physical gratification, and love. Acknowledging that some scholars and prison officials insist that no prison sex is fully consensual, she argued that this view was too simplistic and observed that outside the confines of prison, "the law assumes that most adult sex is consensual as long as nobody complains" (p. 6), a perspective not shared by prison officials.

Shortly after the PREA legislation was passed, Mark Fleisher, PhD, an ethnographer with experience in studying criminal behavior from an anthropological perspective, was funded by the National Institute of Justice to explore the culture and language of prison rape. Fleisher and Krienert (2009) conducted 600 semi-structured interviews from both male and female prisons across the country and concluded that while the "idea" of prison rape exerted a powerful influence on inmates' lives, rape "did not frequently occur" (p. 12). Rather, they asserted that these beliefs arose as much from the influence of the family and neighborhood social life, the county jail, and the media, as they did from direct observation or experience in prison. When rape did occur, they were told by inmates that it was often perpetrated against "easy targets" and was frequently associated with getting another inmate's commissary or as retaliation for unpaid debts.

Finally, as we were developing our study design, the BJS published its first in a series of four studies of prison sexual assault. In this first endeavor, the BJS reviewed actual allegations of sexual violence reported to corrections officials throughout the country in male and female prisons during 2004 and 2005 (see Beck & Hughes, 2005; Beck & Harrison, 2006). These data involved 6,241 allegations in 2005, a rate that was up from 5,286 in 2004. The inmate-on-inmate incidents were substantiated in only 15 percent of the allegations made to officials, and these involved primarily younger white male victims, in jail, being assaulted by an older male of a different racial group. Half of these incidents involved the use of force and in the remaining incidents inmates were talked into it, bribed or blackmailed, or offered protection from other inmates. A similar rate of substantiation was found for the staff-on-inmate incidents; however, in two thirds of these incidents the encounters were described by both participants as being romantic in nature. Most substantiated incidents of staff sexual misconduct involved correctional officers, but 16 percent also involved other prison staff including janitors, cooks, and drivers, and 10 percent involved health care staff including counselors, doctors, dentists, and nurses. Two thirds of the perpetrators were female prison staff with male inmates being the presumed "victim."

Based upon the convergence of these early commentaries, combined with our own experience, we decided to include as our primary outcome measures four different types of sexual behavior we had reason to believe occurred in prison either with other inmates, with correctional staff, or with other prison staff or visitors: consensual sex, bartered sex, and coerced sex either as victim or perpetrator. We realized that this approach would provide us with a comparative platform for examining the behavioral interplay between these different types of sexual behaviors in prison. Moreover, given the emergent impression that the rate of authenticated rape would be very low, we concluded that a more inclusive approach would better capture the concerns regarding forced and manipulated sexuality that lay at the heart of the PREA legislation.

Conclusions

Our research emerged in the context of a decade of legal reviews and enactments that positioned the rights of the prisoner in the domains of international human rights and constitutional law, but which simultaneously sought to curtail their access to the federal courts when their attempts at civil litigation were seen as frivolous or malicious. It was within this multifaceted context that we developed a study to identify relevant static and dynamic risk markers recently identified in the clinical risk assessment literature, using samples of both male and female inmates, with the inquiry occurring in the broader context of the continuum of sexual behavior that occurs in the prison environment. Our experiences in the field, combined with the nascent nature of risk research concerning sexual behavior in prison, convinced us that model generation rather than model testing was the appropriate starting place for this type of empirical undertaking.

References

Beck, A. J., & Hughes, T. (2005). *Sexual violence reported by correctional authorities, 2004* (NCJ No. 020656). Washington, DC: US Department of Justice, Bureau of Justice Statistics.

Beck, A. J., & Harrison, P. M. (2006). *Sexual violence reported by correctional authorities, 2005* (NCJ No. 214646). Washington, DC: US Department of Justice, Bureau of Justice Statistics.

Borum, R., Bartel, P., & Forth, A. (2002). *SAVRY: Manual for the structured assessment of violence risk in youth.* Tampa, FL: Florida Mental Health Institute, University of South Florida.

Columbia Human Rights Law Review (2009). *A jailhouse lawyer's manual* (8th ed.). Available from http://xa.yimg.com/kq/groups/16831155/909208821/name/Jailhouse+Lawyers+Manual.pdf

Fleisher, M. S., & Krienert, J. L. (2009). *The myth of prison rape: Sexual culture in American prisons.* Lanham, MD: Rowman & Littlefield Publishers.

Gaes, G. G., Wallace, S., Gilman, E., Klein-Saffran, J., & Suppa, S. (2002). The influence of prison gang affiliation on violence and other prison misconduct. *The Prison Journal, 82,* 359–385.

Golden, D. M. (2006, June). *The prison litigation reform act: A proposal for closing the loophole for rapists.* Washington, DC: American Constitution Society for Law and Policy.

Hensley, C., Struckman-Johnson, C., & Eigenberg, H. M. (2000). Introduction: The history of prison sex research. *The Prison Journal, 80,* 360–367.

Koscheski, M., Hensley, C., Wright, J., & Tewksbury, R. (2002). Consensual sexual behavior. In C. Hensley (Ed.), *Prison sex: Practice and policy* (pp. 111–132). Boulder, CO: Lynne Rienner Publishers.

Maguire, K., & Pestore, A. L. (1997). *Sourcebook of Criminal Justice Statistics, 442.* Bureau of Justice Statistics, US Department of Justice.

Monahan, J., Steadman, H., Silver, E., Appelbaum, P., Robbins, P., Mulvey, E., et al. (2001). *Rethinking risk assessment: The MacArthur study of mental disorder and violence.* New York, NY: Oxford University Press.

Otis, M. (1913). A perversion not commonly noted. *Journal of Abnormal Psychology, 8,* 113–116.

Puplava, J. A. (1997). Peanut butter and politics: An evaluation of the separation of powers issues in Section 802 of the Prison Litigation Reform Act. *Indiana Law Journal, 73* (1), 329–353.

Ribet, B. (2010). Naming prison rape as disablement: A critical analysis of the Prison Litigation Reform Act, The Americans With Disabilities Act, and The Imperatives of Survivor-Oriented Advocacy. *Virginia Journal of Social Policy and the Law, 17,* 281, 317.

Ristroph, A. (2006). Sexual punishments. *Columbia Journal of Gender and Law, 15,* 139–184.

Smith, B. (2006). Rethinking prison sex: Self-expression and safety. *Columbia Journal of Gender and Law, 15,* 185–234.

Struckman-Johnson, C., & Struckman-Johnson, D. (2002). Sexual coercion reported by women in three Midwestern prisons. *Journal of Sex Research, 39,* 217–227.

Struckman-Johnson, C., Struckman-Johnson, D., Rucker, L., Bumby, K., & Donaldson, S. (1996). Sexual coercion reported by men and women in prison. *The Journal of Sex Research, 33,* 67–76.

Taylor, K. F. (2000). The prison litigation reform act's administrative exhaustion requirement: Closing the money damage loophole. *Washington University Law Quarterly*, *78*, 955–978.

Webster, C. D., Douglas, K. S., Eaves, D., & Hart, S. D. (1997). *HCR-20: Assessing the Risk for Violence* (Version 2). Mental Health, Law, and Policy Institute, Simon Fraser University.

Wooldredge, J. D. (1994). Inmate crime and victimization in a southwestern correctional facility. *Journal of Criminal Justice*, *22*, 367–381.

UNIT IV: CRITICAL THINKING QUESTIONS

1. Explain how current criminal justice policies foster further criminal behavior. Identify affirmative actions the criminal justice system can implement to prevent recidivism.
2. Describe how prison overcrowding is a state fiscal policy concern. Identify strategies for reducing the jail population.
3. Identify gender-focused resources. Explain the necessity for such resources.
4. Describe the differences between male and female leadership. Identify the major characteristics of female leadership.
5. Identify and explain the four interlocking factors that underlie the prison crisis. Discuss the goals of the anti-prison movement.
6. Describe how states contribute to correctional corruption in the private prison industry. Explain the difficulty in investigating this type of corruption.
7. Define "crony capitalism." Explain its effects and influences on the private prison industry.
8. Explain why prison rape is a human rights issue. Discuss the difficulty in passing the Prison Rape Elimination Act.

   Overall

   Using only the information in this unit, how would you describe corrections and punishment in the United States to someone from another country?

UNIT V

Juvenile Justice

Unit Introduction

The juvenile justice system in the United States was first established with the New York House of Refuge in 1824, the first correctional institution for juvenile offenders. Another early milestone came about during the Progressive Era with the Child-Saving Movement. In 1899, the Illinois Juvenile Court Act was passed to remove juvenile offenders from criminal courts. In the history of the juvenile justice system, there has been an ongoing debate about how to define a juvenile offender and the "adultification" of juvenile offenders. In 1974, the Juvenile Justice Delinquency Prevention Act was passed to remove juveniles from adult jails and to separate status offenders from juvenile offenders. This debate was also fueled in the 1990s with "get-tough" policies and mediated by nationwide research. Most recently, reformation in the juvenile justice system has been driven by research toward evidence-based programs (Reading 5.1).

Globally, the U.S. juvenile justice system has been criticized for its punitive legislation, allowing the transfer of juvenile offenders to adult courts, and its unethical policies in violation of the Convention on the Rights of the Child. However, it has been noted that human rights are shaping our legislation toward more progressive reforms which include the CRC (Reading 5.2).

Another aspect of the juvenile justice system is the placement of offenders with the objective of public safety. Practitioners call for a focus on risk assessment to match offenders with program models to help rehabilitate the offender. Other issues that must be considered when placing offenders is culture, gender, sexual orientation, and mental health. As with other areas of the CJS, gender plays a role in the juvenile system, particularly with respect to decision-making and LGBT youth (Readings 5.3 and 5.4).

Just like adults, there are juveniles who have mental health issues for which treatment makes more sense than incarceration. Although cognitive behavioral therapy is used in the juvenile justice system, programs keep looking for alternative strategies such as yoga which can better equip juvenile offenders emotionally (Reading 5.5). However, youths who have not been provided the skills to negotiate their anxiety, depression, etc., have access to a wider variety of drugs than any other generation. It is important that practitioners be aware of current drug trends to help identify and match offenders with the right program (Reading 5.6).

READING 5.1

The Cycle of Reform and Retrenchment in Juvenile Justice

By Edward J. Loughran

The history of juvenile justice in the U.S. dates back to the early 1800s with the opening of the first House of Refuge in New York City, and has evolved through repeated phases of reform and retrenchment. One of the earliest reforms was in Massachusetts. The Westboro School for Boys was constructed in 1846 and then closed with all Massachusetts training schools in the 1970s in a sweeping reform moving youths from institutions to small treatment centers located regionally around the state. The most significant retrenchment was in the 1990s, when the "get tough" movement returned juvenile justice systems to reliance on institutions as placement of choice. Today's emphasis on evidence-based programs is the most recent reform, moving delinquent and at-risk youths into community programs for the best chances of success.

I have experienced more than one of these cycles during my 40 years in the field and lived amidst reform as commissioner of the Massachusetts Department of Youth Services (DYS) at the height of its leadership, when designated as the national model for juvenile corrections by the National Council on Crime and Delinquency. At DYS and in my current role as executive director of the Council of Juvenile Correctional Administrators, I have seen the waves of reform come and go across the country and believe we are learning how to ensure the changes that improve the care, treatment and outcomes for youths and families do not get washed away with the next incoming tide.

Soon after I began my career as the director of a group home in New York City for the New York State Division for Youth, the Juvenile Justice and Delinquency Prevention Act of 1974 passed Congress and required states to remove juveniles from adult jails and to end the practice of housing status offenders with juvenile delinquents in training schools. The requirements of the act ushered in the era of "least restrictive placement" for delinquents and remained the federal government's direction to state systems.

However, the more lenient approach to handling juveniles in trouble with the law was short-lived. Politics, funding and construction dominated policy-making and practice. In 1978, the New York

Edward J. Loughran, "The Cycle of Reform and Retrenchment in Juvenile Justice," *Corrections Today*, vol. 73, no. 1, pp. 6, 12.

State Legislature rushed to pass the Juvenile Offender Act after a 15-year-old boy named Willie Bosket robbed and killed two laborers on successive weekend nights and bragged upon his capture, "You can't do anything to me. I'm only 15." New York, which already tried all 16-year olds charged with a crime in its criminal court, now required the automatic transfer of 13, 14- and 15-year-olds to criminal court for 17 different felony crimes from murder to burglary. Florida soon followed by giving prosecutors the authority to remand to adult court youths between the ages of 14 and 18 who were charged with either a misdemeanor or felony offense. When juvenile crime, then fueled by the lethal combination of drugs and guns in the hands of kids, began to rise in the mid-1980s and finally crested in 1993, virtually every state in the country had followed New York and Florida by passing transfer laws—usually in reaction to a particularly heinous crime by a single youth or group of juveniles acting together.

This time period regarded as the "get-tough" movement or "adultification" of juvenile crime, witnessed more youths transferred to criminal court or given longer confinement in secure juvenile facilities than in any other period since the founding of the juvenile court. Some transferred juveniles received the death penalty; many were given a life without parole sentence. Money followed the legislative and policy changes; panicked legislatures authorized the building of thousands of new secure beds around the country to "get tough." Ironically, most beds did not come on line until well after the juvenile crime rate began its steady drop for 10 uninterrupted years in 1993. But the overbuilding led to poor practices and policies incarcerating many nonviolent youths to fill the "state of the art" secure beds to justify their costs. One state even built a "supermax" juvenile facility in 1999 only to close it a decade later. The second irony is now it is again money—the lack of—driving the closure of large facilities and encouraging reinvestment in less expensive and more effective community programs.

Throughout retrenchment cycles, isolated pockets of reform have happened throughout the country that provide lessons for successful change initiatives. In Massachusetts, DYS' emergence in the early 1990s as a leader and model system led to replication of its reform system replacing large, congregate care training schools with small 15-bed secure treatment programs throughout the state. Just as state officials traveled to Massachusetts in the 19th century to study the Westboro School for Boys, policymakers from other states came again to Massachusetts to learn how and what DYS developed. Missouri sent several teams of judges, legislators and juvenile justice practitioners to Massachusetts, studied the changes and upon their return, adapted the Massachusetts model to the Missouri system, which is recognized as a leader in juvenile corrections today.

Research and data also provided impetus for reform. In 1994, the Office of Juvenile Justice and Delinquency Prevention (OJJDP) launched the congressionally-mandated Conditions of Confinement study to collect data from 1,000 correction and detention facilities nationwide. The study found poor conditions in facilities, including high rates of youth injuries and staff turnover, little mental health services and crowded living. The study also found that facilities accredited by existing standards programs did not fare better than nonaccredited facilities. OJJDP launched the Performance-based Standards (PbS) program to establish and implement national performance standards and outcome data measuring practices. CJCA developed and directs PbS and currently works with more than 200 individual facilities in 28 states and the District of Columbia to align practices with approaches deemed effective by research and to integrate the PbS continuous improvement process with daily operations. Analysis of the national PbS database builds resources the field can use to address conditions of confinement issues. For example, research demonstrates the safest facilities are those where youths report they understand the rules, staff are fair, school is good and they have not been locked up—tangible practices facility staff can address and as a result, see fewer injuries and uses of restraints and isolation.

Research demonstrates the safest facilities are those where youths report they understand the rules, staff are fair, school is good and they have not been locked up—tangible practices facility staff can address and as a result, see fewer injuries and uses of restraints and isolation.

Research identifying what approaches work to rehabilitate young offenders started with studies by Robert Ross and Paul Gendreau, who reviewed 95 intervention programs and found that 86 percent of them reported success. Mark Lipsey's meta-analyses of many rehabilitative programs in the 1990s, which also demonstrated the effectiveness of correctional treatment programs similarly increased understanding and changes in practice. As research, outcome data and effectiveness increasingly entered the discussions of juvenile correctional practice as well as state legislatures, the rigorously-tested interventions of multi-systemic therapy, functional family therapy and multi-dimensional treatment foster care, began to spread across the country to treat youths with emotional and family-related problems in their home communities rather than in far away institutions.

Two philanthropic organizations have developed and invested millions of dollars during the last 15 years in juvenile justice reform initiatives: *The John D. and Catherine T.* MacArthur Foundation and the Annie E. Casey Foundation. Beginning in 1996, the MacArthur Foundation funded the interdisciplinary Research Network on Adolescent Development and Juvenile Justice as well as training, advocacy, policy analysis and public education efforts. These reform-oriented efforts laid the groundwork for the national Models for Change initiative, which promotes juvenile justice reform in 16 states around the country. In 1992, the Casey Foundation launched the Juvenile Detention Alternatives to Incarceration project, which works with local and state pretrial detention authorities to significantly reduce the number of youths confined while awaiting their court process.

The evidence indicates that juvenile justice is recovering from the excesses of the "get-tough" movement. Will the current reforms develop staying power, or will policymakers flinch at the first sign of a rise in juvenile crime? That depends on three things: First, each individual reform must be rigorously evaluated to demonstrate its effectiveness with the juvenile population it was designed to serve. Second, reforms must be incorporated in the everyday operations of a juvenile justice system—not stand as an isolated instance of reform with no connection to the whole entity. Third, reformers must leave their egos at the door and work together with other juvenile justice stakeholders to perpetuate the reforms.

READING 5.2

Globalization and Juvenile Life Sentences

Creating Meaningful Opportunities for Release for Juvenile Offenders

By Beth Caldwell

Although the United States is the only country in the world that currently incarcerates juvenile offenders for life without the possibility of parole, this country appears to be moving towards practices more consistent with the rest of the world. This article discusses these trends and focuses on California's groundbreaking legislative reforms, which have created a schema that provides most juvenile offenders with the opportunity to earn their release from prison after serving between fifteen and twenty-five years in prison. Though the punitive American approach to juvenile justice is out of step with the rest of the world, the national trends are moving this country's treatment of juveniles who break the law closer to the aspirations of the Convention on the Rights of the Child.

The widespread adoption of the United Nations Convention on the Rights of the Child (CRC) has made a tremendous impact on global responses to juveniles—young people under the age of eighteen—who break the law. Although the United States has not ratified this nearly universally accepted Convention, its principles are nonetheless influencing the evolution of American juvenile justice. The U.S. Supreme Court has been influenced by global practices shaped by the CRC in a string of recent Eighth Amendment cases that prohibit the juvenile death penalty and limit juvenile LWOP sentences.

Although the United States is the only country in the world that currently incarcerates juvenile offenders for life without the possibility of parole, we appear to moving towards practices more consistent with the rest of the world. The recent trend to limit and, in many states, eliminate life sentences for juvenile offenders is notable in this regard. Legislation that expands the opportunities for juveniles sentenced to life in prison to obtain release is rapidly unfolding across the country. This article discusses these trends and focuses on California's groundbreaking legislative reforms, which have created a schema that provides most juvenile offenders with the opportunity to earn their release from prison after serving between fifteen and twenty-five years in prison. While some states continue to allow the practice of sentencing juveniles to life without parole (LWOP), the national trend is moving in the opposite direction, bringing American juvenile justice back towards its rehabilitative roots and rendering it more consistent with internationally accepted practices.

Global Trends in Juvenile Justice

When viewed in a global context, the United States' approach to juvenile justice has become quite punitive (Goldson & Muncie, 2006). Although the country's juvenile court system was founded in 1899 based on the idea that juveniles are fundamentally different than adults and should therefore be treated differently when they break the law, punitive reforms throughout the 1990s created numerous exceptions to juvenile court jurisdiction. These ever-widening exceptions opened the doors to allow increasing numbers of teenagers under the age of eighteen to be processed in adult courts each year. By the end of the 1990s, every state in the nation allowed juveniles to be transferred to adult court under some circumstances (Fagan & Zimring, 2000).

What began as an exception, carved out for the "worst of the worst," expanded to have a broad reach. An estimated 250,000 juveniles are tried, sentenced, and/or incarcerated in the adult criminal justice system each year within the United States (Arya, 2011). Once these teenagers enter the adult system, they no longer receive access to the rehabilitative services the juvenile delinquency system was designed to provide. In many respects, these laws have dismantled the juvenile justice system by systematically excluding large groups of young people.

Transferring juveniles to adult courts and, ultimately, to adult prisons, raises serious ethical and public policy concerns given what is known about the experiences of juvenile offenders who are housed in adult facilities. Studies show juvenile offenders are more likely to commit suicide and to be attacked with a weapon when housed in adult facilities (Redding, 2010). Furthermore, removing teenagers from the juvenile court system on such a widespread level reveals a collective belief that they are beyond redemption. The punitive trajectory of American juvenile justice since the 1990s indicates a lack of faith that young people are capable of being rehabilitated as the juvenile court system set out to do.

This punitive approach to juvenile justice stands in stark contrast to global trends. At the international level, countries are moving towards juvenile justice systems that incorporate the principles set forth in the United Nations Convention on the Rights of the Child. Celebrating its twenty-fifth anniversary this year, the CRC has been accepted across the world. According to UNICEF, it "is the most rapidly and widely ratified convention in history" (UNICEF). 192 countries were State Parties to the Convention as of November 2005. The United States and Somalia are the only countries that have not ratified the Convention. The CRC requires due process protections for young people and requires states to use alternatives to incarceration whenever possible for juveniles who break the law. It emphasizes the rehabilitative potential of young people and embraces a philosophy that prioritizes rehabilitation over retribution. The CRC expressly prohibits sentencing juveniles to life without the possibility of parole.

Many countries have dramatically reformed their juvenile justice systems in order to comply with the CRC. I investigated this reform process in Mexico in 2010. Prior to 2005, juveniles who committed crimes in Mexico were either handled in an administrative system that lacked due process protections or through the regular criminal justice s ystem geared for adults. Due to the constitutional reforms, each of Mexico's thirty-one states was required to establish a juvenile delinquency system. In the state of Oaxaca, where I did most of my research, the government hired university professors to research best practices. Informed by this work, and by the CRC, they developed a juvenile justice code that truly embodies the principles of the Convention (Caldwell, 2011).

For example, the CRC prohibits life without parole for juvenile offenders. Oaxaca's code allows for a maximum period of incarceration of ten years for people under the age of eighteen who commit crimes. The CRC states that juveniles should not be incarcerated with adults unless it would be "in the child's best interest." Accordingly, Oaxaca does not allow juveniles to be transferred into adult court or to be housed in adult jails or prisons. Further, the CRC mandates that incarceration be used "as a measure of last resort" and for "the shortest appropriate period of time." Oaxaca's code therefore prohibits the incarceration of children under the age of fourteen and uses detention sparingly for older juvenile offenders, incarcerating a total of twenty-six youth in the entire state in 2009.

Other countries also incarcerate young offenders at much lower rates than the United States. According to the Justice Policy Institute (2011), "[t]he U.S. has almost 6 times as many youth in secure confinement as all comparison nations combined, despite having only a third greater general population." Finland, for example, had a total of six juveniles detained in 2008 (Justice Policy Institute, 2011). New Zealand uses restorative justice circles to respond to most youth crime. There are alternative ways to approaching juvenile crime, and many countries use them. The American approach of sentencing young people to longer and longer prison sentences is not the only way to respond when young people break the law.

Because the United States has not ratified the CRC, we are not bound to follow it. An estimated 2,500 people are incarcerated in the U.S. for LWOP sentences on the basis of crimes they committed when they were under the age of eighteen. Thousands more are serving de facto LWOP sentences—sentences that amount to LWOP sentences because release is extremely unlikely or will not occur within the life expectancy of the juvenile offender. In contrast, no juvenile offenders are serving life without the possibility of parole sentences in the rest of the world. Some countries allow the practice but do not apply it towards juveniles (de la Vega & Leighton, 2009). The United States stands alone in its use of

LWOP sentences for youth; many posit that the country's desire to continue to impose this sentence stands in the way of ratifying the CRC.

Global Trends and the Supreme Court

Although the United States has refused to ratify the CRC, the Convention's core principles are influencing American law. The Supreme Court has considered it in its recent Eighth Amendment jurisprudence on extreme sentences for juvenile offenders. When the Court held in 2005 that the death penalty constitutes cruel and unusual punishment in violation of the Eighth Amendment, it was impressed by the CRS's "express prohibition on capital punishment for crimes committed by juveniles under 18" (*Roper v. Simmons*, 2005, p. 576). The opinion discusses international practices, concluding, "it is fair to say that the United States now stands alone in a world that has turned its face against the juvenile death penalty" (p. 577).

Five years after it outlawed the juvenile death penalty, the Supreme Court banned juvenile LWOP sentences for juveniles who have not committed homicide in *Graham v. Florida* (2010). The Court compared life without parole to a death sentence in that it is the second most severe punishment that can be imposed. International practices informed by the CRC also influenced the Supreme Court in Graham, where the Court explained, "'the overwhelming weight of international opinion against' life without parole for non-homicide offenses committed by juveniles 'provide[s] respected and significant confirmation for our own conclusions'" that life without parole is cruel and unusual punishment (*Graham v. Florida*, 2010, p. 81). As the Court acknowledged in *Roper* (2005), "It does not lessen our fidelity to the Constitution or our pride in its origins to acknowledge that the express affirmation of certain fundamental rights by other nations and peoples simply underscores the centrality of those same rights within our own heritage of freedom." (p. 578).

In *Miller v. Alabama* (2012), the Supreme Court found that "appropriate actions" for imposing the sentence of life without parole "will be uncommon" for juveniles, but it left the possibility open for juveniles who have committed homicide. Under *Miller*, life without parole for juveniles may not be imposed under mandatory sentencing guidelines. Rather, the sentencing court must consider mitigating evidence relating to the defendant's youth prior to imposing a life without the possibility of parole sentence.

There is a great deal of litigation surrounding the question of whether *Miller v. Alabama*'s prohibition on mandatory LWOP sentences for juvenile offenders applies to those 2,500 juvenile offenders who were sentenced to LWOP prior to the *Miller* decision. States are trying to determine whether *Miller* applies retroactively. Though state courts have reached conflicting conclusions on this issue, the majority of the states whose high courts have ruled on the issue have found that *Miller* does apply retroactively. Illinois, Iowa, Massachusetts, Mississippi, Nebraska, New Hampshire, and Texas have found that the case does apply retroactively, and that those sentenced prior to the decision are entitled to resentencing that considers mitigating factors or to the possibility of release. On the other hand, Pennsylvania, Minnesota, Louisiana, and Michigan have determined that *Miller* does not apply retroactively. These states house large numbers of juvenile offenders serving LWOP sentences; there are 355 in Louisiana, 444 in Pennsylvania, and over 300 in Michigan, comprising approximately 44% of total juveniles serving LWOP in the entire country. Nationally, the trend appears to favor limiting life without parole for juveniles, consistent with the CRC and international norms.

Advocates have appealed international human rights bodies to bring state interpretations of the law more in line with international human rights principles. For example, in *Hill v. United States* (2014), the ACLU and the Human Rights Institute of Colombia Law School filed a case with the Inter-American Commission on Human Rights alleging that the United States is in violation of the American Declaration of Human Rights because the state of Michigan continues to incarcerate juveniles with LWOP sentences. This case was pending in front of the Inter-American Commission at the same time that the Michigan Supreme Court was considering whether *Miller* applies retroactively. A hearing was convened in front of the Inter-American Commission the same week that Michigan Supreme Court heard oral arguments. Ultimately, Michigan determined that *Miller* is not retroactive, and the Inter-American Commission case is still pending. It seems likely that the Inter-American Commission will find the United States in violation of human rights principles because it continues to allow juvenile life without parole.

Some states have taken a broader approach than *Miller* requires and are eliminating LWOP as a sentencing option for juvenile offenders, consistent with the CRC's statement that "[n]either capital punishment nor life imprisonment without possibility of release shall be imposed for offences committed by persons below eighteen years of age." The Massachusetts Supreme Court recently held that juvenile LWOP (even for homicide offenders) violates the state's Declaration of Human Rights. Colorado and Texas transformed juvenile LWOP sentences to life with the possibility of parole after 40 years. Wyoming and Delaware did the same, but offer the possibility of release after 25 and 20 years respectively. Delaware's law requires that youthful characteristics be considered in resentencing decisions.

Legislative Reforms in Juvenile Justice

The Supreme Court's acknowledgement of the CRC's core principles is trickling down to the states, spawning legislation that expands the protections available to juvenile offenders beyond the minimal boundaries the Supreme Court has established. Within the past year, states such as California, Hawaii, and West Virginia have passed legislation that requires all juvenile offenders to have "meaningful opportunities to obtain release" from prison. These changes to the law are moving our treatment of juvenile offenders back towards the original goals the juvenile court was founded upon, towards a focus on rehabilitation and redemption rather than permanent incarceration. Oddly enough, American juvenile justice is returning to its roots in part due to the influence of international human rights norms, epitomized in the CRC, as well as international practices.

State legislation that builds on the Supreme Court cases and provides more opportunities for juvenile offenders appears to be gaining momentum. California passed Senate Bill 9 in 2012 followed by Senate Bill 260 in 2013. Together, these bills created opportunities for almost all California juvenile offenders, including those previously sentenced to life without parole, with the opportunity to be released from prison after they have served between fifteen and twenty-five years of their sentences. This legislation effectively transforms California's approach to juvenile justice, which for years had become increasingly punitive. The state currently incarcerates over 6,000 individuals who were sentenced to spend life in prison and will now qualify for release. Senate Bill 9 created a process whereby juvenile offenders serving life without the possibility of parole sentences can petition the court to be resentenced to life *with* the possibility of parole. Under the new law, the court must consider how the crime was influenced by the individual's youth, as well as any evidence of rehabilitation. Senate Bill 260 applies to almost all juvenile offenders with long adult prison sentences, including those with life sentences and those with long term-of-years sentences. It creates a special parole process that for youth offenders; the Board of Parole must consider how "hallmark features of youth" influenced the crime, and evidence of rehabilitation and maturation since the time of the crime. The Parole Board "shall give great weight to the diminished culpability of juveniles as compared to adults, the hallmark features of youth, and any subsequent growth and increased maturity of the prisoner in accordance with the relevant case law." Under SB 260 thousands of young offenders with determinative term-of-years sentences who would have never qualified for parole within their lifetimes will now have Youth Offender Parole Hearings after serving fifteen years in custody.

California's new Youth Offender Parole Hearings are one approach to operationalizing the Supreme Court's directive in *Graham* (2010) that states provide juvenile offenders with a "meaningful opportunity to obtain release based on demonstrated maturity and rehabilitation." The Supreme Court purposefully left the implementation of this meaningful opportunity for release vague, stating, "[i]t is for the State, in the first instance, to explore the means and mechanisms for compliance" (p. 75). Since *Graham* specifically addressed a life without parole sentence, courts are divided as to whether this "meaningful opportunity to obtain release" requirement applies only to those sentenced to life without the possibility of parole. California's Supreme Court has taken a broader view. In *People v. Caballero* (2012), it held that *Graham*'s prohibition on life without parole for juveniles who have not committed homicide applies to those sentenced to *de facto* life sentences. Juvenile offenders sentenced to prison terms that exceed their life expectancies, such as Caballero's 110-year sentence, are now entitled to meaningful opportunities to obtain release in California.

California's approach to offering more juvenile offenders the opportunity to obtain release at younger ages is moving in the direction of international practices. In England, for example, juveniles are not incarcerated for the rest of their lives; the longest sentence imposed on a juvenile offender was 30 years (de la Vega & Leighton, 2008). Similarly, the maximum sentence given to a juvenile in Europe typically would not exceed 25 years (de la Vega & Leighton, 2008). Other countries seem to offer juveniles more meaningful opportunities for release than found in most states in the United States. Although California's legislation goes farther than many other states, others are following suit. West Virginia and Hawaii both passed very similar legislation in 2014.

California's Youth Offender Parole Hearings appear to be accomplishing what they set out to do in that more juvenile offenders are being released at younger ages through the process. Debates about the Supreme Court's loose "meaningful opportunity" standard focus on (1) the age of release; (2) the likelihood of release. Although the Florida Court of Appeals says that offering the possibility of parole after an individual has served seventy years in prison qualifies as a meaningful opportunity for release, it seems that an individual should be released at a younger age in order for the opportunity for release to be truly meaningful. In California, the average age of prisoners granted parole in the first six months of the Youth Offender Parole Hearings is approximately ten years younger than the average age of the general population of parolees.

So far, those who have been granted parole have been incarcerated for at least twenty-five years. While this is less time than other lifers spend in prison in California, it is still longer than a system modeled after the CRC would permit. The CRC requires not only that incarceration be used as a last resort, but also that it be imposed for the shortest time necessary. As previously discussed, twenty-five years is the longest sentence that would typically be imposed on a juvenile offender in Europe. More progressive recommendations for reconsidering the release of juvenile offenders set the timeframe for parole at ten years. Based on the fundamental premise that young people have unique capacities to change as they mature, a Michigan appellate judge drew the line at ten years (although his decision was subsequently reversed) as does the Model Penal Code. In Oaxaca, Mexico, ten years is the longest sentenced a juvenile may receive. Ten years is a logical point for parole or resentencing considerations to take place because a juvenile's brain continues to develop until the age of twenty-five. After spending ten years in custody, a young offender would have matured into adulthood, and many will have grown out of certain hallmark features of youth the Supreme Court has recognized may contribute to crime, including impulsivity, poor decision-making, and susceptibility to influence. The ten-year-mark would provide young offenders with more meaningful opportunities to integrate into society and to build meaningful lives upon their release. This would give them enough time to have children, raise families, and establish meaningful professional careers.

In order to be meaningful, an opportunity for release on parole must be realistic. In *Graham*, Supreme Court clarified that juvenile offenders are not required to be released, but they must have a *realistic* opportunity to be released. Typically, parole grants are unlikely. Nationally, grant rates range between under ten percent to thirty percent. My preliminary research on California's Youth Offender Parole Hearings suggests that those who go through YOPHs are at least twelve percent more likely to be released than their counterparts in the general population. This is a sign that the specialized youth parole hearings are creating more realistic opportunities for juvenile offenders to be released.

In order to earn their release at Youth Offender Parole Hearings, young offenders must demonstrate they have been rehabilitated. Like many other states, California's prison classification ranks prisoners as higher security risks if they are younger, and if they committed an offense while they are under the age of eighteen. This systematically deprives young offenders of many educational, vocational, and rehabilitative opportunities, and exposes them to higher levels of violence. Juvenile offenders tend to be sent to Level IV prisons, the highest security level, when they first arrive in prison. This renders them even more vulnerable to violence than they would be in other adult prison facilities.

In August 2014, California passed legislation to respond to this problem. AB 1276 is currently awaiting the governor's signature to become law. This new law would change the prison classification system to allow young people who are twenty-two years old or younger at the time of their entry to prison to be classified under a specialized system that would channel them into lower security facilities that offer more rehabilitative programming. This approach is more consistent with the CRC's recognition of "the right of every child ... to be treated in a manner ... which takes into account the child's age and the desirability of promoting the child's reintegration and the child's assuming a constructive role in society" (Article 40). Missouri's blended sentencing model, discussed at this symposium, takes this effort to expand rehabilitative opportunities to youth offenders in the adult system even further by housing them in their own facility that is designed to offer rehabilitative opportunities to juvenile offenders. This is a model California and other states should consider in order to allow all young offenders access to the kinds of rehabilitative services our juvenile court system was designed to offer. The Supreme Court has recognized that young people are capable of change, and we have an obligation (and opportunity) to provide them with rehabilitative opportunities even if they are transferred to adult court.

Conclusion

I think—I hope—the American approach to juvenile justice is heading towards a philosophy more rooted in human rights principles, that considers the fundamental differences between youth and adults, and that offers meaningful opportunities to change and become reintegrated into society. California's approach, which offers resentencing opportunities to juveniles serving life without the possibility of parole sentences and provides Youth Offender Parole Hearings after juvenile offenders have served fifteen to twenty-five years of their sentences, is a promising model. The state's recent move to change the prison classification process for young offenders so they can be housed in facilities with greater access to rehabilitative programming is another important step in the direction of offering real opportunities for redemption to people who have made tragic mistakes in their youth. Missouri's blended sentencing model is an even more promising model for offering juvenile offenders with adult prison sentences access to rehabilitative programming.

The punitive American approach to juvenile justice is still out of step with the rest of the world, but I am encouraged by national trends that are moving our treatment of juveniles who break the law closer to the aspirations of the Convention on the Rights of the Child. I hope that our country's responses to juvenile crime will increasingly acknowledge the importance of youth as a mitigating factor and facilitate the social reintegration of young offenders as the CRC would have us do.

References

Arya, N. (2011). State Trends: Legislative Victories from 2005 to 2010: Removing Youth from the Adult Criminal Justice System. Washington DC: Campaign for Youth Justice. Retrieved from http://www.campaignforyouthjustice.org/component/content/article/1-real-life/88-statetrends2013.html

Caldwell, B. (2011). Punishment v. Restoration: A Comparative Analysis of Juvenile Delinquency Law in the United States and Mexico. *Cardozo Journal of International and Comparative Law 20(1),* 105–142.

De la Vega, C. & Leighton, M. (2008). Sentencing our Children to Die in Prison: Global Law and Practice. *University of San Francisco Law Review 42,* 983–1043.

Fagan, J. & Zimring, F. E. (Eds.) (2000). *The Changing Borders of Juvenile Justice: Transfer of Adolescents to the Criminal Court.* Chicago: University of Chicago Press.

Goldson, B. & Muncie, J. (2006). Rethinking Youth Justice: Comparative Analysis, International Human Rights, and Research Evidence. *Youth Justice 6 (2),* 91–106.

Graham v. Florida, 560 U.S. 48 (2010).

Hill v. United States, Case No. 12.866, Inter-American Commission on Human Rights (2014).

Justice Policy Institute (2011). *Finding Direction: Expanding Criminal Justice Options by Considering Policies of Other Nations.* Retrieved from http://www.justicepolicy.org/uploads/justicepolicy/documents/juvenile_justice.pdf

Miller v. Alabama, 132 S. Ct. 2455 (2012).

People v. Caballero, 282 P. 3d 291 (Cal. 2012).

Redding, R. E. (2010). *Juvenile Transfer Laws: An Effective Deterrent to Delinquency.* Washington DC: U.S. Department of Justice, Office of Juvenile Justice & Delinquency Prevention. Retrieved from https://www.ncjrs.gov/pdffiles1/ojjdp/220595.pdf.

Roper v. Simmons, 543 U.S. 551 (2005).

United Nations Convention on the Rights of the Child, *opened for signature* Nov. 20, 1989, 1577 U.N.T.S. 3 (entered into force Sept. 2, 1990).

UNICEF, *Convention on the Rights of the Child.* Retrieved from http://www.unicef.org/crc/.

READING 5.3

New Practices in Juvenile Justice

By Cheryln K. Cherie Townsend

Edward J. "Ned" Loughran, executive director of the Council of Juvenile Correctional Administrators, provides a historical summary of juvenile justice reforms in his Guest Editorial article in this issue of *Corrections Today.* One of the three things that he concludes are necessary to sustain the current reforms being implemented in many jurisdictions in our country is that they be incorporated in the everyday operations of a juvenile justice system. As you read this issue of *Corrections Today,* you will have the opportunity to learn how several jurisdictions are translating the knowledge about what works best with youths in the juvenile justice system into everyday operations. This gives me great hope for the future—not only in terms of the positive public safety outcomes that will result from juvenile justice reforms, but also in terms of the positive life outcomes and opportunities that will be achieved by youths in these systems.

In the 1990s, the *Comprehensive Strategy for Serious, Violent, and Chronic Juvenile Offenders* was developed by John Wilson and James "Buddy" Howell and published by the Office of Juvenile Justice and Delinquency Prevention.[1] This strategy provided a framework that guided many juvenile justice practitioners, communities and jurisdictions as they sought to both prevent youths from becoming delinquent and to improve the system's response to youths who engaged in delinquent conduct. Since the publication of the comprehensive strategy, we have learned a great deal about risk assessment and which program models are most effective with specific youths, what is necessary for longterm positive outcomes and how to achieve public safety outcomes and cost-effectiveness through more balanced investments. Recently, the Center for Juvenile Justice Reform at Georgetown University commissioned a paper incorporating this new information into the comprehensive strategy titled *Improving the Effectiveness of Juvenile Justice Programs: A New Perspective on Evidence-Based Practice.*[2] The paper notes, "The juvenile justice system has made enormous progress in program development and system reforms over the past twenty years. Nonetheless, many systems continue to struggle with achieving a balance of community-based versus institutionally based care and managing the tension between their rehabilitative versus public safety functions."[3] While that challenge exists, you will see in this issue of *Corrections Today* that several jurisdictions representing states, counties

Cheryln K. Cherie Townsend, "New Practices in Juvenile Justice," *Corrections Today*, vol. 73, no. 1, pp. 8, 13.

and all regions of our country are successfully finding the balance. There is a diversity of practices presented in this issue, including evidence-based program models, overall rehabilitation strategies, positive youth development and specialized treatment. You will also see thoughtful and successful organizational changes taking place in these representatives of our nation's juvenile justice systems.

King Whitney Jr. wrote, "Change has a considerable psychological impact on the human mind. To the fearful it is threatening because it means things may get worse. To the hopeful it is encouraging because things may get better. To the confident it is inspiring because the challenge exists to make things better."[4] The individuals who work within all of the systems represented in this issue, and those who live and work within the communities represented, are those who are confident regarding change and who have worked to make things better for youths, their families and their communities. The best news is that they are not the exception, they are the rule. Throughout the U.S., juvenile justice systems are finding success at the individual and organizational level when they utilize data and validated risk/needs assessments to inform decisions regarding individual youths as well as at a program level. They are seeing even more promising results when they use evidence-based and research-informed program models. Finally, they are documenting positive youth outcomes when they develop policies and invest resources in a well-balanced system that addresses the entire comprehensive strategy.

One of the greatest challenges to the juvenile justice system today is that in our commitment to "right a wrong" and to achieve a well-balanced system, we may unintentionally eliminate one or more of the program components of the comprehensive strategy. The strength of the continuum and its ability to produce good, if not great, outcomes for youths is dependent upon our investment in each component based on the needs of youth in our communities. We have also learned through successful reform efforts that the culture of an organization—and the culture of individual programs and/or facilities—are the keys to both positive reform outcomes for youths and staff safety. That learning needs to be applied to each component of the continuum. As we face new challenges with limited resources, it is even more critical that we invest in systemic reform and in positive and healthy cultures within those systems that touch the lives of young people.

Notes

1. Wilson, J. J. anti J. C. Howell. 1993. *A comprehensive strategy for serious, violent, and chronic juvenile offenders.* Washington, D.C.: U.S. Department of Justice, Office of Justice Programs, Office of Juvenile Justice and Delinquency Prevention.

2. Lipsey, Mark W., James C. Howell, Marion R. Kelly, Gabrielle Chapman and Darin Carver. 2010. *Improving the effectiveness of juvenile justice programs—A new perspective on evidence-based practice.* Washington, D.C.: Center for Juvenile Justice Reform, Georgetown Public Policy Institute, Georgetown University.

3. Ibid.

4. Moncur, Michael. *The Quotations Page.* Retrieved from http://www.quotationspage.com/quote/1688.html.

READING 5.4

Gendered Decision-Making Practices in the Juvenile Justice System

By Gavril Paraschiv

Introduction

This research makes conceptual and methodological contributions to the youth's antisocial development, the connections between behavioral onset and its police and judicial analogs, the mechanisms by which juveniles reach criminal court, and LGBT youth involved in the juvenile justice system. The purpose of this study is to examine gendered decision-making practices that influence entry into the juvenile justice system, the sexual orientation and/or gender identity of LGBT youth, the rehabilitative view of the juvenile justice system, and the criminal behavior of juvenile offenders. The mainstay of the paper is formed by an analysis of the differences between the profiles and service needs of girls and boys entering the juvenile justice system, the complexities and limitations of the data-driven movement in juvenile justice, gender inequities in juvenile justice systems, and the rehabilitative goals of the juvenile justice system. The theory that I shall seek to elaborate here puts considerable emphasis on the effectiveness of treatment programs for juvenile offenders, the key role of the treatment component in reducing the subsequent criminal behavior of juvenile offenders, juvenile justice systems in the United States, and prevention as an essential part of an effective strategy for addressing juvenile delinquency in any community.

The Criminal Behavior of Juvenile Offenders

Champion contends that each jurisdiction in the United States[1] has its own methods for processing juvenile offenders. Violations of the laws pertaining only to juveniles are *status offenses*. The juvenile justice system consists of all of the processes involved whenever juveniles come into contact with law enforcement. The concept of juvenile justice has different meanings for individual states and for the federal government. Criminal court actions have harsher long-term consequences for offenders

Gavril Paraschiv, "Gendered Decision-Making Practices in the Juvenile Justice System," *Contemporary Readings in Law and Social Justice*, vol. 5, no. 1, pp. 76-81.

compared with juvenile court proceedings.[2] DeLisi et al. state that the more antisocial the individual,[3] the earlier the onset of antisociality. Criminal onset has been linked to a variety of behavioral, psychological, and dispositional outcomes. An individual's first arrest almost never coincides in time and place with their antisocial behavioral onset. "Early starters are often raised in home environments characterized by multiple forms of family dysfunction, are more likely to display temperamental and self-regulatory deficits, are prone to eliciting and engaging in aversive social interactions, are likely to evince more serious and more sustained conduct problems, and are more likely to experience early contact by and involvement in the juvenile justice system."[4]

As Lipsey et al. put it, the intertwined goals of juvenile justice should be ensuring public safety[5] and altering the life trajectories of those juveniles to reduce further criminal behavior and to improve their chances to prosper as productive citizens. Dealing effectively with juvenile delinquency involves prevention and intervention. Prevention is community-based activities aimed at helping youth avoid delinquent behavior.

All of this can be taken as evidence of the recognition that the focus of prevention efforts is on youth who may be at risk for delinquent behavior. Lipsey et al. explain that juvenile justice interventions involve a supervisory component and a treatment one. The supervisory component consists of some structure for monitoring or controlling the youth's behavior. High-risk juveniles may have high reoffense rates, whereas low-risk juveniles have little likelihood of reoffending even without intervention.[6]

Pennington reports that the juvenile delinquency courtroom becomes a socialization experience[7] for both parents and youth. Some jurisdictions allow parents to participate at multiple stages of the juvenile justice process. The juvenile delinquency court could be a key forum for parents to positively engage with the legal system. Juveniles likely observe the limited role and decision-making power of their parents in the court process.

What matters for the present discussion is that engaging parents in a meaningful way in the juvenile justice process helps build positive views of the law within the family and potentially diminishes delinquent behavior. Pennington says that the current era in the juvenile delinquency court is increasingly punitive. Current juvenile justice policies often take a negative view of parental participation. Direct participation by parents in the delinquent court can benefit the juvenile justice process. The narratives of parents in juvenile court are not part of the dominant courtroom narrative.[8]

Gender Inequities in Juvenile Justice Systems

Schwalbe explains that raw risk scores may be used to group juveniles[9] into ordinal risk classes ranging from low risk to high risk. Gender differences can open a window into the presence of gender biases in juvenile justice decision-making. Risk assessment instruments can increase gender equity in the juvenile justice system.[10]

Squatriglia maintains that lesbian, gay, bisexual and transgender ("LGBT") youth may enter the juvenile justice system for reasons related to their sexual orientation and/or gender identity. When youth feel threatened, they are at-risk for involvement with the juvenile justice system due to truancy. A juvenile justice system that recognizes the difficulties experienced by LGBT youth should successfully guide them towards becoming happy, health and fully realized adults. The sexual orientation and or gender identities of LGBT youth should be fostered as part of the rehabilitative process. The juvenile justice system must support them in the exploration and expression of their sexual orientation and gender identity. As children in the juvenile justice system are less mature than adults, it is unreasonable to hold them to the same level of responsibility for their actions.

It is worth emphasizing that the sexual orientation and gender identity of youth in the juvenile justice system should be supported as part of the rehabilitative process. Squatriglia holds that secure detention is usually reserved for youth with extensive prior involvement in the juvenile justice system[11] or who have committed serious offenses. LGBT youth are overrepresented in populations that are at risk for involvement with the juvenile justice system. The juvenile justice community must implement programs that specifically serve LGBT youth. LGBT youth are at greater risk of entering the juvenile justice system, being more likely to face harassment once in the system.

The preceding considerations suggest that LGBT youth often enter the juvenile justice system for reasons other than delinquency, their sexual orientation being a direct cause of entering the foster care system. Squatriglia insists that youth in the juvenile justice system are completely dependent upon the State for their care. The purpose of the juvenile justice system requires that the sexual orientation and gender identity of LGBT youth be fostered and encouraged as a fundamental part of the rehabilitation process.[12]

Underlying Causes of Juvenile Delinquency

Sherman points out that the restriction on disproportionate minority contact (DMC) addresses racial disparities[13] at all stages of the juvenile justice process. Girls are rarely a high priority for state and local juvenile justice systems, being a subpopulation within juvenile justice requiring specific research, policies, and programs. Juvenile justice systems struggle to craft gender-responsive strategies to deal with runaway girls. Trauma is related to girls' development and triggers their juvenile justice involvement. Gender bias that drives girls into the juvenile justice system may not be the result of intentional discrimination by juvenile justice systems. Gender discrimination in juvenile justice is found largely in the impact or effect of policies and practices.[14] Woolard focuses on girls involved in the child welfare and juvenile justice systems,[15] and in the adult criminal justice system. The juvenile justice system utilizes the state's police power to protect public safety to intervene in children's lives when they commit delinquent acts or status offenses, which are only illegal because the juvenile is a minor. The different systems view girls differently, based on whether they are in the child welfare or the juvenile justice system.[16]

Harrison analyzes the issues raised by gender-segregated juvenile courts[17] in both the dependency and delinquency systems. The triggering events that lead to boys' involvement in the juvenile justice system are different than those affecting girls.[18] Edelman and Watson affirm that the juvenile justice system is ill-equipped[19] to serve girls effectively. The proportion of girls in the juvenile justice system continues to grow. Appropriately serving the girls who are in the juvenile justice system will require significant changes to policy and practice.[20]

Conclusions

These findings highlight the importance of examining gendered juvenile court interventions, the juvenile justice system tendency to divert female offenders more readily compared to male offenders, the emergence of antisocial behavior, and the importance of criminal onset. The results of the current study converge with prior research on the purpose of the juvenile justice system, the relationship between sexual orientation and/or gender identity and involvement of LGBT youth in the juvenile justice system, the presence of gendered decision-making practices in the juvenile justice system, and gender bias for girls in juvenile justice systems. The paper generates insights about underlying causes of juvenile delinquency, the use of the juvenile justice system to protect wayward girls, the mechanisms that perpetuate gender inequity in juvenile justice, and the use of risk assessment instruments in varied juvenile justice agencies with male and female offenders.

References

1. Paraschiv, Daniel-Ștefan (2013), "The Emergence of International Criminal Law as an Aspect of Global Governance: The Case of China," *Economics, Management, and Financial Markets* 8(2): 204–209.
2. Champion, D. J. (2010), *The Juvenile Justice System: Delinquency, Processing, and the Law*. 6th edn. Upper Saddle River, NJ: Prentice Hall, 1–44.
3. Nica, E. (2012), "The Increased Significance of Education as an Investment in Human Capital," *Contemporary Readings in Law and Social Justice* 4(2): 112–117.
4. DeLisi, Matt, Neppl, T. K., Lohman, B. J., Vaughn, M. G., & Shook, J. J. (2013), "Early Starters: Which Type of Criminal Onset Matters Most for Delinquent Careers?," *Journal of Criminal Justice* 41: 12. See also Farrington, D. P. (2012), "Should the Juvenile Justice System be Involved in Early Intervention?," *Criminology and Public Policy* 11(2): 265–273.
5. Berna, Ioana-Bianca (2013), "Democracy and Gender Inequality in China," *Journal of Research in Gender Studies* 3(1): 119–124.
6. Lipsey, M. W., Howell, J. C., Kelly, M. R., Chapman, G., & Carver, D. (2010), "Improving the Effectiveness of Juvenile Justice Programs: A New Perspective on Evidence-Based Programs," Center for Juvenile Justice Reform, Georgetown University. See also Howell, J. C., & Lipsey, M. W. (2012), "Research-based Guidelines

for Juvenile Justice Programs," *Justice Research and Policy* 14(1): 1–18; Lipsey, M. W., & Howell, J. C. (2012), "A Broader View of Evidence-based Programs Reveals More Options for State Juvenile Justice Systems," *Criminology and Public Policy* 11(3): 515–523; Lipsey, M. W. (2012), "Effective Interventions for Juvenile Offenders: Using Meta-analysis to Bridge from Research to Practice," in Bliesener, T., Beelmann, A., & Stemmler, M. (eds.), *Antisocial Behavior and Crime: Contributions of Developmental and Evaluation Research to Prevention and Intervention.* Cambridge, MA: Hogrefe Publishing, 181–198; Welsh, B. C., Lipsey, M. W., Rivara, F. P., Hawkins, J. D., Aos, S., & Peel, M. E. (2012), "Promoting Change, Changing Lives: Effective Prevention and Intervention to Reduce Serious Offending," in Loeber, R. & Farrington, D. P. (eds.), *From Juvenile Delinquency to Adult Crime: Criminal Careers, Justice Policy, and Prevention.* New York: Oxford University Press, 245–277.

7. Carmen, P. (2012), "Fictional Narratives of Embodiment in Robbe-Grillet's Works," *Review of Contemporary Philosophy* 11: 158–163.
8. Pennington, L. J. (2012), "Engaging Parents as a Legitimacy-Building Approach in Juvenile Delinquency Court," *UC Davis Journal of Juvenile Law and Policy* 16(2): 481–534.
9. Berna, Ioana-Bianca (2013), "The Discourse of New Imperialism in Southeast Asia," *Contemporary Readings in Law and Social Justice* 5(1): 70–75.
10. Schwalbe, C. S. (2008), "A Meta-analysis of Juvenile Justice Risk Assessment Instruments: Predictive Validity by Gender," *Criminal Justice and Behavior* 35(11): 1367–1381.
11. Nica, E. (2012), "Driving Forces for the Professionalisation of Human Resource Management in Europe," *Economics, Management, and Financial Markets* 7(4): 134–139.
12. Squatriglia, H. (2008), "Lesbian, Gay, Bisexual and Transgender Youth in the Juvenile Justice System: Incorporating Sexual Orientation and Gender Identity into the Rehabilitative Process," *Cardozo Journal of Law and Gender* 14: 793–817.
13. Rădulescu, A. (2013), "Aspects of Metalinguistic Awareness in Solution-focused Therapy," *Linguistic and Philosophical Investigations* 12: 150–155.
14. Sherman, F. T. (2012), "Justice for Girls: Are We Making Progress?," *UCLA Law Review* 59: 1584–1628.
15. Vasile, M. (2013), "The Gender of Silk," *Journal of Research in Gender Studies* 3(1): 102–107.
16. Woolard, J. L. (2012), "Crossing Over: Girls at the Intersection of Juvenile Justice, Criminal Justice, and Child Welfare," in Miller, S., Leve, L. D., & Kerig, P. K. (eds.), *Delinquent Girls: Contexts, Relationships, and Adaptation.* Dordrecht: Springer, 25–39.
17. Berna, Ioana-Bianca (2013), "The Diplomatic Process within the EU," *Contemporary Readings in Law and Social Justice* 5(1): 64–69.
18. Harrison, K. M. (2012), "A New Approach to Juvenile Justice: An Analysis of the Constitutional and Statutory Issues Raised by Gender-Segregated Juvenile Courts," *UC Irvine Law Review* 2: 773–807.
19. Paraschiv, Ramona-Gabriela (2012), "The Importance of Procedural Justice in Shaping Individuals' Perceptions of the Legal System," *Geopolitics, History, and International Relations* 4(2): 162–167.
20. Edelman, P. B., & Watson, L. (2013), "Improving the Juvenile Justice System for Girls: Lessons from the States," *Georgetown Journal on Poverty Law and Policy* 20: 215–268.

READING 5.5

The Value of Alternative Therapies in Mental Health Treatment for Incarcerated Youths

By Lynn Williams

A growing concern of the criminal justice system is how to effectively treat the high percentage of incarcerated youths who suffer from mental health and substance abuse issues. At present, most juvenile correctional facilities are using cognitive behavioral therapy (CBT) in their treatment. This article discusses an innovative program instituted at Cuyahoga Hills Juvenile Correctional Facility (CHJCF) called the Power Within Me program, which combines mindfulness yoga and meditation techniques as a complementary therapy to CBT in the treatment of juvenile offenders. This article will draw upon psychological literature, a preliminary study of the program's effectiveness, testimony of the participants and personal observation to provide evidence that alternative treatments like those used in the Power Within Me are effective counterparts to more traditional therapies and highly useful as treatment interventions.

Background: Juvenile Offenders and Mental Health

Close to 70 percent of youths in the juvenile justice system have a diagnosed mental health disorder, and approximately 30 percent suffer from a mental illness so severe it impairs their ability to function as a responsible adult.[1] Overwhelming research shows that juvenile offenders suffer significantly higher rates of depression, anxiety, post-traumatic stress disorder (PTSD) and attention deficit hyperactivity disorder (ADHD) than the general population of young people.[2] The rate at which mental disorders affect incarcerated youths is about 70 percent, which far surpasses the normal rate of mental disorders among the general population of teens (approximately 20 percent).[3] Research also indicates that 47 percent of detained boys suffer from moderate to severe levels of depressive

Lynn Williams, "The Value of Alternative Therapies In Mental Health Treatment for Incarcerated Youths," *Corrections Today*, vol. 78, no. 1, pp. 24-28.

symptoms, while the general prevalence of major depression in U.S. teens is estimated to be between 5 percent and 8 percent.[4] The suicide rate of incarcerated youths is found to be two to three times higher than youths in the general population.[5] It has also been discovered that 21.3 percent of boys met criteria for an anxiety disorder, while only 13 percent met the same criteria among the general population of teens.[6] As many as 21 percent of incarcerated male youths have inattention and hyperactivity symptoms associated with ADHD, while normative U.S. samples are estimated to be only 4.1 percent.[7] Some researchers have found that ADHD in juveniles is related to the development of adult antisocial personality disorders.[8]

> *... yoga and mindfulness teach participants to be less reactive to incoming and environmental stimuli and to observe their thoughts and emotions without judgment.*

The majority of juvenile offenders are also victims of early childhood trauma and maltreatment, with extensive abuse and neglect histories.[9] In a large U.S. study of incarcerated youths, virtually all of those studied (90 percent) reported exposure to some type of trauma, and 32.3 percent of boys met criteria for PTSD.[10] These traumatic experiences can cause detrimental effects on brain development, particularly on the cognitive control section, which is responsible for decision-making and regulating emotions.[11] These cognitive processing issues include failure to properly hold attention, work memory and regulate emotion. Researchers have linked these issues to behavioral disorders and have associated them with the development and persistence of antisocial behavior.[12,13]

In addition, substance abuse has been strongly linked with general offending and is often comorbid with other psychiatric disorders.[14] One study found that 77 percent of juvenile offenders used substances within the last six months.[15] The National Center on Addiction and Substance Abuse at Columbia University implicated drug and alcohol use in 64 percent of violent offenses and 72 percent of property offenses among juveniles.[16]

Mental Health Treatment in Juvenile Prisons

These statistics overwhelmingly support the need for extensive and effective mental health treatment in juvenile facilities. CBT has been the predominant method of treatment for youths involved in the criminal justice system and has proved very effective;[17] however, recent studies have found that alternative therapies, such as mindfulness and yoga, can be equally effective in treating anxiety and depression.[18] Because of this, yoga and mindfulness have been incorporated as components of some CBT programs to increase their effectiveness.[19 20] While CBT replaces negative cognitions and emotions with a more optimistic outlook, yoga and mindfulness teach participants to be less reactive to incoming and environmental stimuli and to observe their thoughts and emotions without judgment. This approach also incorporates breathing techniques, which allow the body and brain to go into deep relaxation, thus facilitating an enhanced connection between the body and emotions for better self-regulation. Schools and community programs for teens have begun to implement mindfulness-based approaches to improve adjustment among chronically stressed and disadvantaged youths and enhance self-regulatory capacities. Robin Casarjian of the Lionheart Foundation, who brings emotional literacy programs to prisons, comments, "Mindfulness training helps youths to consider more adaptive alternatives. It creates a gap between triggers for offending behavior and their responses. They learn to not immediately act out on impulse, but to pause and consider the consequences of a potential offending and high-risk behavior."[21]

Yoga has grown so much in popularity in recent years that an estimated 8.7 percent of people in the U.S. (20.4 million) now practice yoga.[22] There is a growing movement toward using yoga as an effective mind-body intervention for children and adolescents to improve specific physical and mental health conditions and as a means of improving overall health, physical fitness and general stress management. Yoga is increasingly being used with youths in a variety of settings, such as prisons, psychiatric hospitals and schools, for its clinical benefits; well-documented studies have confirmed the physical benefits of yoga, such as lower blood pressure, improved heart health, reduced stress levels and a boosted immune system. Research has also found yoga to have many emotional benefits, including reduced anxiety and depression, decreased insomnia, aid in pain management and treatment for PTSD.[23]

To maximize the effectiveness of mental health treatment for incarcerated youths, CHJCF has implemented the Power Within Me program, an innovative yoga program developed by Lynn Williams, Ph.D., to target the specific mental health and behavioral problems related to its juvenile offenders. CHJCF is one of three juvenile correctional facilities under the Ohio Department of Youth Services and serves young men ages 12 to 21; it is a minimum-to-medium-security facility and the national winner of the 2015 Performance-based Standards Learning Institute Barbara Allen-Hagen Award for the second time in three years. "Dr. Williams has implemented a unique and valuable yoga program, in line with our Path to Safer Facilities, seeking to enhance meaningful activities for youths," said Harvey Reed, director of the Ohio Department of Youth Services. "It has helped youths in both expected and unexpected ways, improving self-control and interpersonal flexibility."

Power Within Me Yoga Program and the IAM® Meditation Technique

The Power Within Me program consists of a 10-week curriculum based on an integrative approach that builds on the CBT skills the youths are already receiving. It uses a combination of yoga and mindfulness techniques, or "mindful yoga," to facilitate relaxation, stress management and emotional regulation, while also targeting clinical applications like attention problems, impulsivity, sleep problems, anxiety, depression and trauma. To evaluate the effectiveness of the program, Williams conducted pre- and post-assessments administering the Beck Anxiety Inventory and Beck Depression

Inventory, for which the youths self-reported the symptoms they were experiencing. Williams found that participants of the 10-week program had a significant reduction in anxiety and also lower reports of depression.

The program meets weekly and is part mindful yoga class and part meditation class. Although yoga can be a means of exercise, the emphasis is not on physical fitness but on awareness, or mindfulness. Mindfulness, by definition, is being fully present in the moment with purposeful, nonjudgmental awareness. Mindful yoga uses mindfulness techniques and awareness of the body and breathing to assist youths in learning how to regulate emotional and physiological states. When youths are on their yoga mats, they are instructed to let go of the memories of the past and worries about the future, and to let themselves fully "be" in the present moment. The mindful yoga instruction allows them to tune in to their bodies and follow their natural movement. It also teaches them the use of breathing for better management of emotions, improved impulse control and more effective self-regulation.

The weekly meditation class uses the IAM® (Integrated Amrita Meditation Technique), which was created by world-renowned humanitarian Amma. It is a short and simple meditation that integrates movement, breathing, sound and visualization, and is designed to help practitioners reduce stress, increase productivity and find greater fulfillment in their lives. This meditation practice can increase one's energy and alleviate tension, thus improving mental and physical health. The international journal *Evidence-Based Complementary & Alternative Medicine* published a five-year study which showed that the IAM® meditation technique lowered stress hormones and had a number of psychological, physiological and biochemical benefits.[24]

The Power Within Me curriculum focuses on key socio-emotional themes, such as identity, power, happiness and patience, and integrates principles of yoga that include nonviolence, compassion for all living things, contentment and truthfulness. Through mindful yoga, youths begin to pay attention to themselves and their surroundings in a different way. When they first begin practicing, they are often unaware of their "emotional weather"—their thoughts, moods and energy levels that are constantly fluctuating—and can be very reactive to environmental stimuli. Living in unawareness, they often feel very stressed, anxious or depressed due to this assault of constantly changing stimuli. Through the practice of mindful yoga, they become more of an observer of their emotional weather and external environments, and are able to quiet their minds, relax their bodies and have more mental and emotional space for present-moment awareness. (This is particularly challenging at CHJCF as it is an open dorm-style living arrangement.) Being equipped with more present-centered awareness and attention can improve decision-making and emotional regulation by decreasing impulsivity, risky decision-making and emotional reactivity.[25]

Participants in the program have reported many benefits and have described how it has helped them better develop their socio-emotional skills and improve their ability to face the challenges of incarceration:

"Yoga helps me get away from everything—stress, anger, anxiety—and be in my own world. I feel relaxed and peaceful, and it takes my mind to a different planet."

"Yoga helps me calm down and focus on what's important and what's not important. For example, rather than focusing on all the time I have to do, I can look at all the opportunities I've been given. Rather than focus on the negatives, now I can focus on the positives."

"I can catch myself getting stressed and do yoga things throughout the day, like take a deep breath and rotate my shoulders, and it will help me relax. It helps me take the stress off."

"I have impulse control problems. Yoga helps me release my anger and stress so I can think before I act. When I got denied my early release, instead of flipping the unit, I took a deep breath. Yoga helped me stop and see the bigger picture and that I can still do good."

"Yoga helps me with my anger. It helps me calm down, relax and take my mind off stuff. I told my mama about it; now, she has tried deep breathing and it has helped her. I told her we will do yoga together when I get out."

Conclusion

Incarcerated youths face a number of challenges. The Power Within Me program at CHJCF has been very popular and engaging with the youths and can be a promising addition to traditional CBT and mental health interventions being used in juvenile correctional facilities. Yoga, mindfulness and meditation techniques are increasingly being used in therapeutic ways with youths and are achieving well-documented physical and mental benefits. These complementary techniques can help juvenile offenders learn better emotional regulation, rational decision making and behavioral control, and help reduce impulsivity and improve overall psychological health—which in turn can assist them in decreasing their risk, addressing their mental health needs, increasing resiliency and improving their motivation and ability to reenter their communities as positive, productive citizens.

Notes

1. Meservey, F. and K. Skowyra. 2015. Caring for youth with mental health needs in the juvenile system: Improving knowledge and skills. Office of Juvenile Justice and Delinquency Prevention. Washington, D.C.: U.S. Department of Justice. National Center for Mental Health and Juvenile Justice. Retrieved from http://cfc.ncmhjj.com/wp-content/uploads/2015/05/OJJDP-508-050415-FINAL.pdf.

2. Shufelt, J. and J. Cocozza. 2006. Youth with mental health disorders in the juvenile justice system: Results from a multi state prevalence study. Delmar, N.Y.: National Center for Mental Health and Juvenile Justice.

3. Merikangas, K., J. He, M. Burstein, S. Swanson, S. Avenevoli, L. Cui, C. Benjet, K. Georgiades and J. Swendsen. 2010. Lifetime prevalence of mental disorders in US adolescents: Results from the national

comorbidity study—adolescent aupplement (NCS-A). *Journal of the American Academy of Child and Adolescent Psychiatry,* 49(10): 980–989.

4. Domalanta, D. D., W. L. Risser, R. E. Roberts and J. M. Risser. 2003. Prevalence of depression and other psychiatric disorders among incarcerated youth. *Journal of the American Academy of Child and Adolescent Psychiatry,* 42:477–484.

5. Abram, K. M., J. Y. Choe, J. J. Washburn, L. A. Teplin, D. C. King, M. K. Dulcan and E. D. Bassett. 2014. Suicidal thoughts and behaviors among detained youth. *Juvenile Justice Bulletin.* Washington, D.C.: Office of Juvenile Justice and Delinquency Prevention. U.S. Department of Justice.

6. Teplin, L. A., K. M. Abram, G. M. McClelland, M. K. Dulcan and A. A. Mericle. 2002. Psychiatric disorders in youth in juvenile detention. *Archives of General Psychiatry, 59:*1133–1143.

7. Costello, E. J., S. Mustillo, A. Erkanlt, G. Keeler and A. Angold. 2003. Prevalence and development of psychiatric disorder in childhood and adolescence. *Archives of General Psychiatry,* 60:837–844.

8. Lilienfeld, S. and I. Waldman. 1990. The relation between childhood attention-deficit hyperactivity disorder and adult antisocial behavior reexamined: The problem of heterogeneity. *Clinical Psychology Review,* 10: 699–725.

9. Snyder, H. N. and M. Sickmund. 1999. Juvenile offenders and victims: 1999 national report. Washington, D.C.: Office of Juvenile Justice and Delinquency Prevention. U.S. Department of Justice.

10. Arroyo, W. 2001. PTSD in children and adolescents in the juvenile justice system. *Review of Psychiatry,* 20(1): 59–86. Washington, D.C.: American Psychiatric Publishing.

11. Van Goozen, S. H., G. Fairchild, H. Snoek and G. T. Harold. 2007. The evidence for a neurobiological model of childhood antisocial behavior. *Psychological Bulletin,* 133:149–182.

12. Teplin, L. A. et al. 2002.

13. Cauffman, E., L. Steinberg and A. R. Piquero. 2005. Psychological, neuropsychological and physiological correlates of serious antisocial behavior in adolescence: The role of self-control. *Criminology,* 43:133–176.

14. Elliott, D. S., D. Huizinga and S. Menard. 1989. *Multiple problem youth: Delinquency, drugs and mental health problems.* New York: Springer.

15. McClelland, G. M., K. S. Elkington, L. A. Teplin and K. M. Abram. 2004. Multiple substance use disorders in juvenile detainees. *Journal of the American Academy of Child and Adolescent Psychiatry,* 43(10): 1215–1224.

16. The National Center on Addiction and Substance Abuse at Columbia University. 2004. Criminal neglect: Substance abuse, juvenile justice and the children left behind. New York: Columbia University.

17. Lipsey, M. W. 2009. The primary factors that characterize effective interventions with juvenile offenders: A meta-analytic overview. *Victims & Offenders,* 4: 124–147.

18. Sundquist, J., A. Lilja, K. Palmér, A. Memon, X. Wang, L. Johansson and K. Sundquist. 2015. Mindfulness group therapy in primary care patients with depression, anxiety and stress and adjustment disorders: Randomized controlled trial. *The British Journal of Psychiatry,* 206(2): 128–35.

19. Khalsa, M. K., J. M. Greiner-Ferris, S. G. Hofmann and S. B. Khalsa. 2015. Yoga-enhanced cognitive behavioural therapy (Y-CBT) for anxiety management: A pilot study. *Clinical Psychology and Psychotherapy,* 22(4): 364–71.

20. Piet, J. and E. Hougaard. 2011. The effect of mindfulness-based cognitive therapy for prevention of relapse in recurrent major depressive disorder: A systematic review and meta-analysis. *Clinical Psychology Review,* 31: 1032–1040.

21. James, C. 2013. 'Mindfulness' training improves self-control for youth in jail. Retrieved from www.futurity.org/mindfulness-may-curb-impulses-jailed-youths.

22. Yoga Journal Editor. 2012. New study finds 20 million yogis in U.S. *Yoga Journal.* Retrieved from www.yogajournal.com/uncategorized/new-study-finds-20-million-yogis-u-s.

23. Balasubramaniam, M., S. Telles and P. M. Doraiswamy. 2013. Yoga on our minds: A systematic review of yoga for neuropsychiatric disorders. *Frontiers in Psychiatry,* 3: 1–16 (January).

24. Vandana, B., K. Vaidyanathan, L. A. Saraswathy, K. R. Sundaram and H. Kumar. 2011. Impact of integrated amrita meditation technique on adrenaline and cortisol levels in healthy volunteers. *Evidence-Based Complementary and Alternative Medicine,* 2011: 1–6.

25. James, C. et al. 2013.

READING 5.6

Novel Drugs of Abuse

By Joseph L. Calles, Jr.

Introduction

There is evidence that psychoactive substances have been used by humans for millennia.[1] The original sources of mind-altering drugs were- and still are-found in the natural environment, with the majority being plant-based. It can be argued that the current, worldwide problem with drug abuse has its origins in three interactive factors: our inherent neurochemical makeup (i.e. neurotransmitters, such as dopamine and serotonin), the availability of purer and more potent forms of drugs (e.g. morphine derived from opium), and more efficient delivery systems (e.g. intravenous needles vs. oral ingestion).[2]

What has complicated and exacerbated the contemporary drug problem is the development of multiple synthetic substances that mimic the actions of the traditional drugs of abuse (e.g. marijuana, stimulants, hallucinogens, etc.), but in a much more powerful- and potentially dangerous-manner. As will be described in the chapters that follow, the production of constantly evolving variants of abusable drugs carries with it untold human costs, and creates a myriad of legal issues. This paper will focus on the descriptions of several of the synthetic drugs of abuse that currently are, or may be, used by adolescents, as well as the implications for future drug development and availability.

Cannabinoids

It should come as no surprise that marijuana remains the most commonly abused drug by adolescents, with daily use in a US sample by 1.3%, 3.6% and 6.6% of 8th, 10th and 12th graders, respectively.[3] What is surprising, and very concerning, is that 11.4% of adolescents, from that same sample, had also tried synthetic marijuana.[3] Synthetic cannabinoids (CBs) were developed to further explore the structures and functions of the CB receptors, not as drugs of abuse. Unfortunately, the chemical formulas became available on the Internet, with subsequent production of the actual compounds, by amateur chemists, for recreation and/or profit. The concerns regarding the use of synthetic CBs include the lack of testing in humans for long-term effects, their greater potency when compared to natural marijuana, and emerging reports of serious toxic reactions, including psychosis,[4] seizures,[5] and myocardial infarction.[6]

One of the inherent problems in monitoring the use of, and the adverse effects from, the synthetic CBs is that they are sold as incense under various names, including Spice and K-2, the brand names of which (especially Spice) have come to be generically used to refer to any "incense" blend that contains synthetic CBs. It is obvious that these blends are not incense in the traditional sense, as they are not burned to scent the air, but are smoked to "get high." An important task for clinicians is to try and determine which type of CB has been used by their patients, given the variety of chemical compounds, and their varying strengths of cannabimimetic activity, that are readily available for retail purchase. Table 5.6.1 lists the 9 categories of CBs that were banned by the House of Representatives in Kansas, the first US state to ban CBs by broad chemical classes, rather than by individual compounds.[7]

The active component of marijuana (cannabis) is Δ^9-tetrahydrocannabinol (Δ^9-THC). Its analogues include the antiemetics/appetite enhancers (for those receiving cancer chemotherapy) (-)-Δ^9-THC (dronabinol; Marinol®) and its analogue nabilone (Cesamet®), both of which have low abuse potential.[8,9] Another Δ^9-THC analogue, HU-210, is at least one hundred-times more potent than the natural chemical, has great potential for causing abuse and addiction, and has been found in some Spice blends. This molecule was synthesized in 1988 by Mechoulam, and colleagues, at the Hebrew University (thus the "HU" designation).[8,10]

Several synthetic CBs are designated as "JWH" molecules, as they were synthesized by John W Huffman, a research chemist at Clemson University, in the 1980s.[10] The most extensively studied

Table 5.6.1 Chemical Classes of Cannabinoids[7] and Representative Compounds*

1. Tetrahydrocannabinols (classical cannabinoids)- natural or synthetic analogues, e.g. HU-210, nabilone
2. Naphthoylindoles, e.g. JWH-015, JWH-018, JWH-019, JWH-073, JWH-081, JWH-122, JWH-200, JWH-210, JWH-387, JWH-398, AM-1220, AM-2201
3. Naphthylmethylindoles, e.g. JWH-175, JWH-184
4. Naphthoylpyrroles, e.g. JWH-146, JWH-147
5. Naphthylmethylindenes, e.g. JWH-176
6. Phenylacetylindoles, e.g. JWH-250, JWH-251, JWH-253
7. Cyclohexylphenols, e.g. cannabicyclohexanol (CP 47,497-C8), CP 47,497, CP 55,940
8. Benzoylindoles, e.g. AM-694, RCS-4
9. WIN 55,212-2 (an aminoalkylindole)

* See text for the descriptions of the letters associated with the individual compounds.

compound from that laboratory is the naphthoylindole JWH-018, which continues to appear in Spice blends, despite its illegal status in many countries.[5] The Spice manufacturers have liked using JWH-018 in their blends, as it is very potent when compared to Δ^9-THC. Unlike Δ^9-THC, which is a partial agonist at the CB_1 receptor, JWH-018 is a full agonist, and has a four-times greater affinity for the receptor than does Δ^9-THC.[10] Two newer naphthoylindole cannabimimetic molecules, AM-1220 and AM-2201, were synthesized by Alexandros Makriyannis (therefore the "AM" designation), a bioorganic chemist at Northeastern University. They have recently been showing up in some Spice blends, and AM-2201 was one of the four synthetic CBs identified in the mixture that caused seizures in a young adult male.[5] As can be seen in Table 5.6.1, Drs. Huffman and Makriyannis have synthesized cannabinoid agonist compounds in several other chemical classes.

Another group of research cannabinoids are the cyclohexylphenols, such as CP 47,497, its C8 homologue CP 47,497-C8 (cannabicyclohexanol) and CP 55,940.[8,10] These were developed by the Charles Pfizer ("CP") company (now Pfizer, Inc.) in the 1970s, but have only recently found their way into Spice blends. These compounds are also very potent when compared to the natural Δ^9-THC.

Two other compounds of note are the benzoylindole RCS-4 (an analogue of JWH-018) and the aminoalkylindole WIN 55,212-2. The original source of the RCS series of synthetic CBs is unclear, but it may have been the company named Research Chemical Supplier. Due to its potential hazards to health, the use of RCS-4 has been banned in several countries. The origin of the WIN series is well-known, that being the former Sterling Winthrop Pharmaceuticals company, which is now a part of Sanofi S.A. WIN 55,212-2 is a potent full agonist of the CB1 receptor.[9]

In summary, there are numerous CBs that have been synthesized, e.g. there about 60 compounds in the JWH series and about 40 in the AM series. Given the complexity of the chemical compounds that are discussed in this section, and the multiple ways in which those molecules can be modified, there will undoubtedly be many more cannabimimetic compounds in the future. One of the obvious concerns is the potential for acute and long-term adverse effects, especially given that many of these compounds are several times more powerful than naturally-occurring cannabis, which already contributes to the risk of adolescent users developing neuropsychiatric disorders.[11]

Stimulants

In the recently published Youth Risk Behavior Surveillance (YRBS), researchers found that 3.8% of students had used methamphetamines at least once during their lifetimes.[12] A positive aspect of the report is that from 1999 through 2011, among US high school students, there was a significant linear decrease in the prevalence of use of metha-mphetamines (9.1%-3.8%). Unfortunately, metha-mphetamines are not the only stimulant drugs that can be abused. Comparable to the increased availability of synthetic CBs, in recent years several amphetamine-like compounds have been manufactured abroad and sold

Table 5.6.2 Chemical Classes of Stimulants[19] and Representative Compounds

1. Piperazines
   a. Benzylpiperazines, e.g. BZP, MBZP
   b. Phenylpiperazines, e.g. mCPP, pFPP, TFMPP
2. Phenethylamines
   a. Methyl derivatives, e.g. amphetamine, methamphetamine, phentermine
   b. Hydroxyl derivatives, e.g. phenylpropanolamine, ephedrine/pseudoephedrine
   c. Ketone derivatives, e.g. cathinone and methcathinone, which are derived from the Khat plant (*Catha edulis*), and are naturally occurring analogues of amphetamine. Synthetic versions include methedrone and methylone
   d. Methylenedioxy derivatives, e.g. MDA, MDMA ("Ecstasy")
   e. Methoxy derivatives, e.g. mescaline*
3. Pyrovalerones, e.g. MDPV
4. Naphthylpyrovalerones, e.g. naphyrone, Bromo-Dragonfly*
5. Cocaine and synthetic cocaines, e.g. pFBT, dimethocaine

* These are also hallucinogens.

legally as "party pills," or as "bath salts" which are not put into bathwater, but instead are ingested, inhaled, smoked or injected.

Also comparable to the use of synthetic CBs, the use of "bath salts" can produce several toxic reactions, including agitation, tachycardia, psychosis- and even death.[13] Table 5.6.2 lists the chemical classes of stimulants and some representative compounds.

The piperazine stimulants first appeared in Europe, sold as "party pills" commonly containing benzylpiperazine (BZP) or trifluoromethyl-phenylpiperazine (TFMPP).[14,15] In New Zealand, a product called "The Good Stuff" contained both BZP & TFMPP,[16] which together have demonstrated pharmacologic effects similar to MDMA ("Ecstasy").[17] Another piperazine, meta-chlorophenylpiperazine (mCPP), also has effects similar to MDMA, and in Europe has been sold in combination with MDMA, or in some cases has totally replaced MDMA, in pills sold as Ecstasy.[18] Other drugs of abuse in this family include MDBP (the methylene dioxy analogue of BZP) and 1-(4-methoxyphenyl)piperazine (MeOPP),[19] with the potential for several other analogues to be synthesized. One obvious concern about the use of these drugs is that young people who are purchasing them (often via the Internet) may be getting chemical compounds that can have unintended consequences, including agitation, anxiety, confusion, tremor, insomnia, seizures, and even severe multiorgan toxicity.[15]

The phenethylamines are a diverse group of stimulatory compounds that includes common drugs of abuse, such as the amphetamines, MDMA (Ecstasy), and mescaline.[20] One particular subgroup is the ketone derivatives, which includes cathinone, the major psychoactive alkaloid from the Khat plant (*Catha edulis*), and a naturally occurring analogue of amphetamine. There are many synthetic cathinones that have been produced, several of which have found their way into "bath salts".[21] Another synthetic cathinone group, the pyrovalerones, can be modified to produce the pyrrolidine derivative 3, 4-methylenedioxypyrovalerone (MDPV),[22] which was the active compound found in the "bath salts" used in Michigan and the "primary factor contributing to (the) death" of one of its users[13] Given the potential dangers associated with their use, in late 2011 the US Drug Enforcement Administration temporarily placed the synthetic cathinones mephedrone, methylone, and MDPV into Schedule I of the Controlled Substances Act.[23] There is no doubt that illegal labs will continue to produce variants of these drugs for profit.

Dissociative Anesthetics

The dissociative anesthetics were developed for use during surgical procedures, but their use has been limited by serious adverse effects, including psychosis. One of the popular dissociative drugs has been phencyclidine (PCP; "angel dust"), the use of which had its heyday in the 1970s, but which never went away completely. The use of PCP has enjoyed a slight resurgence in recent years as young people have rediscovered its mind-altering properties (see chapter 11). In the national Monitoring the Future survey, in 2011, 2.3% of 12th graders reported having used PCP at some point during their lifetimes.[3] Of equal concern is that 17.2% of those same respondents said that PCP was "fairly easy" or "very easy" to obtain. Other data are somewhat more reassuring, as the trend for first-use of PCP by young people (aged 12 years or older) is decreasing, from 123,000 individuals in 2002 to 45,000 in 2009 and 2010.[24] However, analogues of PCP have been synthesized (Table 5.6.3), and more are likely to be available in the future, to be used by those who are always looking for "the next high."

Ketamine ("Special K") is a dissociative agent that has legitimate medical uses in humans and in non-human species.[25] It has also become a drug of abuse. In 2011, 1.7% of 12th graders reported having used ketamine at some point during the year preceding the survey.[3] Ketamine offers some advantages over PCP, in that it has a wide margin of safety, even in cases of overdose, as it does not appreciably alter respiratory functions.[25] It should not, however, be considered a benign drug, as it can cause depression, psychosis, and cognitive dysfunction.[25] Recently, in Europe, there have been reports of a ketamine analogue, methoxetamine (MXE), which is available through Internet vendors.[26]

Table 5.6.3 Dissociative Anesthetics and Representative Compounds

1. Phencyclidine (PCP) and analogues, e.g. 4-Methoxyphencyclidine (methoxydine, 4-MeO-PCP), 3-Methoxyphencyclidine (3-MeO-PCP)
2. Ketamine and analogues, e.g. methoxetamine
3. Dextromethorphan (DXM)

Although little is known about this drug, MXE appears to be similar in its effects to ketamine, but with a longer duration of action.

Dextromethorphan (DXM) is used clinically as an antitussive agent, but is included in this section as it, along with PCP and ketamine, derives its psychotropic effects from antagonism of the glutamate N-methyl d-aspartate (NMDA) receptor.

Hallucinogens

The hallucinogens have traditionally been classified by their chemical structures into two broad categories, the tryptamines and the phenethylamines.[27] The tryptamines can be further subdivided into "simple" tryptamines (e.g. psilocybin) and the ergolines (e.g. LSD) (Table 5.6.4). Compared to other psychoactive drugs, the hallucinogens are unique in that the pharmacological effects are very dependent on the expectations (i.e. the mindset) of the user and on the environment (setting) in which the drug is used. Anticipating a negative experience and/or being in negative surroundings can lead to the proverbial "bad trip." Despite that possibility, many youth continue to use hallucinogens, from the 1960s-era classics LSD, mescaline and psilocybin, to newer synthetic drugs. By 2005–06, youth in Los Angeles were already using a myriad of tryptamine and phenethylamine compounds.[28]

Recently there have been reports of new hallucinogenic drugs becoming available for use in Europe. The drugs 4-HO-MET (4-hydroxy-N-methyl-N-ethyltryptamine)[29] and Bromo-Dragonfly (1-(8-bromobenzo [1,2-b;4,5b'] difuran-4-yl)-2-aminopropane[30] are described as producing the same mind-altering effects as LSD. Given that activation of the 5-HT_{2A} receptor seems to be crucial for the clinical effects of the hallucinogens,[31] and that other serotonin receptors (5-HT_{2C} for the

Table 5.6.4 Chemical Classes of Hallucinogens (27, 28) and Representative Compounds

1. Tryptamines:
   a. "Simple" tryptamines, e.g. DMT, AMT, DiPT, 5-MeO-DMT, 5-MeO-AMT, 5-MeO-DiPT, DPT, 5-MeO-DPT, 4-ACO-MiPT, 4-HO-MiPT, 4-HO-DiPT, 4-HO-DPT, 4-HO-MET, ibogaine, psilocybin (the prodrug of the biologically active psilocin)
   b. Ergolines, e.g. LSD and a few very closely related compounds
3. Phenethylamines*
   a. Phenethylamines, e.g. mescaline, 2C-B, 2C-E, 2C-P, 2-CT-7, 2-CT-2, DOI, DOB
   b. Amphetamine, e.g. MDMA, DOM
   c. "FLY" drugs, e.g. 2C-B-FLY, 3C-B-FLY, Bromo-Dragonfly ("B-fly")

* These are also included in the stimulants (see Table 5.6.2 above); most are not hallucinogenic.

phenethylamines and 5-HT_{1A} for the tryptamines), as well as other chemical systems (e.g. glutamatergic) are involved, it is anticipated that more hallucinogenic compounds will be synthesized in the years to come.

Conclusion

The diversity and availability of newer drugs of abuse is increasing. The chemistry of the compounds is complex, but not so much that it hinders their production by clandestine laboratories and amateur chemists. Laws controlling the possession and use of drugs of abuse are being circumvented by modifying them enough to be "legal." By the time that legislation is amended to outlaw certain compounds, untold youth have tried them and placed themselves at risk for experiencing adverse effects, some of which may be serious or permanent. During that same lag in time, drug producers will have come up with other compounds to get around the law- and the cycle will continue. There are at least two ways that this problem can be addressed.

Legally, the passage of laws that outlaw broad categories of drugs should slow down the production of compounds that are modifications of previously banned drugs. Clinically, the early identification of, and intervention with, youth who are at high risk for drug use and dependence needs to be incorporated into our daily practice lives. It is hoped that the information presented in this brief review will lead to a greater awareness, and better treatment, of drug-using youth in the 21st century.

Acknowledgments

This paper is a revised and adapted version of an earlier publication in the book "Substance abuse in adolescents and young adults. A manual for pediatric and primary care clinicians" edited by Donald E. Greydanus, Gabriel Kaplan, Dilip R. Patel and Joav Merrick with Walter de Gruyter in Berlin, 2013.

References

1. Sullivan RJ, Hagen EH. Psychotropic substance-seeking: evolutionary pathology or adaptation? Addiction 2002;97(4):389–400.
2. Nesse RM, Berridge KC. Psychoactive drug use in evolutionary perspective. Science 1997;278(5335):63–6.
3. Johnston LD, O'Malley PM, Bachman JG, Schulenberg JE. Monitoring the future national results on adolescent drug use: Overview of key findings, 2011. Ann Arbor: Institute Social Research, University Michigan, 2012. Accessed 2013 Jan 03. URL: www.monitoringthefuture.org/pubs/monographs/mtf-overview2011.pdf
4. Pierre JM. Cannabis, synthetic cannabinoids, and psychosis risk: What the evidence says. Curr Psychiatry 2011;10(9):49–57.

5. Schneir AB, Baumbacher T. Convulsions associated with the use of a synthetic cannabinoid product. J Med Toxicol 2012;8(1):62–4.
6. Mir A, Obafemi A, Young A, Kane C. Myocardial infarction associated with use of the synthetic cannabinoid K2. Pediatrics 2011;128(6):e1622–7.
7. Committee on Corrections and Juvenile Justice, Kansas House Bill 2049. Accessed 2013 Jan 03. URL: www.kslegislature.org/li/b2011_12/.../hb2049_01_0000.pdf
8. Thakur GA, Nikas SP, Makriyannis A. CB1 cannabinoid receptor ligands. Mini Rev Med Chem 2005;5(7):631–40.
9. Seely KA, Prather PL, James LP, Moran JH. Marijuana-based drugs: innovative therapeutics or designer drugs of abuse? Mol Interv 2011;11(1):36–51.
10. Fattore L, Fratta W. Beyond THC. The new generation of cannabinoid designer drugs. Frontiers Behav Neurosci 2011;5:60.
11. Rubino T, Zamberletti E, Parolaro D. Adolescent exposure to cannabis as a risk factor for psychiatric disorders. J Psychopharmacol 2012;26:177–88.
12. Eaton DK, Kann L, Kinchen S, Shanklin S, Flint KH, Hawkins J, et al. Youth risk behavior surveillance-United States, 2011. MMWR Surveill Summ 2012;61(4):1–162.
13. Centers for Disease Control and Prevention (CDC). Emergency department visits after use of a drug sold as "bath salts"—Michigan, November 13, 2010-March 31, 2011. MMWR Morb Mortal Wkly Rep 2011;60(19):624–7.
14. Cohen BM, Butler R. BZP-party pills: a review of research on benzylpiperazine as a recreational drug. Int J Drug Policy 2011;22(2):95–101.
15. Schep LJ, Slaughter RJ, Vale JA, Beasley DM, Gee P. The clinical toxicology of the designer "party pills" benzylpiperazine and trifluoromethylphenylpiperazine. Clin Toxicol (Phila) 2011;49(3):131–41.
16. Sheridan J, Butler R, Wilkins C, Russell B. Legal piperazine-containing party pills—a new trend in substance misuse. Drug Alcohol Rev 2007;26(3):335–43.
17. Baumann MH, Clark RD, Budzynski AG, Partilla JS, Blough, BE, Rothman RB. N-substituted piperazines abused by humans mimic the molecular mechanism of 3,4-methylenedioxymethamphetamine (MDMA or 'Ecstasy'). Neuropsychopharmacol 2005;30(3):550–60.
18. Bossong MG, Brunt TM, Van Dijk JP, Rigter SM, Hoek J, Goldschmidt HM, et al. mCPP: an undesired addition to the ecstasy market. J Psychopharmacol 2010;24(9):1395–401.
19. Maurer HH, Kraemer T, Springer D, Staack RF. Chemistry, pharmacology, toxicology, and hepatic metabolism of designer drugs of the amphetamine (Ecstasy), piperazine, and pyrrolidinophenone types, a synopsis. Ther Drug Monit 2004;26(2):127–31.
20. Khan JI, Kennedy TJ, Christian DR Jr. Phenethylamines. In: Khan JI, Kennedy TJ, Christian DR Jr, eds. Basic principles of forensic chemistry. New York: Humana Press, 2012:157–76.
21. Prosser JM, Nelson LS. The toxicology of bath salts: a review of synthetic cathinones. J Med Toxicol 2012;8(1):33–42.

22. Coppola M, Mondola R. 3,4-methylene-dioxy-pyrovalerone (MDPV): chemistry, pharmacology and toxicology of a new designer drug of abuse marketed online. Toxicol Lett 2012;208(1):12–5.
23. Drug Enforcement Administration, Department of Justice. Schedules of controlled substances: temporary placement of three synthetic cathinones in Schedule I. Final Order. Fed Regist 2011;76(204):65371–5.
24. Substance Abuse and Mental Health Services Administration. Results from the 2010 National Survey on Drug Use and Health: Summary of national findings. Rockville, MD: Substance Abuse and Mental Health Services Administration, NSDUH Series H-41, HHS Publication No (SMA) 11–4658, 2011.
25. Morgan CJ, Curran HV, Independent Scientific Committee on Drugs. Ketamine use: a review. Addiction 2012;107(1):27–38.
26. Corazza O, Schifano F, Simonato P, Fergus S, Assi S, Stair J, et al. The phenomenon of new drugs on the Internet: the case of the ketamine derivative methoxetamine ('MXE'). Hum Psychopharmacol Clin Exp 2012;27:145–49.
27. Nichols DE. Hallucinogens. Pharmacol Ther 2004;101(2):131–81.
28. Sanders B, Lankenau SE, Bloom JJ, Hathazi D. "Research chemicals": tryptamine and phenethylamine use among high-risk youth. Subst Use Misuse 2008;43(3–4):389–402.
29. Kjellgren A, Soussan C. Heaven and hell—a phenomenological study of recreational use of 4-HO-MET in Sweden. J Psychoactive Drugs 2011;43(3):211–9.
30. Corazza O, Schifano F, Farre M, Deluca P, Davey Z, Torrens M, et al. Designer drugs on the internet: a phenomenon out-of-control? The emergence of hallucinogenic drug Bromo-Dragonfly. Curr Clin Pharmacol 2011;6(2):125–9.
31. Fantegrossi WE, Murnane KS, Reissig CJ. The behavioral pharmacology of hallucinogens. Biochem Pharmacol 2008;75(1):17–33.

UNIT V: CRITICAL THINKING QUESTIONS

1. Discuss the importance of the changes in treatment of juveniles since the 1800s. Identify any negative outcomes from the "get-tough" approach in juvenile justice.
2. Describe how the U.S. juvenile justice legislation is punitive in comparison to global trends. Explain how the Convention on the Rights of the Child shaped legislation.
3. Identify the challenges in reforming the juvenile justice system. Describe the types of cultural issues considered in the reformation of the juvenile justice system.
4. Discuss the importance of the study of gender as related to juvenile justice. Identify groups overrepresented in the juvenile justice system. Explain why they are overrepresented.
5. Identify the types of mental health problems generally found among juvenile offenders. Describe the types of therapy used to treat mental health problems found in the juvenile system.
6. Explain how the choice of drugs affects the increase of drug abuse among today's youth. Identify the types of drugs being used by youth.

   Overall

   Using only the information in this unit, how would you describe juvenile justice in the United States to someone from another country?

UNIT VI

Victimology

Unit Introduction

The final unit begins with a review of "how the intersection of race, gender, and class shape criminological literature" on violence and victimization. The violent victimization of women and girls continues to be pervasive in our society, but the growth of violent female offenders has also increased (Reading 6.1).

Other specialized populations which are examined under victimology include the elderly, LGBTIQ youth, drug addicts, victims of domestic violence and the undocumented. With the growth of the elderly population, we have seen the need for new practices and coordinated efforts between social workers, law enforcement and legal specialists. It has been recommended that to successfully prosecute elder abuse, there must be specialized units and cooperative investigative efforts (Reading 6.2).

As a marginalized population, LGBTIQ youth are most likely to suffer bullying at the hands of their peers. To address this violence, recommendations for growth-fostering relationships and positive school climates are provided (Reading 6.3). Another group that has a high likelihood for violent victimization is drug addicts who traverse into criminal subcultures filled with danger (Reading 6.4).

With the growth of the field of victimology, new theoretical models are being developed. When considering intimate partner violence in the Latino/a community, outreach programs from an epidemiological perspective are being used (Reading 6.5). Finally, a view of how one can look at the migration from Central America to the U.S. is offered, highlighting policy initiatives which have created damaging consequences for undocumented Latinos/as who face violence crossing through Mexico from both the government and cartels (Reading 6.6).

READING 6.1

At the Intersections

Race, Gender and Violence

By Nikki Jones and Jerry Flores

Over the last several decades, scholars have paid increased attention to gender and trends in violent offending and victimization (DeHart and Lynch, 2013; Goodkind, 2009; Males, 2010). Most recently, interest in this area was piqued by changes in arrest statistics for women and girls beginning in the late 1980s and continuing into the early 2000s. During this time, girls' arrests for violent offenses increased more rapidly and decreased more slowly than arrests of boys for similar offenses (Chesney-Lind and Shelden, 2004). Over this time period, more girls entered secure detention for crimes against persons like simple assault and aggravated assault. The number of women incarcerated for violent offenses also increased over the first decade of the twenty-first century from 109,340 in 1999 to 183,986 in 2009 (Bureau of Justice Statistics, 2011). During this time, women also continued to experience high rates of victimization. Women were 45 percent of simple assault victims in 2008 (Bureau of Justice Statistics, 2011). Women remain the most common victims of rape and sexual assault (80 percent). Data from 2009 find that women who reported rapes were raped by men 78 percent of the time and most often by a friend, relative or intimate partner.

These data reveal a complicated trend: women and girls remain common targets of violent victimization, especially at the hands of men and intimate partners, but are also more likely than ever to be arrested and incarcerated for violent offending. This is especially true for poor women of color who are disproportionately represented in the juvenile and criminal justice systems (Renzetti and Maier, 2002). How do researchers account for these recent trends? How are these recent trends in gender, violent offending and victimization patterned by intersections of race, gender and class? How do these explanations challenge or extend previous studies of gender and violence, especially studies of women's experience with violence and victimization? Finally, how do these explanations help us to understand the hype surrounding the so-called "new violent girl" and the punitive institutional responses that have emerged as a result of socially constructing girls as "wild" or "bad"?

In this chapter we review key contributions to the literature on gender, violence and victimization. Instead of providing an exhaustive review of the literature, we highlight key theoretical and empirical contributions that illustrate *how intersections of race, gender and class shape the criminological literature on gender, violence and victimization*, and *the implications of "intersectionality" for helping us to better understand trends in violence and victimization among women and girls*. We begin with a discussion of Dorie Klein's (1973) "The Etiology of Female Crime: A Review of the Literature," which is one of the earliest and most significant reviews of the traditional criminological canon. Klein's critique was among the first to challenge the representation of women in the traditional criminological literature. Subsequent critiques of the literature encouraged the development of gender and crime and feminist criminology as valid areas of study in the criminological literature. These critiques also paved the way for the development of Black feminist criminology (Potter, 2006), which encourages the use of an intersectional analysis to understand trends in violent offending, victimization and institutional responses to each. In contrast to the early criminological works surveyed in the first section of this chapter, recent work on gender, violence and victimization draws on an intersectional framework to explain how categorical variables like race, gender or class, pattern violence and victimization. In addition to explaining differences in patterns across and within groups, these explanations also help us to better understand how race, gender and class inform institutional responses to violence and victimization.

On Etiology: Gender and Criminology

It is almost impossible to disentangle the earliest explanations for women's and girls' experiences with violence—either as victims or offenders—from researchers' essentialist understandings of the inherent biological or psychological qualities of women and girls. Early theorists concerned with delinquent, deviant, or criminal behavior argued that women and girls were "naturally" constrained from engaging in all forms of crime, including violence. These pseudoscientific arguments of the late nineteenth and early twentieth centuries were also racialized. For example, in *The Female Offender*, Lombroso and Ferrero (1895) argued that only "savage" women are capable of violent crimes. Among the so-called savage women cited by Lombroso: the Hottentot, a Negro woman and a Red Indian woman. In contrast, Lombroso argued, "civilized" white women did not use violence because it was inconsistent with their essential female nature.

Dorie Klein's analysis of the representation of women in early criminological theory exposed the taken-for-granted assumptions embedded in essentialist arguments that continued to influence theories about women's offending well into the 1970s. In "The Etiology of Female Crime: A Review of the Literature," Klein (1973) explains how these narrow theories of women's crime, developed from the turn of the twentieth century until the mid-1950s, relied on the fundamental assumption that women's criminal behavior was a result of their deficient biology or individual psychological deficiencies. Among the traditional theorists critiqued by Klein were Lombroso, who once wrote that "the born female criminal is, so to speak, doubly exceptional, as a woman and as a criminal" (Lombroso and Ferrero, 1895, p. 184). In each of these texts, Klein writes, assumptions of inherent biological differences between the sexes manifest themselves into physiological and psychological differences which, while tangentially influenced by social structure, ultimately explain women's offending (Klein, 1973). An example of this type of essentialist theorizing is perhaps best reflected in Otto Pollak's suggestion, published in *The Criminality of Women* (1950), that the majority of women's crime is hidden *and* that women are favorably situated to hide their criminality because of an inherent biological quality particular to women: their need to hide their menstruation from others.

Klein (1973) offers that when read side-by-side these theorists represent "a tradition" of explaining women's criminality that relies on "implicit or explicit assumptions about the *inherent nature of women*" (p. 31). Such theories suggest that women's criminality is inherently physiological or psychological in nature and only partially related to their position within the larger social structure. These theorists, Klein argues, along with their contemporaries, "create two distinct social classes of women: good women who are 'normal' non-criminals, and bad women who are criminals" (p. 31). This type of theorizing reflects, Klein argues, "a moral position that often masquerades as scientific distinction" (p. 31).

In her review of the literature, Klein also reveals how the taken-for-granted sexism of early theorists was joined with racist characterizations of non-white women. A critical review of the literature reveals that the work of many positivist theorists reflected a belief in a racial hierarchy that situated white, upper class men located at the top and Black, lower class women at the bottom. Regarding Lombroso and Ferrero's (1895) classic biological atavistic approach Klein (1973) writes that Lombroso "theorizes that individuals develop differentially within sexual and racial limitations which differ hierarchically from the most highly developed, the white men, to the most primitive, the nonwhite women" (p. 186). Klein (1973) argues that Thomas' socio-psychological explanation for women's criminal offending is also rooted not only in flawed assumptions about biology, sex and gender, but also race. According to Klein (1973), Thomas argues that in civilized nations the sexes are more physically different as are the "races." The implication of the intersection of the two is obvious: "[t]he most highly developed races would therefore have the most feminized women, that is, the most 'good' women and in turn the most 'noncriminal' women" (p. 36). Klein argues that these forms of sexism and racism influenced theories of women's criminal offending into the 1970s.

Klein's critical review was an early feminist critique of the criminological canon; it was also a critique of many of her contemporaries who, Klein argued, were "guilty of the same undocumented and poorly researched work as earlier criminologists" (p. 33). In response to the return of biological theories to explain girls' offending and the persistent emphasis on the role of women's sexuality in contemporary theories of women's offending Klein (1973) concludes, "[t]he road from Lombroso to the present is surprisingly straight" (p. 33). These narrowly focused explanations for women's offending led to narrowly focused strategies to respond to women's offending: strategies developed to solve the problem of women's criminal behavior were largely focused on the individual adjustment of women to "gender appropriate" behavior (Goodkind, 2009; Klein, 1973).

In the years following Klein's (1973) "Etiology," feminist criminologists would rely heavily on her initial critical review of the criminological literature in the development of their own research agendas (Chesney-Lind and Shelden, 2004; Miller, 2001; Naffine, 1987, 1996). In this line of research, scholars deliberately sought to challenge some of the commonsense assumptions about gender and patterns of women's violence and victimization. Ngaire Naffine (1987) extended Klein's critical review of the traditional criminological literature in *Female Crime: The Construction of Women in Criminology*. Naffine (1987) provides a critical review of the construction of women in mainstream criminology and the implications of this construction for criminological theory. Naffine (1987) suggests that, "[i]f one were to typify the average female offender, she would be a once-only shoplifter who tends to steal items of little value" (p. 12). Here, Naffine highlights how women's use of violence and, in turn, women's victimization were routinely ignored and instead replaced with a romanticized version of the delinquent as "the rogue male" while his female counterpart remains, predictably, primarily concerned with the "narrow set of relations with the opposite sex" (p. 11). Naffine expands her critique in *Feminism and Criminology* (1996) where she extends her theoretical critique of criminological theory to a large-scale disciplinary critique of contemporary criminological literature (cf. Leonard, 1982). In a call that is consistent with the intellectual shifts of the time, Naffine argues for greater reflexivity on the part of researchers: not only should researchers rethink how they see women, but they should also think critically about how their own positions or "standpoints" inform their research (Collins 1990; DeHart and Lynch, 2013; Harding, 2004). In contrast to an unreflective embrace of empirical research, Naffine (1996) argues for a feminist criminology that is willing to "put itself about, to engage with its detractors, and to subject itself to precisely the sort of critical scrutiny it has applied to others" (p. 4). It is the role of the feminist criminologist, Naffine (1996) suggests, to critique this tendency within the discipline and to then move beyond this critique and into the "work of criminology."

The shift to reflexivity that Naffine describes led to a number of theoretical and conceptual breakthroughs that have influenced the development of gender and crime over the last quarter of a century. As Daly (1998) writes, a significant "source of field expansion [in the area of gender and crime] comes from feminist scholars" (p. 100) who are concerned with theories of gender and studies of women's lives as well as the application of this research to crime. Daly (1998) explains, "this group is less interested in devising a grand theory of gender and crime, and more inclined to identify the ways in which gender structures men's and women's life worlds, identities, and thinkable courses of action" (p. 100). Scholars writing in this tradition often emphasize the influence of inequality, oppression and marginalization on girls and women's pathways to crime. Early examples of works produced within this tradition include Eleanor Miller's (1986) study of female street hustlers in Milwaukee and Meda Chesney-Lind's (2010) study of the criminalization of girls and women's survival strategies, among others. In the next section, we describe how the theoretical contributions of intersectionality, "race-gender-class" (Daly, 1998) and black feminist criminology (Potter, 2006) have shaped contemporary understandings of gender, violence and victimization.

At The Intersections: Understanding Gender, Violence and Victimization

In the decades following the publication of Klein's "Etiology," feminist criminologists continued to challenge simplistic assertions about gender that characterized the discipline. Feminist criminologists also encouraged a new generation of scholars to account for how *intersections* of gender, race and class patterned violence and victimization among women, especially women of color who were disproportionately represented in arrest and incarceration statistics as the twentieth century neared its end (Britton, 2000; Collins, 2004; Daly, 1997; DeHart and Lynch, 2013; Renzetti and Maier, 2002; Shelden, 2010). Sally Simpson's (1991) direction to fellow criminologists was one of several calls to expand the criminological literature in this way:

> Criminologists have been mistaken to ignore important variations in criminal behavior among females. The simplistic assertion that males are violent and females are not contains a grain of truth, but it misses the complexity and texture of women's lives. A review of the empirical literature on violence reveals the confounding effects of gender, race, and class. Although their combined influences are difficult to tease out, a firm understanding of how they interact is fundamental for a more inclusive and elegant criminological theory.
>
> *(p. 129)*

In an early examination of the variation in causal factors for Black women and white women's offending Hill and Crawford (1990) also argue for a more careful examination of the intersections of race, gender and class within studies of gender and crime. In the introduction to their analysis the authors write that theories about female criminality "are theories about white females" (Hill and Crawford, 1990, p. 603). The authors later conclude that Black women "fit less" into current theoretical models and that "the empirical neglect of the Black female offender has had important consequences for the development of theory" (Hill and Crawford, 1990, p. 621). In "Different Ways of Conceptualizing Sex/Gender in Feminist Theory and the Implications for Criminology" Daly (1997) suggests that these types of empirical and theoretical challenges to the literature, "were part of a general mood to unsettle social theory and to re-engage a critique of positivist social science" (Daly, 1997, p. 33). One of the most influential concepts to arise out of these challenges to both mainstream social science and feminist theory was what Daly (1997) terms "class-race-gender." On the conceptualization of multiple inequalities Daly (1997) writes, "[c]lass-race-gender conceptualizes inequalities, not as additive and discrete, but as intersecting, interlocking and contingent" (p. 33). This concept has been particularly influential on Daly's (1997) work: "My work has been most influenced by class-race-gender or what I have come to term multiple inequalities" (p. 33). Daly (1997) continues, "In the 1980s, it was ... Black women whose critique of feminist thought had the greater influence on my thinking" (p. 33).

Over the last two decades, researchers have adopted an intersectionality framework to explain variations in violence and victimization across and within groups. In "Caste, Class and Violent Crime: Explaining Difference in Female Offending" Simpson (1991) explores differences in violent offending both within and between gender and racial groups. Regarding the peculiar position of black women, Simpson (1991) writes, "Black females appear to respond differently to conditions of poverty, racism, and patriarchy than their class, gender, and racial counterparts. Race and gender merge into a theoretically interesting and important case, one that deserves more systematic inquiry" (p. 116). Simpson's (1991) examination of trends in the literature that address variations in violent offending by gender and race suggests that:

> Black women, especially those in the "underclass" engage in what might be considered anomalous behavior for their gender (i.e., violent crimes) but not their race. ... On the other hand, given the high level of violence among black males, black female rates of violent crime are relatively low.
>
> *(p. 116)*

Like Daly, Simpson (1991) offers that "[c]lass, gender and race are best understood as intersecting systems of dominance and control" (p. 125). This type of theorizing, Simpson (1991) suggests, can better explain variations in black women's and white women's willingness to "buy into" the dominant "patriarchal power system" which may exert some control over women's use of interpersonal violence (p. 127). Regarding culture and violent offending in particular, Simpson (1991) suggests that, "As structural conditions increasingly preclude mobility for the bottom of the surplus population, cultural redefinitions and adjustments may influence perceptions of, and beliefs about, the emergence and appropriateness of violence" (p. 128). Here, Simpson (1991) suggests that it is the varying structural positions of white women and Black women, and their dynamic interaction with culture, that explain, at least in part, why white women and Black women apparently use and experience violence differently: "Class is an oppressive structure for both black and white females, but black women's experiences of their material circumstances and their perceptions of self and choice vary qualitatively from those of whites" (p. 128). Simpson (1991) concludes:

> The observed gender differences in how violence is interpreted and incorporated into one's behavioral repertoire emerge from the contradictory cultural tendencies of caste (i.e., female = nonviolent, black = violent; Lewis 1981). Black

> females ... are more apt than black males to delegitimate violence. However, given their racial oppression and differential experience of patriarchy, in the family, black females are perhaps less apt to delegitimate violence than their white counterparts.
>
> *(p. 129)*

Over the last two decades, feminist criminologists and gender and crime scholars have examined women's and girls' experiences with aggression and violence with increasing complexity.[1]

Meda Chesney-Lind's studies of delinquent girls reveal how gender specific violence shapes girls' pathways to delinquency (DeHart and Lynch, 2013; Bosworth and Fili, 2012; Chesney-Lind and Shelden, 2004; Daly, 1997, 1998); and feminist criminologists using Collins' concept of "intersectionality" (Collins, 2004) have contributed new insights into the study of women's experiences with violence by challenging the "universality" implied by popular theories on the relationship between gender, violence and victimization (Daly, 1997). Scholars have shown how intersections of race, gender and class expose women to unique life experiences, which, in turn, may influence and shape their social relationship to violence (Renzetti, 2004; Simpson 1991; Simpson and Elis, 1995).[2]

An understanding of how material circumstances influence women's and girls' relationships to violence is illustrated in Beth Richie's (1996) study of black battered female offenders. Richie's analysis examines the impact of what she describes as "multiple marginality." Richie's analysis of the life histories of African American battered women incarcerated at Riker's Island Correctional Facility in New York City also blurs the boundaries between victim and offender—a common experience for incarcerated African American women. Richie argues that African American women were "compelled to crime" by a range of structural and personal circumstances that included pressures to adhere to socially appropriate gender roles. Richie describes how the ability of women to adequately respond to the violence they experienced at the hands of their partners was made more difficult by simultaneous experiences of racism. Black gender ideologies (Collins, 2004) also placed pressure on women to demonstrate loyalty to their black male partners. These experiences were compounded by poverty, which limited the options available to women to respond to the violence in their lives. Under these conditions, women often chose survival strategies, like using violence against their male partners, which increased their social isolation and made them more vulnerable to criminal sanctions, including long periods of incarceration.

Recent contributions from Jody Miller, Gail Garfield, Hillary Potter and Nikki Jones echo Richie's argument and further demonstrate how intersections of race, gender and class shape violence and victimization in the lives of African American girls who come of age in distressed urban neighborhoods. In *Getting Played: African American Girls, Urban Inequality, and Gendered Violence* (2008), Miller draws on an analysis of surveys and interviews conducted with at-risk and delinquent African American youth to explain how structural circumstances foster troubling cultural adaptations that result in the prevalent threat of gender-specific violence for girls and the normalization of participation in this violence for boys. Miller's analysis reveals how violent victimization in urban settings is shaped by extreme poverty. Girls' and boys' accounts of violence reveal both their vulnerability and marginality in these settings. The violence reported by girls includes verbal harassment, unwanted touching, and sexual assault. Miller reports that over half of the 75 girls interviewed experienced some form of sexual coercion or assault; nearly a third of interview respondents reported multiple experiences of victimization. Generally, girls were hesitant to report gender-specific harassment or violence to institutional authorities.[3]

Miller's work highlights how intersections of gender and class shape experiences of violence and victimization among poor urban youth of color. Recent work from Hillary Potter and Gail Garfield extends her analysis by emphasizing how intersections of race, gender and class shape violent victimization and the use of violence among African American women and girls. In her research on black women and intimate partner abuse, *Battle Cries: Black Women and Intimate Partner Abuse* (2008), Hillary Potter reports on how intersecting identities shape women's experience with violence and victimization. Among the contributions of Potter's work is her explanation of how images and expectations of the "Strong Black Woman" shape how women make sense of the abuse in their lives. Potter writes that the women in her study confronted numerous forms of domination and discrimination "because of their abusive circumstances and their interwoven identities due to race, gender and other social, cultural, and individual circumstances" (pp. 9–10). Potter introduces the concept of "dynamic resistance" to explain how these intersections shape women's responses to the abuse in their lives, including ways that challenge typical notions of mainstream femininity, like fighting back against their abuser. She explains:

> The women's self-perception as Strong Black Women, and not as victims, is considered to account for their efforts to resist abuse and other life distress. Included in this resistance is the propensity for the women to verbally and physically retaliate against their abusers.
>
> *(Potter, 2008, p. 10)*

Potter's use of Black Feminist Criminology (Potter, 2008) also helps to uncover how intersecting oppressions (Collins, 2004) pattern black women's experiences with violence and victimization over the life course. Potter explains that Black feminist criminology "extends beyond traditional feminist criminology to view African American women (and conceivably, other women of color) from the multiple marginalized and dominated positions in society, culture, community and families" (2006, p. 107). Potter (2006) argues that much of contemporary criminology fails to address how multiple forms of oppression influence the experiences of women. These experiences shape the meanings of violence among Black women and the set of responses available to women who want to end the violence in their lives. Potter encourages other scholars to draw on Black feminist criminology when examining how black women experience and respond to crime and victimization (Potter, 2006).

Gail Garfield takes an approach that is consistent with Black feminist criminology in her examination of African American women's experiences with violent victimization. In *Knowing What We Know: African American Women's Experiences of Violence and Violation* (2005), Garfield draws on an intersectionality framework introduced by legal scholar Kimberlé Crenshaw and other feminist scholars: "Kimberlé Crenshaw suggests that the social, personal, and physical dimensions of uneven power relations intersect rather than stand as isolated or discrete relations. And through this intersection, differences are created that give texture and shape to women's day-to-day experiences" (Garfield, 2005, p. 3). Garfield also draws on an intersectionality framework in her study of violence in the lives of African American men in *Through Our Eyes: African American Men's Experiences of Race, Gender and Violence.* Garfield extends her analysis of the "relational context of violence and violation" and uses the life histories of African American men to complicate common images of Black manhood and masculinity. Her work reveals the "tensions, dilemmas, and contradictions" that characterize African Americans' experiences with violence. Her work provides a unique perspective on men who are actively involved in creating a more progressive manhood that is less harmful to others and to their own sense of self. These studies reveal the benefit of interrogating experiences of violence and victimization at the intersections of race, gender, class and other categorical identities. As we describe in the following section, an intersectional analysis is especially useful in understanding the underlying dynamics that have contributed to recent increases in arrests for violent offenses among women and girls.

Race, Gender and The New Violent Girl

Over the last decade, researchers have focused more attention on girls' participation in violent acts, and the subsequent victimization that results from these physical encounters (Jones, 2010; Schaffner, 2006). Some popular and scholarly explanations for recent trends in girls' violence and victimization reflect the same sort of essentialist understandings of gender and race that informed the earliest explanations of women's and girls' offending. For example, popular explanations of girls' changing nature suggest that girls today are "moody," "insecure" and "meaner" than ever before, making them more likely to participate in crime and violence (Wiseman, 2002). Psychologists Dellasega and Nixon (2003) claim that this generation of girls is "rotten" and has simply gone "wrong" because of the increased "bullying" that happens among teenage girls. They attribute this behavior to "superstar singers acting like sexy schoolgirls and movie stars firing machine guns or using martial arts on opponents while wearing skintight jumpsuits," paying little attention to poverty, discrimination and inequality (Dellasega and Nixon, 2003, p. 3). Some explanations are reminiscent of the "liberation hypothesis" (Adler, 1975), which offered that the women's movement "freed" women to participate in crime, especially crimes dominated by men. For example, Prothrow-Stith and Spivak (2005) have argued that encouraging girls to participate in sports and excel in academics has also made them more competitive and aggressive, which in turn encourages girls' violent behavior.

These explanations ignore recent self-report data that do *not* reveal a dramatic change in girls' behavior (Males, 2010, p. 27). These explanations also fail to uncover the social meaning of violence for girls in distressed urban neighborhoods, and neglect recent changes in institutional responses to girls' violent or aggressive behavior. Recent research has filled this gap in the literature. In *Between Good and Ghetto: African American Girls and Inner-city Violence* (2010) Jones draws on an intersectional framework to examine the social meaning of violence and victimization among African American adolescent girls. Her ethnographic study reveals how gender patterns girls' use of violence in ways that are similar and distinct to boys' use of violence in the same settings (cf. Jones, 2008). Her analysis also reveals variation in the use of violence among similarly situated African American girls. The study reveals how growing up in neighborhoods characterized by concentrated poverty and a visible and unpredictably violent drug trade pushes both adolescent boys and girls into a preoccupation with survival. Girls' accounts reveal the array of interpersonal and situational strategies they draw on to manage the violence they confront in neighborhood and school settings where interpersonal violence is governed largely by a hyper-masculine, eye-for-an-eye ethic that Elijah Anderson has described as the "code of the street." A form of street justice, the code emerges where the presence of civil law is weak and thrives in settings where social institutions like schools or the police have abdicated responsibility for ensuring the well-being of inner city residents (Anderson, 1999, p. 10). While adolescent girls in these settings have no manhood to defend, girls' accounts reveal that they do have many reasons to be preoccupied with protecting themselves from threats of violence. The need to avoid or overcome dangers throughout their adolescence presents a gendered challenge for inner-city girls whose experience is complicated by intersections of gender, race and class.

Jones explains that African American inner-city girls who live in distressed urban neighborhoods must learn how to effectively manage potential threats of interpersonal violence—that is, they must work the code of the street—at the risk of violating mainstream and local expectations regarding appropriate feminine behavior.[4] The gendered expectations surrounding girls' and women's use or control of violence are perhaps the most constraining. Girls are expected to use relational aggression—as popular media suggests—and fight with words and tears, not fists, knives or box cutters. Inner-city girls, like most American girls, feel this pressure to be "good," "decent" and "respectable." Yet, like some inner-city boys, they may also feel pressure to establish a "tough front" in order to deter potential challengers on the street or in the school setting. Girls who are deeply invested in crafting a public persona as a tough girl or a "fighter," as some in Jones's study did, are especially open to being evaluated by peers, adults, and outsiders as "street" or "ghetto." Such distinctions are powerful, Jones argues, because community members and institutional actors—teachers, judges, police officers—use them as a basis for understanding, interpreting, and predicting their own and others' actions, attitudes, and behaviors, especially when it comes to interpersonal violence (Anderson, 1999). These understandings help to pattern institutional responses to girls' violence as well, including expulsion, arrest and entry into secure detention.

Recent research, including chapters in this volume, also reveals how responses to girls' violent behavior are patterned by intersections of race, gender and class (Chesney-Lind and Jones, 2010). These studies find that girls' arrests for violent offenses like simple assault or aggravated assault are influenced by policy shifts implemented over the last several decades, including a shift in responses to domestic violence incidents (Chesney-Lind, 2010) and "zero-tolerance" policies toward fighting in schools (Losen and Skiba, 2010). In one of the most definitive studies in this area, Darrell Steffensmeier and colleagues (2005) dismissed claims that the twenty-first century girl is committing more crimes than girls in previous periods. Instead, girls' arrests for violent offenses like simple assault or aggravated assault are artifacts of "recent changes in public sentiment and enforcement policies for dealing with youth crime and violence that has elevated the visibility and reporting of girls' violence" (Steffensmeier, Schwartz, Zhong and Ackerman, 2005, p. 356). Steffensmeier and colleagues describe the increased arrests of girls for violent offenses as a consequence of a "net-widening effect": girls today are much more likely to receive an official criminal sanction for behavior that would not have been addressed by law enforcement in years past. Policy shifts in responding to student behavior in school is an example of this net-widening effect. Steffensmeier and colleagues (2005) explain:

> Many schools, especially in the large urban centers, have adopted zero tolerance policies toward violence ... Both male and female youth are being arrested in substantial numbers for behavior that, before these preventive measures, would have likely been handled as a school disciplinary matter.
>
> *(p. 366)*

These changes in policies and practices have "disproportionately escalated girls' arrests for violent crimes," the researchers continue, "particularly for assaults involving minor physical confrontations or verbal threats—most frequently with another girl—that in the past would have been ignored or responded to less formally" (Steffensmeier et al., 2005, p. 367). The authors conclude that the rise in girls' violence is "more a social construction than an empirical reality."

Girls today are no more violent than in years past. However, girls' violent or aggressive behavior is more likely to trigger an official sanction from the juvenile or criminal justice system than in years past. This is especially true for girls of color. For example, in a recent study Tia Stevens, Merry Morash and Meda Chesney-Lind used data from the National Longitudinal Youth Survey to examine the probability of conviction and institutionalization for violent behavior among youth in 1980 and 2000 (Stevens, Morash and Chesney-Lind, 2011). The researchers found that while self-reports of attacks on other people did not increase over this time period, "an increased proportion of youth penetrated into the juvenile justice system in 2000." In 2000, girls were "nearly twice as likely as girls in 1980 to report they had been charged with a crime." These changes were particularly dramatic for black girls: "Black girls in 2000 were nearly seven times more likely as their 1980 counterparts to have been charged with a crime" (Stevens et al., 2011, p. 19). Stevens et al. (2011) conclude that "the justice system is getting tougher on girls but girls do not appear to be getting tougher" (p. 22).

It might also be said that the justice system is getting especially tough on girls of color. Changes in policies and institutional practices have led to increases in the involvement of African American, Latina and Native American girls in the justice system (Bosworth and Fili, 2013). Girls who enter institutions of confinement are increasingly being arrested for behavior that previously did not warrant criminal sanctions: "once these girls enter the system, they tend to stay in the system, despite fairly clear evidence that in previous decades their behavior would not have warranted a criminal justice response, much less an arrest" (Chesney-Lind and Jones, 2010, p. 4). In turn, entry into secure detention often increases girls' vulnerability to a unique set of risks, including exposure to violence and victimization (Bosworth and Fili, 2013; Schaffner, 2006). Empirical research conducted in the US suggests that emotional, physical and sexual abuse of inmates is ubiquitous in institutions of confinement (Friedman, 2003). Schaffner (2006) found that girls regularly encountered violence and the threat of violence while incarcerated in California. In secure detention settings, girls must contend with threats of violence from other girls and, at times, from correctional staff. In a review of the literature in this area Burton-Rose (2003) found that girls and women across the US face the constant threat of sexual and physical assault inside of detention facilities by correctional staff. Girls and women in detention are more likely than males to experience verbal abuse by staff members for behavior that is deemed "unladylike" (Bosworth and Fili, 2013; Goodkind, 2009). Researchers have also documented the frequency of child abuse and neglect inside group homes in the US and Canada (Chesney-Lind and Shelden, 2004). In an ethnographic study of a Canadian group home Brown (2010) found that girls constantly worried about potential threats of violence. They continually shifted from using violence to being victims of violent acts perpetrated by staff members and other residents (Brown, 2010). Crosland et al. (2008) found that staff members in American group homes are often ill equipped and under-trained to deal with these types of situations, which tends to exacerbate already volatile situations.

These challenges are exacerbated for youth who are perceived by institutional actors to be "gender non-conforming." Recent studies of LGBT youth in detention have shown LGBT youth are likely to receive additional sanctions for behavior that is otherwise age-appropriate (Estrada and Marksamer, 2006). This secondary punishment—the punishment delivered to those who violate gender norms—is built into the earliest phases of the system. In a study of gender non-conforming youth in the juvenile justice system, Angela Irvine (2010) found that LGBT youth are twice as likely to be detained during pre-trial for nonviolent offenses like truancy, running away and prostitution. These youth are also much more likely to be subject to verbal and sexual harassment and to experience violence at the hands of other youth while in detention (Estrada and Marksamer, 2006). Lisa Pasko's recent research on the experiences of LBQ girls in custody also reveals how girls' lesbian identities are pathologized or minimized among correctional staff. Her work also documents how recent policy interventions like the Prison Rape Elimination Act have had the unintentional consequence of intensifying punitive responses to sexual activity among incarcerated girls (Pasko, 2011).

Conclusion

Dorie Klein's (1973) critique of the etiology of criminological theory reveals how taken-forgranted assumptions about women distorted explanations for women's offending, including women's experiences with violence and victimization. Since the publication of Klein's critical review, the field of gender and crime has expanded significantly. Feminist contributions have been especially important to the development of this area: "feminist researchers have made women offenders and victims visible" partly by demonstrating how "girls are penalized for behavior which is condoned or encouraged in boys" (Morris and Gelsthorpe, 1991, p. 4). Feminist scholars have also complicated the study of women's lives by integrating understandings of "intersecting oppressions" and "class-race-gender" into theory and methods. An early example of this approach includes Simpson's (1991) use of Black feminist thought in her examination of gender and race variation in violent offending. In recent years, this work has been extended and complicated by scholars like Jody Miller, Hillary Potter, Beth Richie, Nikki Jones and others who have drawn on an intersectionality framework to provide more nuanced accounts of how race, gender and class shape experiences of violence and victimization. Such approaches to understanding violence and victimization are necessary in order to adequately explain recent trends in the arrest and detention of women and girls for violent offenses. For example, in contrast to popular and scholarly claims about a new violent girl, the best available data reveal that girls' behavior has not changed in any substantial ways over the last several decades. However, it is clear that institutions and adults have changed the way we respond to violent or aggressive behavior among women and girls. This is especially true for girls of color who are overrepresented at every stage of the juvenile justice system. Future research should continue to explore the social meaning of violence among women and girls along with the consequences of punitive policies and practices for women and girls. Researchers should also continue to examine how intersections of race, gender, class and sexuality pattern trends in gender, violence and victimization.

Notes

1. See Dana Britton's "Feminism in criminology: Engendering the outlaw" (2000) for an analysis of how Black feminist thought and feminism, respectively, can influence criminological theory and research. For recent studies of gender, crime, violence and victimization see *Gender and crime: Patterns of victimization and offending* (Heimer and Kruttschnitt, 2005).

2. The introduction of the ethnomethodologically driven concepts of "doing gender" and "doing difference" also helped to complicate criminological theories on gender and violence (Fenstermaker and West, 2002;

Topical Box 6.1.1 Gender-Motivated Hate Crimes

Jessica P. Hodge

The gendered nature of hate crime perpetration and victimization is clearly evident when looking at both federal and state statistics. Similar to other types of crimes, particularly violent crimes, the majority of hate crime offenders and victims are male. For example, in the state of New Jersey in 2006, there were 320 male victims and 340 male hate crime offenders, compared to 179 female victims and 71 female hate crime offenders (New Jersey State Police Bias Incident Summary Report, 2007). However, the gendered nature of hate crime changes when looking specifically at gender-motivated violence, which is why one of the most controversial issues of bias crime legislation is whether gender should be included as a protected group.

Until the passage of the Matthew Shepard and James Byrd, Jr Hate Crimes Prevention Act (HCPA) in 2009, the Department of Justice was only required to collect data on hate crimes motivated by race, ethnicity, religion, disability, and sexual orientation (Federal Bureau of Investigation, 2007). With the passage of the HCPA, however, the US Attorney General is now required to collect data on the new categories of gender and gender identity crimes (Anti-Defamation League, 2010). These new categories may include crimes such as the assault against a woman because she is female, or when a transgendered man is attacked because he identifies as a woman. Despite the fact that 49 states have some form of a hate crime law (Wyoming being the exception), only 26 states and Washington, DC currently include gender as a protected group in their hate crime statutes (Anti-Defamation League, 2008).

Because of the extent of violence towards women in the US, arguments against the addition of gender as a protected group maintain that these crimes would overwhelm already congested courts and would make statistics gathering too cumbersome. Furthermore, opponents argue that gender-motivated crimes do not fit the "typical" hate crime criterion; in other words, factors used to assess whether bias was involved in an offense are largely irrelevant to crimes such as domestic violence or rape. Another argument is that those who do commit crimes against women do not really "hate" women, "at least in the same sense that white supremacists hate blacks and Jews" (Gerstenfeld, 2004, p. 49). If a hate crime is due to an offender's prejudicial attitudes or animus towards another individual or group, critics question how one can argue that a man hates all women, or that crimes of rape and domestic violence are always motivated by hatred towards women.

However, many scholars point out the difficulty of finding a sexual assault or domestic violence case that is not motivated in part by an inherent gender bias, and argue that such crimes are used as means by which to intimidate women and to reinforce a sexually stratified social hierarchy (Weisburd and Levin, 1993–94, p. 38). Indeed, sexual assaults and domestic violence are often analogized to such crimes as cross-burnings and lynchings, crimes historically used to intimidate less powerful groups and enforce a racially stratified social hierarchy (Angelari, 1994; MacKinnon, 1991). Like other "traditional" bias crimes against racial, ethnic, or religious minorities in which violence is used to enact revenge over an entire group of individuals, men often utilize gender-motivated violence as a means to punish all women. Proponents also assert that the current laws addressing domestic violence and sexual assaults do not cover all possible forms of gender-bias crimes. In the 1989 case of Marc Lepine, for example, he purposely murdered 14 women at the University of Montreal because he blamed his academic and personal failures on women. Another example occurred in 2009 at a Pittsburgh health club. George Sodini entered an aerobics class he purposely selected due to the attendance of all women, and opened fire, randomly killing three women and injuring 11 more before killing himself ("Three Pennsylvania Women Killed in Hate Crime," 2009). It was discovered soon after the murder spree that Sodini had maintained an internet blog detailing his hatred for women and his plans for seeking revenge against them.

While not ignoring the fact that same-sex violence occurs in both domestic assaults and sexual assaults, or that women can also be violent, the gender disparities involved in such violence are clearly evident: men are overwhelmingly the perpetrators of violence against women. Moreover, research demonstrates that when women are violent within intimate relationships, they use violence to defend themselves or their children, or as a means to express anger or frustration based on past abuse (Miller, 2005), whereas men use violence to assert dominance, and to control or punish their partner (Barnett, Lee and Thelan, 1997; Hamberger, Lohr, Bonge and Tolin, 1997). Because violence directed at women by men continues to be a serious issue, affecting millions of women, it is critical that we continue to find ways to eradicate such violence. Counting gender-motivated crimes as part of hate crime statutes is one way to highlight such clear gendered behavior.

References

Angelari, M. (1994). Hate crime statutes: A promising tool for fighting violence against women. *American University Journal of Gender & the Law*, *2*, 63–105.

Anti-Defamation League (2008). *Anti-Defamation League state hate crime statutory provisions*. Washington, DC: Author. Retrieved from www.adl.org/99hatecrime/state_hate_crime_laws.pdf.

——(2010). *ADL urges FBI to begin collecting hate crimes data on new categories*. New York: Author. Retrieved from www.adl.org/combating_hate/hate_crimes_data.asp.

Barnett, O. W., Lee, C. Y. & Thelan, R. E. (1997). Gender differences in attribution of self-defense and control in interpartner aggression. *Violence Against Women*, *3*(5), 462–81.

Federal Bureau of Investigation (2007). *Hate crime statistics, 2006*. Washington, DC: Author. Retrieved from www.fbi.gov/ucr/hc2006/index.html.

Feminist news (2009, August 6). *Three Pennsylvania women killed in hate crime*. Retrieved from www.feminist.org/news/newsbyte/uswirestory.asp?id=11865.

Gerstenfeld, P. B. (2004). *Hate crimes: Causes, controls, and controversies*. Thousand Oaks, CA: Sage.

Hamberger, L. K., Lohr, J. M., Bonge, D. & Tolin, D. F. (1997). An empirical classification of motivations for domestic violence. *Violence Against Women*, *3*(4), 401–23.

MacKinnon, C. A. (1991). Reflections on sex equality under law. *Yale Law Journal*, 100(5), 1281–328.

Miller, S. L. (2005). *Victims as offenders: The paradox of women's violence in relationships*. New Brunswick, NJ: Rutgers University Press.

New Jersey State Police (2007). Bias incident summary. In *Crime in New Jersey: 2006 uniform crime report, for the year ending December 31, 2006*. Trenton: NJ: State of New Jersey, Office of the Attorney General. Retrieved from www.state.nj.us/lps/njsp/info/ucr2006/pdf/2006-sect-12.pdf.

Wiseman, R. (2002). *Queen bees and wannabes: Helping your daughter survive cliques, gossip, boyfriends, and other realities of adolescence*. New York: Three Rivers Press.

Biographical Box 6.1.1 *Susan Caringella*

My interest in the area of rape and sexual assault arose when I discovered that the state I was living in, Michigan, had the most radical rape reform legislation. Being aware of the disparity between law on the books/in theory and law in action/daily practice I wanted to research how the "model" reforms withstood implementation.

Feminists had increased awareness about "double victimization" of raped women where prosecution of rape offenders was commonly sacrificed through the persecution of victims. Many of us were spurred on to generate/apply feminist theory and garner evidence to prove how and why our society, legal system and individuals respond to raped females, and males, in such unique, prejudicial and punishing manners.

My contribution, pièce de résistance, is *Addressing Rape Reform in Law and Practice* in 2009 (Columbia University Press). This book is a critical, intricate analysis of rape reform law and its effects, where I move beyond critique to present an alternative model for change. This work owes much to the pioneers who carved out foundations for studying rape. I see this book as the culmination of Susan Brownmiller's classic treatise and Susan Estrich's insightful arguments for legal change. There are scores of empirical researchers such as Mary Koss, Diana Russell, Martha Burt, Lynda Lytle Holmstrom and Ann Wolbert Burgess, Walter DeKeseredy and Martin Schwartz, Jody Miller, Raquel Kennedy Bergen, along with the more theoretical work of Herman and Julia Schwendinger and Catherine MacKinnon to name but a select few who have been major contributors in the field.

Unfortunately, I have serious reservations about where the field is *not* headed. The reemergence of myths about rape has gone virtually unnoticed, not to mention unanswered. What is more, with some feminist success surrounding the recognition of women's equality, some alleged "feminists" have contorted attitudes such that old myths intersect with new myths about women's power and sexual agency to yield a "Catch 22." For example, women who take precautionary measures like not drinking or dressing "sexily" are condemned for self-imprisonment, while empowered women who engage in such behaviors are disparaged for precipitating their own rapes.

Second, I don't think the proclivity to emphasize privileged groups of college students has been recognized. This propensity is understandable given the availability of students for research, but is nonetheless problematic.

Although I sometimes feel like Don Quixote fighting windmills in trying to facilitate inroads against rape, perhaps history yields more optimism about the future. There is the Hegelian dialectic, and there is the pendulum. The past begets change in the future that swings first to one side, "radical" reforms such as affirmative consent states, and then to the other, like legislators and judges trying to preclude use of the very words "rape" and "victim." This gives momentum to further change that reflects remnants of the new and old (e.g., of reform and backlash laws and attitudes), bringing forth still newer forms approaching justice for women, and men. My work I dedicated to "reinvigorating the movement" (as Susan Estrich put it) towards matching the ideal with the real, the laws on the books with the practice of law towards "equality and justice" for all.

West and Zimmerman, 1987; for a comprehensive review and critical analysis of feminist criminologists' use of "doing gender" see Miller, 2002).

3. Miller's earlier work explored how gender patterns the use of violence among gang-involved and non-gang-involved girls. For more details see Miller, J. (2001) *One of the guys: Girls, gangs and gender*. New York: Oxford University Press.

4. For further discussion see Mullins, C. W., Wright, R., and Jacobs, B. A. (2004). Gender, streetlife and criminal retaliation, *Criminology*, *42*(4), 911–40.

References

Adler, F. (1975). *Sisters in crime.* New York: McGraw-Hill Press.

Anderson, E. (1999). *Code of the street: Decency, violence, and the moral life of the inner city.* New York: W. W. Norton and Company.

Bosworth, M. & Fili, A. (2013). Corrections, gender-specific programming and offender re-entry. In C.M. Renzetti, S.L. Miller and A.R. Gover (eds), *Routledge international handbook of crime and gender studies* (pp. 231–242). New York: Routledge.

Brown, M. (2010). Negotiations of the living space: Life in the group home for girls who use violence. In M. Chesney-Lind and N. Jones (eds), *Fighting for girls: New perspectives on gender and violence* (pp. 175–99). Albany: State University of New York Press.

Britton, D. M. (2000). Feminism in criminology: Engendering the outlaw. *Annals of the American Academy of Political and Social Science, 57*(1), 571–92.

Bureau of Justice Statistics. (2011). *Criminal victimization in the United States 2008.* Washington, DC: US Department of Justice.

——(2011, September 15). *Federal criminal case processing statistics.* Retrieved from http://bjs.ojp.usdoj.gov/fjsrc/var.cfm?ttype=trends&agency=USMS&db_type=ArrestsFed&saf=IN.

Burton-Rose, D. (2003). Our sisters' keepers. In T. Herivel and P. Wright (eds), *Prison nation: The warehousing of America's poor* (pp. 258–61). New York: Taylor and Francis.

Chesney-Lind, M. (2010). Jailing "bad" girls: Girls' violence and trends in female incarceration. In M. Chesney-Lind and N. Jones (eds), *Fighting for girls: New perspectives on gender and violence* (pp. 57–79). Albany: State University of New York Press.

Chesney-Lind, M. & Jones, N. (eds) (2010). *Fighting for girls: New perspectives on gender and violence.* Albany: State University of New York Press.

Chesney-Lind, M. & Shelden, R. G. (2004). *Girls, delinquency, and juvenile justice* (3rd edn). Belmont, CA: Wadsworth Cengage Learning.

Collins, P. H. (1990). *Black feminist thought: Knowledge, consiousness, and the politics of empowerment.* New York: Routledge.

——(2004). *Black sexual politics: African Americans, gender and the new racism.* New York: Routledge.

Crosland, K. A., Dunlap, G., Sager, W., Neff, B., Wilcox, C., & Blanco, A. et al. (2008). The effects of staff training on the types of interactions observed at two group homes for foster care children. *Research on Social Work Practice, 18*(5), 410–20.

Daly, K. (1997). Different ways of conceptualizing sex/gender in feminist theory and their implications for criminology. *Theoretical Criminology, 1*, 25–51.

——(1998). Gender, crime and criminology. In M.H. Tonry (ed.), *The handbook of crime and punishment* (pp. 85–110). New York: Oxford University Press.

DeHart, D. & Lynch, S. (2013). Gendered pathways to crime: The relationship between victimazition and offending. In C.M. Renzetti, S.L. Miller and A.R. Gover (eds), *Routledge international handbook of crime and gender studies* (pp. 120–133). New York: Routledge.

Dellasega, C. & Nixon, C. (2003). *Girl wars: 12 strategies that will end female bullying.* New York: Simon and Schuster.

Estrada, R. & Marksamer, J. (2006). The legal rights of LGBT youth in state custody: What child welfare and juvenile justice professionals need to know. *Child Welfare League of America, 85*(2), 171–94.

Friedman, A. (2003). Juveniles held hostage for profit by CSC in Florida. In T. Herivel and P. Wright (eds), *Prison nation: The warehousing of America's poor* (pp. 164–65). New York: Taylor and Francis.

Garfield, G. (2005). *Knowing what we know: African American women's experiences of violence and violation.* New Brunswick, NJ: Rutgers University Press.

Goodkind, S. (2009). "You may even be president of the United States one day"? Challenging commercialized feminism in programming for girls in juvenile justice. In L.M. Nybell, J.J. Shook, and J. L. Finn (eds), *Childhood, youth, and social work in transformation* (pp. 364–384). New York: Columbia University Press.

Harding, S. G. (ed.) (2004). *The feminist standpoint theory reader.* New York: Routledge.

Heimer, K. & Kruttschnitt, C. (eds) (2005). *Gender and crime: Patterns in victimization and offending.* New York: New York University Press.

Hill, G. & Crawford, E. (1990). Women, race and crime. *Criminology, 28,* 601–23.

Irvine, A. (2010). We've had three of them: Addressing the invisibility of lesbian, gay, bisexual and gender non-conforming youths in the juvenile justice system. *Columbia Journal of Gender and the Law, 12*(3), 675–700.

Jones, N. (2008). Working "the code": On girls, gender, and inner-city violence. *Australia and New Zealand Journal of Criminology, 41*(1), 63–83.

——(2010). *Between good and ghetto: African American girls and inner-city violence.* New Brunswick, NJ: Rutgers University Press.

Klein, D. (1973). The etiology of female crime: A review of the literature. In B. R. Price and N. J. Sokoloff (eds), *The criminal justice system and women* (pp. 30–53). New York: McGraw-Hill.

Leonard, E. (1982). *Women, crime and society: A critque of theoretical criminology.* New York: Longman Inc.

Lombroso, C. & Ferrero, G. (1895). *The female offender.* New York: D. Appleton and Company.

Losen, D. J. and Skiba, R. (2010). *Suspended education: Urban middle schools in crisis.* Montgomery, AL: Southern Poverty Law Center.

Males, M. (2010). *Girls myths.* Retrieved September 1, 2010, from www.youthfacts.org/girlphob.

Miller, E. M. (1986). *Street woman.* Philadelphia, PA: Temple University Press.

Miller, J. (2001). *One of the guys: Girls, gangs, and gender.* New York: Oxford University Press.

——(2002). The strengths and limits of "doing gender" for understanding street crime. *Theoretical Criminology,* 6, 433–60.

——(2008). *Getting played: African American girls, urban inequality, and gendered violence.* New York: New York University Press.

Morris, A. & Gelsthorpe, L. (1991). Feminist perspectives in criminology: Transforming and transgressing. *Women and Criminal Justice, 2*, 3–26.

Mullins, C. W., Wright, R. & Jacobs, B. A. (2004). Gender, streetlife and criminal retaliation. *Criminology, 42*(4), 911–40.

Naffine, N. (1987). *Female crime: The construction of women in criminology*. Boston, MA: Allen & Unwin.

——(1996). *Feminism and criminology*. Philadelphia, PA: Temple University Press.

Pasko, L. (2011). Setting the record "straight": Girls, sexuality and the juvenile correctional system. *Social Justice, 37*(1), 7–26.

Pollak, O. (1950). *The criminality of women*. Philadelphia, PA: University of Pennsylvania Press.

Potter, H. (2006). An argument for black feminist criminology. *Feminist Criminology, 1*(2), 106–24.

——(2008). *Battle cries: Black women and intimate partner abuse*. New York: New York University Press.

Prothrow-Stith, D. and Spivak, H. R. (2005). *Sugar and spice and no longer nice: How can we stop girls' violence?* San Francisco, CA: Josey-Bass Press.

Renzetti, C. M. (2004) Feminist theories of violent behavior. In M. Zahn, H. Brownstein, and S. Jackson (eds), *Violence: From theory to research* (pp. 131–143). Cincinnati, OH: Anderson Publishing.

Renzetti, C.M. & Maier, S. (2002). "Private" crime in public housing: Violent victimization, fear of crime and social isolation among women public housing residents. *Women's Health and Urban Life, 1*, 46–65.

Richie, B. (1996). *Compelled to crime: The gender entrapment of battered black women*. New York: Routledge.

Schaffner, L. (2006). *Girls in trouble with the law*. New Brunswick, NJ: Rutgers University Press.

Simpson, S. (1991). Caste, class and violent crime: Explaining differences in female offending. *Criminology, 29*, 115–35.

Simpson, S. & Elis, L. (1995). Doing gender: Sorting out the castle and crime conundrum. *Criminology, 33*, 47–81.

Stevens, T., Morash, M. & Chesney-Lind, M. (2011). Are girls getting tougher, or are we tougher on girls? Probability of arrest and juvenile court oversight in 1980 and 2000. *Justice Quarterly, 28*(5), 719–44.

Steffensmeier, D., Schwartz, J., Zhong, H. & Ackerman, J. (2005). An assesment of recent trends in girls' violence using diverse longitudinal sources: Is the gender gap closing? *Criminology, 43*(2), 355–406.

Weisburd, S. B. & Levin, B. (1993–94). "On the basis of sex": Recognizing gender-based bias crimes. *Stanford Law & Policy Review, 5*(2), 21–47.

West, C. & Fenstermaker, S. (1995). Doing difference. *Gender & Society, 9*(1), 8–37.

West, C. & Zimmerman, D. H. (1987). Doing gender. *Gender & Society, 1*(1), 125–51.

Wiseman, R. (2002). *Queen bees and wannabes: Helping your daughter survive cliques, gossip, boyfriends, and other realities of adolescence*. New York: Three Rivers Press.

READING 6.2

Elder Abuse and the Criminal Justice System

An Uncertain Future

By Candace J. Heisler

Training and inter-agency cooperation have improved when it comes to identifying and prosecuting elder abuse, but public safety and other agencies have taken a hit in the recession, impeding progress.

More than a decade ago, *Generations* published an article about the criminal justice system, describing the then-recent phenomenon of criminalizing elder abuse and neglect (Heisler, 2000). The article highlighted obstacles and knowledge gaps confounding effective intervention by professionals and agencies that investigate and prosecute these cases; several promising approaches and practices were described. This article is an update on efforts to protect victims of elder abuse and hold their perpetrators criminally accountable. While there are promising and successful developments, the future presents significant challenges to professionals, to funders, and to the community at large.

Changing the Understanding of Elder Abuse

Early efforts to define elder abuse as criminal conduct have continued and increasingly focus on effective identification, investigation, and prosecution of perpetrators. Criminal justice intervention is now more frequent and convictions more common. Goals of stopping the abuse, protecting victims, holding offenders accountable, and attempting to make victims whole through the criminal justice process are realized more often than a decade ago. Many efforts have led to progress.

Candace J Heisler, "Elder Abuse and the Criminal Justice System: An Uncertain Future," *Generations*, vol. 36, no. 3, pp. 83-88.

Specialized Investigation and Prosecution Units

Elder abuse cases are complex and fraught with legal, investigative, and practice hurdles. While multiple systems are often involved in cases, all too often those systems do not understand one another, their principles, or their goals and motivations. Cases may begin with non-criminal justice professionals, reporting may be delayed, and evidence may be in the possession of people unfamiliar with the demands of criminal law. Various agencies may have concurrent but different responsibilities. Especially in cases involving facilities, critical documents may be unfamiliar to criminal investigators and the prosecution. The victim may have unique needs for immediate and longer-term assistance to achieve safety, recoup losses, protect assets, assist with decision making, and understand and participate in the criminal process.

The complexity of elder abuse cases requires the involvement of various specialists and experts to help interpret information, conduct capacity assessments, and follow money trails. Coordinated effort is critical to protecting and supporting the victim, and locating crucial evidence and records. These experts and programs include civil bar members specializing in family and elder law; Adult Protective Services (APS) and the Long-Term Care Ombudsman Program; domestic violence and sexual assault programs; regulatory agencies; aging services organizations; and members of the faith and financial communities. Investigators and prosecutors who do not routinely handle elder abuse cases rarely possess such relationships and knowledge.

Effective prosecution requires expert prosecutors who expedite case handling and charging and use specialized procedures to memorialize testimony, such as direct and cross-examination of an older victim who may not survive until a prosecution is completed. Unfortunately, legal tools that may be available in elder abuse cases, such as conditional examinations or depositions and the right to an early trial setting, may be unfamiliar to attorneys who do not regularly handle elder abuse cases (Heisler, 2007).

Specialization may be key to overcoming these considerable hurdles. Over the last decade, various law enforcement, prosecution, and victim assistance agencies have established (or expanded) specialized units to handle elder abuse cases and their victims. Examples of such units are in San Diego, San Bernardino, Orange, and San Francisco counties in California; King County (Seattle) in Washington; and Brooklyn and Manhattan in New York. Some units are associated with forensic or family justice centers; others are not. When specialized units are co-located with community and governmental organizations, they are positioned to offer a broad array of victim services and assistance at a single location.

Increased Knowledge of Forensic Issues

Knowing whether an injury or wound is the result of abuse or neglect—rather than an outcome of aging, underlying medical condition, or medications—is critical to proving criminal conduct. Over the last decade, the number of medical professionals with expertise in geriatrics has slowly increased. Courses in medicine, nursing, and social work programs have increased the pool of potential experts to identify, report, and testify.

There are common indicators for various forms of abuse (Brandl et al., 2007; Stanford School of Medicine, n.d.). Critical research has revealed characteristics of accidental versus intentional bruising, and refuted beliefs about bruises associated with aging (Mosqueda, Burnight, and Liao, 2005; Wiglesworth et al., 2009). Applying what has been learned about strangulation and suffocation in younger populations to older cohorts has led to the identification of crimes that in the past were likely undiscovered. Information from wound-care specialists and other medical professionals about pressure ulcers (bedsores) and standards of care, proper treatment, causation, and prevention has led to convictions for cases of caretaker neglect that previously were regarded as just poor care or unavoidable outcomes.

Elder abuse cases are complex and fraught with legal, investigative, and practice hurdles.

Similarly, expanding the criminal justice system's knowledge about capacity and its role in consent has been critical in financial, neglect, and sexual abuse cases. Prosecutors have increased their successful prosecution of cases through reliance on medical and mental health experts who assess victims' current and past decision-making capacity and susceptibility to undue influence.

What previously had been described as "civil" (or non-criminal) conduct is prosecuted more frequently, thanks to enhanced knowledge and cooperation between criminal justice practitioners and geriatric mental health professionals. The well-publicized case of the exploitation of Brooke Astor highlighted the connection between mental incapacity and alleged consent. Evidence from various health professionals and people involved in her life over many years was critical to proving lack of consent and criminal financial exploitation by her son.

Collaboration with Teams and Forensic Centers

According to Dyer and colleagues: "Elder abuse and neglect cases often pose multiple, complex issues that may be social, medical, ethical, legal, and financial in nature, and which require expertise beyond that available from any single discipline" (Dyer et al., 2005). A recent response has been the growth of multi-disciplinary efforts, including teams, and the participation of criminal justice professionals within them. Teams focus on such problems as identifying and responding to problematic situations, preserving assets, managing and building cases, and supporting prosecution efforts. Criminal justice professionals benefit from the varied experience, knowledge, training, and resources of team members.

Efforts may be based in medical settings or through a variety of other agencies and nonprofit organizations. Medical setting–based teams exist in Minnesota, New Jersey, California, and Texas. Some teams have evolved into forensic centers that are essentially "a 'one-stop shop' where the consumer is an agency working through an elder abuse case and needing the assistance of other agencies with expertise in abuse." Members make home visits with APS to conduct psychological and medical evaluations, "lessening the burden of multiple interviews for the alleged abuse victims, and gathering evidence for possible prosecution" (Schneider et al., 2010). Such forensic centers began at the University of California, Irvine, and now exist in Los Angeles, San Francisco, and New York.

Law enforcement–led teams take several forms. They may focus on rapid response to elder abuse calls in which APS and law enforcement may jointly respond to alleged financial abuse cases (Heisler and Stiegel, 2002). Law enforcement may team with a victim advocate: the officer focuses on the criminal investigation, and the advocate attends to the victim's needs. Elsewhere, local code-enforcement teams include law enforcement, animal control, and public health personnel, as well as fire marshals, city attorneys, and APS. Teams investigate locations, including nursing facilities, to identify problems and remedial actions, and, when necessary, seek to close the facility or ensure its supervision by the court (Heisler, 2007).

Prosecution-led teams focus on identifying criminal cases, case-building, and meeting victims' needs. Examples include the San Bernardino District Attorney's Office in California, the Kennebec County Prosecutor's Office in Maine, and in New York, the Manhattan Elder Abuse Case Consultation and Review Team, and the Brooklyn Multidisciplinary Team.

Knowing whether an injury or wound is the result of abuse or neglect is critical to proving criminal conduct.

Some teams focus on a specific type of elder abuse. Fiduciary Abuse Specialist Teams bring together law enforcement, mental health service providers, APS, and other healthcare practitioners, prosecutors, and experts from financial institutions to consider financial exploitation referrals, determine if criminal conduct is present, review evidence, and meet victims' needs (Brandl et al., 2007). One program in Oregon has recruited retired people with expertise in financial matters to review and analyze transactions and assist law enforcement and prosecutors in developing cases (Heisler, in press).

Elder Fatality Review Teams focus on suspicious deaths of older adults to identify criminal conduct and systemic failures that may contribute to fatalities (Stiegel, 2005). Teams now operate in numerous states including Maine, California, Arizona, Arkansas, Montana, Texas, Kentucky, and Michigan.

In San Diego, a Medical Examiner–Adult Protective Services Response Team ensures that older adult death cases referred to the medical examiner are cross-checked with APS files to identify those with prior abuse investigations. Thus armed, the medical examiner's office can make more informed decisions about whether to conduct autopsies in elder death cases. A similar project exists in Indianapolis.

Collectively these efforts share at least one purpose—to ensure that criminal matters are recognized and critical evidence is identified and collected so cases that should be handled by the criminal justice system can be. The involvement of varied disciplines and professionals means the additional expertise often required to prosecute elder abuse matters can be marshaled.

Training and Education

Criminal justice professionals require added knowledge and skills in order to handle elder abuse cases effectively. Training and education efforts have been focused at the federal, state, and local levels.

At the federal level, the Office on Violence Against Women (OVW) oversees the Enhanced Training and Services to End Violence and Abuse of Women Later in Life Grants Program, which has funded the creation of national curricula on elder abuse for law enforcement, prosecutors, and judicial officers. The OVW has funded training courses delivered locally for law enforcement on detecting and responding to elder abuse cases; national courses for prosecutors on elements of effective elder abuse prosecution; and national courses for judges on making informed decisions in elder abuse matters. The program also funds development of coordinated community responses focused on systems change, victim services training, and some direct services—all of which can improve the response of the criminal justice system in responding to elder abuse cases.

The Office on Victims of Crime has created a multi-day training course on elder abuse for victim advocates and has funded the development of cutting-edge video materials on elder abuse for courts, criminal justice, corrections, and victim services professionals. The National Center on State Courts has created an Elder Abuse Prosecution Toolkit with funding from the Bureau of Justice Assistance (Uekert et al., 2012).

For more than three years, the National Family Justice Center Alliance has included elder abuse training at its annual conference. The National District Attorneys Association also includes elder abuse presentations at its annual domestic violence conference.

At the state level, California, for example, requires that officers and field supervisors complete elder abuse training (Heisler and Stiegel, 2002). For more than a decade, the California District Attorneys Association has held an annual multi-day elder abuse training conference.

Allied professionals critical to identifying, reporting, and handling elder abuse cases historically have been offered little elder abuse training. These include medical examiners and coroners who decide if elder deaths are autopsied. The University of California, Irvine, Program in Geriatrics and Forensic Center now offers an elder death investigations course (Girondo et al., 2010). Nurses are often uniquely situated to identify and report elder abuse, yet little formal training had been available. The International Association of Forensic Nurses has recently created "Nursing Response to Elder Mistreatment Curriculum," which is available at *iafn.org/displaycommon.cfm?an=1&subarticlenbr=459.*

Despite Progress, Challenges Lie Ahead

While there are many positive developments in the criminal justice system's response to elder abuse, at least two significant challenges must be acknowledged: changes in case law regarding admissible evidence, and staffing and financing of public safety.

Changes in Case Law

Since 2004, case law has changed how elder abuse (and other) cases must be proven. Beginning with the United Supreme Court's decision in *Crawford v. Washington* (2004), long-established rules regarding admissible evidence have been turned upside down. Previously, prosecutors could present out-of-court statements shown to be reliable and made to law enforcement officers by the victim or witness about the crime, even if the victim later was unable to testify in court. This was particularly important in elder abuse cases where between the crime's occurrence and the court date, victims died or suffered health setbacks so significant that they could not attend proceedings, or were no longer legally competent to testify.

The International Association of Chiefs of Police estimates some 10,000 positions have been lost in the recession.

After the Crawford decision and the many related decisions that have followed, those once-admissible statements are inadmissible for the truth of their content unless the elder (declarant) is currently unavailable and, at some point during the life of the case, that declarant did testify and was subject to cross-examination. While there are some exceptions, the Crawford decision has greatly restricted the ability to prosecute elder abuse cases unless the declarant actually testifies and is cross-examined.

While efforts have always been made to build solid cases that reduce reliance on the elder person's testimony, the reality is this case law has made the prosecutor's job much more difficult. Because this is a United States Supreme Court decision, which interprets the Constitution's right of a defendant to confront (cross-examine) witnesses against him or her, the decision applies in every criminal courthouse nationwide.

Staffing and Funding

Over the last decade, all aspects of government have sustained cutbacks, including public safety. Law enforcement and prosecution agencies have seen significant reductions in staffing and funding. As an example, between 1986 and 2008, law enforcement agencies experienced a steady increase in the number of sworn and civilian employees (U.S. Department of Justice, Office of Community Oriented Policing Services, 2011).

The recession that began in 2008 has led to layoffs, mandatory furloughs, and hiring freezes. Federal support that funds the hiring of officers has also been reduced. The International Association of Chiefs of Police estimates some 10,000 positions have been lost. Agencies have reduced the types of cases they respond to, are requiring victims to submit reports by telephone or online, have discontinued or reduced training programs, have not ordered new technology, and have reduced the number of follow-up investigations they conduct. One study found these reductions were applied to property crimes, financial crimes, non-felony domestic assaults, and computer crimes. Some agencies have discontinued specialized units. Volunteers and civilian employees are handling assignments previously handled by officers. Some agencies have consolidated their functions with others (U.S. Department of Justice, Office of Community Oriented Policing Services, 2011).

The impact of these changes and of the Crawford case law on elder abuse cases have not been specifically studied. That said, they are sobering realities that must be evaluated as we consider future criminal justice responses to elder abuse. Much time and effort have gone into educating the criminal justice system that elder abuse is criminal conduct; in developing specialized prosecutors, law enforcement, and teams; and in developing and delivering training to improve its investigation and prosecution of abuse. It would be a sad thing if, after all of this progress, the doors to the courthouse would swing shut.

Expanding Response to Elder Abuse Is Key for the Future

The criminal justice system's response to elder abuse is at a critical crossroads. There is increasing consensus that some cases are so serious that this system must be involved in protecting the victim and the community, and holding the offender accountable. Many innovative approaches have been developed, resulting in more cases being investigated and prosecuted. Involvement of new partners and allies, specialized handling, and training and education have improved the effectiveness of the criminal justice system. At the same time, the work has grown more difficult. Our future success will be determined by how we overcome the challenges and expand responses that work.

References

Brandl, B., et al. 2007. *Elder Abuse Detection and Intervention: A Collaborative Approach.* New York: Springer.

Crawford v. Washington. 2004. 541 U.S. 36, 124 S. Ct. 1354.

Dyer, C. B., et al. 2005. "Community Approaches to Elder Abuse." *Clinics in Geriatric Medicine* 21(2): 429–47.

Girondo, M. W., et al. 2010. "Education and Training of Mandated Reporters: Innovative Models, Overcoming Challenges, and Lessons Learned." *Journal of Elder Abuse & Neglect* 22(3–4): 340–64.

Heisler, C. J. 2000. "Elder Abuse and the Criminal Justice System: New Awareness, New Responses." *Generations* 24(2): 52–8.

Heisler, C. J. 2007. "Elder Abuse." In Davis, R. C., Lurigio, A. J., and Herman, S., eds. *Victims of Crime*, 3rd ed. Los Angeles: Sage.

Heisler, C. J. In press. "Elder Abuse." In Davis, R. C., Lurigio, A. J., and Herman, S., eds. *Victims of Crime.* 4th ed. Los Angeles: Sage.

Heisler, C. J., & Stiegel, L. A. 2002. "Enhancing the Justice System's Response to Elder Abuse: Discussions and Recommendations of the 'Improving Prosecution' Working Group of The National Policy Summit on Elder Abuse." *Journal of Elder Abuse & Neglect* 14(4): 31–54.

Mosqueda, L., Burnight, K., & Liao, S. 2005. "The Life Cycle of Bruises in Older Adults." *Journal of the American Geriatrics Society* 53(8): 1339–43.

Schneider, D. C., et al. 2010. "Elder Abuse Forensic Centers." *Journal of Elder Abuse & Neglect* 22 (3–4), 255–74.

Stanford School of Medicine. n.d. "Elder Abuse: Signs and Symptoms of Abuse." elderabuse.stanford.edu/screening/signs.html. Retrieved July 1, 2012.

Stiegel, L. A. 2005. *Promising Practices in the Development of Elder Abuse Fatality Review Teams: A Replication Manual.* Washington, DC: American Bar Association.

Uekert, B. K., et al. 2012. *Elder Abuse Toolkit for Prosecutors.* Williamsburg, VA: National Center for State Courts. eldersandcourts.org/Elder-Abuse/Elder-Abuse-Standards-and-Model-Programs.aspx. Retrieved July 1, 2012.

U.S. Department of Justice (DOJ), Office of Community Oriented Policing Services. 2011. *The Impact of the Economic Downturn on American Police Agencies.* Washington, DC: DOJ. cops.usdoj.gov/files/RIC/Publications/e101113406_Economic%20Impact.pdf. Retrieved July 2, 2012.

Wiglesworth, A., et al. 2009. "Bruising as a Marker of Physical Elder Abuse." *Journal of the American Geriatrics Society* 57(7): 1191–6.

READING 6.3

Peer Victimization and Resilience Among LGBT Youth

By Michele E. Stathatos, Ryan J. Watson, and Michael L. Sulkowski

One third of U.S. high school-age children are victimized by their peers (Sulkowski, Bauman, Wright, Nixon, & Davis, 2014). Of these, over 85% of youth report being verbally harassed because of their actual or perceived sexual orientation, 44% are physically aggressed for the same reason, and 90% have heard their peers use "gay" pejoratively (Kosciw, Greytak, & Diaz, 2009). Thus, victimization related to actual or perceived sexual orientation is a common experience for many heterosexual students—not just lesbian, gay, bisexual, and transgender (LGBT) students—in U.S. schools.

Peer Victimization, Psychosocial Risk, and Shifts to A Focus on Resilience

Marginalized students (e.g., LGBT youth, students from immigrant families, students with disabilities) have been found to be especially vulnerable to peer aggression (Rose, Espelage, Aragon, & Elliott, 2011; Sulkowski et al., 2014). Recent research has elucidated that LGBT youth (and heterosexual youth perceived as LGBT) are particularly vulnerable to peer aggression and victimization. Moreover, bias-based harassment or victimization based on one's actual or perceived sexual orientation has been found to be especially detrimental for the health and well-being of boys. In one study by Swearer, Turner, Givens, and Pollack (2008), boys who were called "gay" reported higher levels of psychological distress and more negative attitudes about school when compared to students who were victimized for other reasons exclusive of being called gay. Additionally, the negative effects associated with being victimized because of one's sexual orientation often last into adulthood and years after the harassment occurred (Espelage, Aragon, Birkett, and Koenig, 2008).

Research has established that victimized LGBT youth are at risk for academic underachievement, lower motivation to pursue secondary education, experiencing mental health problems, abusing substances, exhibiting sexual risk-taking behavior, and engaging in suicidal behavior (Bontempo & D'Augelli 2002; D'Augelli, 2002; Garofalo, Wolf, Kessel, Palfrey, & DuRant, 1998; Kosciw, Greytack, Bartkiewicz, Boesen, & Palmer, 2012). However, it is noteworthy that much of the research conducted on establishing these risks is more than a decade old and was conducted during a time that emphasized risk factors to the neglect of resilience. In general, few studies have focused on resilience in LGBT youth; interesting results emerge from the studies that do exist. In general, research finds that when youth come out they also report positive adjustment. For example, one study found that coming out was related to later life psychosocial adjustment: Being out in high school was related to positive psychosocial adjustment in young adulthood (Russell, Toomey, Ryan, & Diaz, 2014). These students perceived their school climate to be more positive when compared to their LGBT peers who did not come out. In another study, youth reported higher grades and less victimization when they were not managing their sexual identity disclosure: Youth who were out to all contexts (e.g., parents, friends, teachers) reported earning the highest grades compared to youth who were out to some and not others (Watson, Wheldon, & Russell, 2015). Overall, research has highlighted the benefits to building a positive school climate in which students can openly express themselves, as well as the positive effects of coming out during adolescence.

School connectedness and social support are protective factors that contribute to a student's positive psychological functioning at school. When students feel socially supported by their teachers and peers at school, they are more likely to feel connected to their school as well as stay engaged academically.

Resiliency Among LGBT Youth

Despite facing adversity, many marginalized and at-risk youth overcome substantial challenges (Cutuli et al., 2013). Resilience refers to the existence of healthy adaptation during or after experiencing threats or disturbances to one's well-being (Masten, 2001). Therefore, resilience is the healthy adaptation in response to challenging and hostile experiences. Resilience-related protective factors are attributes in an individual, family system, community, and society that help with effectively managing stressful events and with mitigating and eliminating risk. Thus, building skills, strengths, and providing resources and supports are all protective factors that can help an individual remain buoyant in the face of adversity. Collectively, as members of school communities that support all students, school psychologists can be key stakeholders to support the resilience of LGBT students through firming up the previously mentioned protective factors.

Protective Factors

Protective factors are generally discussed as being a part of an ecological model, which serves to help facilitate positive outcomes in the face of adverse circumstances. Individual, relational, and contextual factors are associated with the ability to function under adversity (Masten, 2011). Protective factors take the form of individual relationships (such as relations with peers), school engagement, participation in community activities, or policies and programs, among others. Especially important is support from parents and caregivers; this support crucially influences healthy development of self-esteem and impacts students' positive physical, mental, and emotional health. However, parental support of LGBT youth is oftentimes compromised because these youth are afraid to come out or because they have come out and experienced negative repercussions from disclosing their sexual identity. Students need to feel safe and comfortable at school, as it may not be safe to express their identity in the home environment.

Growth-fostering relationships, school connectedness, and social support are protective factors that foster a safe learning environment and contribute to student resiliency. Growth-fostering relationships are characterized as high quality interpersonal connections that are characterized by empathy, mutuality, and empowerment. Mereish and Poteat (2015) found that LGBT youth have better psychosocial outcomes and experience less psychological distress when involved in a growth-fostering relationship. Additionally, growth-fostering relationships increase a student's feelings of connectedness to school and they provide an extra layer of social support. Overall, school connectedness and social support are protective factors that contribute to a student's positive psychological functioning at school. When students feel socially supported by their teachers and peers at school, they are more likely to feel connected to their school and learning environment as well as stay engaged academically.

Facilitating Resiliency in LGBT Youth

The protective factors mentioned above impact students' resiliency by fostering the growth of strong peer and teacher relationships. These factors can be implemented at schools with a specific focus on LGBT students through LGBT education, advocacy, and support. Schools with these social support structures report having fewer rates of reported LGBT slurs, fewer incidences of homophobic victimization, more feelings of safety, and more supportive conversations with teachers at school (Kosciw, Greytak, & Bartkiewicz, 2014). Research has found that the exclusion of positive information about LGBT people is likely related to discriminatory practices that compromise school safety and students' ability to learn (Crocco, 2001). When schools teach a LGBT-inclusive curriculum, all students, including heterosexual, LGBT, and gender nonconforming students felt safer, experienced less victimization, reported hearing fewer homophobic slurs, and experienced greater peer acceptance (Russel et al., 2014).

Five Suggestions for Facilitating Resiliency

Many ways exist for school psychologists, teachers, and other staff to build relationships with LGBT youth so that they feel supported and positively reinforced. The Gay, Lesbian, and Straight Education Network (GLSEN) is an organization that works to create positive change in schools. To support LGBT students, GLSEN recommends that schools and educators to do the following: Use inclusive language, know that many of your students identify as LGBT, teach materials that are inclusive of the LGBT community, and intervene during name calling. Each of these recommendations is further delineated below.

- Use inclusive language. Using inclusive language involves using language that does not specify gender, sex, or sexual orientation. For example, one may use the words "partner" or "significant other" rather than "girlfriend" or "boyfriend" inside and out of the classroom.
- Know that many youth identify as LGBT. Most classes have LGBT students, and it is important not to assume that students are heterosexual.
- Teach material that is inclusive of the LGBT community. The majority of published books, movies, news stories, and current events include hetero-sexist stories and themes, which excludes LGBT students' experiences. As previously stated, schools that have implemented LGBT education report fewer LGBT slurs, fewer incidences of homophobia, and more feelings of safety (Kosciw et al., 2014). When possible, material or textbooks should be chosen that highlight the accomplishments of LGBT role models, public figures, and politicians (such as Ellen Page, Harvey Milk, Frank Ocean, and Janet Mock).

Table 6.3.1 Steps to Establishing a GSA

Follow school protocol	Establish your GSA the same way you would any other club by following the school handbook.
Find a faculty advisor	Identify a teacher or staff member who is supportive of or has shown support toward the LGBT community.
Inform administration of your plans	Tell administrators what you are doing. If administration is hesitant or resistant, remind them that forming a GSA is protected under the Federal Equal Access Act.
Inform staff of your plans	Tell staff that they can inform students who may be interested in attending or participating in the GSA.
Pick a meeting location	The meeting place should offer privacy and confidentiality.
Advertise	Make flyers, posters, and announcements, and offer free food.
Hold your first meeting	Establish ground rules, explain why the group is important, and plan future events.
Register your GSA	https://gsanetwork.org/register-your-gsa

Table 6.3.2 Nationally Recognized LGBT Resources and Organizations

Organization	School-Wide Events/ Resources	Additional Resources
GLSEN (Gay, Lesbian, and Straight Education Network)	Ally Week, Think B4 You Speak, Day of Silence, Safe Space Kit, No-Name Calling Week	Educator guides (School Climate and HIV Risk; LGBT History Month; Get the Facts: Realities of LGBT Students; Valentine Road: Watch, Discuss and Act; Working with LGBT Students of Color) LGBT-inclusive curriculum, and lesson plans on bullying, bias, and diversity
GSA Network	How to start a GSA, creating an inclusive GSA, GSA actions and events	Legal resources, research and reports
PFLAG (Parents, Families, and Friends of Lesbians and Gays)		Cultivating respect: Safe Schools for All; One Voice Can Change The World; PFLAG Scholarships; Welcoming Faith Communities; Straight for Equality; PFLAG Diversity Network; Make it Count

- Intervene during name calling. Through intervening when a student is being called a name or acting as an active bystander, educators set the tone that harassment will not be tolerated. This begins with educating others when hearing noninclusive language, derogatory jokes, and using incorrect assumptions and stereotypes about the LGBT community.
- Help establish a gay–straight alliance (GSA) at your school. Many benefits are related to having a GSA. Research illustrates that harassment, bullying, and peer victimization of LGBT youth can be reduced by providing resources and information on LGBT issues in the classroom (GLSEN National Climate Survey, 2008). Additionally, the emergence of clubs—such as high school GSAs—that allow individuals to access information and resources in their school helps with the dissemination of key information and the improvement of school climate. Furthermore, having GSAs present helps with establishing a safe space for students to go and discuss topics surrounding LGBT issues at school, at home, and in their communities.

GSAs can function as support groups in which LGBT students can receive social support, feel accepted, and develop friendships. They also act as a way to build a sense of belongingness and decrease the sense of social isolation. Schools with GSAs have been found to have higher perceived levels of safety and lower rates of harassment and victimization for LGBTQ youth (O'Shaughnessy, Russell, Heck, Calhoun, & Laub, 2004). Similarly, a study by Toomey, Ryan,

Diaz, & Russell (2011) found that there is a positive association between the presence of a GSA at school with school belongingness and GPA. In addition, Lee (2002) found that the presence of a GSA is associated with positive developmental outcomes such as higher academic achievement and greater personal comfort with one's own sexual orientation. Thus, as a critical way to support LGBT students, school psychologists should support the establishment of GSAs as well as support their existence. Table 6.3.1 lists distinct steps related to establishing and implementing a school-based GSA, and Table 6.3.2 provides a list of LGBT resources and organizations.

Practice Applications

As caring members of school communities, the onus is on school psychologists to help maintain a safe and LGBT-supportive school climate. To help in this regard, school psychologists can appeal to some of the 10 domains of the NASP *Model for Comprehensive and Integrated School Psychological Services* (NASP, 2010). In this regard, relevant domains include Domain 6: Preventive and Responsive Services; Domain 8: Diversity in Development and Learning; and Domain 9: Research and Program Evaluation.

Domain 6: Preventive and Responsive Services

Domain 6 requires school psychologists to uphold their knowledge of principles and research related to resilience and risk factors so that they can help implement multitiered systems of support for students. LGBT students can be supported in numerous ways to help build their resiliency (see above). Additionally, school psychologists are responsible for collaborating with other staff to promote service delivery, which also involves advocating for the implementation of LGBT organizations and LGBT-relevant information in the curriculum.

Domain 8: Diversity in Development and Learning

Domain 8 encourages school psychologists to obtain knowledge of individual differences, abilities, disabilities, and other areas of diversity within our students and to educate themselves about effectively working with diverse student populations. Thus, it is important for school psychologists to seek competence related to unfamiliar issues, topics, and populations to promote fairness and social justice in school policies and programs.

Domain 9: Research and Program Evaluation

Domain 9 focuses on research and program evaluation, which encourages school psychologists to be involved with research, inform their practice with empirical findings, and be effective consumers of research. Therefore, school psychologists should stay current with research about the LGBT community to ensure that they are well prepared to facilitate effective service delivery and intervention.

Conclusion

Awareness of peer victimization and resilience among LGBT youth is important to our practice as competent school psychologists. Research illustrates the negative effects attributable to peer victimization and social risk. This paper highlights how building resiliency and fostering protective factors can help reduce peer victimization and its deleterious effects on LGBT students. Building and facilitating resiliency through fostering protective factors can be done in numerous ways and school psychologist can be key stakeholders in these efforts. More specifically, school psychologists can ensure that teachers and staff are using inclusive language in the classroom, make teachers aware that many youth identify as LGBT, provide resources for teachers to teach LGBT inclusive material in the classroom, promote intervention during bullying and name calling, and help to set up a Gay–Straight Alliance club at school.

References

Bontempo, D. E., & D'Augelli, A. R. (2002). Effects of at-school victimization and sexual orientation on lesbian, gay, or bisexual youths' health risk behavior. *Journal of Adolescent Health, 30*(5), 364–374. doi:10.1016/S1054-139X(01)00415-3

Crocco, M. S. (2001). The missing discourse about gender and sexuality in the social studies. *Theory into Practice, 40*, 65–71. doi:10.1207/s15430421tip4001_10

Cutuli, J. J., Desjardins, C. D., Herbers, J. E., Long, J. D., Heistad, D., Chan, C., … Masten, A. S. (2013). Academic achievement trajectories of homeless and highly mobile students: Resilience in the context of chronic and acute risk. *Child Development, 84*, 841–857. doi:10.1111/cdev.12013

D'Augelli, A. R. (2002). Mental health problems among lesbian, gay, and bisexual youths ages 14 to 21. *Clinical Child Psychology and Psychiatry, 7*, 433–456. doi:10.1177/1359104502007003039

Espelage, D. L., Aragon, S. R., Birkett, M., & Koenig, B. W. (2008). Homophobic teasing, psychological outcomes, and sexual orientation among high school students: What influence do parents and schools have? *School Psychology Review, 37*, 202.

Garofalo, R., Wolf, R. C., Kessel, S., Palfrey, J., & DuRant, R. H. (1998). The association between health risk behaviors and sexual orientation among a school-based sample of adolescents. *Pediatrics, 101*, 895–902.

Gay and Lesbian Straight Education Network. (2008). *National Climate Survey.* New York, NY: Author.

Kosciw, J. G., Greytak, E. A., & Bartkiewicz, M. J. (2014). Failing progress: Changes in school climate for LGBT youth over time. In E. Meyer & D. Carlson (Eds.), *Gender and sexuality in education: A reader* (pp. 188–201). New York, NY: Peter Lang.

Kosciw, J. G., Greytak, E. A., & Diaz, E. M. (2009). Who, what, where, when, and why: Demographic and ecological factors contributing to hostile school climate for lesbian, gay, bisexual, and transgender youth. *Journal of Youth and Adolescence, 38*, 976–988. doi:10.1007/s10964-009-9412-1

Kosciw, J. G., Greytak, E. A., Bartkiewicz, M. J., Boesen, M. J., & Palmer, N. A. (2012). *The 2011 National School Climate Survey: The experiences of lesbian, gay, bisexual and transgender youth in our nation's schools.* New York, NY: Gay, Lesbian and Straight Education Network.

Lee, C. (2002). The impact of belonging to a high school gay/straight alliance. *The High School Journal, 85*, 13–26. doi:10.1353/ hsj.2002.0005

Masten, A. S. (2001). Ordinary magic: Resilience processes in development. *American Psychologist, 56*, 227–238. doi:10.1037/0003-066X.56.3.227

Masten, A. S. (2011). Resilience in children threatened by extreme adversity: Frameworks for research, practice, and translational synergy. *Development and Psychopathology, 23*, 493–506. doi:10.1017/S0954579411000198

Mereish, E. H., & Poteat, V. P. (2015). A relational model of sexual minority mental and physical health: The negative effects of shame on relationships, loneliness, and health. *Journal of Counseling Psychology, 62*, 425–437. doi:10.1037/cou0000088

National Association of School Psychologists. (2010). *Model for comprehensive and integrated school psychological services.* Retrieved from https://www.nasponline.org/assets/Documents/Standards%20 and%20Certification/Standards/2_PracticeModel.pdf

O'Shaughnessy, M., Russell, S., Heck, K., Calhoun, C., & Laub, C. (2004). *Safe place to learn: Consequences of harassment based on actual or perceived sexual orientation and gender non-conformity and steps for making schools safer.* San Francisco, CA: California Safe Schools Coalition.

Rose, C. A., Espelage, D. L., Aragon, S. R., & Elliott, J. (2011). Bullying and victimization among students in special education and general education curricula. *Exceptionality Education International, 21*, 2–14.

Russell, S. T., Toomey, R. B., Ryan, C., & Diaz, R. M. (2014). Being out at school: The implications for school victimization and young adult adjustment. *American Journal of Orthopsychiatry, 86*, 635–643. doi:10.1037/ort0000037

Sulkowski, M. L., Bauman, S., Wright, S., Nixon, C., & Davis, S. (2014). Peer victimization in youth from immigrant and non-immigrant U.S. families. *School Psychology International, 35*, 649–669. doi:10.1177/0143034314554968

Swearer, S. M., Turner, R. K., Givens, J. E., & Pollack, W. S. (2008). "You're so gay!": Do different forms of bullying matter for adolescent males? *School Psychology Review, 37*, 160.

Toomey, R. B., Ryan, C., Diaz, R. M., & Russell, S. T. (2011). High school gay–straight alliances (GSAs) and young adult well-being: An examination of GSA presence, participation, and perceived effectiveness. *Applied Developmental Science, 15*, 175–185. doi:10.1080/10888691.2011.607378

Watson, R., Wheldon, C., & Russell, S. T. (2015). How does sexual identity disclosure impact school experiences? *Journal of LGBT Youth, 12*(4), 385–396. doi:10.1080/1 9361653.2015.1077764

READING 6.4

The Drug Addict as a Victim

A Link to Explore

By Laura M. Nunes[1] and Ana Sani[2]

Introduction

Victimization is a phenomenon that appears in different settings and includes several dimensions, which themselves also differ according to the type of victim and their specificities. Certain populations have heightened vulnerability, which increases their exposure to the experience of victimization situations. Among these population types, we can also mention those who tend to engage in criminal behaviors but at the same time present characteristics which render them susceptible to victimization. We are talking here about the drug addict, who often has two roles: on the one hand s/he may commit illegal and violent actions, and on the other, s/he may also be the victim of crime and violence.

Drug addiction is one of those behaviors that is related to crime and can at the same time lead to victimization experiences. Several studies (Brochu 2006; Nunes 2011a; Seddon 2006) have been developed with the purpose of examining the link between drug addiction and criminal behavior. Today this drug-crime link is considered unquestionable, although it is also well known that there is no causal relationship between those two behaviors (Bean 2014).

However, it is also understood that the victimization of drug addicts often occurs, and there are not enough studies dedicated to this different mode of connection between drugs and crime. Following this, some authors (MacCoun, Kilmer and Reuter 2003) have stressed the need to study the drug addict, not just because there is a link with criminal behavior, but also considering the victimization suffered by those individuals. It is important to study the victimization of those who, as drug users, are exposed to the violent drug markets, have a high-risk lifestyle, and are under the psychopharmacological effects of the drugs (Goldstein 1985). It is undeniable that these factors increase the vulnerability of this population. Over the last few years, a number of researchers (Goldstein 1985; MacCoun, Kilmer and Reuter 2003; Nunes 2011a; 2011b) have highlighted the urgency of studying drug addict victimization, but the reality is that this domain has received little attention.

Laura M. Nunes and Ana Sani, "The Drug Addict as a Victim: A Link to Explore," *Journal of Drug Addiction, Education, and Eradication*, vol. 11, no. 3-4, pp. 333-342.

In this chapter, we will present some theoretical models regarding the drug-crime link, and explore some approaches to addiction-related violence, in order to explain why it is important to analyze this phenomenon. We will also highlight how these theoretical models are suitable for the possible explanation of the frequent victimization of the drug addict. We will go on to present briefly an integrated model of the drug addict's victimization (Nunes and Sani 2013), and explain the importance of developing modes of evaluation, through victimization surveys, specially designed for drug addicts (Nunes and Sani 2014).

Broadly, the aim of this chapter is to understand victimization from the drug addict's perspective, and raise awareness of a problem that is rarely investigated and not covered by most drug addict support programs.

Drug Addiction and Violence—A Lifestyle Based in Deviant Routines

There is extensive evidence that drug abuse and violence are linked (Caridade and Nunes 2014), and there are analyses that support empirically the link between drug abuse and criminal practices (Brochu 2006; Nunes 2011a). The relation between violent practices and use of drugs is well known. It is also known that drug consumption can be on the part of the offender, on the victim, or both (Fagan 1993; Kleiman and Heussler 2011). So, there are criminal occurrences in which the victim is an individual under the influence of drugs.

Explanations of this link between drugs and violence have focused on aggression patterns rather than the pattern of victimization. Although it is known that drug consumption increases some violent behaviors (Howard and Wang 2003a, 2003b), the reality is that drug effects/consequences also can lead to victimization vulnerabilities. The drug addict is, in effect, an individual with special characteristics which may render him fragile in the face of victimization situations. Indeed, we know that drug use can potentiate the occurrence of victimization experiences (Whitbeck, Hoyt and Yoder 2001). Moreover, while studies have been conducted on the drug-crime link, possible links between drug consumption and victimization experiences (Stevens et al., 2007) have not been so widely explored, and this constitutes a serious failure in analysis of the phenomenon of drug addiction.

Indeed, there are a considerable number of reasons to believe that the drug addict is particularly vulnerable to victimization, especially when those individuals are under the effects of intoxicating substances. This can be explained by different arguments (MacCoun, Kilmer and Reuter 2003):

1. because the person under the intoxicating effects of drugs is an easy target for actions such as robbery, rape, and other crimes;
2. because intoxicated individuals often take on an unsettling demeanor, for example in terms of their appearance, behavior, and speech;

3. because the state of intoxication leads to unpredictable and ambiguous behavior manifestations;
4. because the abovementioned conditions weaken the perception of signals and stimuli, and diminish the capacity of transmission signals to others (i.e., the intoxicated state leads to poor communication);
5. finally, because it is not uncommon in the illegal drug market to find that the individual selling the product, being in possession of large sums of money, is also intoxicated.

These elements make the addict a fragile and desirable target. Indeed, the very lifestyle of these individuals makes them vulnerable to victimization, and the environment they frequent is also frequented by those who may commit crimes against them.

Routine Activities Theory and Drug Addicted Vulnerability

According to Wolfgang (1957), certain crime situations are precipitated by the victim. We can therefore inquire as to whether the drug addict, with all the characteristics mentioned above, is not one of those individuals who create situations which may precipitate their own victimization. As noted, some of these characteristics can indeed enhance such individuals' own victimization, and thus we often find that victims of murder and assault, for example, show signs of having used drugs and having previously been involved in conflicts leading to a physical attack.

Fagan and Chin (1990), in their studies, affirm the vulnerability to victimization situations of those who take drugs. The authors argue that some substances induce behavioral changes that may result in situations with characteristics that potentiate victimization by aggression, for example, carried out by those who are free of the effects of substances. Other authors (Stevens et al., 2007) have found elevated levels of violent victimization among drug users. In order to better analyze this phenomenon, it is necessary to look at the routines of the drug users, in places where there are drugs to buy and sell, with illegal transactions conducted in a highly conflictive context. Indeed, we must take into consideration the fact that the drug user and the criminal exist in the same illicit markets, and that they both have an interest in one product: the drug. So, these two deviant figures turn out to cross each other's paths in the same contexts and confront the same interests.

The theory of routine activities developed by Cohen and Felson (1979) provides an explanation for the occurrence of crime centered in criminal circumstances and contexts. According to this approach, there are three important elements which take place at the same time promoting the criminal occurrence. Those three factors are (i) a motivated offender, (ii) a vulnerable target or possible victim, and (iii) the absence of guardians able to prevent the occurrence. Those three factors work together to create the opportunity for crime.

This theoretical perspective argues that the choices of an individual can influence the possibility of becoming a desirable target (Doerner and Lab, 2012) for a motivated offender who is ready to commit a crime, and is waiting for the most favorable criminal opportunities in a context with no-one to prevent the crime being committed. Thus, an addict may be an appropriate target because of his or her vulnerable state, arising either from being under the influence of drugs or in a state of abstinence. In fact, given the elements explained earlier there are many factors which put the drug addict at high risk of being deceived or attacked (Wilcox 2010).

All of this is also related to the individual's lifestyle, which, in the case of the addict, is highly risky. According to Hindelang, Gottfredson, and Garofalo (1972), the risk of victimization is very much associated with the lifestyle of the people who, in fact, can influence/affect the opportunities for crime, by creating favorable criminal conditions. A drug addict, by virtue of his lifestyle at the margins of society, is generally represented as a deviant individual and therefore at greater risk of being subjected to violent reactions from others. There is an increased likelihood of the addict being involved in crime, either as victim or offender, or even as a witness, because of the places that this population frequent, especially at night, and because of the relationships that these individuals establish with people closely linked to drug misuse and criminal contexts (Kennedy and Forde 1990; Nofziger 2009; Nofziger and Stein 2006).

Thus, direct and/or indirect victimization eventually integrate the everyday life and routines of the drug addict, who has regular contact with deviant and criminal individuals. Also, by dint of their lifestyle the drug addict will tend to have much less protection, especially in the form of formal protection from the social control system, for fear that their deviant activity is discovered by the authorities (Wilcox 2010).

Taken together, this lack of protection, the perceived vulnerability, the motivation of others to engage in criminal practices, and the other factors discussed above, can all explain why someone with a lifestyle linked to drug dependence can be seen as very easily engaged in victimization situations.

Approaches to The Drug-Crime Link and Drug-Victimization Connection

Some theoretical models explain the drug-crime link and drug-related violence from a deterministic point of view, based on the powerful effects of the substances on behaviors.

One such approach is the *Chronic Effects Model*, which suggests that drug addiction becomes chronic and causes neuropsychological functioning changes, developing pathological conditions that contribute to the adoption of violent actions (Rothman, Reyes, Johnson and LaValley 2012). This model focuses mainly on violence developed in the context of intimate relationships. We can look at this theoretical approach as a possible explanation for the violent acts of the drug addict, in the context of close relationships—even though this model can also be applied to violence in other relational contexts. There are models which focus on the generic relation between drugs and crime. Thus, another explanation, the so-called *Psychopharmacological Model*, tries to explain criminal behavior due to the pharmacological effects of the substances (White and Gorman 2000). In this point of view, the intoxicated state can cause behavioral changes and lead to violent actions, and the toxic effects can also lead to criminal behaviors. This is true, but intoxication also tends to leave individuals prostrate, and therefore in a situation of greater vulnerability to victimization (Nunes and Sani 2013). We can therefore say that this model, which explains the link between drugs and crime and violent behaviors, can also support an explanation of the link between drugs and victimization.

Another approach attempts to explain how violence in intimate relationships may be associated with drug use. The *Model of Proximal Effects* refers to the psychopharmacological power of substances, which gradually leads to a reduction of cognitive functioning capacities, and increases impulsivity, which tends to mediate the aggressive behavior (Shorey, Stuart and Cornelius 2011). It seems that some of the factors used to explain this problem are indirectly linked to drugs, but we also can say that the reduction of cognitive capacities can lead to more risky behaviors, and can be exploited by others who would victimize the drug user.

Another model, very close to the one just presented, is the *Economic-Compulsive Model*, which points to drug dependence as a cause of acquisitive crime. This model suggests that crime related to drug addiction occurs because the drug user needs money to buy drugs. However, this argument may be a form of rationalization often presented by addicts about their own criminal behaviors (MacCoun, Kilmer and Reuter 2003). On the other hand, the economic situation of the drug addict, together with the need to maintain the addiction, and abstinence syndrome, may lead individuals to situations that weaken them in a deviant world where they can easily become a victim. Because of this fragility, we can conclude that the reasons behind the criminal practices developed by drug users are the same factors that can expose them to a victimization experience.

Related to the lifestyle perspective, and considering the places where those individuals develop their routine activities, the *Systemic Model* refers to the violence associated with illegal drug markets. This model can help to explain both the criminal behavior and the victimization of the drug addict. This theoretical point of view explores the violence of the drug markets that can potentially lead addicts to violent behaviors in order to protect themselves, as well as to situations in which they are the victims of violent actions (Goldstein 1985). Thus, the study of those violent behaviors, in systemic terms, should emerge as a priority for analysis of the drug-crime phenomenon (Goldstein, Brownstein and Bellucci 1989). However, it is also important to study the victimization of drug users who are exposed to these violent markets (Goldstein 1985). From a systemic and environmental perspective, we can say that the places the drug addict visits frequently are the same places where s/he can commit or become a victim of crime.

Another model presents an integrated perspective. This is the *Tripartite Model* proposed by Goldstein (1985), which points to the combined influence of the factors mentioned earlier. This theory tries to explain the drug-crime link, but it also provides an explanation for the frequent victimization of the drug addict. The author combines three reasons for such linkage: (i) the psychopharmacological effects of the product; (ii) the high costs of certain illegal substances; and (iii) the violence in illegal drug markets. According to the author, those factors could affect the individual's behaviors. So, this could contribute to crime, committed by different types of offender, with different types of victim (Goldstein, Bellucci, Spunt and Miller 1991). As we can see, the reasons that the literature points to for the drug-crime link can also explain the vulnerability of the drug addict to victimization.

Other authors have presented theoretical approaches that take a different, less deterministic perspective, instead taking a processual point of view centered on the lifestyle of the drug addict. From this perspective, we can say that lifestyle, as presented by Faupel (1987; 1981), can relate to the issues associated with the individual's routines that have already been pointed out in this chapter as something to consider.

Faupel presented a model based on analysis of the life structure and career of the individual who uses drugs, and specifically heroin. Faupel (1987) emphasized the link between drug abuse and criminal practices as a process through four stages affected by different variables, such as availability of the substances, the individual's motivations, and their deviant skills. According to the author, the structure of life is related to the standard daily occurrences associated with areas such as labor, domestic and private life, etc. Then, Faupel (1987) argued, there would be four stages: (i) the *casual user*, with low availability of substances and a high life structure; (ii) the *stabilized junkie*, with high availability of substances and a high life structure; (iii) the *free-wheeling junkie*, with high availability of substances but a low life structure; and, at last, (iv) the state of the *street junkie*, with no life structure and no access to substances. This individual is an outsider both in the normative society and in the deviant subculture. He has no place in any social group.

The *street junkie* is lonely and fragile, and exceptionally vulnerable to victimization situations. Indeed, this individual is completely alone, without support or group belonging. At the *free-wheeling junkie* stage the individual has access to drugs but not to a life structure. So, this will be a state in which the addict is at the mercy of illicit drugs markets. In such markets there are high probabilities of being a victim of crime, as we have already seen. These individuals will be subjected to illegal drug market fluctuations, and will obviously be vulnerable to victimization situations in this particularly dangerous environment.

Following what has been said above, we draw attention to an integrated model, proposed by Nunes and Sani (2013). This theoretical approach tries to consider most of the factors that have already been highlighted by the conceptualizations previously developed.

This integrated model argues that it is possible to adopt the Goldstein idea, and take into consideration the fact that drug addicts have constraints related to substances' costs. Because of this, addicts can more easily succumb to forms of criminal or deviant behaviors, such as participation in drug trafficking, and other criminal actions. Furthermore, it is not uncommon for those individuals to have no ways to pay their accounts with their drug suppliers. In those cases, the addict is at the mercy of violent methods used to settle the accounts and resolve conflict. In the illegal context of drug markets these kinds of problems are resolved by violent and unlawful methods.

Considering Faupel's stages, and looking to the problems present in the drug addict's life, including lifestyle and routines in dangerous and illegal business as well as in violent places, it is clear that it only makes sense to think about the problem of drug addiction by integrating these models into a global perspective which integrates all of these described factors (Nunes and Sani 2013).

Reasons to Evaluate the Victimization of the Drug Addict

There are several factors that make it important to evaluate the victimization experiences of the drug addict population, and the violence of illegal drug markets is one of them, since it exposes the addict to numerous risks. This violence relates to the following aspects (MacCoun, Kilmer and Reuter 2003):

1. First, the youth of the participants involved in those transactions (approximately 18–22), can lead to easier involvement in violent actions, and certain markets of some drugs have very young sellers;
2. Second, the price of the drugs, which can be so high as to create competition situations which lead easily to violent occurrences;
3. Third, these illegal transactions are conducted under conditions of pressure and uncertainty, and regulation of the conduct and protection of the business are carried out by violence;
4. Fourth, some drugs turn their users more violent and ready for precipitated behaviors in a conflict situation. It is important to note that, according to some delinquency studies, drug user on drug user crime is very frequent.

On the other hand, and according to Goldstein (1985), it is very difficult to access information about the victimization of drug addicts because these kinds of victims are not interested in talking about it with the police; they do not remember details of the crime or the offender; most victimization questionnaires only ask about drug consumption in general, and not about the role of drugs in the specific offense; in this context, the victim may have instigated some kind of provocation that might have precipitated the crime. So, emphasizes Goldstein (1985), in the face of all this, we cannot overestimate the importance of the drug addict's victimization.

Alcohol-related crime and violence and the victimization associated with alcohol abuse are topics that have been widely studied. However, the relation between illegal drugs consumption and victimization experiences has not had much attention. According to various authors (e.g., MacCoun, Kilmer and Reuter 2003; Nunes 2011b), these are some of the reasons why it is urgent to study drug addict victimization.

Final Notes

As we said at the beginning of this chapter, over the last few decades science has tried to explain the idea that the victim of ongoing violence can sometimes develop a drug abuse problem, in order to develop better methods of support for individuals in such situations. The social sciences have also studied the use of drugs by the offender, as well as the phenomenon of the link between drug abuse and crime. But very few studies have focused on the drug addict as a victim of crime and violence, considering the conditions and lifestyle of those individuals.

Having presented some of the theoretical models relating to the drug-crime link and attending to evidence already revealed in studies pertaining to the victimization of the drug addict, it seems urgent to start studying the experience of victimization situations among drug users. The urgency of such investigation lies in the fact that these individuals not only have potential for delinquent actions, but are also exposed to very difficult situations that can lead to victimization experiences.

In effect, the drug addict is a kind of victim who, for obvious reasons, has no interest in reporting the crime they have suffered to the authorities. However, they are victims of severe situations, and rehabilitation programs should take this into account. For this reason, this is a phenomenon which should be studied with great attention.

To do so, we need to develop victimization surveys specially designed for this very specific population, such as the questionnaire developed by Nunes and Sani (2014) for the Portuguese drug addict population. On the other hand, the general drug addict evaluation should include an analysis of possible situations of victimization so that intervention can be designed to take into account the specificities of these cumulative experiences. It is also imperative to know the role of drugs in the occurrence of crime and to ascertain the influence of substances on the offender's behavior, and also the potential vulnerability of this kind of person to be a victim.

This association between substance abuse and victimization is noteworthy. Investigation of this association is the study of the potential risk of a victimization experience leading to involvement in consumption behaviors, often at early stages of the development of the individual. Drug use can be preceded and contributed to by victimization experiences, and can be a factor which exposes the individual to risks of becoming a victim of violence and crime. Thus, evaluation must consider the register of the consumption, and the consumption history of each individual. It is also very important to analyze the situations of victimization that could have arisen prior to the drug abuse period, as well as after the addiction problem. Only with this kind of information can we design proper intervention programs that consider all of the various dimensions of the drug-violence link. It is imperative to treat this population by acknowledging that most of their problems and victimization experiences are too severe and cause too much damage to be ignored in the treatment processes.

It is impossible to understand those individuals and provide appropriate support without looking at all of the dimensions involved, and victimization risks are one of those factors. The prevention of this population's victimization also necessitates that attention be paid to the routines and lifestyles of the drug addict, and that these persons are able to report these criminal situations to the relevant assistance institutions without fear.

References

Andrews, D., & Bonta, J. (2010). *The psychology of criminal conduct* (5th Ed.). New Jersey: Matthew Bender, & Company.

Bean, P. (2014). *Drugs and crime*. New York: Routledge.

Brochu, S. (2006). *Drogue et criminalité. Une relation complexe* (2ª Ed.). Montréal: Les Presses de l'Université de Montréal.

Caridade, S., & Nunes, L. (2014). Violência nas relações íntimas juvenis e abuso de substâncias: vitimação, agressão e género. *Psiquiatria, Psicologia e Justiça, 6*, 167–189.

Cohen, L., & Felson, M. (1979). Social change and crime rate trends: A routine activity approach. *American Sociological Review, 44*, 588–608.

Doerner, W., & Lab, S. (2012). *Victimology*. 6ª edição Cincinnati: Anderson Publishing.

Fagan, J. (1993). Interactions among drugs, alcohol, and violence. *Health Affairs, 12*(4), 65–79.

Fagan, J., & Chin, K.-L. (1990). Violence as regulation and social control in the distribution of crack. In M. De La Rosa, E. Lambert, & B. Gropper (Eds.). *Drugs and violence: causes, correlates, and consequences* (pp. 8–43). Rockville: U.S. Department of Health and Human Services. National Institute on Drug Abuse.

Faupel C. (1987). Drug availability, life structure, and situational ethics of heroin addicts. *Journal of Contemporary Ethnography, 15*(3/4), 395–419.

Faupel C. (1991). *Shooting dope: career patterns of hard-core heroin users*. Gainesville: University of Florida Press.

Goldstein P. (1985). The drugs/violence nexus: A tripartite conceptual framework. *Journal of Drug Issues, 39*, 143–174.

Goldstein P., Brownstein H., & Bellucci A. (1989). Crack and homicide in New York city, 1988: A conceptual based event analysis. *Contemporary Drug Problems, 16*(4), 651–687.

Hindelang, M., Gottfredson, M., & Garofalo, J. (1978). *Victims of personal crime: An empirical foundation for a theory of personal victimization*. Cambridge, MA: Ballinger.

Howard, D., & Wang, M. Q. (2003a). Risk profiles of adolescent girls who were victims of dating violence. *Adolescence, 38*, 1–14.

Howard, D., & Wang, M. Q. (2003b). Psychosocial factors associated with adolescents boys' reports of dating violence. *Adolescence, 38*, 519–533.

Kennedy, L. W., & Forde, D. R. (1990). Risky lifestyles and dangerous results: Routine activities and exposure to crime. *Sociology and Social Research, 74*, 208–228.

Kleiman, M., & Heussler, L. (2011). Crime-minimizing drug policy. *Journal of Criminal Justice, 39*, 286–288.

MacCoun R., Kilmer B., & Reuter P. (2003). Research on drugs-crime linkage: the next generation. In J. Ashcroft, D. Daniels & S. Hart (Eds.). *Toward a Drugs and Crime Research Agenda for the 21st Century: Special Report* (pp. 65–90). Washington: U.S. Department of Justice Office of Justice Programs.

Nofziger, S., & Stein, R. (2006). To tell or not to tell: Lifestyle impacts on whether adolescents tell about violent victimization. *Violence and Victims, 21*, 371–382.

Nofziger, S. (2009). Deviant lifestyles and violent victimization at school. *Journal of Interpersonal Violence, 24*(9), 1494–1517.

Nunes, L. (2011a). *Droga-crime: (des)construções.* Porto: Edições UFP.

Nunes, L. (2011b). O toxicodependente sob a perspectiva da vitimação. In A. Sani (Ed.), *Temas da vitimologia: realidades emergentes e respostas sociais* (pp. 241–266). Coimbra: Almedina.

Nunes, L., & Sani, A. (2013). Victimization of the drug addict. *Journal of Modern Education Review, 3*(9), 243–250.

Nunes, L., & Sani, A. (2014). Toxicodependência e vitimação: inquérito dirigido a indivíduos dependentes de drogas. *Análise Psicológica, 1*(32), 79–90.

Rothman, E., Reyes, L., Johnson, R., & LaValley, M. (2012). Does the alcohol make them do it? Dating violence perpetration and drinking among youth, *Epidemiologic Reviews, 34*(1), 103–119.

Seddon, T. (2006). Drugs, crime and social exclusion: social context and social theory in British drugs-crime research. *British Journal of Criminology, 46*(4), 680–703.

Shorey, R., Stuart, G., & Cornelius, T. (2011), Dating violence and substance use in college students: A review of the literature. *Aggression and Violent Behavior, 16*, 541–550.

Stevens, A., Berto, D., Frick, U., Kerschl, V., McSweeney, T., Schaaf, S., Tartari, M., Turnbull, P., Trinkle, B., Uchtenhagen, A., Waidner, G., & Werdenish, W. (2007). The victimization of dependent drug users. Findings from a European study, UK. *European Journal of Criminology, 4*(4), 385–408.

Whitbeck, B., Hoyt, R., Yoder, K., Cauce, A., & Paradise, M. (2001). Deviant behaviour and victimization among homeless and runaway adolescents, *Journal of Interpersonal Violence, 16*(11), 1175–1204.

White H., & Gorman D. (2000). Dynamics of the drug-crime relationship. *Criminal Justice, 1*, 151–218.

Wilcox, P. (2010). Victimization, theories of. In B. Fisher, & S. Lab (Eds.), *Encyclopedia of victimology and crime prevention* (pp. 978–986). Thousand Oaks: SAGE Publications.

Wolfgang, M. (1957). Victim precipitated criminal homicide. *The Journal of Criminal Law, Criminology, and Police Science, 48*(1), 1–11.

READING 6.5

Crime and Victimization Among Latinas

By Venus Ginés and William Hervey

Introduction

> [After John raped me] he pushed me away.... [That] make me feel really bad.... I went to the kitchen to drink water.... And I turned my back and I—the first thing I saw was the knife. Then I took it and I was just angry.... I went to the bedroom and I told him—he shouldn't do this to me.... I asked him if he was satisfied with what he did. Then he said he doesn't care about my feelings. He did say that and I ask him if he has orgasm inside me because it hurt me when he made me do that before. He always have orgasm and he doesn't wait for me to have orgasm. He's selfish. I don't think it's fair, so I pull back the sheets and then I did it.
>
> (Reardon 1996)

On 23 June 1993, Lorena Bobbitt, a timid, petite immigrant from Ecuador, severed her husband's penis with a kitchen knife while he was passed out in a drunken stupor. The story garnered national attention, enabling women's groups and the news media to bring to the public consciousness the emotional, physical, and sexual abuse many women suffer for years before snapping. In addition to her husband's physical and sexual abuse, Lorena Bobbitt had also been coerced into having an abortion. Her trial in January 1994 became a rallying point for many other women who had suffered such abuse to speak out on the lack of attention for victims of domestic violence. In the end, Bobbitt was acquitted because she was suffering from post-traumatic stress disorder (PTSD), but her case was only a symptom of a larger problem that must be addressed for any real progress to occur in rectifying a situation in which many women, especially Latinas, are the victims of violent crimes or feel compelled to commit crimes themselves in order to survive.

Bobbitt's actions became a major media story, with the entire nation knowing what she had done and what had happened to her. Almost 20 years later, her last name is still a slang phrase for the severing of a man's penis. It must be remembered that her story is not an isolated one, but is representative of the plight of domestic violence suffered by many Latinas. However tempting it might be to individualize Bobbitt's story, this case and other similar, though less sensationalized, cases are really the cumulative effect of numerous societal factors. Most pertinently, one must examine the society she lived in, her psychological state of mind, her biomedical state, and the environmental factors that aggravated an already volatile situation.

Taken collectively, these factors, embedded within the epidemiological criminology paradigm, may help explain or frame how to better understand Bobbitt's situation and response. Moreover, if properly analyzed they can equip public health providers to intervene with programs that steer victims of domestic violence in a more positive direction before the situation comes to a tragic conclusion. This is true not only in situations of domestic violence but also for Latinos and crime in general, both as victims and as perpetrators.

Latinos are now the fastest-growing population in the United States. As of 2010, Latinos/Hispanics numbered 50.4 million and are projected to increase to 108.2 million by 2040 (US Census Bureau 2008, 2011). However, it is important to note that this is not a homogeneous group. Latinos immigrating to the United States come from 22 different countries of origin and have specific demographic patterns and degrees of acculturation, causing difficulty in making broad assumptions about Latinos, although enough commonalities exist that it is possible to look at crimes *against* Latinas, crimes committed *by* Latinas, and how gender and culture place them in disparate risk for becoming victimized.

Latinas as Offenders

Although the demographics are gradually changing, the majority of female offenders in the United States criminal justice system are minority, economically disadvantaged, and single mothers (Sentencing Project 2007). In addition, they are disproportionately undereducated and unskilled, with sporadic employment histories. The life issues relevant to this analysis that propel women into crime include family violence, substance abuse, and economic issues. Specifically, women in the criminal justice system are more likely to have come from single family homes, or to have lived in foster care or group homes at some point in their childhood.

Economic factors, in addition, can often drive women to commit crimes, and these crimes are often accentuated when the women are unable to remove themselves from an impoverished living environment and an environment fraught with drug and alcohol abuse. Generally, women offenders often grow up in families where drugs or alcohol are abused. Incarcerated women also report a history of either physical or sexual abuse from a family member. What complicates this population of women even more is that many of the women who enter the criminal justice system have had prior-diagnosed mental health issues. For example, 25 percent of women in state prisons have been identified as experiencing depression stemming from PTSD, a condition often seen in women who have suffered sexual abuse and other similar traumas (Gaines and Miller 2013).

Many factors influence Latinas who commit violent crimes, including stress deriving from society in general, their families, the acculturation process, and from poor parenting problems and skills. From a criminal justice perspective, culturally competent law enforcement training programs are generally lacking when dealing with these crimes and criminals, which leads to a lack of social and legal justice. For instance, Latina women who are isolated from their homeland, their culture, their community, and their family often become depressed and vulnerable to all manner of abuse. Language barriers often exist that can cause misunderstandings or even deliberate deceptions by the abuser, as in the case of Lorena Bobbitt. This vulnerability can lead to abuse by others, including husbands, lovers, and the criminal subculture to which they may be become acculturated. From an epidemiological criminology perspective, it is critical to identify an operant balance for Latinas that does not tip away from a healthy lifestyle to a behavior that is more criminal in nature and context. Yet it is critical to examine the acculturation process for the Latino women that take into account biopsychosocial and environmental factors that can influence the behavior of the Latina.

Latinas as Victims

The involvement of women in the criminal justice system has largely been as victims of crime rather than as criminals, with women making up about half of violent crime victims but representing a minority of offenders. Women from low-income households are four times more likely to experience violence than women in the income bracket above $50,000 (Craven 1996). And, as undocumented aliens have been increasing nationally, this has possibly seeded a growing anti-illegal-immigrant sentiment that has also led to an increase in the number of hate crimes directed at Latinos since around 2000, with many believing the numbers are actually underreported, owing to a fear of repercussions (NIJ 2011; Costantini 2011). This increase is especially disconcerting for Latinas, who fall victim to a variety of crimes, most notably sexual crimes, harassment, assault, rape, and sodomy. According to the Bureau of Justice Statistics' National Crime Victimization Survey (NCVS), the percentage of violent victimizations reported to police against white non-Latino (50 percent), black non-Latino (48 percent), and Latino (53 percent) males was similar in each case, but with Latinos showing a small increase. In contrast, for females the percentage of violent victimizations reported to the police against white non-Latinas (52.4 percent), black non-Latinas (55.4 percent), and Latinas (62.5 percent) was also similar in each case, though Latina females experienced a higher percentage of violence as victim (BJS 2011a).

As has already been alluded to, the issue around violence is even worse for undocumented immigrants. Battered undocumented immigrant women in the borderlands are pushed and pulled across the United States–Mexico border in search of socioeconomic stability and advancement, maintenance of sociocultural ties, and physical security for themselves and their children. Ethnographic research on domestic battery among immigrants in Phoenix, Arizona, has shown that battering contributes to further illegal activity, while, at the same time, national immigration policies can be a contributing factor to domestic battery (Salcido and Adelman 2004). This awareness is consistent with one of the structural elements in the epidemiological criminology paradigm, which addresses the importance of one's environment as a factor for contributing to either a healthy or a criminal lifestyle. For example, many battered immigrant women feel that they have no place to go, or fear that there is no other safe haven for them and their children, since most shelters are run by non-Latinos. As a result, they generally stay with their abuser. For cultural, social, and economic reasons, Latinas are more likely to stay in an abusive relationship.

Some of the issues that may impact the Latino family home environment may begin with the low self-esteem of the men, who feel they are disrespected at work, which can exacerbate their aggressive behavior toward the wife and children at home. Latinas in these abusive relationships fall victim to the cycle of domestic violence because of their culturally imposed role as self-sacrificing martyrs who must preserve the family at any cost, even their life. The most common scars in these situations may not be physical but, rather, primarily emotional, psychological, and moral abuses. These are critical factors that need to be understood, as they tend to go unanalyzed by mainstream researchers. Factors that influence a Latina woman to stay in an abusive relationship can include the following:

- The family comes first.
- These battering incidents must be kept private.
- He is the macho and "boys will be boys."
- The family is economically deprived.
- He holds the paperwork to her immigration status.
- There is no facility with Latino social workers or advocates.
- The law enforcement officer would not understand her language or culture.
- She is unable to speak the language to defend herself.
- She believes that the family must stay together because the Church forbids divorce.
- She has a genuine fear that the abuser will hurt the children.
- She fears that she will be blamed for not keeping home and hearth intact.
- She feels guilty about turning against the man who brought her to the United States.

Latina Prisoners

There are approximately 344,400 Latinos and Latinas in federal and state prisons and local jails, making up slightly over 24 percent of the inmate population. Latino males and females have seen a marked percentage change over the past 10 years in their rate of incarceration, accounting for an increase of

3.1 percent and 28 percent, respectively (BJS 2011b). In federal and state prisons, Latina women are imprisoned and held in custody at a rate of 133 per 100,000. This is approximately 1.5 times greater than for white females, who have a rate of 91 per 100,000. The largest incarceration rate of Latina women is of those between 25 and 34 years of age, which accounts for, on average, 320 per 100,000 (BJS 2011c).

When Latina women are subjected to incarceration, they invariably leave behind their culture, family, social support networks, and identity. If the Latina had been victimized by violent acts that prompted a response to fight back, she often viewed as responsible for breaking up the family. Yet, as was alluded to previously, many Latina women are subjected to all manner of mental and physical abuse, socioeconomic deprivation from their male counterpart, and, invariably, drug and sexual abuse. All of these factors or co-occurring disorders need to be examined in the context of how the criminal justice system might be able to provide primary, secondary, and/or tertiary prevention interventions to try to address these life events.

The Epidemiological Criminology Response

When we examine the applicability of the epidemiological criminology model for better understanding the Latina woman, we are compelled to address these issues not as separate events but as a tapestry of complex events that need to be addressed collectively. The Latino culture tends not to break down such post-traumatic issues so neatly. Rather, a more holistic approach is the best, an approach that takes into account both the public and the mental health side of the equation, along with the criminal justice side. Today, as the American criminal justice system attempts to interpret the application of contemporary US law and its adaptability to cultural shifts and changes, a subtle criminogenic health disparity continues to exist against Latinas. That is, a barrier to justice may include the lack of accessible, culturally and linguistically relevant programs. From the moment of their arrest, to their court appearance, to post-adjudication and sentencing, and reentry back into the community, Latinas lack targeted programs that provide the education, job skills, and training necessary to improve their situation and enable them to break away from this pattern of violence.

For example, when a Latina is in need of shelter, because of abuse or to access mental health services, too few are available to accommodate these women and their children, let alone have bilingual and bicultural staff. However, since 1997 a national non-profit organization, Día de la Mujer Latina, Inc. (Day of the Latin American woman), has focused on providing Latinas with a dedicated day of early detection screening for chronic diseases, mental health, and domestic violence counseling, and an opportunity for them to learn about their legal rights. On many occasions, the stories of abuse told by the Latino women were similar, regardless of whether it was Houston, Miami, or Atlanta. The women had more in common than the abuse, with most of the victims being petite in stature, caught between culture and religion, fearful and mistrustful of law enforcement, controlled by the men in their life (mostly because of economics rather than love), and for the most part feeling powerless. The majority of the violent episodes, which also included rape, were provoked by the substance abuse of their partner.

This pattern was evident in the case of Lorena Bobbitt, but at that time there was no scientifically emerging model, such as epidemiological criminology, to help frame a complex analysis. In short, Lorena had no social support, was economically challenged, lived in a foreign country with no family or social support network to defend her, suffered from spousal abuse, and was still recovering (emotionally and physically) from a coerced abortion. This type of scenario continues to subject victims, such as Bobbitt, to criminal behavior both as the victim and as the perpetrator—two sides of the same coin.

A possible solution to help the number of Latinas who are victims of crime, or who are neglected or who have fallen through the cracks of the justice system, is to develop a balanced solution for intervening, such as through the integration of the Community Health Workers and Promotores model. The Promotores and Community Health Workers are oftentimes used in the Latino community to serve as patient navigators—that is, to help patients navigate the complex maze of the health system by providing counseling, serving as interpreters, and acting as advocates, as needed. From our perspective as practitioners, these are trusted members of the Latino community who can be trained to motivate victims to seek help when they experience physical and emotional abuse, inform them of available resources, navigate them through the complicated legal system, and raise their education level with training to improve marketable skills. It is almost 20 years since the young, reserved Lorena Bobbitt came onto the scene with a tragic story and the dramatic trial that kept so many captivated and intrigued (Margolick 1994). The good news is that this victim, and perpetrator, is now a licensed realtor and founded a non-profit organization, Lorena's Red Wagon Foundation, that seeks to provide food, shelter, toys, and other items to victims of domestic violence.

Conclusion

The epidemiological criminology model can serve as a guiding post for researchers interested in not tipping the balance away from a healthy and safe lifestyle to a more criminal subculture among at-risk Latinas. The Latino culture is rich in heritage and is the fastest-growing racial group and cultural ethnicity in the United States. When one is working with Latinos broadly and Latina women specifically, it is critical to examine the co-occurring conditions to which they might be subjected: drug, mental, physical, and sexual abuse; economic deprivation; cultural isolation; and other maladies. Any analysis that requires a criminological or criminal justice approach or examination should take into account such co-occurring conditions. Unlike standard mental health counseling, the Latino culture does not typically segment these conditions, but rather suppresses them collectively, thereby requiring a collective and interdisciplinary examination.

Crime is a disease that plagues every corner of American society, and, as with a disease, it is foolish only to treat the symptoms. The root cause of the problem must be addressed for there to be any real and lasting change. Violence and criminal behavior are the symptoms of a larger disease, and while the symptoms cannot be ignored or left untreated, unless the root causes of the disease are cured, the symptoms will only reappear and worsen. Regardless of race or ethnicity, everyone who becomes a victim of crime (or is accused of a crime) is entitled to equal justice. In a country as rich and powerful as the United States, more resources need to be allocated to provide everyone with the same opportunities for life, liberty, and the pursuit of happiness.

References

Bureau of Justice (BJS) Statistics (2011a, September) *Criminal Victimization in the United States, 2010*, National Crime Victimization Survey NCJ 235508. Washington, DC: US Department of Justice. Online, available at: http://bjs.ojp.usdoj.gov/content/pub/pdf/cv10.pdf (accessed 14 November 2013).

Bureau of Justice Statistics (2011b, December; revised 2012, February) *Prisoners in 2010. Office of Justice Programs—Bulletin*, NCJ 236096 Washington, DC: US Department of Justice. Online, available at: http://bjs.ojp.usdoj.gov/content/pub/pdf/p10.pdf (accessed 14 November 2013).

Bureau of Justice Statistics (2011c, December) *Correctional Populations in the United States, 2010*, Office of Justice Programs. NCJ 236319 Washington, DC: US Department of Justice. Online, available at: http://bjs.ojp.usdoj.gov/content/pub/pdf/cpus10.pdf (accessed 14 November 2013).

Costantini, C. (2011) "Anti-Latino hate crimes rise as immigration debate intensifies", *Huffington Post*. Online, available at: www.huffingtonpost.com/2011/10/17/anti-latino-hate-crimes-rise-immigration_n_1015668.html (accessed 14 November 2013).

Craven, D. (1996) *Female Victims of Violent Crime*, Washington, DC: Bureau of Justice Statistics, US Department of Justice.

Gaines, L. K. and Miller, R. L. (2013) *Criminal Justice in Action*, 7th ed., Belmont, CA: Wadsworth.

Margolick, D. (1994) "Lorena Bobbitt acquitted in mutilation of husband", *New York Times*, 22 January. Online, available at: www.nytimes.com/1994/01/22/us/lorena-bobbitt-acquitted-in-mutilation-of-husband.html?pagewanted=allandsrc=pm (accessed 14 November 2013).

National Institutes of Justice (NIJ) (2011) *Research Briefing: Understanding Trends in Hate Crimes against Immigrants and Hispanic-Americans*, Washington, DC: Office of Justice Programs. Online, available at: www.nij.gov/topics/crime/hate-crime/immigrants-hispanics.htm#stateselection (accessed 14 November 2013).

Reardon, D. C. (1996) "A story of destruction: The testimony", *Post-Abortion Review*, 4(2–3) (Spring and Summer). Online, available at: http://afterabortion.org/1996/a-story-of-destruction-the-testimony/ (accessed 14 November 2013).

Salcido, O. and Adelman, M. (2004) "'He has me tied with the blessed and damned papers': Undocumented-immigrant battered women in Phoenix, Arizona", *Human Organization*, 63: 162–173.

Sentencing Project (2007) "Women in the criminal justice system: Briefing sheet", Washington, DC: Sentencing Project. Online, available at: www.sentencingproject.org/doc/publications/womenincj_total.pdf (accessed 14 November 2013).

US Census Bureau (2008) *Population Projections*, Washington, DC: US Department of Commerce. Online, available at: www.census.gov/population/projections/data/national/2008/summarytables.html (accessed 14 November 2013).

US Census Bureau (2011) *The Hispanic Population: 2010*. Washington, DC: US Department of Commerce. Online, available at: www.census.gov/prod/cen2010/briefs/c2010br-04.pdf (accessed 14 November 2013).

READING 6.6

"Between a Rock and a Hard Place"

The Plight of Irregular Central American Migrants

By Santiago Baruh

The last two years have seen a succession of migrant and refugee crises around the world as a result of religious persecution, ongoing civil conflicts, crime, and economic or political instability. The three major situations that have captured the public eye are the Syrian refugee crisis, the Rohingya people's plight, and the record number of unaccompanied minors arriving to the United States from Central America during 2014. While the Syrian crisis mushrooms and the Rohingya crisis in South East Asia has all but disappeared from the pages of newspapers and media outlets, the Central American migration crisis has been all-but displaced from the mind of the U.S. audience. This is because the management of the Central American crisis has been outsourced to Mexico since July 2014.

This "outsourcing" has taken the form of Mexico's controversial *Frontera Sur (Southern Border)* program, which was implemented in July 2014. While this initiative has been successful in detaining more Central American migrants than ever before, it has also replicated the negative effects of U.S. border control strategies. This is a tactic based on "border enforcement through deterrence," which, while having some positive effects (e.g. a 73 percent increase in the detention of migrants since the policy was first implemented), has produced a number of damaging consequences for irregular migrants. These include forcing them to employ migrant smugglers in higher numbers, and to attempt crossing into the United States through more perilous locations, raising the number of immigrants who have died due to exposure and other environmental factors.

This article will focus on the issue of "irregular migrants". In the terminology of human migration in the 21st century, irregular migrants are those people whose movement from one country to another takes place outside the regulatory norms of the sending, transit or receiving countries. Irregular migrants from Central America are escaping the political instability and high levels of criminal violence that have pervaded the countries of the Northern Triangle, composed of El Salvador,

Santiago Baruh, "'Between a Rock and a Hard Place:' The Plight of Irregular Central American Migrants," *Washington Report on the Hemisphere*, vol. 35, no. 20, pp. 8-11.

Guatemala, and Honduras. The Northern Triangle countries currently possess some of the highest murder rates in the world, which are compounded by high levels of state violence.

Although the decision to migrate is normally a personal choice, as stated by Cornell University Law Professor Chantal Thomas, the ongoing trend is a result of factors that are affecting the population in the region at large. This article explores the "push" and "pull" factors compelling thousands of Central American migrants to leave their countries for the United States and how an array of border policies in the region have affected them.

"Push" and "Pull" Factors in Central American Migration

Long exceeded in importance by Mexican immigration to the United States, more than half a century of migration by Central Americans to the United States has grown as a result of the civil conflicts of the 1970s and 1980s, Hurricane Mitch in the 1998, and chronically high levels of crime and poor economic opportunities in the Northern Triangle. An estimated 80 percent of the millions of Central American migrants living abroad have chosen to reside in the United States.

"Push" and "pull" factors in international migration refers to those factors that drive migration at the structural level as opposed to more personal or temporary reasons. In the case of Central America, Push factors include persistent political instability, high levels of violence, and lack of employment possibilities; pull factors include the existence of social networks in the United States and the promise of a better life there.

Economically, the region is in a crisis: Guatemala (2011) and Honduras (2013) have high levels of poverty, with 53.7 and 64.5 percent of their respective populations living below the national poverty line.

Another key push factor in the region is the pervasiveness of violence, a trait that has been exacerbated since the civil wars of the 1980s. Even though Honduras was not the site of a civil conflict, a combination of domestic and international factors that has driven the rise in violence over the past 10 years. Among these factors are rising unemployment rates (especially among young adults); the deportation of gang members from the United States that started in the 1990s and changes in the transnational drug trade, which has made Central America one of the most important points in trafficking routes to the United States (not only for narcotics but also for guns and human-trafficking or people smuggling). These factors have contributed to a growth in the number of homicides in the country, which has been estimated to be at around the 66 per 100,000 people level in 2014. *InSight Crime*, an international NGO working on crime reporting and prevention, also reports that Guatemala had a homicide rate of 31 per 100,000 people. El Salvador, on the other hand, had an estimated homicide rate of 90 out of 100,000 people.

Caught in The Middle

As a result of the push and pull factors previously mentioned, hundreds of thousands of Central Americans are fleeing from the region. The journey is rife with dangers that have increased since the introduction of the *Frontera Sur* program in July 2014. Similar to what happened to irregular migrants trying to cross the U.S.-Mexican border in the 1990s and early 2000s, the introduction of border enforcement strategies based on deterrence has forced migrants to take more risks (including contacting people-smugglers traffickers and attempting to cross through more isolated places along the border), and has reduced the number of state assistance mechanisms available to migrants.

The combination of the effects of the policy shifts mentioned above has made irregular migrants more invisible and, therefore, harder to research, engage, and aid. Another consequence of this increased invisibility has been a higher rate of victimization at the hands of criminals (both organized and opportunistic ones) and state-forces, notorious for being highly violent and corrupt in Mexico and Central America. In relation to this, the Inter-American Commission on Human Rights (IACHR) has reported that Mexican state security forces enjoy high levels of impunity, which explains why migrants are reluctant to contact them or those in positions of authority in the event of a crime. The situation has become so dire that in a recent opinion article, Sonia Nazario stated that, "the [Mexican] government push has been interpreted as open season on migrants who have become prey to an exploding number of criminals and the police who rob, rape, beat and kill them."

The victimization of irregular migrants and the violation of their human rights in their journey from their native countries to Mexico and, ultimately, the United States is a direct violation of the

United Nations conventions regarding both migrants and refugees, of which El Salvador, Guatemala, Honduras, and Mexico are a part. The United States is not a part of either of these conventions and has historically been reluctant to receive refugees, as described by Maria Cristina Garcia in *The Washington Post.* This is confirmed by a report from the Department of State that shows that the number of refugees that arrived in the first two months of FY2016 is 8,856, of which only 1.9 percent have come from Latin America and the Caribbean.

This problem is exacerbated by the U.S. Congress' emphasis on aid programs that focus on security issues (such as the *Central American Regional Security Initiative or CARSI)* as opposed to the White House's interest in approving an aid package in which these policies play but a small part of the total. The Obama administration has begun requesting more funds from Congress for aid programs rather than security-based initiatives, as was the practice in the past: the Foreign Operations Budget Request for FY2016 highlights the importance of engaging with structural issues to understand and target the root causes of the migratory crisis. This shows a shift in Washington's emphasis from attacking the problem to addressing its causes. That the Chairman of the United States' Senate Homeland Security and Governmental Affairs Committee has acknowledged not only the existence of push and pull factors, but also the role of U.S. demand for illegal drugs in relation to migration and border security seems to signal the possibility of a future approach that is more comprehensive in its scope. In spite of these changes, the White House's budget request has been held up in Congress, where there are different propositions as to how much funding should be allocated and to which programs or areas.

Finally, while Mexico's Southern Border program might have succeeded in reducing the number of Central American migrants caught at the U.S. border, statistics from the U.S. Border Patrol indicate an increase in the detention of families and unaccompanied minors at the US-Mexico Southwest border during the first month of FY2016 when compared to the same month for FY2015. This might signal either a decrease in the effectiveness of Mexico's *Frontera Sur program,* or an improvement in the tactics used by migrants, people-smugglers, and human-traffickers to traverse through Mexico.

So migrants are caught, as the popular saying goes, "between a rock and a hard place." On one hand, they are forced to migrate due to factors virtually beyond their control or ability to change and, on the other hand, they have to face the hostility from receiving and transit countries and the increasingly perilous journey in search of a better life for them and their families. The United States and Mexico have proven to be quite reluctant to receive asylum seekers/refugees from the region or to assign this status to migrants from Central America. Although the United States was quick to take asylum seekers during the Nicaraguan civil conflict in the 1970s and 1980s, and during the Hurricane "Mitch" crisis in 1998, this is no longer true even though many consider contemporary Central American migrants refugees.

Implications for the United States and Irregular Migrants

The current Central American migration crisis can be considered the result of a combination of structural factors and misguided policy choices. In recent months the media has focused on the issue of unaccompanied minors, Syrian, and Cuban migrants crossing through the region. This has shifted the focus away from the larger problem of irregular migration originating in the Northern Triangle and has consequently harmed these migrants.

It is imperative that the United States take responsibility for its role in creating and perpetuating the root causes of the Central American migration crisis by implementing a more comprehensive strategy to address the issues of poor governance, insecurity, and poor economic performance in the region. The United States' recognition of these shortcomings will not only help "Northern Triangle" countries, but will also better assuage U.S. concerns about immigration in the long run.

UNIT VI: CRITICAL THINKING QUESTIONS

1. Define "intersectionality." Explain how the concept of intersectionality contributes to our understanding of violent victimization and offending.
2. Describe the issues associated with investigating and prosecuting elder abuse. Explain how Crawford v. Washington (2004) affects the prosecution of elder abuse.
3. Identify the types of issues LGBT youth suffer when they are bullied and victimized by their peers. Describe what factors create a positive school climate for LGBT youth.
4. Discuss how a drug addict is likely to become a victim. Include the types of victimizations a drug addict may experience.
5. Explain the three aspects of the epidemiological criminology paradigm and why it must be considered in dealing with intimate partner violence. Although Latina women are known to stay in abusive relationships, discuss why any woman would prefer to remain in an abusive relationship.
6. Describe the Frontera Sur (Southern Border) program. Explain how the Frontera Sur program affects migration to the U.S.

   Overall

   Using only the information in this unit, how would you describe the field of victimology in the United States to someone from another country?

CONCLUSION

This text is about the "present" and how one currently views or thinks about the CJS. As today's students of the CJS know, the system, though simplistic in design, is not so in practice. The three main subsystems—police, courts, and corrections—each play a role in meeting the overall goal of the system, which itself is debatable. However, each has its own practice methods and goals. Furthermore, the diversity of each can lead to issues and problems for itself and the system. With additional elements such as juvenile justice and victimology, the amount of study and understanding is more extensive.

This text presents perceptions, views, and opinions about the various issues the system and its subsystems have encountered. Readers are encouraged to not accept anything at face value but to critically think about what was offered. To critically think means to ask questions, seek further clarity, and form perspectives, views, and opinions of one's own beyond the preliminary information provided by others. What is taken away by the reader is based on the reader's choice. We ask that the choice involves critical thought with a greater desire to further explore what has been read in this text. Ultimately, the desire is improvement in the CJS by those who think and make logical, rational decisions wherever possible, decisions that begin with critical thinking.

—M.L. Dantzker, Ph.D. and Rosalva Resendiz, Ph.D.
Co-editors

Printed in the USA
CPSIA information can be obtained
at www.ICGtesting.com
LVHW080033190824
788631LV00009B/91